Hotel and Food Service Marketing

Other Hotel and Catering Texts available from the Publisher

Hotel and Catering Case Studies
Peter Abbott and John Shepherd

Computer Systems in the Hotel and Catering Industry
Bruce Braham

The Management of Hotel Operations
Peter Jones and Andrew Lockwood

Food Service Operations, Second Edition
Peter Jones

The Management of Catering Operations
Paul Merricks and Peter Jones

People and the Hotel and Catering Industry
Andrew Lockwood and Peter Jones

Principles of Hotel and Catering Law, Second Edition
Alan Pannett

The Hotel Receptionist, Second Edition
Grace and Jane Paige

Book-keeping and Accounts for Hotel and Catering Studies
Grace and Jane Paige

Catering Costs and Control, Second Edition
Grace Paige

Hotel and Food Service Marketing

A Managerial Approach

FRANCIS BUTTLE, BSc (Hons), MA

Lecturer in Marketing
Department of Hotel, Restaurant
and Travel Administration
University of Massachusetts, Amherst

Cassell Educational Ltd: Villiers House,
41–47 Strand,
London WC2N 5JE

British Library Cataloguing in Publication Data
Buttle, Francis
    Hotel and food service marketing: a managerial approach.—(Holt
    hotel and catering)
    1. Hotel management   2. Caterers and
    catering   3. Marketing
    I. Title
    647'.94'0688   TX911.3.M3

ISBN: 0–304–31533–8

Reprinted 1988, 1990, 1991

Contents

For Linda, Emma and Lewis

Acknowledgements

The author and publisher wish to thank the following who have kindly given permission for the use of copyright material:

Advertising Research Foundation; Advertising Association; Allyn & Bacon Inc.; B. T. Batsford Ltd; Blackie & Son Ltd; Booz Allen & Hamilton Inc.; British Institute of Management; British Tourist Authority; CACI; CBS College Publishing; Collins Publishers; Controller of Her Majesty's Stationery Office; Countryside Commission; *Harvard Business Review*; Horwath & Horwath (UK) Ltd; Huddersfield Polytechnic (Hotel & Catering Research Centre); Institute of Marketing; JICNARS; Kendall–Hunt Publishing; Lexington Books; McGraw-Hill Book Co.; A. C. Nielsen Co. Ltd.; Northern Ireland Tourist Board; Prentice–Hall Inc.; Research Services Ltd; Scottish Tourist Board; Wales Tourist Board; Wiedenfeld & Nicholson Ltd.

Full references to these copyright materials appear in the text or in the references section at the end of each chapter. Whilst every effort has been made to trace copyright owners, this has not always been successful. The author and publishers apologise for any infringement of copyright or failure to acknowledge original sources. Any corrections advised to the publishers will be included in further printings.

Preface

The long-term survival of a hotel or food service organisation operating in a competitive environment depends on its ability to satisfy customers' demands efficiently and effectively. So many new businesses, particularly in food service, open in a blaze of publicity only to close in ignominy shortly afterwards. Whilst inadequate marketing does not account for all of these failures, it certainly explains many. Customer dissatisfaction with location, product quality, service standards and price, or even simple lack of awareness, speeds the demise of the business.

Marketing can provide security, longevity and profitability.

Much of this book concerns the marketing of hospitality products for profit. But there is also an important non-profit sector which includes, for instance, hospital and school catering. The book also investigates how the basic principles of marketing apply when the profit motive is absent.

Like most new products, the book has been produced to fill an observed gap in the market. The text has been written primarily for students pursuing BTEC Higher Diplomas or Degrees in Hotel, Restaurant, Catering, Hospitality or Institutional Management. Candidates preparing for the professional examinations of the HCIMA will find the book particularly useful for foundation studies unit B3 (Marketing 1) and elective studies unit B16 (Marketing 2). In addition, some chapters, particularly those dealing with identification of target markets, planning, pricing, advertising, selling, sales promotion, merchandising and public relations offer guidelines and systematic procedures which can be immediately applied by practising managers.

The book is organised into three parts. Part I examines the character of the hotel and food service industry before introducing the basic concepts of marketing. Strategic marketing planning occupies Part II, whilst Part III is concerned with a more detailed analysis of product development and management, pricing, distribution planning and the promotion of hospitality demand.

Before putting fingers to word processor keyboard—the 1980s' equivalent of pen to paper—I established some principles which were to guide the production of the book. It is for you, the reader, to decide whether they have been achieved.

- Completeness. A full review of principles and practice. It assumes no previous knowledge of marketing.
- Theoretical strength. A number of chapters are concerned specifically with theoretical issues. These precede others on management techniques.
- Managerial orientation. As opposed to mere description the text has an analytical, planning and decision-making focus.
- Relevance. The book draws on practice in the hospitality industry to illustrate general marketing principles and uses research from leisure, tourism and hospitality to build the theoretical base.
- Logical sequence. The book progresses from general to specific and from abstract to concrete.

- Standard chapter structure. Each chapter consists of preview, learning objectives, text, review, questions/exercises and references.

Some new products, particularly service products, move very rapidly from conceptual status to full commercial launch into the market-place; the opposite is true of this book. The idea for the book arose when fruitlessly trying to find a suitable text which spanned both marketing principles and hospitality applications. The production of the manuscript took well over two years and although I take full responsibility for the finished product with all its faults of omission and commission, I owe an enormous debt of gratitude to the former and present colleagues, clients, students and employers who have contributed in so many ways. Worthy of particular mention are: David Airey, Army Catering Corps, Burger King, The Creative Business, Crest Hotels, Dorchester Hotel, English Tourist Board, Paul Gamble, David Gilbert, Holt, Rinehart & Winston's anonymous reviewers, Hotel Industry Marketing Group, Institute of Marketing, Richard Kotas, Simon Lake, Marriott Hotels, Victor Middleton, Ogilvy & Mather, Mike Riley, Wales Tourist Board, Steven Wanhill, Alan Wolfe.

Many thanks, too, to the team which converted my word processing output, typescript and scrawl into a form suitable for editorial consumption: Amanda Butcher, Caroline Casey, Sue Hiscock, Hazel Jones, Caroline Miller, Gaye Mortali, Nickie Street.

—PART 1—

Fundamentals of Marketing

Part I of this book comprises five chapters. The first presents an overview of the service sector of the economy and the hotel and catering industry in particular.

The second introduces the reader to marketing, its scope and applications the marketing concept and the marketing environment.

Chapter 3 is about marketing research, introducing the reader to its value, applications and techniques.

The fourth chapter attempts to synthesise the current level of understanding about consumer behaviour. It looks at issues such as consumer motivation and decision making. These chapters fit together logically. Since the main role of hotel or food service marketers is to influence demand, they must understand the nature of consumer behaviour and, to do so, almost invariably need to themselves use, or evaluate others' use of marketing research techniques.

The final chapter in Part I examines one of the marketing manager's most important tasks—the identification of the markets in which he wishes to influence demand. His ability to do so is the outcome of his understanding of consumer behaviour and his use of marketing information.

—1————————————————

The Service Sector and Hospitality

1.1 CHAPTER PREVIEW

This chapter performs two tasks. It introduces you to both the service sector of the economy in general and the hotel and catering industry in particular.

The aim is to assess the size, significance and contribution of both to the economic well-being of the country.

A selection of data, mostly collected by government agencies, give substance to the description.

In particular we attempt to answer these questions: what is a service? what significance has the service sector in comparison to extractive and manufacturing industry? what role does the hotel and catering industry play in the service sector? is service marketing different from the marketing of other products?

The information in this chapter serves as a background against which later discussions of marketing management practice are set in context.

Readers who are familiar with the industry may wish to skip later parts of the chapter, but should read through the sections entitled 'The Service Economy' and 'Services Defined'.

1.2 LEARNING OBJECTIVES

By the end of this chapter you should be able to:
1. Define the terms:
   industry.
   hospitality.
   hotel.
   catering.
2. Explain why the debate about the meaning of the term 'services' is widely regarded as sterile.
3. Demonstrate statistically the significance to the economy of the service sector in general and the hospitality industry in particular.
4. Distinguish between primary, secondary and tertiary industry.
5. Define the functional characteristics which are said to differentiate goods from services.
6. Identify the core products offered by the hospitality industry.
7. Explain the connections between tourism, leisure and hospitality.

1.3 THE SERVICE ECONOMY

In most developed economies, services are a major form of economic activity, contributing significantly to wealth and employment.

A common process of economic development has been experienced by many (though not all) countries. The first phase of this is pre-industrial where the focus of economic activity is agriculture. This is termed primary industry. Secondary industry is manufacturing; this emerged during the industrial revolution and still contributes in a major way to our national economic health.

The tertiary sector of the economy is also termed 'post-industrial' and is based on the output of services. A number of indicators of the significance of the service sector are tabled below. Approximately 56 per cent of employees earn their income from the service sector; this proportion has been growing in recent years (see Table 1.1). Over the three years tabled, the proportion employed in primary and secondary industry has fallen, whilst if public employees are regarded as part of the service sector then its proportion has risen from 61 per cent to 64 per cent (exclusion of public employees gives a shift from 54 per cent to 56 per cent.)

The contribution of the service sector to Gross Domestic Product (GDP) is shown in Table 1.2. GDP is the sum total of the goods and services produced by an economy's residents calculated at the market prices they command. In the UK, annual statistics are released in the Central Statistical Office's publication *National Income and Expenditure*. Table 1.2 shows what has happened to GDP over three years, 1981 to 1983. Consumer expenditure on services approximates 16 per cent of GDP; this is equivalent to 26 per cent of total consumer expenditure.

Table 1.1   *Pattern of employment (UK).*

	1981		1982		1983	
	'000	percentage	'000	percentage	'000	percentage
Total (all industries)	21,870	100	21,473	100	21,210	100
Agriculture, horticulture, forestry, energy supply, fishing	2,710	12.4	2,624	12.2	2,405	11.3
Manufacturing	5,710	26.1	5,387	25.1	5,264	24.8
Services	11,825	54.1	11,869	55.3	11,941	56.3
Public administration and defence	1,625	7.4	1,593	7.4	1,600	7.5

Source: CSO: Annual Abstract of Statistics, 1985. (Table 6.2 Employees in Employment).

Table 1.2   *Gross domestic product (UK).*

	Total GDP at market prices	Total consumer expenditure		Consumer expenditure on services other than rent and rates		
	£m	£m	as percentage of GDP	£m	as percentage of total GDP	as percentage of total consumer expenditure
1981	254,203	152,125	59.8	38,773	15.3	25.5
1982	277,334	166,477	60.0	42,776	15.4	25.7
1983	301,298	182,427	60.5	47,464	15.8	26.0

Source: CSO: National Income and Expenditure, 1984.

Services also make a significant contribution to the Balance of Payments (BOP). BOP is the term used to describe an economy's imports and exports of both goods and services. In economic parlance these are called visibles and invisibles. A measure of the contribution of services to BOP appears in Table 1.3. It shows the service sector to make a positive net contribution to BOP.

Table 1.3   *Balance of payments.*

	1981	1982	1983
Visible trade			
Exports (fob)[1]	50,977	55,565	60,625
Imports (cif)[2]	47,325	53,181	61,341
Visible balance	+3,652	+2,384	−716
Invisibles			
Credits	29,644	31,307	34,975
Debits	26,075	24,485	31,343
Invisible balance	+3,569	+6,822	+3,632
of which:			
Services balance[3]	+4,485	+3,706	+3,902

Source: CSO: Annual Abstract of Statistics 1985.
[1] fob;   Free on Board. Value at point of export. Assumes buyer meets shipping charges beyond point of departure.
[2] cif;   Cost Insurance Freight. Assumes overseas exporter pays all costs up to arrival at UK point of entry.
[3]   Services balance exceeds invisibles balance in 1981 and 1983 because other invisibles make negative contribution to BOP.

1.4 SERVICES DEFINED

What is it that makes a 'service' special? Are services really different from other products?

Gershuny, a major contributor to our understanding of the service economy, distinguishes between 4 conceptions of the term 'service': service industries, service products, service occupations and service functions[1]. Service industry covers all those firms and employees whose major final output is some intangible or ephemeral commodity or, alternatively, that residual set of productive institutions whose final output is not a material good. Service products, however, are not all necessarily produced by service industries; manufacturing firms frequently produce services and sell them to consumers either packaged with other goods, or more exceptionally, on their own. Workers employed in tertiary or service occupations exist in all industries and perform non-production jobs such as cleaning, teaching or catering. Finally whilst service functions involve individuals in service work this need not take place within the money economy, for example, voluntary help or housework.

Levitt[2] distinguishes between tangibles and intangibles whilst Christopher[3] suggests that the distinction is that 'service products are those which produce a series of benefits which cannot be stored'.

However, not all authors agree with the notion that differences exist. Wyckham[4], for example, flatly states that 'services are not different from products'.

One attempt to clear the confusion which surrounds the service marketing debate is made by Blois[5]. His review of the literature isolates 4 approaches which have attempted to settle the issue of whether services are different. Those approaches are based upon:

1. Definitions of services.
2. Classification of products into goods or services.
3. Isolating distinctive functional differences.
4. Development of conceptual frameworks.

Many authors and practitioners have attempted the first approach—yet there is still no consensus definition. Even the *Service Industries Journal*, which sets out to be a forum for discussion and debate on the nature and role of the service sector, does not offer an editorial definition. Blois asserts that two knowledgeable observers, presented with the same set of products, would not agree which were services.

The classification approach arranges items (products in this case) into groups on the basis of their character. A new product can then be identified as a member of a particular group, say industrial product, consumer good or service on the basis of its characteristic similarity to other group members. Blois comments that those taxonomies which do exist are ambiguous.

The third approach is to isolate those characteristics of services which seem to cause differences in the management of their marketing. Blois points out the tautological nature of this approach. To identify functional differences requires the *prior isolation* of 'services' from all other marketed products, yet such isolation is the intended *outcome* of this process. The characteristics which are commonly cited as making the marketing of services different are:

1. Heterogeneity.
2. Intangibility.
3. Perishability.
4. Inseparability.

Heterogeneity implies variance and a lack of uniformity in the standard of the service output. A bank teller is less courteous to customer A than to customer B; a hairdresser makes a better job of Mrs Smith's head than of Mrs Jones'. With heterogeneity of output, quality control becomes a major problem for management.

Services are also said to be intangible. Customers can neither properly evaluate nor sample prior to purchase. The marketing problem which arises from intangibility is centred on how to communicate the benefits of a service to a consumer.

Services are also said to be perishable. They can not be stored. If a dentist's chair is empty for half an hour it is business lost for ever. The marketing problem is how to generate sufficient demand and control or synchronise this demand so that it is felt at the times desired by the marketer.

Inseparability of production and consumption is held to be the fourth distinctive characteristic of services. Consumption of most services takes place on the producer's premises although some exceptions like television repairs or management training take place in the home, on the customer's premises or elsewhere. For marketing management this poses problems of distribution—the purchaser needs to come to the producer in order to experience the benefits of consumption: here hotels and restaurants are examples.

There has been recent criticism of this functional approach. A number of commentators such as Bonoma and Mills[6], Middleton[7] and Goodfellow[8] have shown that many so-called services do not exhibit one or more of these characteristics whereas a number of physical goods do.

The fourth approach to understanding the nature of services involves the development of conceptual frameworks. Blois reports two such frameworks: Shostack[9] organises market offerings along a continuum according to their degree of tangibility whilst Gronroos'[10] approach is to consider the relative importance of buyer/seller interactions during the purchase process. Conceptual frameworks act as a means of organising the world and can therefore reduce complex issues to manageable, understandable proportions.

A third conceptual framework provided by Middleton[11] is most helpful, building a common system of classification for both goods and services. Underlying his approach is a classification system long used for distinguishing between different types of physical goods. Middleton regards both goods and services as ranging along a continuum from convenience products to shopping products, having the characteristics shown in Figure 1.1.

Convenience products are frequent purchases involving the customer in relatively little comparison of alternatives. Shopping products are generally more expensive, less frequent purchases involving the customer in rather more time and effort making comparisons between alternatives.

Middleton's proposition is that all products are better described in terms of their position along this continuum than they are in terms of being either goods or services. Thus, urban bus transport, commuter train transport, bank services, post-office services, take-away foods, detergents, petrol, cigarettes all tend towards the convenience end of the spectrum whilst holidays, hotel accommodation, air transport, private education, cars, freezers, carpets and furniture cluster at the other end.

Such a conceptual framework renders the debate over the distinguishing features of services redundant.

Why does this confusion about the nature of services exist? Firstly, the field of service marketing is emergent, it does not have the history of study and practice of consumer goods marketing. The notion that planned marketing can be equally applied in services

CONVENIENCE PRODUCTS	SHOPPING PRODUCTS
mainly low unit value/price	mainly high unit value/price
mainly perceived necessities	

CONVENIENCE PRODUCTS	SHOPPING PRODUCTS
Low problem solving	high problem solving
low information search	high information search
low customer commitment	high customer commitment
high purchase frequency	low purchase frequency
high brand loyalty	low brand loyalty
high speed decision process	low speed decision process
high rapidity of consumption	low rapidity of consumption
extensive distribution expected	limited distribution expected

Figure 1.1 Product continuum.

has taken a long time to gain acceptance. Secondly, many ostensibly tangible goods contain elements of service. A company buying a fork-lift truck will receive financial advice before, as well as driving instruction and maintenance arrangements after, the purchase. A household purchasing kitchen furniture will receive planning and colour scheming advice before purchase and installation afterwards. In these examples, the benefits the buyer experiences are delivered by both tangible and intangible components of the purchase.

Lovelock remarks that all services deliver a number of utilities and that before purchasing consumers will evaluate alternatives against them:

1. Form utility (physical elements of the service such as food, room or swimming pool).
2. Place utility (convenience of location).
3. Time utility (open when needed).
4. Psychic utility (feelings about the service or establishment).
5. Monetary utility (cost and value for money).[12]

In general, the field of service marketing is confined to those exchanges in which the service element is the core. Shostack calls these 'service dominant'.[13]

Much information published about industry is collected by the government, and categorised using the Standard Industrial Classification (SIC). The introduction to the 1980 revised edition states that:

> The United Kingdom economy is made up of a wide range of economic activities through which goods are produced or services rendered by firms and other organisations. For analytical purposes, economic activities of a similar nature may be grouped together into 'industries', for example into agriculture, motor vehicle manufacture, retail distribution, catering, national government service. A system used to group activities in this way is described as an industrial classification. 'Industry' in this context is not restricted to extractive or production activities but extends to the provision of goods and services of all kinds.[14]

The SIC identifies 4 categories of service industry (from a total of 9 categories).

Division Number	Description
6.	Distribution, hotels and catering, repairs.
7.	Transport and communication.
8.	Banking, finance, insurance, business services and leasing.
9.	Other services.

1.5 HOTEL AND CATERING INDUSTRY

The hotel and catering or food service industry, now quite widely also called the *hospitality* industry, is a key member of the service sector. It is a far from homogenous group of firms and establishments linked by their common economic activity. Industries can be classified by production process (e.g. metal fabrication), raw material (dairying) economic function (e.g. retailing) or type of output. The hospitality industry is identified by its output of products which satisfy the demand for accommodation, food and beverage away from home.

The Standard Industrial Classification (SIC), revised edition 1980, attempts to draw boundaries which describe the industry. Like its predecessor, the 1968 version, it has been widely used to classify official statistics.

Table 1.4 details all the activities listed in the 1980 SIC Class 'Hotels and Catering'. It includes all restaurants, snackbars, cafes (both licensed and unlicensed), take-away shops, public houses and bars, nightclubs of every kind, other licensed clubs, canteens and messes, catering contractors, hotels licensed and unlicensed, camp sites, caravan sites, holiday camps and a variety of other forms of short-stay accommodation.

However a number of hospitality activities are listed elsewhere. Division 9 of the 1980 SIC, Other Services, includes the following:

Catering services ancillary to higher education institutions (activity 9,310)
Catering services ancillary to schools (activity 9,320)
Catering services ancillary to educational and vocational training not elsewhere specified (activity 9,330)
Soup kitchens (activity 9,611)
Social and residential homes (activity 9,611)

A useful indication of the value of an industry is its investment in fixed assets. Businessmen will invest when they have confidence in a profitable return on that investment. Table 1.5 shows the extent of fixed capital formation, i.e. annual investment in new buildings and works, plant, machinery and vehicles, over the three year period 1981–83 for a number of industries including hotels and catering.

The hospitality industry has experienced steadily climbing fixed capital formation not unlike the pattern in food manufacturing. The metals manufacturing industry by comparison has been in steady decline.

A further indication of the economic significance of hospitality is shown in Table 1.6. This charts consumer expenditure on hotel and catering products as a percentage of total consumer expenditure over a period of three years.

The figures show that household expenditure on hospitality is steady at between 5 per cent and 6 per cent of total consumer expenditure. The total market is currently approaching £9 billion annually.

No single source of information provides an authoritative picture of the structure of the hospitality industry. Table 1.7 brings together information from two sources.

In total, the 248,100 establishments service the hospitality needs of a population of 55 million people and overseas tourists to Great Britain.

Considered in total, the industry is complex and heterogeneous. Consider the following variations in type of operation:

• catering only or accommodation also.
• profit- or cost-orientation.
• sole trader catering or subsidised government–controlled operations.
• single hotel business or multisite operators.
• captive market or selective custom.
• fish and chips or cordon bleu.
• vending machine or silver service.
• eating for pleasure or eating for survival.

The hospitality industry delivers a product with three principal components:

Table 1.4 *Standard industrial classification, revised 1980.*

DIVISION 6			
Class 66	Group	Activity	
			HOTELS AND CATERING
	661		RESTAURANTS, SNACK BARS, CAFÉS AND OTHER EATING PLACES
		6611	Eating places supplying food for consumption on the premises

1. Licensed places

Eating places licensed to provide alcoholic liquor with meals but not normally providing regular overnight accommodation. Any entertainment provided is incidental to the provision of meals. Railway buffets and dining car services are included. Hotels are classified to heading 6650 and night clubs etc to heading 6630

2. Unlicensed places

Eating places which do not provide alcoholic liquor: ice-cream parlours and coffee bars

6612 Take-away food shops

Fish and chip shops, sandwich bars and other premises supplying prepared food for consumption off the premises

662 6620 PUBLIC HOUSES AND BARS

Establishments wholly or mainly engaged in supplying alcoholic liquor for consumption on the premises; the provision of food or entertainment is ancillary and the provision of overnight accommodation, if any, is subordinate

663 6630 NIGHT CLUBS AND LICENSED CLUBS

Establishments providing food, drink and entertainment to their members and guests, including residential clubs. Sports and gaming clubs are classified to heading 9791

664 6640 CANTEENS AND MESSES

1. Catering contractors

School canteens, industrial canteens and other catering establishments operated by catering contractors. Canteens run by industrial establishments for their own employees are classified with the main establishment

2. Other canteens and messes

Separately identifiable service messes, university and other canteens not elsewhere specified

665 6650 HOTEL TRADE

1. Licensed premises

Hotels, motels and guest houses providing overnight furnished accommodation with food and service which are licensed to serve alcoholic liquor (inc. bed and breakfast places)

2. Unlicensed premises

Hotels, motels and guest houses providing overnight furnished accommodation with food and service but are not licensed to serve alcoholic liquor (including bed and breakfast places)

667 6670 OTHER TOURIST OR SHORT-STAY ACCOMMODATION

1. Camping and caravan sites

The provision of camping and caravan sites for rent. Rented caravan or chalet sites providing food supplies from a retail shop only are classified here but if the site includes a place providing prepared food it should be classified as a holiday camp

2. Holiday camps

Provision of chalet or caravan accommodation having on the site a place providing prepared food

3. Other tourist or short-stay accommodation not elsewhere specified

Holiday centres, conference centres, holiday houses, apartments, flats and flatlets. Youth hostels, non-charitable holiday homes, private rest homes without medical care. Charitable rest homes are classified to heading 9611 and convalescent homes and rest homes with medical care to heading 9510.

Source: CSO: Standard Industrial Classification, Revised 1980.

Table 1.5   *Industrial fixed capital formation (£ million).*

Year	1981	1982	1983
Hotels and catering	662	691	737
Food manufacturing	598	697	684
Metals manufacturing	298	263	245

Source: CSO: National Income and Expenditure 1984

Table 1.6   *UK Consumer Expenditure on Hospitality.*

	Total consumer expenditure (£m)	Catering expenditure (meals and accommodation)	
		(£m)	(percentage of total)
1981	152,125	8,112	5.3
1982	166,477	8,683	5.2
1983	182,427	9,967	5.5

Source: CSO: Annual Abstract of Statistics 1985.

Table 1.7   *Hospitality outlets in Great Britain (1981).*

Hotels, Guesthouses, Hostels, Holiday Camps[a]	33,200
Restaurants, Cafes, Snackbars[a]	52,200
Public Houses[a]	60,800
Nightclubs and Licensed Clubs[a]	33,200
Industrial catering[b]	24,100
Hospitals and Homes[b]	8,900
Schools, colleges, etc[b]	35,700
	248,100

Source: [a] *Hotel & Catering Establishments in Great Britain: A Regional Analysis.* HCITB, 1985.
   [b] *Food Service Insight—The Business Outlook for Suppliers to the UK Food Service Industry to 1987.* BIS Marketing Research Ltd.

- Accommodation.
- Food.
- Beverage.

These are the essential core products of the industry. The infinite variation with which hospitality marketers combine these core products to meet the demand of customers suggests that consumers seek rather more than the utilitarian satisfaction of a comfortable bed and full stomach. These 3 core products are enhanced, made more attractive, by being tailored to satisfy the demands of specific sources of custom. Furthermore consumption often takes place in an environment which is also tailored to deliver satisfaction. The atmosphere of a Wimpy Bar or high-class restaurant may be as deliberately designed and managed as the contents of menu and wine list. Some marketers regard atmosphere/environment as equal in importance to the 3 core products in attracting customers and providing satisfaction.

Demand for accommodation is a function of travel and tourism. A tourist is defined as:

an individual spending at least 24 hours away from home for the purposes of pleasure, holiday, sport, business or family reasons.[15]

Journeys of less than 24 hours, although making a major contribution to the turnover of caterers at destinations, are excluded from most statistics. This short duration traveller is termed an excursionist. Excursionists are the source of much revenue and employment at coastal resorts within easy travelling distance of centres of population.

An overseas visitor who spends 12 months or longer at a destination is generally classified as a resident. A tourist, then, is a traveller spending at least 24 hours but less than one year away from home.

A broad distinction can be made between travel for business purposes and travel for pleasure/holidays. Some trips, of course, are made with both purposes in mind. A further distinction can be made between domestic and international travel. The business demand for travel is described by Medlik and Airey as comprising:

> a small number of travellers making frequent journeys of short duration.[16]

Business journeys may be made for a large number of reasons—meeting suppliers and customers, conferences, seminars or exhibitions for example.

The pleasure/holiday sector is made up of a larger number of people making journeys away from home for amusement or relaxation. A major reason for travel is to visit friends and relatives. Some experts treat this as part of the pleasure/holiday sector. Others regard it as a separate sector.

Demand for food and drink is of two kinds. Firstly, it may be connected with staying away from home. Secondly, it may be an activity in its own right. Food and drink establishments satisfy two motives—they serve as a source of pleasure and entertainment as well as being a 'substitute domestic activity' meeting nutritional needs.

1.6 THE LEISURE INDUSTRY[17]

To a large extent corporate success in the hospitality industry is dependent upon satisfying leisure needs and wants.

As with hospitality, there is no single definition of the term leisure. What is leisure for one person may be work for another.

In the UK, the proportion of household disposable income expended on leisure was about 24 per cent in 1979. Leisure activities can be roughly divided into the following overlapping categories:

- passive at-home entertainment (e.g. watching TV, listening to records and tapes, reading books and newspapers);
- home-based activities (e.g. gardening, do-it-yourself, artistic activities and hobbies of all kinds, including many things done largely for pleasure which in other circumstances might be considered work—such as special types of cooking, needlework and decorating);
- social activities at home or at the homes of friends and relatives;
- social activities outside the home (meals out, dancing, clubs, etc);
- cultural away-from-home activities (cinemas, theatres, museums, amateur dramatics);
- spectators at sports and similar events, and related gambling;

- participants in sports and other active pursuits (ranging from football to fishing, from swimming to skiing);
- participants in less active games and pursuits (ranging from billiards to chess);
- day or other short trips away from home (picnics, outings, etc—especially by car);
- longer holiday trips away from home (including foreign tourism and camping);
- use of second homes, boats with sleeping accommodation, etc.

A number of these leisure activities involve tourism directly and therefore have implications for the hotel sector; others, whilst not involving overnight accommodation are of significance to the catering sector.

A number of factors contribute towards the amount of leisure time available:

1. the shorter working week and the consequent longer weekend.
2. the rising proportion of females in the workforce, which is in turn affected by smaller family sizes, labour saving devices in the home and women's attitudes towards their domestic and working roles.
3. the general level of unemployment.
4. the reduction in time required for housekeeping duties.
5. longer paid holidays.
6. the shorter working day.

The general trend is towards increased leisure time at a forecast rate of increase in the UK of 0.6 per cent per annum for the period 1980–1990, whilst leisure spending is forecast to rise at 2.8 per cent per annum over the same period.

This augurs well for hospitality marketers.

1.7 THE HOTEL SECTOR

A Hotel is

> an establishment of a permanent nature, of four or more bedrooms, offering bed and breakfast on a short-term contract and providing certain minimum standards.[18]

The term 'hotel' covers boarding-houses, inns, guesthouses, bed-and-breakfast establishments, unclassified hotels, in addition to 1, 2, 3, 4 and 5 star hotels which may or may not be licensed to serve liquor. Hotels vary by location (coastal, countryside, small towns, large towns, cities), demand (business or holiday), size (4 bedrooms to several hundred bedrooms), standard (unclassified to 5 star), ownership (independent, franchised or group operated, for example) and atmosphere (busy/efficient or relaxed/homely).

The national tourist boards collect data about the size of the hotel industry in the UK, but, because there is no compulsory registration scheme for hotels throughout the country, the information may be incomplete. Table 1.8 lists the numbers of hotels in England, Scotland, Wales and Northern Ireland which have registered with their national tourist boards. The UK hotel market comprises some 20,000 establishments offering approximately 670,000 bedspaces. The bulk of these are in England (almost 80 per cent), where the geographic dispersion is evidence of the location of demand. Twenty per cent of bedspaces are located in London and a further 19 per cent in the

Table 1.8   *The UK hotel industry*

	No. of hotels[3]	Bedspaces[4]	Bedrooms[5]
England[1]	15,896	535,208	—
Scotland[7]	2,996	88,117[6]	44,522[6]
Wales[2]	1,321	42,964	22,194
Northern Ireland[2]	141	—	3,412

Source: *British Tourist Authority Digest of Statistics No. 11.*
[1] figures are the 1983 stock of hotels, motels, inns and guest houses
[2] represents only those hotels registered in 1982 with national tourist boards. This is voluntary in Wales but compulsory in Northern Ireland
[3] includes establishments of 1–3 bedrooms
[4] not collected for Northern Ireland
[5] not collected for England
[6] based upon data collected from 2,454 hotels and thus represents 82 per cent of stock
[7] figures refer to 1982

West Country, a popular holiday region. There are a large number of small establishments in the West Country, two-thirds of the hotels having 10 bedrooms or less.

The majority of England's largest hotels are located in London however, there are 113 establishments of 201 or more bedrooms in England and of these 77 are London-located.

Table 1.9 lists the UK's top 20 hotel groups.

In the UK, we currently have a buyer's market, in other words, supply of accommodation exceeds demand.

Table 1.9   *United Kingdom's top 20 hotel groups (1985).*

Hotel	Rooms	Units	AA classifications
1. Trusthouse Forte Hotels	20,798	191	2, 3, 4, 5 star
2. Ladbroke Hotels	6,105	48	2, 3, 4 star
3. Crest Hotels	6,023	52	2, 3, 4 star
4. Mount Charlotte Hotels	5,834	51	1, 2, 3, 4 star
5. Queens Moat Houses	4,612	58	2, 3, 4 star
6. Thistle Hotels	4,511	35	3, 4 star
7. Swallow Hotels	3,190	31	2, 3, 4 star
8. G. W. Hotels	2,947	35	2, 3, 4, 5 star
9. Imperial London Hotels	2,778	7	Unclassified
10. Embassy Hotels	2,558	39	2, 3, 4 star
11. Stakis Hotels	2,408	27	2, 3, 4 star
12. Rank Hotels	2,247	6	4, 5 star
13. Commonwealth Holiday Inns	2,034	9	4 star
14. Metropole Hotels	1,965	6	4 star
15. Holiday Inns	1,891	8	4 star
16. Butlin's Hotels	1,483	7	Unclassified
17. Intercontinental Hotels	1,461	4	4, 5 star
18. Sheraton Hotels	1,443	5	4, 5 star
19. Hilton International Hotels	1,440	3	4, 5 star
20. Anchor Hotels	1,333	29	2, 3 star

Source: Huddersfield Polytechnic's Hotel & Catering Research Centre.
   Ownership changes cause rapid dating of such tables.

As noted earlier, demand for accommodation is a function of travel and tourism. The British Tourist Authority annually publishes a digest of statistics drawn from a number of sources such as the World Tourism Organisation, the OECD Tourism Committee, the UK Department of Trade and Industry's *International Passenger Survey*, the Central Statistical Office, the Department of Employment, the survey of Overseas Motoring Visitors to Britain and the British Tourist Authority's *British National Travel Survey* and *British Home Tourism Survey*. These figures are evidence of the significance of tourism to the economy.

Over recent years the number of overseas visitors to the UK has been static at about 11 or 12 million per annum. However their expenditure, as shown in Table 1.10, has been rising.

Table 1.10   *Overseas visitors to UK.*

	No. of overseas visitors[1]	Expenditure (£ million)	Expenditure per visitor (£)
1981	11,452	2,970	259
1982	11,636	3,168	272
1983	12,499	3,655	292

Source: International Passenger Survey (Business Monitor MQ6)
[1] Number of visits. Anyone entering more than once is counted on each occasion.

UK residents made over 21 million trips overseas during 1983; this represents an increase of greater than 50 per cent over 1978. Expenditure overseas was £4,054 million in 1983 compared to £1,549 million in 1978.

Not all accommodation demand is generated by overseas tourists. The *British Home Tourism Survey* estimates that British residents made a total of 133 million tourist trips in 1983, passing a total of 545 million nights away from home and spending some £5,350 million. These figures, which are put into recent historical context in Table 1.11, include business and holiday tourism plus visits to friends and relatives. Holiday tourism data appear separately in Table 1.12.

The hotel sector is labour intensive and this is obviously reflected in employment statistics. Table 1.13 shows that the sector employs a rising proportion of the total workforce (1.4 per cent in 1983).

Table 1.11   *All domestic tourism by British residents.*

	Estimated no. of trips[1] (millions)	Estimated no. of tourist nights[2] (millions)	Estimated expenditure[3] (£m)
1981	126	520	4,600
1982	123	505	4,500
1983	131	545	5,350

Source: British Home Tourism Survey 1983.
[1] Rounded to 1.0 million
[2] Rounded to 5.0 millions
[3] Rounded to 25 millions

Table 1.12   *Domestic holiday tourism by British residents.*

	Estimated no. of trips[1] (millions)	Estimated no. of tourist nights[2] (millions)	Estimated expenditure[3] (£m)
1981	72	385	3,075
1982	72	375	3,100
1983	78	410	3,625

Source: British Home Tourism Survey 1983.
[1] Rounded to 1.0 million
[2] Rounded to 5.0 millions
[3] Rounded to 25 millions

Table 1.13   *Employment in Hotels, UK ('000).*

	Total employed	Total hotel employees[1]	Percentage of total
1981	21,870	272	1.2
1982	21,473	279	1.3
1983	21,210	290	1.4

Source: CSO Annual Abstract of Statistics, 1984 & 1985 (Table 6.2).
[1] Hotels and other residential establishments.

1.8 THE CATERING SECTOR

Caterers are defined as:

> those organisations that provide food for consumption outside individual or family dwelling.[19]

Catering comprises two main sectors—organisations which cater for profit and those which cater at cost; the latter form is also known as welfare catering. The 'Welfare' or 'at cost' sector includes self-operated canteens and messes, hospitals, state schools, private schools, colleges and universities, the armed services and prisons. The 'for profit' sector includes restaurants, cafes, snackbars, fish and chip shops, take-away shops, licensed hotels, some motels, holiday camps, other hotels, boarding and guesthouses, public houses and bars, retail stores, catering contractors and licensed and registered clubs.

As with hotels establishments vary by location, demand, size, standard, ownership and atmosphere. The size of an industry is in part indicated by the number it employs. Table 1.14 shows that the numbers employed in catering in the UK rose between the years 1981 and 1983.

Table 1.14   *Employment in catering, UK ('000).*

	Total employed	Total catering	Percentage of total
1981	21,870	646	3.0
1982	21,473	689	3.2
1983	21,210	673	3.2

Source: CSO Annual Abstract of Statistics, 1984, & 1985 (Table 6.2).

A second set of statistics concerning the numbers of businesses registered for Value Added Tax (VAT), and their turnover appears in the *Annual Abstract of Statistics*. The data, which appear in Table 1.15, show that a total of 113,000 grossed revenue of £15 billion (inclusive of VAT) in 1982.

The largest proportion of revenue, 40 per cent of the total, was earned by Britain's 40,000 VAT registered public house businesses. The data in Table 1.15 are not the same as those in Table 1.7. Table 1.7 lists the number of hospitality outlets, Table 1.15 the number of VAT registered businesses; in addition to differences caused by multiple-outlet business and non-registered outlets the two sources quoted do not define types of outlet in the same way.

Each year, a survey is made into the food purchases of a sample of British households over a one-week period. A special report issued in 1981 showed that the average person

Table 1.15 *No. of catering businesses in Great Britain, and their turnover.*

	Year	No. of businesses[1]	Turnover (inclusive of VAT) (£m)
Total catering	1980	109,471	12,424
	1981	111,532	13,627
	1982	113,333	14,926
Hotels and other residential establishments	1980	14,281	2,483
	1981	13,929	2,752
	1982	13,385	2,880
Holiday camps, camping and holiday caravan sites	1980	1,587	405
	1981	1,565	421
	1982	1,542	390
Restaurants, cafes, snackbars, etc, selling food for consumption on the premises only	1980	11,512	1,431
	1981	11,735	1,529
	1982	11,817	1,639
Fish and chip shops, sandwich and snack bars and other establishments selling food partly or wholly for consumption off the premises	1980	22,715	1,103
	1981	24,980	1,284
	1982	26,256	1,497
Public houses[2]	1980	40,608	4,857
	1981	40,145	5,273
	1982	41,457	6,002
Clubs (excluding sports clubs and gaming clubs)	1980	17,571	1,570
	1981	17,873	1,718
	1982	17,568	1,776
Catering contractors	1980	1,196	575
	1981	1,304	650
	1982	1,308	743

Source: Annual Abstract of Statistics 1985.
[1] Only organisations registered for value added tax are recorded.
[2] Figures include, besides those businesses registered as Public Houses, brewers known to operate Public Houses. These 40 to 50 businesses account for about ⅓ of the total activity of Public Houses in each of these two years.

eats about 3.25 meals per week in which the food content is not from the household supply. This average varies between: geographic areas—4.27 in Greater London compared to 2.86 in the survey's most rural area; income group—4.91 for the large-income earners compared to 1.08 for old age pensioner households; housing tenure—6.45 for those living in rented, furnished accommodation compared to 2.9 for those living in unfurnished council property; age group—4.48 for households in which the housewife is under 25 years old compared to 1.71 where the housewife is 75 years and over[20].

The general profile of the consumer of catering products is a young, relatively affluent, city dweller living in rented accommodation.

1.9 CHAPTER REVIEW

1. The service sector of the economy employs over 56 per cent of the working population of the UK.
2. The employment share of services is growing.
3. Over one quarter of consumer expenditure is on services.
4. Exports of services are greater than imports.
5. Services are widely thought to require a marketing approach which is different from that used for physical goods.
6. The issue of whether services are different from physical goods can be approached from 4 points: attempts can be made to define 'service', products can be sorted into taxonomies which distinguish between goods and services, functional differences between goods and services can be isolated and all products can be categorised by reference to conceptual frameworks which transcend the 'is it a good or is it a service?' argument.
7. There is no consensus definition of 'service'.
8. Four functional differences are said to distinguish services from goods—services are heterogeneous, intangible, perishable, inseparable.
9. One conceptual framework categorises all products into 'shopping' products or 'convenience' products.
10. The confusion surrounding the validity of the concept of service marketing arises out of its recent emergence, its lack of history and marketers' recognition that many physical goods contain elements of service.
11. Service marketing literature is generally concerned with products which are 'service dominant'.
12. The Standard Industrial Classification (SIC) distinguishes between 4 forms of service industry.
13. The SIC does not group all hospitality activities together.
14. The hotel and catering industry is also known as the hospitality industry.
15. The hospitality industry includes all organisations whose output satisfies the demand for accommodation, food and beverage away from home.
16. The level of UK investment in hospitality fixed capital is rising.
17. UK consumers spent £10 billion on hospitality in 1983.
18. The 3 core products offered by hospitality marketers are accommodation, food and beverage. A fourth product, atmosphere/environment, is felt, by many marketers, to be equally important.
19. Demand for accommodation is a function of travel and tourism.
20. Tourists may travel for business or holiday/pleasure reasons and may be domestic or international.
21. Demand for food and drink may be connected with staying away from home or may be an activity in its own right.

22. Success in the hospitality industry may be dependent upon satisfying consumer leisure needs and wants.
23. Both hotels and catering establishments vary by location, demand, size, ownership and atmosphere.
24. An hotel is 'an establishment of a permanent nature, of 4 or more bedrooms, offering bed-and-breakfast on a short term contract and certain minimum standards.'
25. The UK hotel market comprises some 20,000 establishments containing 670,000 bedspaces.
26. The locational pattern of hotels is a function of demand.
27. There are between 11 and 12 million overseas visitors to the UK per annum.
28. British domestic tourists spent over 500 million nights away from home in 1982; of these, 75 per cent were spent by holidaymakers.
29. Hotels employ about 1.4 per cent of the UK working population.
30. Caterers are 'those organisations that provide food for consumption outside individual or family dwellings'.
31. Caterers may operate 'for profit' or 'at cost'.
32. 'At cost' caterers are also known as welfare caterers.
33. Catering establishments employ 3.2 per cent of the UK working population and grossed £15 billion in 1983 (only VAT registered businesses).
34. The general profile of the consumer of catering products is a young, relatively affluent, city dweller living in rented accommodation.

1.10 QUESTIONS

1. How useful is the distinction between holiday and business travel? What relevance does it have for hospitality management?
2. Is 'hospitality' a better way to describe the industry than 'hotel and catering'? Why?
3. Why do some marketers regard the distinction between goods and services as unhelpful? How valid is the distinction?
4. Hospitality makes a direct contribution to the trading health of the economy. Does it also make an indirect contribution?
5. Attempt to define the term 'service' and distinguish it from 'good'.
6. What are the connections between tourism and hospitality, leisure and hospitality, leisure and tourism?
7. The functional differences said to distinguish between goods and services—heterogeneity, intangibility, perishability and inseparability—appear to be uncharacteristic of some services. Consider banking, hairdressing, take-away food service, window-cleaning, dry-cleaning, management consultancy and private education. Do these distinctions apply?

REFERENCES

[1] Gershuny, J. I. and Miles, I. D., *The New Service Economy* (1983) Frances Pinter.
[2] Levitt, T. (1981) Marketing intangible products and product intangibles. *Harvard Business Review*, May–June.
[3] Christopher, M., McDonald, M. and Wills, G. (1980) *Introducing Marketing*. London: Pan Books.
[4] Wyckham, R. G., Fitzroy, T., and Mandry, G. D. (1975) Marketing services. *European Journal of Marketing*, **9**(1).
[5] Blois, K. (1983) Service marketing—assertion or asset. *Service Industries Journal*, **3**(2), July, 113–20.
[6] Bonoma, T. V. and Mills, M. K. (1980) *Services Marketing*. Working Paper, Harvard Business School, Cambridge, MA.

[7]   Middleton, V. T. C. (1983) Product marketing—goods and services compared. *Quarterly Review of Marketing*, **8**(4), July, 1–10.
[8]   Goodfellow, J. H. (1983) The marketing of goods and services as a multidimensional concept. *Quarterly Review of Marketing*, **8**(3), April, 19–27.
[9]   Shostack, G. L. (1977) Breaking free from product marketing. *Journal of Marketing*, **41**(2).
[10] Gronroos, C. (1980) *An Applied Service Marketing Theory*. Working Paper No. 57, Swedish School of Economics and Business Administration, Helsinki.
[11] Middleton, V.T.C. (1983) op. cit.
[12] Lovelock, C. H. (1979) Theoretical contributions for service and non-business marketing, in Ferrell O.C. (ed.) *Conceptual and Theoretical Developments in Marketing* (Proceedings series): AMA, 147–65.
[13] Shostack, G. L. (1982) How to design a service. *European Journal of Marketing*, **16**(1).
[14] *Standard Industrial Classfication* (rev. 1980). London: Central Statistical Office.
[15] Hotel and Catering Economic Development Committee (1976). *Hotel Prospects to 1985*. London: NEDO.
[16] Medlik, S. and Airey, D. W. (1978) (2nd edn.) *Profile of the Hotel and Catering Industry*. London: Heinemann.
[17] This section draws heavily on *Leisure Spending in the European Community: Forecasts to 1990*, EIU Special Report No. 93, Economist Intelligence Unit, 1981.
[18] Hotel and Catering Economic Development Committee (1976) op. cit.
[19] Hotel and Catering and Food Manufacturing Economic Development Committees (1971) *Convenience Foods in Catering*. London: NEDO.
[20] *Household Food Consumption and Expenditure, 1981*. London: MAFF.

—2———————————————

First Principles

2.1 CHAPTER PREVIEW

This chapter introduces the basics of marketing; it defines what is meant by the term marketing and differentiates it from selling. It presents marketing in both a business and a non-business context, drawing conclusions about the tasks common to all marketing managements. The aim is to show that marketing is:
- a set of skills and techniques
- a way of doing business

2.2 LEARNING OBJECTIVES

By the end of this chapter you should be able to:
1. Define the following:
   - marketing.
   - marketing orientation.
   - marketing concept.
   - market.
2. List the four elements of the marketing mix.
3. Distinguish between marketing, selling and advertising.
4. List and describe the main environmental factors which can affect marketing decisions.
5. Identify instances in which the marketing concept has been adopted in the hospitality industry.
6. Explain why a marketing orientation isn't always best.
7. Critically evaluate the marketing concept.
8. Identify and characterise eight different demand management tasks.
9. Explain why marketing management *is* demand management.

2.3 MARKETING DEFINED

Whether we recognise it or not, we are all involved willingly or unwillingly in marketing. We are involved as buyers, sellers and consumers of goods and services. We are involved as shoppers, readers of advertising and as advisers of friends.

But not only are we involved in marketing through these consumption-related activities, even in a social sense we may be involved in marketing. For example, if we were to ask a draughtsman friend to produce a drawing of a planned restaurant extension so that we can meet the local authority planning committee's requirements, we may well have to market the proposal. It will almost certainly involve diplomatic yet persuasive communication with the friend and an offer to reimburse out-of-pocket expenses. Many social transactions involve exchanges of this sort, and the concept of exchange is central to marketing.

A definition will make this point more clearly. Marketing has been defined in many ways which often appear to conflict.[1] Earlier definitions tended to emphasise marketing as a business function with profit as the end-purpose of marketing and activities such as selling or advertising as the means by which this profit is created. Because marketing skills are now widely applied outside the profit-oriented business environment, this is no longer acceptable.

The definition which best describes all the marketing activities featured in this book is:

Marketing is the process by which exchange of mutual satisfiers occurs.

There are several aspects of this definition which are worth noting. First, it is a 'process', a series of measures, changes, activities, or events. The marketing process typically involves a series of identifiable stages. Since this book is largely (but not exclusively) concerned with the marketing for profit of hotel and catering products, let us now put this marketing process into a business context. It normally involves:
- finding or creating a dissatisfied group of consumers
- designing a product or service to satisfy their wants
- selling it at a price the consumers are willing to pay
- making it conveniently accessible for purchase

A new hospitality product, Comfort Inns, was launched in 1984. These are 120-room hotels based at motorway junctions, offering up-market amenities at 2-star prices. The market is price-conscious UK businessmen.

A second feature of the definition is that marketing involves 'exchange'. Not only does exchange include the customary business exchanges of goods and services for money, but also barter and swapping. It is possible for any exchange activity to be analysed in marketing terms. Barter, as a form of exchange, does have a number of advantages over more prosaic marketing methods.[2] Currently international barter is enjoying popularity. Nearly half of American purchasing agents have engaged in some form of barter.[3] Britain's export barter trade is valued at over £3 billion per annum (1983 figures). Bartering also occurs in the hotel and catering industry. A hotel will house a sales conference for its linen supplier in exchange for a year's free laundry supply. A restaurant will offer free hospitality to a local radio station and its guests in exchange for unpaid advertising time. Hospitality barter agreements are also called 'trade-outs', particularly in the USA. In some industries barter is so commonplace that several forms exist.[4]

A third aspect of our definition of marketing is that the exchange involves 'mutual satisfiers'. This is quite clearly demonstrated by the barter examples where one item is exchanged for another, both parties to the exchange obtaining their 'satisfier'. In a business sense a company is satisfied by achieving its objectives: making a profit, achieving a targeted turnover and paying a reasonable dividend to shareholders; the consumers' wants are satisfied by the acquisition and consumption of the product and by experiencing the benefits that the product brings.

Philip Kotler, the noted American marketing scholar, offers the following definition of marketing:[5]

> Marketing is a social process by which individuals and groups obtain what they need and want through creating and exchanging products and value with others.

Both Kotler's and our own definition stress the mutual exchange process which is central to marketing.

The Institute of Marketing, which is the main British professional body for practising marketers, proposes the following definition:

> Marketing is the management process responsible for identifying, anticipating and satisfying customer requirements profitably.

One criticism of this definition is that it limits marketing activities to those organisations which have profit as their objective. Non-profit-making organisations also market their wares—charities, sports clubs and religious denominations all perform marketing activities; they are involved in exchange.

2.4 HOSPITALITY MARKETING

Marketing has a role to play in both the profit and the welfare sectors of the hospitality industry. In the profit sector marketers strive to improve room-occupancy levels and the number of covers by devising products which appeal to customers. In the welfare sector marketing's main function is to maximise customer satisfaction within the constraint of a given budget. The customer may be a patient, prisoner, pensioner, pupil or employee, but the organisation which houses and/or feeds him has generally to keep within specified cost limits.

The school meals service, which turns over £500 million per annum and serves 6 million meals per day, is the major sector of the hospitality industry.[6] One review of the school meals service found a high degree of waste, and proposed changes which 'will result in a school meals service producing cost effectively what the customer wants rather than an academic and outmoded idea of what the customer needs'.[7]

Research has also shown that if patients feel at ease in hospitals, they recover sooner. Bad-quality food deeply dissatisfies patients and delays recovery. It has been proposed that 'the patient should be offered a limited à la carte menu based on market research and experience', and that 'there must be a possibility for the walking patient to eat his meal in different situations, room or restaurant, with or without service'.[8] Since only 1 patient in 10 has a special diet, it has been observed that the majority of patients could have meals suited to their normal eating patterns, including full family meals for parents visiting children, birthday cakes for children and wine to celebrate wedding anniversaries. The costs of a non-marketing approach are said to be dissatisfied patients, wasted resources and lost professional reputations of catering staff.[9]

The industrial catering market is a major welfare catering sector. It is estimated that there are between 15,000 and 35,000 units with catering outlets. There is little doubt that the impact of satisfactory industrial food service on worker productivity has been inadequately researched, but 'catering at work is indivisible from the work experience and in consequence is an integral part of industrial relations'.[10]

2.5 INTERNATIONAL VARIATIONS

It is notable that the role of marketing in business varies between types of economy. Marketing, as applied in most capitalist businesses, is aimed at producing satisfied consumers for a satisfactory return to the business proprietors. This is not the aim of marketing in socialist Eastern Europe. The Socialist Marketing Association of Poland (Stowarzyszenie Socjalistycznego Marketingu) defines marketing thus:[11]

> Socialist marketing is that set of integrated activities having as their aim the organization of production from the point of view of domestic and foreign markets and the interests of the national economy.

Evidently this is a radically different view of marketing in which the emphasis is upon achievement of harmonious production in the interests of the state. Yet in one way these two conceptions of marketing are similar: both recognise that marketing attempts to shape or influence demand. The East European definition, however, stresses only the needs of the state-owned producer, not the satisfaction of consumer wants.

2.6 EXPANDING THE DEFINITION OF MARKETING

The traditional conception of marketing is narrow. It views marketing skills as applicable only to consumer or industrial goods and services for the creation of profit. Lately this view has been challenged, particularly by marketers whose skills are being applied in different business environments.

'Meta' is a Greek word, meaning 'beyond', 'after', or 'over'. Metamarketing is the term which has been coined to describe the performance of marketing activities outside a business context.[12] Marketing has matured within the business environment where the skills and techniques of marketers have been put to their most sophisticated use. However, marketing techniques can be used by any organisation or individual wishing either to encourage or discourage an exchange. In many instances the aims and objectives of the metamarketer are non-profit-oriented.

Marketing techniques are being applied in these areas:
- activity marketing (pony-trekking, hang-gliding)
- cause marketing (cancer research, Greenpeace)
- idea marketing (e.g. de Bono's 'lateral thinking')
- organisation marketing (universities, clubs)
- person marketing (sports and pop-music personalities)
- place marketing (Stratford-upon-Avon, Costa Brava)

In addition, there is the marketing of goods and services.

A major metamarketer is the International Management Group, which markets many current and past sports and media personalities such as Arnold Palmer, Björn Borg, Mats Wilander, Jackie Stewart, Martina Navratilova and Michael Parkinson. The company arranges endorsements, exhibitions, tournaments, special events, overseas literary efforts and develops sports films and television programmes.

2.7 THE MARKETING CONCEPT

Marketing is more than a set of skills and techniques used in the process of delivering mutual satisfaction; in many companies it represents a basic way of doing business.

These companies, which are sometimes claimed to have better sales and profit records, have adopted marketing as their 'business logic'—they have adopted the marketing concept.

The marketing concept consists of three interdependent propositions; when a company operationalises them, it is said to have adopted the marketing concept as its fundamental business orientation. The 3 propositions are:

1. A customer or consumer orientation should be the focal point for company decision-making.
2. Such decision-making should produce profitable sales.
3. The entire company should be aware of customers' needs and wants and should be organised and integrated to ensure that the consumer's requirements are met.

If these three conditions are satisfied, it can be claimed that the company is fully marketing-oriented.

In recent years, however, the marketing concept has received much criticism. The most significant of these criticisms are:

1. The limited focus of marketing-oriented companies.

The marketing concept focuses attention on a small group of people—the company's consumers. Other groups can be adversely affected by this limited focus. Much marketing activity produces pollution. This pollution, which can occur during the development, manufacture, transport, selling, consumption, or disposal of a product, is a social cost which has to be carried by society as a whole, and not simply the company's customers.

2. The emphasis on *profitable* sales volume.

The marketing concept demands that the satisfaction of consumer wants shall be profitable. Where a want exists but the marketing opportunity appears unprofitable, the marketer generally will not produce the item. Consequently restaurants have been slow to offer high-fibre, low-salt, or low-fat items on their menus; demand, until recently, has been low. Nor have hotels been designed to accommodate the physically handicapped.

3. The 'cultural carnage' created by some international marketers.

The marketing concept has meant that consumer wants are sometimes met regardless of their cultural consequences (when there exists a profitable sales volume). The *New Internationalist* has investigated the marketing activities of powdered milk manufacturers:[13]

> Our investigation showed that companies like Nestlé were busy persuading poor and often illiterate mothers to abandon breast feeding in favour of powdered milk foods which, in most cases, they did not need, could not afford and were unable to use safely. As a result, unknown thousands of babies were being fed over-diluted milk from unsterilised bottles and were therefore exposed to disease and malnutrition.
>
> These facts are known to the European and American baby food companies like Nestlé and Abbott Laboratories, American makers of a milk brand called 'Similac'.
>
> Yet they continue to promote their products on radio and in newspapers and on hoarding-boards with seemingly no regard for the misery they are inflicting on mothers and children.

The basic issue in all these criticisms is that *marketing has lacked a societal concern*. Marketers are becoming more aware of this and some have responded by suggesting the need for a special 'society-oriented' definition of marketing, such as this:[14]

Marketing is a matching process, based on goals and capabilities by which a producer provides a marketing mix that meets consumer needs *within the limits of society*.[14]

Or this:[15]

The societal marketing concept holds that the organization's task is to determine the needs, wants and interests of target markets and to deliver the desired satisfactions more effectively and efficiently than competitors in a way that *preserves or enhances the consumers' and society's well being*.[15]

Marketing is able to provide three types of satisfaction:
- personal
- social
- societal

Personal satisfaction occurs when the consumers of a product experience gratification from its ownership and/or consumption. Social satisfaction occurs when the consumer's immediate circle of acquaintances, for example, his family or friends, approve of the purchase, as when children tell parents that they enjoyed a trip to the local family restaurant. Societal satisfaction occurs when society as a whole approves of the purchase and consumption of the product. With a 'product' such as education, the whole of society benefits from its consumption, even though only a minority are currently instructed. The societal marketing concept suggests that marketers should stress the delivery of societal satisfactions in consumption whilst also delivering personal and social satisfactions.

Whilst adopting a new definition of the marketing concept may be a sound academic response, there has been only a small voluntary shift in marketing practice. Government controls have been introduced to police marketing behaviour. Some professionals regard this as a reflection of marketing's inability to 'put its own house in order'. Government now has controls over product safety, labelling, pricing, selling methods and several other aspects of marketing. Marketers are more aware of the social responsibilities which have been imposed upon them. Industry watchdog groups, such as the Consumers' Association, now vigorously hound marketers of products considered unsafe. Codes of practice for advertising and sales promotion are now stronger and more readily enforced than previously.

Property developers, including those in the hotel sector, are widely regarded in some sections of the community as bringing more harm than good to society. Green fields and clean beaches are transformed into landscapes of concrete and litter as hotels are built and tourists arrive. The natural beauty and quality of the environment is lost for ever as a minority of developers, proprietors and holidaymakers benefit. Developers retort that hotels create employment and wealth, enriching society. Criticism can be especially severe of international developments; the need to satisfy tourists means that local customs and indigenous values may be trivialised or subjugated. Eventually, some critics claim, the world will be impoverished by its cultural monotony.

2.8 MARKETING ORIENTATION

Marketing orientation is the term used to describe the way of doing business characterised by those companies who have adopted the marketing concept.

Express Catering Foods provides one example of marketing orientation. This company had noticed that much of the content of foil-wrapped, single-portion butter pats bought by caterers was wasted. Diners would use only a part of the prepacked portion and the rest was thrown away. Caterers were paying for butter which their customers, in turn, were not using. Express Catering Foods obtained exclusive rights to a manufacturing system which enabled them to offer a uniquely packaged, smaller single-serve butter pat to caterers. For the caterer it has meant smaller portions, less waste, more cost efficiency and improved profitability. For Express it has meant a greater share of sales in a market where volume sold had been static for some years.

The marketing orientation, as a way of doing business, is appropriate for much of today's industry and commerce. However, it is not always the best. Many companies are orientated, frequently with success, towards different functions. Most common are the production orientation and the sales orientation.

The production orientation is often found in companies serving markets in which demand exceeds supply. Here technological advances may have dramatically changed the face of industry. When transistors were widely being adopted by companies as a much-improved advance over the traditional valve, electrical component manufacturers struggled to produce at a volume to match demand. Similar circumstances exist for the silicon chip, which is widely regarded as a universal replacement for the traditional electrical circuit board. Volume production is vital if the adoption of innovations is to be both widespread and rapid. High volume normally produces economies of scale which are reflected in low prices. Additionally, the innovative silicon chip manufacturer can discourage market entry by new competitors by adopting efficient, low-cost manufacturing systems giving cost advantages and consequent low prices.

A production orientation is much more likely to be successful where the product is essentially the same as those of competitors (i.e. there is little product differentiation) or where there is a technological lead time over competitors as may be afforded by the protection of a patent. Much welfare catering is production-oriented; management is concerned primarily with costs and volume—customer requirements are secondary considerations.

The sales orientation tends to be found in companies with a large fixed capital investment in plant, building and technology, serving markets in which supply exceeds demand. Here the emphasis is on producing a high volume of sales in order to return a fair profit in relation to the capital employed. Because of the large fixed investment, development of new products can be a costly, long-term venture which can only be financed by cash flow resulting from aggressive selling of the existing product.

Much of the hotel industry is sales-oriented. Supply of accommodation exceeds demand. Since hotels are immobile and structural alterations costly, they can neither be moved to locations where demand is higher nor are they readily converted to new uses such as offices, flats, or retail outlets without considerable expense. Hotel marketers frequently need to demonstrate selling skills to build demand for unfavourably located premises in order to finance new long-term ventures.

The sales orientation is frequently a mid-point in a shift from production to marketing orientation. Medlik has noted this pattern in the hotel industry.[16] In today's economic climate the marketing orientation is commonly lauded as the best possible assurance for long-term corporate survival.

Some marketers believe that a marketing orientation is the only right 'logic' for a business whilst other orientations are wrong. This is not necessarily so; others have their place and all can be profitable. Even a technical orientation can be profitable. However, it should be stressed that companies which do not, at an early stage in their planning, consider the needs of the consumer are dicing with financial death.

2.9 MARKETING MANAGEMENT

The main task of marketing, to influence the volume and value of exchanges, requires effective deployment of resources—i.e. people, machinery, finance and materials. Effectiveness is best obtained through skilled management.

Even managers from totally different industries will find that there is some degree of similarity between their job specifications. Every manager is involved in some form of:
- analysis of his decision environment
- planning for future achievements
- implementation of plans
- control of plans and staff

Marketing management is generally concerned, for example, with:

analysis of target markets, competitive marketing strengths, the impact of advertising legislation on promotional activities, marketing opportunities.

planning of marketing strategies to achieve marketing objectives, channels of distribution, advertising campaigns.

implementing marketing strategies, salesforce training schemes, creative advertising solutions to marketing problems.

controlling the marketing budget, the calling frequency of salesmen, advertising expenditure.

This answers the question of what marketing managers do, but it does not answer the question of why they do what they do.

2.10 DEMAND MANAGEMENT

The four management activities listed above relate to two key exchange functions of marketing. These are, for most companies, *facilitation* and *stimulation of consumption*.[17]

Most companies want to improve their business performance—increased sales, increased profits and a rapid rate of growth are the signals of success. Marketing can be the means to this end; marketing can through astute pricing, promotion and distribution of a product stimulate consumers to buy or use more, and make it easier for them to do so.

Sales promotions and advertising are time-honoured ways of stimulating consumption whereas consumption of fast food is facilitated by locating outlets at key strategic points. This suggests that most marketing decisions are directed towards creating a growth in consumption levels. Whilst this is true for most profit-oriented businesses, it is not true for all types of marketing organisations. Kotler[18] has identified and categorised 8 different marketing management problems according to whether demand in the market matches the demand level desired by the marketer (Table 2.1).

Table 2.1 *Demand management.*

	Demand state	Marketing task
1	Negative demand	Disabuse demand
2	No demand	Create demand
3	Latent demand	Develop demand
4	Falling demand	Revitalise demand
5	Irregular demand	Synchronise demand
6	Full demand	Maintain demand
7	Overfull demand	Reduce demand
8	Unwholesome demand	Destroy demand

Where demand states 1–4 occur, a company is primarily interested in facilitating and stimulating consumption, actual demand being less than the level desired by the company. Irregular demand (state 5) suggests that the company manipulates the temporal flow of demand. Full demand (state 6) occurs when actual demand is perfectly satisfactory to the marketer. Demand states 7 and 8 are both examples of situations in which the primary role of marketing management is to inhibit consumption. Let us examine each type of marketing task in greater detail.

Where negative demand exists, marketers attempt to create or develop a want in consumers who positively dislike or avoid the product. For example, a number of vegetarian restaurants may co-operate in promotions to persuade meat-eaters to sample their food. Where consumers are disinterested in the product or service being offered, marketers must try to create a demand. For example, a tour operator specialising in skiing holidays but located well away from the ski slopes could attempt to stimulate demand among a disinterested city public by building an artificial ski slope and providing free skiing lessons.

Latent demand could be exploited if there were a product or service to meet consumer wants. However, as the phrase 'latent demand' suggests, there is no such product. Until recently latent demand existed for special-interest weekend breaks. Driven by the need to fill empty beds over weekends, hoteliers have developed weekend break schemes incorporating accommodation, food and occasionally travel. Frequently the schemes are themed around sports, recreational, or cultural activities. There are gourmet, bridge, gardening and theatre weekend breaks. Demand for short breaks was latent until product development enabled its exploitation.

Where demand is falling, revitalisation is required. Remarketing, the term used to describe the revitalisation of demand, is the question all marketers face when they have a product whose sales volume is declining. Berni Inns recently invested £3 million in revitalising demand for its product. Demand for its traditional fare had been falling. The company spent £300,000 researching the market prior to replacing its set-price menu with a three-tier approach to eating. The three products, all designed to satisfy different groups of customers, are branded the Burgundy Room, Berni and Eleven Eleven. The first offers smart waiter service, a leather-bound menu and a wide choice of dishes; the second has a family appeal; and the third has a wine-bar format aimed at the younger consumer.[19]

Where demand occurs in an irregular seasonal pattern, as does the demand for greetings cards, ice-cream and hotels, the marketing task is to redistribute demand more evenly or to create new types of demand for the off-season. Thus a coastal hotel offers conference facilities during winter, and an ice-cream manufacturer concentrates on the take-home and catering markets during the winter months when he cannot rely on single-serve impulse sales.

Fluctuations in demand can cause considerable management difficulties. During periods of low utilisation capacity remains unused, but permanent staff still have to be paid and other fixed costs are incurred. During periods of high demand extra staff may have to be recruited and trained or further assets purchased or hired to satisfy the inflated demand. Management, according to one observer, can respond to these fluctuations either by manipulating demand so that seasonal irregularities are levelled out or by making supply so flexible that peaks of demand are profitably accommodated.[20] A number of strategies are proposed for each alternative. To manipulate demand a business can:

- Introduce differential pricing to discourage overdemand during seasonal peaks and encourage demand during troughs
- Develop new products to exploit unused capacity
- Promote off-peak sales
- Develop complementary products which can absorb overdemand—a restaurant may open a bar to hold excess demand until tables are vacated
- Create reservation systems to presell capacity; these systems can deflect excess demand to slack periods

To manipulate supply a business can:

- Use part-time employees at peak time
- Strive for maximum efficiency at peak time
- Increase customer participation so that demand on employees' time is reduced—restaurants may introduce self-service, salad bars, smorgasbord, or a buffet
- Share capacity with competitors—during periods of high demand it may be possible to use competitors' staff or equipment
- Invest in the 'expansion ante'—when constructing new facilities, flexibility could be built in; buildings become multi-purpose; restaurants be partitioned when catering for smaller parties; or hotel rooms subdivided to accommodate additional guests

According to one National Economic Development Office (NEDO) report hotels, particularly those dependent upon the holiday market, cope with fluctuations by reducing the room inventory. Either rooms or floors are closed off during the low season or entire hotels close down. They report that some 36 per cent of hotels are closed for 3 or more months each year and 44 per cent for at least one month.[21]

Where demand is full and there is no difference between actual and desired demand levels, the job of the marketer is to maintain this position. Full demand generally signifies a profitable market. Profitable markets attract competition, which launches similar products, lower-cost versions, or new and improved versions in order to take a profitable share. A marketer can only avoid this erosion of demand by himself offering improved customer satisfaction.

Demarketing is necessary when the actual demand level is too high for the marketer. The primary task in demarketing is to reduce demand to a level acceptable to the marketer. During the oil crisis in the 1970s the government demarketed oil by encouraging conservation. Destruction of demand is the principal management task where demand is undesirable from the point of view of consumer, manufacturer, government, or society. Countermarketing, the term used to describe this activity, has recently been employed to combat drug abuse.

The tasks of marketing management might vary, yet they are all similar in one respect. All marketers try to create a desired volume and value of exchanges by influencing demand: *marketing management is demand management.*

2.11 THE TOOLS OF THE TRADE

The marketing mix is the term used to denote the battery of instruments and tools that the marketer uses to influence demand. For any marketer, whether attempting to achieve non-profit or profit objectives, the battery is basically the same.

It has become customary to consider the marketing mix as the Four Ps—product, price, promotion and place.[22] Listed below are examples of some of the dimensions of the Four Ps which the marketer can manipulate in order to influence the exchange behaviour of his market.

Product

Features which are tangible such as size, colour, flavour, odour, quality, name and durability; and intangibles like image, warranty, or guarantee.

Price

Recommended retail price or rack rate; discounts for volume purchase; settlement discounts; differentiation of price in order to appeal to specific groups of customers; and price promotions.

Promotion

Personal selling; telephone selling; advertising; direct mail; sales promotion; public relations; publicity merchandising; and sponsorship.

Place

Facilities location; and inventory level.

In later chapters we shall refer to these components of the marketing mix in much greater detail, discussing the benefits, costs and uses of each.

It should now be clear that selling is not the same as marketing; selling is just one part of the promotion component of the marketing mix. Many people regard marketing as a fancy word for selling. It is not. Selling concentrates on moving what *is* produced; marketing helps to determine what *should be* offered for consumption. Levitt makes these comments:[23]

> Selling . . . is not marketing. Selling concerns itself with the tricks and techniques of getting people to exchange their cash for your product. It is not concerned with the values that the exchange is all about. And it does not, as marketing invariably does, view the entire business process as consisting of a tightly integrated effort to discover, create, arouse and satisfy consumer needs.

Nor is marketing another word for advertising. This too is simply one element in the promotion component of the marketing mix.

2.12 THE MARKETING ENVIRONMENT

Marketing is unlike any of the other major functions in a company—finance, production, personnel, and research and development—in one major way. Marketing is the function through which a company's relationship with the market-place is managed. All the other functions are predominantly inward-looking whilst marketing is primarily outward-looking.

This means that marketing management operates in environments over which it lacks full control. Although the task of the marketing mix is to provide a degree of control, it is rarely, if ever, total. Indeed there are some elements of the business and marketing system which are beyond the control of any marketer.

Business—a system

It is possible to represent a single business as one part of a larger system. The full system can be viewed as having three environments: an internal organisational environment; an operational environment; and an extraneous environment. This is shown symbolically in Figure 2.1.

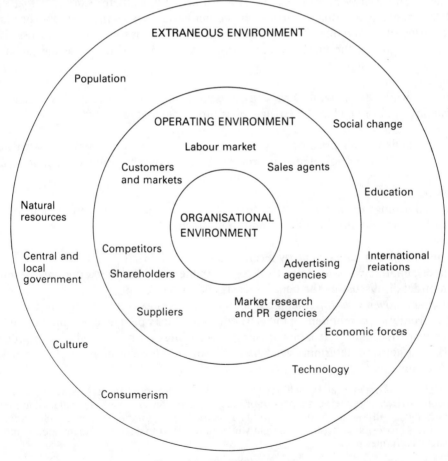

Figure 2.1   The business system.

The organisational environment includes the company, its areas of functional specialisation such as marketing, finance, the roles of the managers and the formal and informal network of relationships between them. The operating environment consists of the organisations and individuals outside the internal environment of the company with which it has close contact in the conduct of its day-to-day business activities. Thus it includes customers, markets, agents, shareholders, advertising agencies, marketing research and public relations agencies, the labour market, competition, material and equipment suppliers.

All businesses, including those in a firm's operating environment, have to cope with the largely unmanageable impact of changes on a national, international, or global scale. This extraneous environment includes trends in population; natural resource utilisation and consumerism; the effects of local and national government decisions; and technological, economic, social and educational change.

Businesses operate under the influence of change in all three environments, and unless such change is accommodated by the business, its survival may be threatened. This is one of the major reasons why a large number of firms employ researchers to scan the environment for changes and trends which impinge upon the profitable deployment of their resources.

Management decisions are often made in response to environmental threats; for example, a hotel's marketing management might lobby local government to prevent planning permission being granted to a competitor whilst work study and personnel deal with threats from the organisational environment such as inefficiency in operations and dissatisfaction of employees.

Marketing is the function of a company which has most dealings with the operating and extraneous environments, including its communications with the environment in the form of salesmen, advertising, public relations and publicity, its distributors and agents who sell the company's products and its research which determines the goods or services to be offered to the consumer. Marketing is, therefore, the organisation's keenest interface with the operating and extraneous environments. Within these environments are many uncontrollable threats to the company's performance; perversely these threats may also present opportunities for an entrepreneurial marketer, as we shall see in the review which follows.

2.13 OPERATING ENVIRONMENT

(1) The Market

A market can be defined as potential or actual demand. Over time a market may expand, shrink, collapse, or boom. A market can contract in one geographic area whilst expanding in another.

Markets can change overnight—a new competitor, a technological breakthrough, or a price alteration may suddenly affect the nature of demand in a market. More often, however, changes are slow. For example, changes in exchange rates are normally gradual and predictable. American demand for British hotel accommodation is highly correlated to the relative strength of the pound against the dollar. When the pound is weak against the dollar, Americans take advantage of the opportunity for a cheap vacation. In 1983 the dollar bought 34 per cent more than it had in 1981. Conversely, between 1981 and 1983, the number of Britons holidaying in the USA dropped dramatically as the pound weakened.

(2) The customers

The type of person who is the customer for a product varies over time. Early in the life of a new product purchases are made by innovators who tend to be risk-takers. Later groups of first-time purchasers tend to be more conservative. For instance, the laggards—the group last adopting an innovation—tend to be older, tradition-bound and sceptical of new products and to live outside the metropolitan areas.

Recently in the UK there has been a widespread increase in the number of wine drinkers. About 25 million people now drink wine, and more are added annually, making a substantial and growing sector for caterers, hoteliers, vintners and marketers of the wine buff's paraphernalia. More important, the perceived snobbery attached to wine-drinking is collapsing and many new consumers have swelled the market, particularly young people. The wine-drinker profile has changed dramatically.

(3) Material supply

Not only is the relationship between a company and its material suppliers of critical importance, but the willingness of a firm to adopt innovative materials may also contribute significantly towards profitability. Many fast-food caterers employ food scientists and quality control staff who not only specify in detail the ingredients of, say, buns and meat pasties, but ensure that standards are maintained by suppliers and that product development is undertaken to improve business performance. Marketers clearly need to be alert to supply deficiencies, sudden price movements, material substitution and political problems in materials supply.

(4) Labour supply

The supply of skilled or trained labour is scarce in some sectors of hospitality, particularly in high average-spend restaurant operations where well-known chefs are in demand. If a company cannot obtain skilled labour in its own area, it can respond by:
- producing a training programme
- importing labour

The marketer needs to be aware of possible problems in labour supply, and its impact upon production and marketing.

(5) Sales agents

In some markets distributors exert great power over their suppliers. Multiple travel agents such as Thomas Cook are highly selective about the products they display and sell. Increasingly retailers are exerting more power in the travel market.

When the Association of British Travel Agents (ABTA) refused to permit members to sell Skytrain Holidays after the £280 million collapse of Laker Airways, Sir Freddie Laker opted to sidestep the normal channels for the sale of holidays and recruited hairdressers, postmasters and newsagents into a novel, although eventually unsuccessful, channel of distribution. Distribution channels are evolutionary. Marketers can obtain a competitive advantage by selling through innovative channels, by breaking with tradition and by tying distributors to exclusive contracts which prevent them handling competitors' products.

(6) Competition

One highly important element of the operating environment is competition. Marketers need to monitor competitors' products, markets, production, marketing and distribution methods. A company seeking an advantage for its products in a competitive market is well advised to maintain a library of competitive intelligence material.

2.14 EXTRANEOUS ENVIRONMENT

(1) Government

The influence of government, both national and local, on the environment into which a company sells is, of course, enormous. Government creates the economic, legal and administrative framework within which business operates. Its influence extends from legislation and financing of business to actually being a major consumer of goods and services in its own right.

Many examples of local government influence on the business environment may be seen daily in the press. Rates affect profitability, planning regulations determine investment decisions and traffic management may influence the number of customers for a business.

The marketer can learn of possible impacts of government activity upon his enterprise by scanning the business press, by co-operating with competitors in an industry-wide organisation through which to lobby government and by maintaining close contacts with the Member of Parliament responsible for the constituency in which the company is located.

The extent of legislation which contains the behaviour of marketers is impressive:
Advertisements (Hire Purchase) Act 1967
Betting and Gaming Act 1960
Bills of Sale Acts, 1878, 1882, 1893
Carriage by Air Acts, 1961, 1962
Carriage by Railway Act 1972
Carriage of Goods by Road Act 1968
Carriage of Goods by Sea Acts, 1920, 1971
Carriers Act 1830
Consumer Credit Act 1974
Consumers' Protection Act 1961 (amended 1971)

Consumer Safety Act 1978
Copyright Act 1958
Fair Trading Act 1973
Food Act 1984
Hire Purchase Act 1973
Lotteries and Amusements Act 1976
Merchandise Marks Acts 1887, 1953
Misrepresentations Act 1967
Patents Act 1949
Prices Act 1974
Race Relations Acts 1964, 1976
Restrictive Trades Practices Acts 1956, 1968, 1976
Sale of Goods Act 1893 (plus amendments)
Sound Broadcasting Act 1972
Supply of Goods (Implied Terms) Act 1973
Television Act 1954
Trade Descriptions Acts, 1968, 1972
Trading Stamps Act 1964
Unfair Contract Terms Act 1977
Unsolicited Goods and Services Act 1971 (amended 1975)

This is not an exhaustive list; indeed many acts which do not appear in the list may be of relevance to marketing practitioners. Lawyers should be able to advise on the significance of these and other Acts of Parliament for particular industries.

Five Acts have particular influence upon the hospitality industry:

Hotels Proprietors Act 1956
Innkeepers Act 1878
Licensing Act 1964 (England and Wales)
Licensing Act 1976 (Scotland)
Food Hygiene Regulations 1970

The European Economic Community (EEC) is a third tier of government, beyond local and national, which also affects business. There is, for example, the European Regional Development Fund, which has granted funds for the protection and creation of jobs within the UK.

(2) Social change

Whilst customer analysis (see p. 34) focuses upon the social changes within customer groups, it does not tell the marketer much about broad social changes within the country as a whole. Such changes can have considerable impact upon sales and achievement of objectives.

Public attitudes change over time. For example, in recent years there has been increasing concern for the welfare of animals. The Ministry of Agriculture, under pressure from concerned members of the public and organised groups such as the Farm Animal Welfare Council, has published codes of conduct for livestock farmers, which in the long term may have repercussions for the catering industry. Britons are now more health and diet conscious than ever before. It reflects in the numbers of health-food stores and the huge variety of wholefoods which are available.

Brewers are trying to develop new markets for their public houses. Male manual workers have propped up profits for many years, but now male roles are changing. Men are expected to play a more active and supportive role within the family. Consequently women and families are becoming the focus of marketing activity.

Reliable information about social change in the UK is available in government publications: *Social Trends*, revised annually by the Central Statistical Office, provides in over 300 tables a comprehensive picture of social change over the previous decade. The Office of Population Censuses and Surveys collates data on national and regional population, migration, births, deaths and medical issues. A rich source of data is the Statistics and Market Intelligence Library in London which collects data and publications on trading and population from around the world.

(3) Population

Demographically change is slow and predictable. Recently we have seen a decrease in trade for funeral directors, caused, it is thought, by the numbers who died prematurely in two world wars. Due to improved medical care and diet, the average lifespan has increased, creating a higher demand for private nursing facilities than has been previously experienced—this is a growth sector in the catering and accommodation markets.

(4) Technology

Computer-based technology has dramatically affected much of Britain's business. Retailers, wholesalers and catering suppliers are adopting the bar coding system under which a code is attached to product packaging. Each product and variant has a unique 13-digit number, which is read by a scanning device incorporated into store checkouts. Electronically items are recorded on a till receipt together with their price. There is a virtual elimination of human error: 'For manufacturers and retailers the system will facilitate product ordering, invoicing, inventory control, reordering and analysis and monitoring of sales.'[24] This is achieved by continuous electronic monitoring of stock levels.

Hospitality is also in the vanguard of technological change. Holiday Inns pioneered a computerised reservation system called Holidex in the 1960s which can now instantly confirm bookings in over 1,700 Holiday Inns worldwide. The company also part-owns a satellite which offers video conferencing facilities and can deliver television broadcasts to guests' rooms.[25]

(5) Consumerism

Consumerism is by no means a recent phenomenon. However, the organisation of consumers into powerful bodies capable of influencing the marketing activities of major producers is relatively new. There have long been complaints about misleading advertising but the modern consumerism tackles much wider issues such as pollution, sexism, product formulation, health and safety in product design, packaging information, selling methods and employees' conditions of work.

President John F. Kennedy first recognised the political significance of consumerism when he introduced the 1962 Bill of Consumer Rights, which said that consumers had a right to safety, a right to information, a right to choose and a right to be heard. These principles still underpin the consumer movement.

Marketers have responded somewhat lethargically to this perceived threat although there is some degree of self-regulation. Government has legislated against some aspects of marketing activity. The Office of Fair Trading, for instance, which was established under the Fair Trading Act 1973, regulates mail-order companies, investigates monopolies and mergers, establishes codes of practice and investigates restrictive trade practices. Locally Trading Standards Officers are the guardians of consumer interest.

Consumers themselves have banded together. The Consumers' Association, with three-quarters of a million members, conducts product tests and issues reports through its monthly publication *Which*? Other groups of consumers have formed around specific issues such as conservation, animal welfare, nuclear disarmament and apartheid. The marketing behaviour of companies may be the subject of their criticism. The nutritional value of some fast foods has been questioned by consumer groups.

Tideman has identified the principal environmental influences upon both business and recreational travel.[26]

Business travel
- The level of production; as capacity or demand rises, businessmen travel more
- Telecommunications; as these become more sophisticated, the demand for travel falls
- Transport; as the speed, frequency and efficiency of air, rail and road transport systems improve, fewer nights will be spent away from home; if congestion increases, the demand for overnight accommodation will rise
- Taxes; government legislation on travelling expense allowances against business/personal taxation
- Structure of trade; if industry becomes more regionally concentrated, the pattern of business travel will change

Recreational travel
- Population; travel will increase as population increases
- Age; the birth rate in countries which are major sources of recreational travellers is falling, resulting in a reduced rate of increase in recreational travel
- Leisure time; the balance of positive influences (increasing life expectancy, early retirement, reduced working week, increased holiday entitlement in employment contracts) and negative influences (continuing education, older school children, working women) will determine recreational travel
- Level of education; the more education, the higher is the propensity to travel
- Transport prices; fuel prices are driving up the cost of travel
- Real disposable income; as this rises, so travel increases
- Possession of durables; ownership of cars, caravans, boats and second homes increases the demand for travel

- Attitudes build travel; travel is no longer unusual, holidays become regarded as a right

Clearly, these influences are important for hospitality marketers whose demand is largely derived from the demand for travel. Tideman comments: 'We believe that the number of national and international business travellers is more likely to decrease in the near future. Regarding travel for recreation we can be more optimistic.'

The NEDO has commented:[27]

the future prospects of the hotel industry are like those of any other industry, subject to extraneous factors such as world economic forces and the development of the national economy generally. The factors which [are] felt likely to have a significant effect on the future demand for accommodation [include] the following: population growth, gross domestic product, consumers' expenditure, volume of exports, volume of imports, management population index, household car ownership index, average paid holiday entitlement, prices, unemployment.

2.15 CHAPTER REVIEW

1. Marketing is both a set of skills and techniques and a way of doing business.
2. Marketing is the process by which exchange of mutual satisfiers occurs.
3. Marketing has application in both profit and non-profit environments.
4. Barter and swapping are forms of marketing.
5. Marketing has a role in both profit and welfare sectors of the hospitality industry.
6. The purpose of marketing is different in capitalist and socialist environments.
7. Marketing techniques can be applied to goods, services, activities, causes, ideas, organisations, people and places.
8. The marketing concept consists of three interdependent propositions: the consumer should be the focal point for company decision-making; the aim should be profitable sales volume; and the entire company should be organised to satisfy consumers.
9. The marketing concept is criticised for its limited focus, its profit orientation and its lack of concern about its cultural effects.
10. Marketing provides personal, social and societal satisfaction.
11. Marketing orientation is the term used to describe the way of doing business characterised by those companies who have adopted the marketing concept.
12. There are a number of business orientations—marketing, sales, production and technological.
13. The marketing orientation is not always optimal.
14. Much of the hotel industry is sales-oriented.
15. Much welfare catering is production-oriented.
16. Managers are responsible for the deployment of resources.
17. Every manager is involved in some form of:
    - analysis of his decision environment.
    - planning for future achievements.
    - implementation of plans.
    - control of plans and staff.
18. Most commercial hospitality marketers try to facilitate and stimulate consumption.
19. Not all marketing strives to increase demand. Sometimes marketers try to maintain, reduce, destroy, or otherwise regulate demand.
20. Marketing management is best characterised as demand management.
21. The marketing mix comprises the Four Ps—product, price, promotion and place. These are the tools used by marketers to manage demand.
22. The marketing environment consists of the organisational environment, the operational environment and the extraneous environment.

23. Changes in the operating and extraneous environments make uncertain the outcomes of marketing decisions.
24. The operational environment includes a business's market, customers, material suppliers, labour source, distributors and competitors.
25. The extraneous environment includes the macroinfluences of government, social change, population, technology and consumerism.

2.16 QUESTIONS

1. Of the Four Ps—product, price, promotion and place—which are most significant when trying to:
   - increase the number of customers at a fast-food outlet?
   - create a meal to satisfy the chronically ill?
   - raise occupancy levels during the late autumn in a Lake District boarding-house?
2. Why, if marketing is concerned with the management of demand, do we never see job advertisements for demand managers?
3. Distinguish between selling and marketing. Some people say that good marketing makes selling simple. What do you think they mean?
4. To what extent can the principles of marketing be extended to the marketing of people, ideas and causes?
5. Imagine you own a small high-quality restaurant. How might you use barter?
6. 'The marketing concept has not been widely adopted in the hospitality industry.' To what extent is this true?
7. The sales orientation can be a productive business 'logic' for the hospitality industry. In what circumstances is this true?
8. Every manager is involved in some form of:
   - analysis of his decision environment.
   - planning for future achievements.
   - implementation of plans.
   - control of plans and staff.

   What elements of the business environment should be analysed by
   (a) the general manager of a country club five miles outside a city?
   (b) the proprietor of a disco/dine club in a city-centre cellar?
   What sources of information should he use?
9. In what circumstances might a hospitality marketer expect to
   (a) reduce demand?
   (b) destroy demand?
10. How might a 4-star hotel in a city-centre location gather information about its city-centre competitors?

REFERENCES

[1] Crosier, K. (1975) What exactly is marketing? *Quarterly Review of Marketing*, Winter.
[2] Kaitaka, J. G. (1976) The reincarnation of barter trade as a marketing tool. *Journal of Marketing*, April.
[3] See: Barter American style. *The Economist*, 31 March 1979, 55.
[4] See: Chemicals in the East explode West. *The Economist*, 10 February 1979, 84–5.
[5] Kotler, P. (1984) (5th edn) *Marketing Management: Analysis, Planning and Control.* Englewood Cliffs, NJ: Prentice-Hall.
[6] Kipps, M. and Thomson, J. (1980) The future of the school meals service. *Hospitality*, June, 10–14.

[7] Smith, A. (1980) The future of the school meals service. *Hospitality*, May, 25–30.
[8] Reuland, R. and Cassée, E. (1983). Hospitality in hospitals, in Cassée, E. and Reuland, R. (eds) *The Management of Hospitality*. Oxford: Pergamon, 143–63.
[9] Rice, J. (1982) Marketing challenge. *Hospitality*, January, 12–18.
[10] Hawkes, G. (1983) 'Industrial catering' in Cassée E. and Reuland R. (eds) op. cit., 165–87.
[11] Taken from Waniewski, J. (1976) *The Importance of Marketing in Production: Its Significance for Turnover and for the Market*. Warsaw: Stowarzyszenie Socjalistycznego Marketingu.
[12] The term was reputedly first used by Kelley, Eugene J. (1965) Ethics and science in marketing, in Schwartz, G. *Science in Marketing*. London: Wiley.
[13] *New Internationalist*, March 1975, 13–15.
[14] Rosenberg, L. J. (1977) *Marketing*. Englewood Cliffs, NJ: Prentice-Hall.
[15] Kotler, P. (1984) op. cit.
[16] Medlik, S. (1980), *The Business of Hotels*. London: Heinemann, 108.
[17] Buttle, F. (1975) The fieldmouse and the barnowl. *Marketing Forum*, 2, March–April, 11–16.
[18] See Kotler, P. (1984) op. cit.
[19] See; Berni stakes out new ground. *Marketing*, **17**(7), August, 23 ff.
[20] Sasser, W. E. (1979) Match supply and demand in service industries, *Harvard Business Review*, November–December.
[21] Hotel and Catering Economic Development Committee (1976) *Hotel Prospects to 1985*, London: NEDO.
[22] McCarthy, E. J. (1964) (2nd edn) *Basic Marketing: A Managerial Approach*, Homewood, IL: Irwin.
[23] Levitt, T. (1975) Marketing myopia. *Harvard Business Review*, September–October, 26 ff.
[24] See: *Background Information concerning the Article Numbering Association*. London: ANA, 5.
[25] Upton, G. (1984) New links in the chain, *Marketing*, **16**(10), March, 29–31.
[26] Tideman, M. C. (1983) External influences on the hospitality industry, in Cassée, E. and Reuland, R. (eds) op. cit., 1–23.
[27] *Hotel Prospects to 1985*. op. cit.

—3—

Marketing Research

3.1 CHAPTER PREVIEW

Marketing management makes strategic and tactical decisions intended to produce customer and corporate satisfaction. Decisions made in an information vacuum are much more likely to be inadequate—hence the role of marketing research.

In this chapter we define marketing research, explain its role in marketing management and look at the motives for undertaking research. We suggest a number of reasons why the relationship between manager and researcher is not always easy, and we profile the British market research industry. However, the bulk of the chapter is concerned with the actual procedure of conducting research. We examine information sources and the means of collecting information, and consider how to evaluate the quality of information.

The chapter focuses especially upon survey research and experimentation, the two data-collection techniques most common in hospitality marketing.

3.2 LEARNING OBJECTIVES

By the end of this chapter you should be able to:
1. Define marketing research.
2. Distinguish between descriptive, exploratory and causal research.
3. Explain why marketing management does not always apply research findings.
4. Obtain details about the services offered by members of the Market Research Society.
5. Describe the five main steps in research procedure.
6. Distinguish between recurrent and occasional marketing decisions.
7. Define what is meant by 'good' information.
8. List topics or fields investigated by marketing researchers.
9. Distinguish between primary and secondary data.
10. Identify the main internal sources of information in the hospitality industry.
11. Identify the principal sources of secondary information outside the organisation.
12. Distinguish between reactive and non-reactive methods of data collection.
13. Follow a flowchart in survey design.
14. Design an experiment.
15. Identify potential problems in operating a group discussion.
16. Distinguish between univariate, bivariate and multivariate data-analysis techniques.
17. Define the terms 'reliability' and 'validity'.

3.3 WHAT IS MARKETING RESEARCH?

When a marketer makes a decision, say, to promote to the business traveller or to open a fast-food outlet, he is rarely certain that the venture will succeed. Indeed, the unpredictable marketing environment, as we saw in Chapter 2, can confound even the best-laid plans. However, managers are paid to make decisions and they will draw upon whatever information they can acquire cost effectively in performing that role.

Decision-making under conditions of uncertainty is the convention for marketers—the fundamental role of marketing research is to reduce the uncertainty. Consequently we find that marketing research has been defined as:[1]

> the systematic and objective search for and analysis of information relevant to the identification and solution of any problem in the field of marketing.

Marketing research is systematic, in that it is planned, following a sequence of logically ordered steps, starting with problem definition and ending with its use in problem solution. Marketing research, at best, is objective—data are collected using scientific methods and are analysed using proven statistical processes. Marketing research can be used to investigate any area of marketing activity from the analysis of sales performance to evaluating the effectiveness of advertising.

It now should be clear that market research and marketing research are distinct. Market research simply aims to describe markets—their size, location and pattern of development. Marketing research is much wider in application. Marketing is not an exact science; any problem has a number of alternative solutions. Marketing research is used to select the best option.

There are a number of modes of decision-making when uncertainty about the outcomes exists. Most widely applied in marketing appears to be the Bayesian approach in which the manager judges the likelihood (probability) of alternative courses of action being successful and attempts to calculate the associated financial payoff.

Before illustrating the process, we should consider probability. If an event is certain to happen, the probability assigned is 1. If, on the other hand, the event is certain not to happen, the probability is 0. Consequently a probability of 0.2 means that a given outcome will occur 2 times in 10. If a coin is tossed, the probability of it coming down 'heads' is 0.5.

A restaurant manager may want to know whether a new format he is planning to introduce will provide a better financial return than his existing operation. If following a Bayesian approach, he acts as follows:
1. Collect historical data about current operation.
2. Research the market for the new format.
3. List a range of outcomes (levels of sales) for each format (e.g. £10,000, £20,000, £30,000, etc.).
4. Assign a probability to each outcome, based upon the analysis in steps 1 and 2.
5. Multiply each outcome by the associated probability.
6. Sum the total for each format to obtain the expected value.
7. Select the alternative with the highest expected value.

This is a simple introduction to a complicated and contentious subject. Interested readers may wish to follow up the references given at the end of the chapter.[2]

3.4 RESEARCH MOTIVES

There are several reasons why marketing research is undertaken:
- Much research is descriptive. For example, it may enable the manager to establish how his business is doing in terms of market share, sales volume, or other performance criteria; it may describe competitors' products or advertising strategy; and it may describe new market segments which are being considered for exploitation.
- Research may also be exploratory, in the sense that it attempts to formulate hypotheses about why certain events are occurring. Such research may suggest reasons why sales are below budget; for example, salesmen might appear unmotivated or there may be a low level of awareness about the product. Exploratory research often precedes causal research.
- Causal or diagnostic research is undertaken to test the hypotheses generated by exploratory research. Causal research tests relationships between variables—for example, studying sales response to advertising.
- Marketing managers may believe that research is a sign of a 'professional'; somehow management which does not use marketing information is held in lower esteem. Axler attributes a high failure rate and poor profitability in the food service industry to inadequate marketing research: 'Those food service operations that have achieved outstanding success without a planned programme of market[ing] research were either established during a period of less rigorous competition and consumer demands or are blessed with management capable of amazing feats of intuitive judgement.'[3]

Even given good reasons for conducting research, there is no guarantee that management will actually use the information in decision-making; when the manager is his own researcher, that is he doesn't have staff to conduct research for him or use an outside agency, the likelihood of applying the information is greater.

There are a variety of reasons which have been put forward for the apparent lack of application of research findings:
- Despite there being a code of practice and training programme for members of the Market Research Society (the principal representative body for marketing researchers in the UK), the calibre of researchers is uneven.
- Clients mostly commission research with a view to obtaining early results. Late results do not enhance the reputation of the marketing researcher.
- Professional marketing researchers often appear highly concerned with technical and statistical procedures whilst giving insufficient attention to interpreting data for client users. Consequently research reports, whilst replete with technical footnotes, frequently contain inadequate recommendations for action. Indeed there is some disagreement amongst marketing researchers about whether the researcher should take some responsibility for the decisions based on his work. On the one hand, some believe that the researchers' role ends with the presentation of a report; on the other, some, like a major British research company, believe that 'the gaining of information is never an end in itself. We will assist you in using the information'.[4]
- Management looks for certainty in research findings, yet researchers present

probabilities. Perfect or near-perfect research, in which full confidence can be placed in the results, is very expensive.

- Clients think in deterministic terms and researchers think in probabilistic terms. In other words, researchers would tend to report that a mixture of factors A, B and C has caused D to occur, whereas clients have an expectation of being told that A causes D. Inevitably action on probabilistic findings is difficult to formulate.

3.5 THE MARKETING RESEARCH INDUSTRY

Complete information about the size of the industry is unavailable. Many larger- and medium-sized companies employ their own research staff and do not disclose their budgets or expenditures. However, the Market Research Society, which is the incorporated professional body for those using survey techniques for market, social and economic research, has over 4,000 individual members. It also issues the annual publication *Organizations in the UK and Republic of Ireland Providing Market Research Services*, which lists some 200 agencies. These agencies received commissions valued at £150 million in 1983,[5] an increase of £24 million over 1982 which was itself, in real terms, 80 per cent more than in 1969.[6]

Agencies fall into 2 categories—the generalist and the specialist. The names of the agencies which offer a wide range of services tend to be better known to the general public—Gallup, Social Surveys, National Opinion Polls, British Market Research Bureau are instances.

Gallup Social Surveys Ltd, for example, which is perhaps best known for its Gallup Poll, the political opinion polling service, operates a number of other services. Included are advertising and communications research, radio research for Radio Luxembourg, international research through Gallup offices in 38 countries, pharmacy prescription monitoring, survey analysis using Gallup's own computer programs, and catering research, together with a European Omnibus in which several clients enter questions into a shared survey.

Other agencies specialise in industry, market, technique or area of the marketing mix:

- *Industry*
  Medical Market Studies specialises in the pharmaceuticals industry; Produce Studies Ltd specialises in the agricultural, horticultural and primary food industries.
- *Market*
  CWA specialises in children's markets; Carrick James specialises in teenage markets.
- *Techniques*
  Retail Audits Ltd specialises in retail auditing; Marketing Research Enterprises specialises in telephone interviewing.
- *Marketing mix*
  KAE specialises in new product development; Pricing Research Ltd specialises in pricing.

A number of agencies conduct research into the hospitality industry. Amongst them are

Gallup (*Eating Out*), National Opinion Polls (*Alcoholic Drinks Survey*), Insight Research (*The Catering Industry: Basic Market Data*), RSGB (*Catering Omnibus Survey*) and Travel and Tourism Research.

3.6 RESEARCH PROCEDURE

Marketing researchers tend to conform to a standard procedure, as shown in Table 3.1, when conducting research.

Table 3.1   *Research procedure.*

I	Analysis of information needs
II	Finding information sources
III	Collecting the information
IV	Analysing the information
V	Using the information

The rest of this chapter will be devoted to a review of each of these stages in research procedure.

3.7 RESEARCH PROCEDURE: ANALYSIS OF INFORMATION NEEDS

The manager's first task is to decide upon what type and quality of information he needs to make sound decisions. Obviously he must be aware of the range of decisions he will have to make. These may be described formally in his job description, learnt informally from peers, or received as instructions from superiors.

Decisions can be classified as recurrent or occasional. Examples of both types appear in Table 3.2. Recurrent decisions generally involve continuous inputs of information gathered in an established, systematised manner. Occasional decisions may require the design of an ad hoc data-collection plan.

Table 3.2   *Frequency of marketing decisions.*

Recurrent hospitality marketing problems requiring continuous information inputs:
- regular appraisal of salespersons' performance
- analysis of actual sales of accommodation, food and beverage against forecast sales
- tracking of seasonal patterns in sales
- setting monthly sales targets for regional sales offices
- monitoring actual promotion expenditure against budget
- considering whether to match changes in competitors' bar prices

Occasional hospitality marketing problems requiring ad hoc information inputs:
- whether to co-operate with adjacent hotels in joint promotion
- whether to sponsor a sporting event
- whether to launch a new food and beverage format
- whether to close a floor during winter
- to discover the reasons for poor sales performance from a particular office
- to see if profitable opportunities exist in franchising a fast-food format

Information derives from many sources—e.g. past experience, marketing research, or conjecture. It can be accurate or inaccurate, reliable or unreliable and subjective or objective. However, good information, such as that expected from marketing researchers, is information which is PATU—a mnemonic where the letters signify:
- pertinent
- accurate
- timely
- usable

Pertinent information is relevant to the problem or decision facing the manager. Irrelevancies are costly and time-consuming. When data are analysed by computer, it is simple to output a wide variety of tables. A good researcher needs to be a rigorous editor.

Accuracy is relative. For some major problems, generally those of an occasional nature, high levels of accuracy are required. An hotel group considering the investment of millions of pounds in a flagship hotel unit will want a high level of accuracy in research reports on the venture. On the other hand, if little is at stake, the acceptable level of accuracy is lower.

Timely information is available when needed; but not too long before because of the danger of the information dating, nor after the decision has to be made.

Usable information is information presented in language understood by the manager with no unnecessary complications or technicalities and with clear guidance for decision-making.

Marketing research provides information about two areas:
- the marketing environment
- the marketing mix

(1) The marketing environment

Research into the environment takes a number of forms, as outlined below.

Market research
Market size and location, area attractions.
Market development—growth, contraction and stability.
Market segments: are all consumers alike?
Market share: how important is each competitor?

Customer and motivational research
Why customers buy.
Why prospects do not buy.
Purchasing behaviour.
Source of custom.

Business and economic studies
Legal investigations.
Economic and social trends.
Financial performance studies—internal and comparative.

International markets—comparative studies.
Operational research studies.
Company image studies.
Economic studies.

Feasibility studies (see Chapter 9)
Demand for proposed ventures.
Financial implications of such ventures.

(2) The marketing mix

Every aspect of the marketing mix can be researched, as outlined below.

Product research
Ideas for new products.
Screening ideas for new products.
Experimentally controlled launch of new products on a limited scale to test consumer acceptance.
Brand name selection.
Competitive product comparisons.
Brand image studies.
Taste tests.

Pricing research
Competitive price studies.
Testing the effect of price changes on demand.
Testing alternative discount structures.

Advertising research (see Chapter 17)
Generating creative ideas for advertising material.
Testing alternative commercials for consumer understanding, recall, etc.
Gauging advertising/sales effects.
Competitive advertising studies.
Audience/readership studies.

Sales research
Sales analysis: rooms, food and beverage.
Sales forcasting (see Chapter 6).
Interdepartmental comparisons.
Testing sales aids and selling methods.
Testing alternative remuneration systems for sales staff.
Salesperson's performance comparisons.
Locating sales prospects.

Distribution research
Changes to the location pattern of hotels.

Distribution cost studies.

Location studies for restaurants, hotels and warehouses.

Distribution effectiveness studies: are own sales offices more effective than use of hotel representatives?

Once the manager has determined his information needs following an appraisal of the decisions he has to make and the problems he is likely to encounter, a matter of priorities has to be settled. Few research budgets are large enough to provide pertinent, accurate, timely and usable information for all decisions, so it is necessary to decide how to allocate funds to research.

3.8 RESEARCH PROCEDURE: FINDING INFORMATION SOURCES

Having decided what is needed, it becomes necessary to locate sources of information. Again the issue of funds is important. It is normally cheaper to look for and use information that has already been collected (secondary information) than it is to collect new information (primary information). If fortunate, the user may find that secondary information is sufficiently pertinent, accurate, timely and usable. Secondary information is normally cheaper and quicker because it involves less search time, little or no fieldwork (interviewing), or data analysis.

Secondary information may be internal or external to the organisation. Hotels are fortunate to have a wealth of information about existing customers, sales and operations.

Customer records include:

(1) The hotel register
This is a legal requirement in most countries and normally records name, address, date of arrival, post-code, the number in party and allocated room.

(2) Reservation requests
These often detail date of request, source of reservation (e.g. direct, through travel agent or hotel representative), method of reservation (e.g. phone, telex, or letter), the type of guest (corporate, association, or private), any special rate or package which may apply to the guest and length of stay.

(3) Guest index
This is an alphabetical card listing of current guests duplicating key information from the register and reservation details, adding mode of travel (car, train, or plane) and purpose of visit (business or pleasure).

(4) Guest master-file
This is a file containing the name, address, occupation, phone number, room preferences, record of previous visits, complaints history and idiosyncrasies of all guests who have stayed in the last 12 months.

Registrations can provide a wealth of useful material. Geographic sorting tells the manager the source of his business; he can pick out repeat clients and lapsed repeaters, marking their location on a map. This enables the hotel to target its marketing efforts. Simultaneous geographic and chronological sorting will establish if there is heavy use at certain times by guests from a particular area. The guest master-file enables the hotel to provide a high level of individual service to guests; this practice is almost exclusively undertaken in 5-star properties.

Sales records normally take the form of an integrated system of records, usually held on paper but increasingly computerised. Medlik identifies 6 types of sales information:[7]

(a) guest bills or folio forms show all the charges incurred, method of payment and the outstanding balance, and are presented to guests for settlement on departure

(b) duplicate bills or a visitors' ledger which reproduce in tabular form individual accounts for a day at a time are retained by the hotel

(c) vouchers from sales outlets originate charges and provide the authority for entries in guests' accounts

(d) daily summary book in which are collected the analysed daily sales totals for monthly transfer to sales ledger account gives a sales analysis by day and by type of charge

(e) sales ledger which contains individual sales accounts of the hotel and personal accounts of all debtors, including guests whose credit extends beyond departure

(f) cash books and receipt books which are the main records of settlement

Operations records include the following:

(1)   In-room questionnaires
Many hotels use these to judge customer satisfaction with their operations; however, 'the data they generate are, more often than not, unreliable and statistically invalid'.[8] The main concern is that such questionnaires, if completed at all, tend to obtain extreme rather than representative responses.

From the hotelier's point of view consumer feedback should be unit specific (i.e relate to one hotel or one outlet within the hotel), actionable, representative of the feelings of the majority of guests, valid and reliable, allow the hotel to monitor trends and be a good predictor of repeat business, and be inexpensive to install, operate and maintain. The customer wants such a system to be interesting and simple to use, monitor his real needs and wants, be anonymous and credible in the sense that management is felt to be acting upon the information.[9]

Frequently marketing researchers are involved neither in questionnaire design nor data analysis, and the results are quite unsuitable as a guide to executive action. A secondary role for these questionnaires has been as a device to convince guests that the hotel takes a genuine interest in their welfare, even though the results may not be acted upon.

One survey of American practice revealed that 92 per cent of hoteliers use in-house guest surveys as a means of judging the hotel's performance, guest satisfaction, grading management and comparing properties.[10]

(2)   Departmental reports
These are weekly or monthly reports recording actual sales against budget, promotion plans and inventory levels. Computerisation of hotel front offices and reservation

systems has greatly simplified file creation and handling. Many of the above paperwork system components have electronic equivalents.

Restaurants are not normally so well equipped with internal records about customers, sales and operations. Customer orders are the prime source of information about food preferences; occasionally a restaurant will conduct a survey of guest satisfaction. The questionnaire is generally offered to the guest to complete at home.

Service staff can enhance information by recording not only the order of each cover, but the number of guests in a party, time of order, sex and approximate age. Bills and delivery notes from supplying organisations may form the basis of operational records. The larger the catering organisation, the more likely is it to possess formalised internal information sources.

External secondary information is available from a large number of sources:

Marketing research firms
Many marketing research organisations conduct syndicated research available to subscribers.

Government
There is a wide variety of regular and occasional government publications:
Annual Abstract of Statistics
British Business
British Tourist Authority: National Travel Survey and Tourism Intelligence Quarterly
Business Monitor
Censuses of Distribution, Production and Population
Department of Employment Gazette
English Tourist Board: British Home Tourism Survey
Household Food Consumption and Expenditure
Monthly Digest of Statistics
National Income and Expenditure (Blue Book)
NEDO reports (particularly the Hotel and Catering Economic Development Committee)
Social Trends
Trade and Industry
The government also publishes a comprehensive guide entitled *List of Principal Statistical Series and Publications.*

International sources
The European Economic Community, World Tourism Organisation, International Monetary Fund and the United Nations are often used to obtain international comparisons. A comprehensive list is available in the Central Statistical Office's publication *International Organizations and Overseas Agencies Publications.*

Trade associations
Three trade associations are the Hotel, Catering and Institutional Management Association, which has an information services department; the British Hotels, Restaurants and Caterers' Association; and in the USA the Hotel Sales Management

Association. The Industrial Market Research Association's Foodservice Industry Group and the Institute of Marketing's Hotel Industry Marketing Group are sources of UK trade data.

Educational institutions
The sixteen educational institutions offering degrees in hotel and catering management maintain well-stocked libraries.

Company annual accounts
Limited companies are obliged to lodge accounts with Companies House.

Directories
There are a number of directories such as Kompass, Kelly's and Dun and Bradstreet which provide details about companies.

Other publications
Media Expenditure Analysis Ltd reports on advertising expenditure. *British Rate and Data* is the bible for advertising media buyers and planners, and other publications include *Caterer and Hotelkeeper, Hospitality, Marketing Pocket Book* and *Annals of Tourism Research.*

Other organisations
Chambers of commerce, British Institute of Management, Institute of Marketing, convention bureaux, tourist offices and consultancies such as Pannel, Kerr & Foster and Horwath & Horwath.

Secondary sources may provide exactly the information which the marketer needs. But more often than not, this is not the case, although secondary sources can help researchers in a variety of other ways. For instance, they may identify appropriate data-collection methods for primary research or help in the development of testable hypotheses.

3.9 RESEARCH PROCEDURE: COLLECTING THE INFORMATION

Having decided what information is needed and from where it is available, the next stage is to collect the information. In secondary research the task is simple since the researcher often only needs to use reference library and interlibrary loan facilities. Four such libraries are listed in Table 3.3.

The task is more complex for primary research. However, in this section we shall examine the collection of both types of information.

Reactive and non-reactive methods

Much marketing research is undertaken using *reactive* methods, that is methods in which the researcher somehow intrudes into the environment in order to collect the

Table 3.3 *Libraries which provide secondary information.*

The British Library (Reference Division) Great Russell Street London WC1 01–636 1544	City Business Library Gillett House Basinghall Street London EC2V 5BX 01–638 8215
British Overseas Trade Board Statistics and Marketing Intelligence Library (SMIL) 1 Victoria Street London SW1H 0ET 01–215 7877	Patent Office Library 5 Southampton Buildings London WC2A 1AW 01–405 8721

information. Examples include surveys, experiments and participant observation. However, there is another set of information-collection techniques which are *non-reactive* and sometimes overlooked by marketing researchers.

The major problem in using only reactive collection methods is that a variety of sources of error arise which may make the results of such research less reliable and plausible.[11] The three classes of error in reactive research are:

(a) respondent error
(b) investigator error
(c) sampling error

Several sources of error may occur within each class.

(1) Respondent error

(a) The testing effect. If people know that they are being watched, their behaviour may change. If a hotel executive watches a guest completing an in-room questionnaire, there is a danger that the guest will not record his true feelings. The response to being observed may be energetic or inconspicuous. The normal solution to this problem is to guarantee anonymity to the respondent, but the only true measure of the 'guinea-pig' effect is to compare the data collected with other information obtained through non-reactive methods.

(b) Role-selection effect. The process of being interviewed and observed forces a respondent to ask the question 'What sort of person should I be as I answer these questions or perform these tasks?'

In a gourmet restaurant a diner asked his opinion about the food may be critical even though the food is of higher quality than that prepared at home. He has adopted the role of gourmet, rather than the role of family member. Different standards apply in different roles. Selection to take part in a survey actually implies a distinction from other non-participants, particularly if the questionnaire starts: 'You have been scientifically selected to take part in a survey of . . . It is very important that you answer the questions as completely as possible.'

Interviewees may view themselves in a different role, as a special person.

(c) Measurement effect. Imagine that you are researching fast-food brand awareness before and after an advertising campaign. Before and after the campaign, you interview

a sample of people, asking: 'Can you tell me the names of any fast-food shops?' The pre-campaign questioning may actually make respondents more likely to notice advertising or other material carrying brandnames. Consequently any post-campaign measurement will not accurately indicate the effectiveness of the campaign, but will be contaminated by the measurement effect.

(d) Response sets. Yea-saying is a common phenomenon which reflects in participants' willingness to endorse rather than refute a statement. This is known as an acquiescence response set. A second response set is the common tendency to endorse strong rather than moderate or indecisive statements. Third, when a series of questions follows a standard scaling format, there is a tendency to endorse either the left or right side of the scale. Fourth, the longer the questionnaire, the more likely are boredom and decreasing attention to introduce error.

(2) Investigator error

(a) Interviewer effect. Respondents may respond to visible cues provided by the interviewer—e.g. facial expressions or tone of voice. The race, sex and age of the interviewers may introduce biased responses.

(b) Instrument effect. To what extent is the data-collection instrument the same at all points in the research? Repeated exposure to a questionnaire becomes uninteresting for respondents. Interviewers may not read questions in exactly the same way every time—they too become bored. Alternatively, the interviewer may become more skilled at each reading as he becomes used to the sequence and wording.

(c) Recording error. This is a problem if interviewers have to write down verbatim responses to questions. Inevitably this involves reduction and translation, both are sources of error.

(3) Sampling error
In most reactive research only a fraction (sample) of the population of interest to the investigator is observed, interviewed, or used as experimental subjects.

(a) Sampling-frame error. A sampling frame is a list of the population to be investigated. If this list is out of date, contains omissions, duplications, or errors, then the sample selected from it will be unrepresentative. Use of an inappropriate sampling frame can also introduce error—not all homes are equipped with telephones, not all companies are listed in directories.

(b) Sample bias. Are interviewees different from those who have steadfastly refused to be interviewed? If using an in-home survey, with repeated callbacks to interview not-at-homes, some sample members will still not be accessible—they may be in hospital, prison, or away on business or holiday. These omissions introduce error. Other problems may arise with illiterates who are unable to complete questionnaires, and volunteers whose motives may be different from non-volunteers.

(c) Administration error. Are the results of a survey administered in the street on a rainy day different from those obtained on a fine day? Are weekend results different from weekday? Are there geographic differences which might cause variations in responses? These considerations need to be built into a research plan.

Non-reactive measures

Despite these sources of error, there is no doubt that most ad hoc and continuous research applies reactive measures. The alternative is to use either non-reactive data-collection methods or a mixture of reactive and non-reactive.

The 3 main types of non-reactive measures are:

Physical traces
  - erosion
  - accretion

Archives
  - continuous
  - episodic
  - private

Observation
  - simple
  - contrived

(1) Physical traces

Physical traces can be used by an alert and creative researcher as a useful source of information. The two types—erosion, where there is some degree of wear to an object; and accretion, where some deposit of materials occurs—are both very low-cost means of collecting information. Examples will help to show their value:

Erosion: a worn carpet tile reveals the most popular seating position in a restaurant.

Accretion: a count of discarded fast-food containers indicates which competitor is the best seller.

Some erosion and accretion measures occur naturally but it is often possible to contrive situations.

(2) Archives

Three types of archive material exist: continuous, episodic and private. We have referred largely to episodic and continuous sources of information in our discussion of secondary data. Government records, actuarial records, records of meetings and association minutes, Hansard, national audio and video archives, proceedings of professional bodies, judicial records, newspapers and magazines are all rich sources of information. Collecting episodic information, that is material which is not part of a series but publicly available, can be time-consuming without the assistance of an experienced archivist. Personal archives, such as diaries, letters, essays, unpublished manuscripts, company sales records, insurance documents, artwork, doodles and private collections, may be of value.

(3) Observation

Observation, with or without the contrived assistance of hardware such as a camera or microphone, may also be of use. Observation may take place in respect of internal operations or customers. Management may conduct a pantry audit or dustbin check to observe waste or count traffic in order to judge the value of a prospective location. Observation of customers may help to assess reactions to a new menu item or the attractiveness of a food display.

For observation to be classified as non-reactive the observer must not exert an influence upon the behaviour of those who are being observed. The influence of a visible observer tends to reduce over time, but the early set of observations may be grossly invalid. A solution to this dilemma is for the observer to be a participant in the events he is studying. Hotel X may send an employee researcher to stay in Hotel Y.

Another form of observation is conversation sampling. If a marketer wants to obtain information about the attitude of diners to a new menu item, he can arrange for a trained listener (waiter) to note reactions at the table.

Reactive measures

The most popular reactive data-collection methods are:
- surveys
- experiments
- group discussions
- projective techniques

Reactive measures: Surveys

A survey is a technique in which members of the population of interest are interviewed. If all members are surveyed, it becomes a census; if only a portion, it is a sample survey. Of all data-collection techniques, survey work is probably the most practised and most abused. Used unwisely, many sources of error and bias can combine to invalidate the findings.

Figure 3.1, which is based upon an approach used in Britain by the Countryside Commission, shows the stages through which a survey must pass from project initiation to report-writing. Five main stages exist:

Stage 1   Preparation
Stage 2   Preliminary decisions
Stage 3   Design and test
Stage 4   Main run
Stage 5   Producing results

Stage 1, preparatory work, involves setting research objectives and defining the information that is needed to meet them. For example, a survey whose objective is to assess likely demand for a new school meals service would want to obtain information about
- the numbers of children dining at school
- parental attitudes towards school meals
- children's attitudes towards school meals

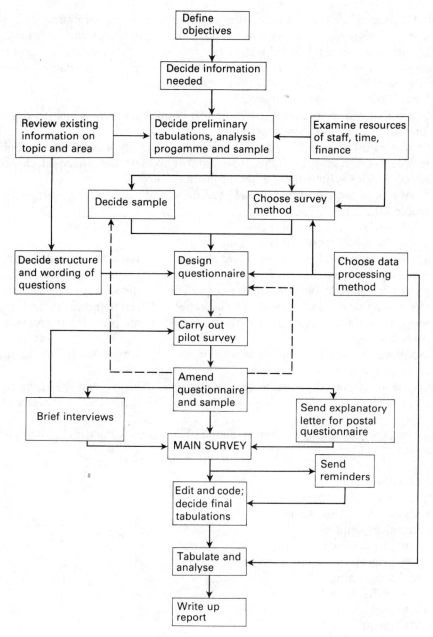

Figure 3.1 Survey stages.

- satisfaction with the present product
- reactions to the new proposal

Stage 2, preliminary decisions, begins with a review of secondary information and an appraisal of constraints. These two factors, taken with the stage 1 preparatory work, enable the researcher to decide how the final report is to be formatted. It is good discipline to design empty tabulations for which the main survey should provide the data because, once again, this helps in question design and data-analysis decisions.

A major issue at stage 2 of the survey design is sampling. The preliminary review of sampling issues involves obtaining answers for these questions:

- What is our *population* of interest?
- Can we obtain an accurate *listing* of this population from which to draw the sample? (known as a sampling frame)
- Should we use a *probability sample* or a non-probability sample? In a probability sample every member of the population of interest has an equal chance of selection. This is not true of a non-probability sample.
- What *size* of sample should we select? The size of a sample is governed by two simple laws. They are:
    - (a) the law of statistical regularity
    - (b) the law of inertia of large numbers
    The first of these holds that any subset of a population selected at random will tend to possess the same characteristics as the larger group. The second holds that large groups are more stable than small groups. They are less likely to be significantly affected by random and irrelevant fluctuations. Taken together, these two laws suggest that the larger the sample, the more likely is it to provide valid and reliable data.
- What should be the sampling *unit*? A person or a householder? Who should answer the questions?

Sampling is an advanced science requiring statistical skills beyond the scope of this book, but readers may wish to follow up some of the references at the end of the chapter.[12]

However, the principles are relatively simple. There are several varieties of each type of sample.

Probability samples
- (a) simple random sample
- (b) systematic random sample
- (c) stratified sample
    - proportionate
    - disproportionate
- (d) Multistage sample
    - cluster sample
    - area sample
- (e) Multiphase sample

Non-probability samples
- (a) quota sample
- (b) convenience sample
- (c) judgemental sample

For probability sampling to take place an accurate, complete sampling frame is necessary. Technically, if a survey uses a non-probability sample, it is not appropriate to draw inferences about the population as a whole; this is only feasible using data from a probability sample.

The main points about each type of sample are listed below.

(1) Probability samples

(a) Simple random sample. Sample members are selected using either a lottery method or a random number method. Random number tables are available from stationers. They are computer-generated lists of numbers which, once the sampling units have all been numbered, can be used in any convenient or systematic way to select sample members.

(b) Systematic random sample. Where a large population exists, this form of sampling is most convenient. An inverse sampling fraction (k) is calculated using the formula:

$$k = \frac{N}{n}$$

where N = size of the population
n = size of the sample

A randomly chosen number (i) between 1 and k is selected. Given a sequentially numbered sampling frame, sample unit $i, i + k, i + 2k, i + 3k \ldots i + (n - 1)k$ are selected for inclusion in the sample. Systematic sampling is wise only if the sampling frame is itself randomly ordered or unrelated to the purpose of the survey.

(c) Stratified sample. There are two forms of stratified sample: proportionate (PSS), and disproportionate (DSS). This form of sampling can help to improve the representativeness of the sample. Simple random sampling and systematic sampling cannot guarantee that all sectors of the population are in the final sample. Stratified sampling improves the likelihood of this happening.

The population is divided into strata selected by the researcher as relevant to his purpose—e.g. age-groups, marital status, or a mixture of both. Random sampling takes place within strata.

When the same sampling fraction is used for selection within each stratum, this is PSS; if this is not the case, it is DSS. The DSS form is preferred where the researcher believes that there is likely to be great within-stratum variation in responses or if he has a particular interest in one or more strata. How this affects the distribution of a sample between strata is shown in Table 3.4. The population has been stratified into age-groups. The researcher is investigating attitudes to a new health-food operation aimed specifically at those aged 25 and under. Use of a common sampling fraction would give insufficient data about the attitudes of the two younger strata; the researcher elects to use different sampling fractions whilst retaining the same overall sample size.

(d) Multistage sample. In multistage sampling a population is divided into progressively smaller groups according to principles of randomness until the final sampling unit is

Table 3.4　*Proportionate and disproportionate stratified sampling.*

Age stratum	Population size	Proportionate stratified sampling		Disproportionate stratified sampling		Variation in sample size (DSS−PSS)
		k	Sample size	*k*	Sample size	
Under 16	6 000	1/100	60	1/50	120	+60
16–25	10 000	1/100	100	1/50	200	+100
26–39	10 000	1/100	100	1/125	80	−20
40+	24 000	1/100	240	1/240	100	−140
	50 000		500		500	0

reached. The two main types of multistage samples are *cluster* samples and *area* samples.

In area sampling the basis for dividing the population into groups is geographic area, the final sampling unit being a comparatively small area. It, therefore, helps to reduce fieldwork costs. Using the electoral roll, it is possible to create a 4-stage sample:

Stage 1　Divide country into constituencies.
　　　　　Randomly select constituencies.
Stage 2　Divide constituencies into wards.
　　　　　Randomly select wards.
Stage 3　Divide wards into polling districts.
　　　　　Randomly select polling districts.
Stage 4　Divide polling districts into groups of households.
　　　　　Randomly select household groups and interview all members.

In cluster sampling the same principle is applied, but not necessarily to geographic areas.

(e) Multiphase sample. In multiphase sampling the whole sample provides basic information, but smaller subsets of this sample (subsamples) are randomly selected to provide more detailed information. The main advantages of this method are that it reduces the burden on the sample members and reduces the costs of information collection and analysis.

(2) Non-probability samples

(a) Quota sample. Quota sampling is very common. In it interviewers are instructed to find a number of respondents with particular characteristics. These characteristics are known as quota controls. For example, the interviewer may be told to interview 20 males, or 20 males under 30. In much the same way as strata are chosen for stratified sampling quota controls must be relevant to the research task.

(b) Convenience sample. This is probably the least satisfactory form of sample for most types of research. However, for exploratory work and hypothesis generation it may be quite sound to use the most convenient group of people available.

(c) Judgemental sample. This is a loose form of quota sample in which the researcher's judgement replaces any overt attempt to find relevant quota controls.

Another major preliminary decision in stage 2 of survey design is to select the survey method; and, once again, there is a variety of choices, each with its own strengths and weaknesses. There are three main survey methods (see Table 3.5):

1. Face-to-face methods
   - personal interview
   - group-administered questionnaire
   - self-administered questionnaire
2. Telephone interview
3. Mail questionnaire

Face-to-face methods are those in which interviewer and interviewee actually meet.

The personal interview may be undertaken with or without a rigid format such as is followed when using a questionnaire. In exploratory work informality may be preferred. In a group-administered questionnaire the whole sample or parts of it are assembled, given instructions on completion of the questionnaire and told to do so independently of one another. This method is valued by advertising researchers who wish to pre-test commercials. In a survey using a self-administered questionnaire the researcher personally delivers the questionnaire to each sample member, normally at home or at work, explaining the objectives of the survey and giving instructions on how to complete the questionnaire. This is then either collected or mailed back to the researcher. It is not uncommon to have a callback 4 times in order to obtain a 75 per cent response rate.

The telephone interview is often used where local calls are free; this is not the case in the UK since not all households have telephones; surveys of the total population should not use this method. It is normally necessary to phone back several times before contact

Table 3.5 *Comparison of survey methods.*

Basis for comparison	Face to face			Telephone interview	Mail questionnaire
	Personal interview	Group-administered questionnaire	Self-administered questionnaire		
Is questionnaire used?	Sometimes	Yes	Yes	Normally, yes	Yes
Response rate	High	High, once assembly problem overcome	75% with 4 callbacks	75% with 3 callbacks	25–70%
Cost per usable response	High	Low-medium	Medium	Low	Low
Speed of survey conclusion	Slow	Fast	Medium	Medium	Medium
Control of response quality	High	Medium	Low	Medium	Low
Opportunity to probe?	Yes	No	No	Yes	No
Depth of results	Deep	Shallow	Shallow	Medium	Shallow
Complex instrument usable?	Yes	No	No	Yes	No
Presence of interviewer bias	Yes	Slightly, yes	No	Yes	No
Level of rapport with respondent	High	Medium	Low	Medium	Low

is made with the right person. It is not uncommon to encounter refusals, mid-interview terminations and not-at-homes.

Mail surveys can only be used with literate populations. Even in Europe and North America many people have reading problems which preclude the use of this method.

Most of the 10 criteria listed on the left-hand side of Table 3.5 are self-explanatory. However, 'response rate' means the number of usable responses obtained from the total sample; 'response quality' becomes an important issue if the respondent is likely to mislead the interviewer; 'probing' refers to the interviewer asking supplementary questions; and a 'complex instrument' is one which enables detailed information to be obtained.

Questionnaires can be either structured or unstructured. With the former, questions are formally framed and sequenced. With the latter, there may be a number of headings or topics for the interviewer to investigate, using his discretion about wording and sequence.

The main disadvantage of personal interviews is the high cost per usable response. In some surveys where depth of response is required there is no real alternative. Richness of results and control are sacrificed in group- and self-administered questionnaires, but replaced by lower-cost and speedier conclusions.

The telephone interview's main advantages are low cost and (given a trained interviewer) flexibility. Mail questionnaires are frequently used where the budget is limited. There are a variety of techniques which are recommended for increasing the mail questionnaire response rate:

- send a 'warning' card mentioning imminent arrival of the questionnaire
- send the questionnaire with covering explanatory letter
- have each letter personally addressed and signed
- offer a small gift for taking part in the survey
- assure confidentiality of results
- use the shortest questionnaire possible
- word questions simply
- keep to questions which require concrete, not abstract, responses
- include a stamped addressed envelope
- send reminders to non-respondents
- be rigorous in screening out sample members from whom responses are not required

Stage 3 in survey design is entitled 'Design and test'. It is during this stage that the questionnaire is designed and piloted to ensure that there are no problems or misunderstandings. Figure 3.2 shows how questionnaires can be developed and piloted. Having decided upon the need to use a questionnaire, the first stage is to group and sequence questions. The normal procedure is to sequence them as follows:

1st: Easy questions which establish rapport.
2nd: Factual questions.
3rd: Attitudinal questions.
4th: Personal questions.

In quota sampling personal questions may need to be placed first in order to establish whether the respondent fits the specified quota controls. Question framing (wording)

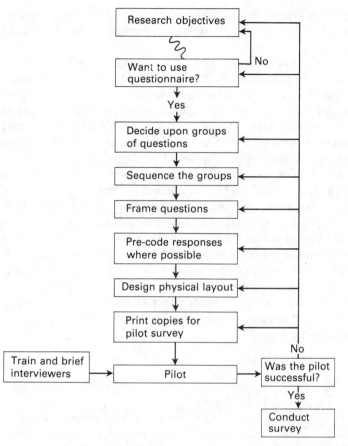

Figure 3.2 Drafting the questionnaire.

and questionnaire design is a developing art. The critical issue to remember is that the questionnaire must be written in a language which is understood by all members of the sample.

Question types
A basic distinction that can be made between questions is the difference between *open* and *closed questions*. A closed question is one to which the respondent gives his answer in the form chosen by the questioner. An open question, by comparison, is one which enables the respondent to give an unguided response.

A closed question providing 3 or more alternative replies is often called a *multiple-choice question*.

Questions which help the respondent to remember something are known as *prompts*. The prompt is an aid to memory; it is not intended to structure the answer so much as to help the respondent call to mind issues or facts that he would not be able to recognise, or recall, without help.

A question which suggests the answer, or biases the respondent in favour of one answer above any others, is a *leading* question. Usually questionnaires are carefully designed to avoid leading the respondent. Particular care is needed when using prompts.

A *probe* is a type of question or remark used to obtain further detail on an answer. The probe gives the questioner the chance to explore further a respondent's reply.

Funnel sequences are so named because a funnel starts off with a very broad question, and then progressively narrows down the scope of the subsequent questions until it comes to a very specific point. The purpose of this procedure is to reduce the likelihood of asking leading questions and to increase the likelihood of the respondent giving a spontaneous answer to the issues explored in the questionnaire.

A *filter* question is one which excludes certain respondents from answering subsequent questions which might be irrelevant to them.

Of course, many questions posed in questionnaires display the characteristics of several of the types of question that we have described above; these are *polymorphous* questions. Many questionnaires use *scaling techniques*, which permit the respondent to express the intensity of his opinion at a point upon a graduated scale. Most frequently applied in hospitality markets are Likert scales and the 'semantic differential'; for information about other forms of scale readers should consult any basic marketing research text. In a Likert scale respondents are exposed to a number of statements with which they are asked to agree or disagree. The responses are then scored on a 5-point scale, summed and analysed. An example appears in Table 3.6.

Table 3.6 *Likert scale.*

	Strongly agree	Agree	Uncertain	Disagree	Strongly disagree
1 I enjoy school meals		√			
2 School meals are fattening			√		
3 A packed lunch is better than a school meal					√
4 School meals are good value for money	√				

Note: Positive statements (nos 1 and 4) are scored 5, 4, 3, 2 and 1 from left to right. Negative statements (nos 2 and 3) are scored 1, 2, 3, 4 and 5 from left to right. This respondent has scored 17 out of a possible 20, indicating a favourable attitude.

One commentator has observed that Likert scales are the most widely used scaling technique because they are so easy to construct, but stresses the need for care in statement wording, analysis and conclusion-drawing.[13]

The semantic differential is a fairly recent scaling innovation, developed by Osgood, Suci and Tannenbaum.[14] Basically it comprises a number of 7-point scales with bipolar terms (adjectives or phrases) at opposite ends. Weights are assigned to positions along the scale $(3, 2, 1, 0, -1, -2, -3)$. It is, therefore, possible to compute mean scores for a sample or the sum of an individual's ratings. The example in Table 3.7 is a selection of scales used to measure the image of an hotel. Repeated administration of the semantic differential over time permits judgements to be made about respondents' changing

Table 3.7 *Semantic differential.*

Modern	....	Old-fashioned
Convenient	....	Inconvenient
Well-decorated	....	Badly decorated
Reasonably priced	....	Expensive
Clean	....	Dirty
Good restaurant	....	Bad restaurant

perceptions of the object under investigation. Similarly, it can be used to map perceptions of competing objects (hotels and restaurants).

Question wording

The wording of questions is an art. However, there are a number of golden rules:

1. Avoid *leading questions* such as 'Which menu items do you totally dislike?'
2. Avoid *double-barrelled questions* such as 'Do you like lobster and crayfish dishes?'
3. Avoid a *partial listing* of alternative responses in a questionnaire. Either a complete list or no list at all is preferable. Items in a partial list tend to have greater drawing power.
4. Avoid *difficult words* as in 'Do you generally approve of the use of monosodium glutamate?' unless questioning experts.
5. Avoid *long sentences*, sentences with several qualifying clauses, or sentences which are grammatically difficult.
6. Avoid *double* and *triple negatives* such as 'Is it not true that you have not eaten pasta this week?'
7. Avoid *ambiguous words* such as 'dinner' or 'tea'.
8. Avoid *emotive words* such as 'purity' or 'wholesome'.
9. Avoid questions which demand too much of the interviewee's *memory*. For example, 'How often have you dined out in the last 12 months?'
10. Avoid questioning completely when *secondary sources* can provide the required information.
11. Avoid *hypothetical questions* such as 'Would you stay in an hotel at the junction of the A3 and M25 if one were built?'
12. Avoid questions which *challenge* the respondent such as 'Can you tell me what this French menu item means in English?'
13. Avoid *vagueness* in questions; be specific. Avoid questions like 'What do you think of the canteen?'
14. Avoid asking questions which require *calculations*.

After wording the questions, as many as possible should be precoded. This means that questions are phrased as closed questions whenever possible. Then the layout is physically planned to appear attractive and easy to complete. Too many questionnaires intimidate respondents.

The final part of stage 3 in survey design is piloting—i.e. testing the survey and subsequently emending the questionnaire if necessary. Piloting should be undertaken using a sample drawn from the same population as the main survey sample. Stage 4 of survey design, the main run, puts into full-scale practice the preliminary decisions and results from the pilot. Finally, stage 5 involves editing and analysing the findings and reporting them in a form usable by the manager. We shall return to the issue of data analysis later in the chapter.

Reactive measures: experiments

An experiment, defined as a test of a hypothesis requiring the manipulation of at least one variable is most often undertaken in causal research—e.g. when a researcher wants to discover the effect of a change in advertising expenditure on sales volume.

There are many varieties of experimental design which are comprehensively covered elsewhere.[15] We shall discuss only those in most common use:

Pre-experimental designs
- one-shot case study
- one-group pre-test–post-test design
- static group comparison

True experimental designs
- pre-test–post-test control-group design
- Solomon four-group design
- post-test only control-group design

Throughout this discussion the following symbols will be used to describe each type of experiment:

R = random selection of subjects to participate in the experiment

X = exposure of subjects to the experimental variable whose effect is being measured (known as the condition)

O = some process of observation or measurement

(a) Pre-experimental designs

The one-shot case study:

$$X \qquad O$$

In this pre-experimental design the effect of the condition on the subjects is only measured once, after exposure to the condition. This is of practically no value, except perhaps as a benchmark against which future experimental effects can be measured. Imagine that X represents expenditure of £10,000 on advertising and O represents a brandname recall level of 30 per cent: what does this tell us? It tells us nothing about the effects of advertising because a wide range of causes may have resulted in the measured recall level. In this case measure O is not a valid indicator of the effect of condition X.

The causes of invalidity in this and other experimental designs derive from 5 main sources:
- the history effect—any environmental circumstances between administration of the condition and the subsequent measurement of its effect; in the advertising example above the recall level could have been caused by word of mouth communication
- the maturity effect—these are changes in the experimental subjects which may lead to invalidity of findings; e.g. forgetting, tiring, or ageing
- the testing effect—we have already discussed how initial exposure of subjects to a test or observation can result in learning or modification of behaviour which, in turn, leads to invalid results on subsequent testing occasions

- the instrument effect—this source of invalidity in experimental results occurs when the instrument used to measure the effects of the condition is subject to variation, as discussed earlier
- the selection effect—only experimental results obtained from randomly selected subjects can be used to draw wider inferences; all pre-experimental designs are non-random; in the advertising example subjects were not randomly selected

The one-group pre-test–post-test design:
$$O_1 \qquad X \qquad O_2$$
In this design a measure (O_1) is taken before administration of the condition; a measure (O_2) is taken afterwards. The belief that $O_2 - O_1$ is the result of X is invalid because of the presence of selection, history, testing, maturity and instrument effects, all of which could contribute to the difference $O_2 - O_1$.

Many studies have been conducted using a time-series variation of this design in which several pre-test and post-test measurements are taken:
$$O_1 O_2 O_3 \qquad X \qquad O_4 O_5 O_6$$
This design, in which either the pre-test trend is compared with the post-test trend or the pre-test average compared with the post-test average, suffers from the same problems as the previous design in which only one measure is taken before and after.

Static-group comparison. The third pre-experimental design which also demonstrates some of these invalidating factors is the static-group comparison:
$$X \quad O_1$$
$$O_2$$
The effect of the condition is measured on the experimental subjects (O_1) whilst, at the same time, a measurement is taken of others who have not been subjected to the condition (O_2). Once again, the assumed effect of X is $O_2 - O_1$. This design means that the testing, instrument, maturity and history effects are controlled. There is no testing or instrument effect because the subjects are only once measured. There is no history effect, provided that the environment for both groups of subjects is the same; and there is no maturity effect since only one measure is taken of each group. However, random selection of subjects has not taken place, therefore, the selection effect persists.

(b) True experimental designs
True experiments are those in which the precise effect of the condition is isolated without any contamination by the 5 sources of invalidity. The first point to note is that all true experimental designs require random selection of participants; the second point to note is that all true experiments have both a set of test subjects on whom the condition is imposed (the test group) and a set of subjects on whom the condition is not imposed (the control group). Third, subjects are randomly allocated to either test or control groups.

The pre-test–post-test control-group design:
$$R\,O_1 \quad X \quad O_2$$
$$R\,O_3 \qquad O_4$$

Measures O_1 and O_3 are taken at the same point in time, as are O_2 and O_4. The effect of X is measured by:

$$(O_2 - O_1) - (O_4 - O_3)$$

The history effect is controlled because any events causing a difference in $O_2 - O_1$ would also have appeared in $O_4 - O_3$. Similarly, maturity, instrument and testing effects would be present in both $O_2 - O_1$ and $O_4 - O_3$. An extension of this design is a time-series version in which a series of measurements is taken of both groups after the condition has been imposed. Sometimes they can be combined with a series of pre-test measures, as shown below:

$$R\ O_1\ O_2\ O_3\ O_4 \quad X \quad O_5\ O_6\ O_7\ O_8$$
$$R\ O_9\ O_{10}\ O_{11}\ O_{12} \qquad O_{13}\ O_{14}\ O_{15}\ O_{16}$$

Solomon four-group design. In this true experimental design 4 randomly selected groups take part; two are subjected to the condition, two are not:

$$R\ O_1\ X\ O_2$$
$$R\ O_3 \quad\ \ O_4$$
$$R \quad\ X\ O_5$$
$$R \quad\quad\ O_6$$

Measures O_1 and O_3 are taken at the same point in time, as are O_2, O_4, O_5 and O_6. In this design the effect of X can be assessed in 4 ways: by comparing O_2 with O_1; O_2 with O_4; O_5 with O_6; and O_5 with O_3. If each of these comparisons shows agreement about the direction of the influences of X (e.g. if $O_2 > O_1$, $O_2 > O_4$, $O_5 > O_6$ and $O_5 > O_3$), then a much stronger inference can be made about its effect. (The symbol $>$ means 'is greater than'.) The formulae below all show the effect of X; by combining and averaging them a more valid impression of the condition's effect will be obtained, in which all 5 sources of invalidity are controlled:

$$(O_2 - O_1) - (O_4 - O_3)$$
$$(O_2 - O_4)$$
$$(O_5 - O_6)$$

The post-test only control-group design:

$$R\ X\ O_1$$
$$R \quad\ O_2$$

This experimental design shows that it is not necessary to conduct pre-tests in order to judge the effect of a condition. In this design all 5 causes of invalidity are controlled. It is the same design as the static-group comparison, with one exception. The selection effect is controlled through random selection of subjects and random allocation to test and control groups. The true effect of X is $O_2 - O_1$.

In all the experimental designs examined so far we have assumed that the researcher is only interested in investigating the effect of one condition. Often this is not the case—e.g. a researcher may want to establish the interactive effects of variations in price and advertising expenditure. Two types of experimental design are of value in these situations: factorial designs, and latin square designs. Both of these experimental designs require advanced analytical skills and are beyond the scope of this book.[16]

Reactive measures: group discussions

The third reactive data-collection method is the group discussion, also known as the 'focus group interview'. Whereas the data generated by surveys and experiments are largely quantitative, group discussions excel in producing qualitative data.

In group discussions a gathering of 7–12 people join together to discuss a chosen topic. The group is managed by a sensitive moderator who is able to extract relevant information during the course of exchanges between group members.

Group discussions are most popular for exploratory work—e.g. in problem definition or hypothesis formulation, but rarely providing data in causal research. The principle underlying group discussions is that a diversity of rich, detailed views can be obtained through group interaction. However, the method is not without problems:

- Group moderators who are skilled and experienced are hard to find; hotel management is unlikely to perform well.
- In any group process dominant figures emerge; moderators must be able diplomatically to reduce that person's dominance whilst valuing his contribution; equally, submissive group members must be encouraged.
- Recordings of the proceedings can be tedious and incomplete without the use of a tape recorder, yet this in turn may inhibit some respondents.
- Interpretation is a major difficulty; the tendency to seek a vote on major issues must be avoided if it is likely to lead to reticence in some group members, yet interpretation is difficult without discovering whether there is a consensus on some issues; interpretation of well-conducted group discussions can only be qualitative.
- Discussion groups can be difficult to organise: how likely is it that an attempt to assemble former hotel guests will succeed?

Reactive measures: projective techniques

Psychologists, particularly those investigating motivation, have encountered difficulties in discovering the true causes of human behaviour. Often respondents will deliberately conceal or repress the true motive; on other occasions they may simply be incapable of expressing or recognising it. To counter these problems a number of projective techniques have been developed.

These barriers between the 'expressed' motive and the 'true' motive are erected for several reasons.[17]

1. Fear of self-incrimination. How many motel rooms have been booked ostensibly for afternoon 'business meetings'?
2. Intellectual deficiencies. The respondent may have highly complex motives which are difficult to explain.
3. Politeness. Respondents may feel inhibited in expressing motives to a stranger.
4. Lack of comprehension. The respondent simply may not understand why he acts as he does.
5. Concealment of abnormal behaviour. The respondent may wish to conceal his own deviant behaviour or, less extremely, not admit to less-than-ideal behaviour.
6. Admission of irrationality. We seem to live in a society which holds rationality in high esteem; respondents may not want to admit their behaviour is emotional or irrational.

The projective techniques detailed below, whilst producing rich and deep information, are fraught with analytical problems; both experts and laymen may differ in their interpretation of the data produced.

1. Sentence completion
The respondent spontaneously completes a battery of incomplete sentences such as: 'Wimpy has a reputation for . . .' Generally the earlier stems (incomplete sentences) in a battery are broader than the later stems, which tend to concern specific issues.

2. Word association (free association)
The respondent gives his instant response to a number of stimulus words spoken by the researcher. In a list of 20 there are likely to be 4 or 5 key words. Hesitations and blocking (when the respondent does not respond) are regarded as pointing to emotional significance.

3. Thematic apperception test (TAT)
In TAT the respondent is shown an ambiguous pictorial stimulus, such as a picture of a restaurant dining room, and is asked to describe what is happening and the attitudes of characters in the picture. Word bubbles might be drawn for the respondent to fill in with imagined conversation. A number of related pictures may be shown.

4. Third-person test
Respondents are asked to explain the motives of a third person in a hypothetical situation. The assumption is that the respondent will project his own motives into the situation, assigning them to the third person. Instead of asking directly: 'Why do you, a successful businessman, stay in a budget hotel?', the respondent is asked to explain why a successful businessman might stay in such a hotel.

3.10   RESEARCH PROCEDURE: ANALYSING THE INFORMATION

The purpose of analysis is to provide meaning; without it, data have no sense, no form and no understandable structure—unanalysed data are meaningless. There are a large number of techniques of analysis; however, statistics is not the subject of this book and readers are advised to follow up references at the end of the chapter.[18]

Analytical techniques can be classified as *univariate, bivariate* and *multivariate*:
- Univariate techniques analyse data relating to a single variable such as sales, coupon response rates, or consumer complaints.
- Bivariate techniques analyse data relating to two variables and look to establish relationships such as correlation or time order between them. Such studies would include price–sales relationships and salespersons' responses to financial incentives.
- Multivariate analysis, the most complicated set of techniques, seeks to establish relationships of a causal or correlative nature between at least 3 variables. Marketing simulations, in which the combined interactive effects of marketing mix decisions on sales and profitability are computed electronically, are a highly developed form of multivariate modelling.

3.11 RESEARCH PROCEDURE: USING THE INFORMATION

No amount of marketing research can make decisions for a manager. It is his task to be the decision-maker.

In deciding what course of action to take the manager must consider the validity and reliability of the findings. He must consider a variety of sources of invalidity such as:
- respondent error
- investigator error
- sampling error and selection effects
- history effects
- maturity effects
- testing effects
- instrument effects

Reliability is reflected by stability in the research findings. If two surveys of household eating-out behaviour were undertaken in swift succession, each producing different results, then the findings would be regarded as unreliable. Of course, if the variance reflected a real-life change, then the reliability level is acceptable.

Findings are valid if the research instrument used to collect the data actually measures what it is intended to measure.

For instance, if a manager wants to discover the attitudes of customers towards a new product, then the attitude-measuring questionnaire must reflect all dimensions of the attitude. It must measure the beliefs and feelings which consumers hold about the innovation, the strength of these beliefs and feelings and the intended purchasing response when the innovation is marketed. All these are dimensions of the construct 'attitude'; if the instrument does not measure all these dimensions, then the results are invalid.

If the manager is assured of the reliability and validity of the findings, he can make decisions with confidence. This, after all, is the primary purpose of marketing research.

3.12 CHAPTER REVIEW

1. Marketing research is the systematic and objective search for, and analysis of, information relevant to the identification and solution of any problem in the field of marketing.
2. There are a number of modes of decision-making under conditions of uncertainty. Most widely encountered in marketing is the Bayesian approach.
3. Marketing research can be descriptive, exploratory, or causal.
4. Market research is not the same as marketing research.
5. Marketing management and marketing researchers often form an uneasy alliance.
6. Marketing research is a £150 million industry.
7. Research agencies can be categorised as general or specific.
8. There are a number of agencies specialising in research for the hospitality industry.
9. There are 5 main steps to research procedure:
   (a) analysis of information needs.
   (b) finding information sources.
   (c) collecting the information.
   (d) analysing the information.
   (e) using the information.

10. Decisions can be classed as occasional or regular; research can be classed as ad hoc or continuous.
11. Good information is pertinent, accurate, timely and usable.
12. Marketing researchers investigate:
    (a) the marketing environment.
    (b) the marketing mix.
13. Marketing environment research comprises feasibility studies and market, customer and motivational research; and business and economic research.
14. Marketing mix research comprises product, pricing, advertising, sales and distribution research.
15. Marketing budgets are seldom large enough to provide information pertinent to every marketing problem.
16. Secondary data are data which have already been collected; primary data are data not previously collected.
17. The hospitality industry, particularly the accommodation sector, is well funded with data about customers, sales and operations.
18. Customer records include the hotel register, reservation requests and guest indices.
19. Sales records include bills, visitors' ledger, vouchers from sales outlets, daily summary book, sales ledger and cash or receipt books.
20. Operations records include in-room questionnaires and departmental reports.
21. External secondary information can be obtained from marketing research companies; governmental and international sources; trade associations; education institutions; published accounts; directories; and other organisations and publications.
22. Data-collection methods can be classified as reactive and non-reactive.
23. Reactive methods suffer from 3 types of error: respondent, investigator and sampling.
24. Respondent error derives from the testing effect, role-selection effect, measurement effect and the response sets of the respondent.
25. Investigator error derives from interviewer and instrument effects and recording errors.
26. Sampling error derives from sampling-frame error, sample bias and administration errors.
27. There are 3 main types of non-reactive measures: physical traces, archives and observation.
28. There are 4 main types of reactive measures: surveys, experiments, group discussions and projective techniques.
29. Survey design is a process which can be broken down into 5 stages: preparation, preliminary decisions, design and test, the main run and production of results.
30. A good sampling frame is an up-to-date list of the researcher's population of interest with no omissions, duplications, or errors.
31. A probability sample is one in which every member of the population stands an equal and positive chance of selection.
32. There are 5 main types of probability sample: simple random samples, systematic random samples, stratified samples, multiphase samples and multistage samples.
33. There are 3 main types of non-probability samples; quota, judgemental and convenience samples.
34. There are 3 main types of survey method:
    (a) face-to-face methods.
      • personal interviews.
      • group-administered questionnaires.
      • self-administered questionnaires.
    (b) telephone interviews.
    (c) mail questionnaires.
35. Questionnaires need to be constructed with care since they can be sources of error.
36. There are a number of types of question: open, closed, multiple choice, prompts, probes, funnels, filters and scales.
37. The two most popular scaling devices are the Likert scale and the semantic differential.
38. There are many potential pitfalls to be avoided in question-wording.
39. Experimental methods can be classified as pre-experimental or true experimental designs.

40. Group discussions, which are useful for hypothesis generation, are not without problems.
41. Projective techniques can be used to counter psychological barriers erected by respondents.
42. A basic distinction made between data-analysis techniques is concerned with the number of variables analysed—one (univariate), two (bivariate) and three or more (multivariate).
43. The two principal concerns of management when deciding whether to use research findings are the validity and reliability of the data.

3.13 QUESTIONS

1. For the research problems listed below would you use primary or secondary data? If primary, how would you construct your sampling frame? What would be your sampling unit and your data-collection method?
   (a) The potential conference market for an Eastbourne (coastal) 3-star hotel.
   (b) Customer opinions about competing budget hotels.
   (c) Patient attitudes to hospital food.
2. What applications can you find for projective techniques in the hospitality industry?
3. Draft a questionnaire to investigate student attitudes towards on-site food service.
4. How could non-reactive data-collection methods be used in the following circumstances?
   (a) To measure the effectiveness of a take-away food bar's anti-litter campaign.
   (b) To assess the effect of a theme park development on local hotels.
   (c) To assess whether the installation of contract caterers, as opposed to own canteen employees, has enhanced shopfloor worker morale?
5. What criteria would you use to evaluate the value of data collected and analysed on your behalf by the marketing research company?

REFERENCES

[1] Green, P. E. and Tull, D. S. (1978) (4th edn) *Research for Marketing Decisions*. Englewood Cliffs, NJ: Prentice-Hall.
[2] Enis, B. M. and Broome, C. L. (1973) *Marketing decisions: A Bayesian Analysis*. London: Intertext; see also Green, P. E. and Tull, D. S. (1978) op. cit.
[3] Axler, B. H. (1979) *Food Service: A Management Approach*. Lexington, MA: D.C. Heath.
[4] Retail Audits Ltd, brochure.
[5] See: Nielsen backs its new data ploy. *Marketing*, 20 September 1984, 8.
[6] Simmons, M. (1983) The UK market research scene. *Survey*, 1, June, 28–9.
[7] Medlik, S. (1980) *The Business of Hotels*. London; Heinemann.
[8] See Yesawich, P. C. (1978) Post-opening marketing analysis for hotels. *Cornell Hotel and Restaurant Administration Quarterly,* **19**(3), November, 70-81.
[9] One novel attempt to obtain representative responses proposes the use of a data entry terminal, allowing 3 alternative responses to 10 questions, situated in the hotel lobby; see: The push-button questionnaire. *Cornell Hotel and Restaurant Administration Quarterly,* **19**(4), February 1979, 70–9.
[10] Lewis, R. C. and Pizam, A. (1981) Guest surveys: a missed opportunity. *Cornell Hotel and Restaurant Administration Quarterly,* **22**(3), November, 32–44.
[11] For a review of reactive and non-reactive data collection methods see Webb, E. J., Campbell, D. T., Schwartz, R. D., and Sechrest, L. (1966) *Unobtrusive Measures: Non-Reactive Research in the Social Sciences*. Chicago: Rand McNally.
[12] See Green, P. E. and Tull, D. S. (1978) op. cit. Chisnall, P. M. (1981) (2nd edn) *Marketing Research: Analysis and Measurement*. London: McGraw-Hill; Luck, D. J., Wales, H. G., Taylor, D. A., and Rubin, R. S. (1982) (6th edn) *Marketing Research*. Englewood Cliffs, NJ: Prentice-Hall; and Zaltman, G.and Burger, P. C. (1975) *Marketing Research: Fundamentals and Dynamics*. Hinsdale, IL: Dryden Press.

[13] Worcester, R. M. and Burns, T. R. (1975) A statistical examination of the relative precision of verbal scales. *Journal of the Market Research Society*, **17**(3), July.

[14] Osgood, C. E., Suci, G. J., and Tannenbaum, P. H. (1957) *The Measurement of Meaning*. Urbana, IL: University of Illinois Press.

[15] Campbell, D. T. and Stanley, J. C. (1966) *Experimental and Quasi-Experimental Designs for Research*. Chicago: Rand McNally.

[16] But see Green, P. E. and Tull, D. S. (1978) op. cit.

[17] See also Oppenheim, A. N. (1969) *Questionnaire Design and Attitude Measurement*. London: Heinemann.

[18] See Letchford, S. (1980) *Statistics*. London: Gee; Greensted, C. S., Jardine, A. K. S., and MacFarlane, J. D. (1978) (2nd edn) *Essentials of Statistics in Marketing*. London: Heinemann; Hoinville, G. (1980) *Survey Research Practice*. London: Heinemann. See also Green, P. E. and Tull, D. S. (1978) op. cit.; Chisnall, P. M. (1981) op. cit.; Luck, D. J. *et al.* (1982), op. cit.; and Zaltman, G. and Burger, P. C. (1975) op. cit.

—4—

Consumer Behaviour

4.1 CHAPTER PREVIEW

Marketers are managers of demand. Demand is a form of behaviour. Marketers study consumer behaviour in order to be able to understand and, if possible, predict and control that demand.

This chapter defines consumer behaviour and outlines the sources of information about, and discusses the key concepts of, consumer behaviour. We refer to involvement, information processing, decision-making processes and learning, and to personality, needs, values and attitudes towards and social influences upon consumer behaviour such as reference groups, the family, social class and organisation membership. The influence of culture is also discussed. Finally, we outline a number of attempts to model consumer decision-making processes and the environmental influences upon them.

4.2 LEARNING OBJECTIVES

By the end of this chapter you should be able to:
1. Define and explain these terms: involvement, information processing, decision-making, learning, personality, needs, values, attitude, reference groups, social class and culture.
2. Explain the relationship between involvement, decision-making and information processing.
3. Describe the essentials of individual, family and organisational buying behaviour.
4. Discriminate between complex buying behaviour, variety-seeking buying behaviour, dissonance-reducing buying behaviour and inertia.
5. Explain the principal criticism of the inferential models of consumer behaviour.

4.3 WHY STUDY CONSUMER BEHAVIOUR?

In Chapter 2 we claimed that the principal task of marketing management was to influence demand, so that it reached a satisfactory level for the marketer. Unless possessed of remarkable intuition and protected by good luck, marketers must rely on their understanding of the processes customers go through in buying and consuming hospitality products. A very high proportion of new restaurants close within weeks of opening in a blaze of publicity. Why? Often because the proprietors have not considered consumer needs, wants and behaviour; instead the restaurant reflects the owner's ego.

If marketers understand the who, what, where, when, how and why of consumer behaviour, then the probability of marketing success is enhanced—there is less waste in the marketing budget, products are developed to satisfy well-researched needs and plans are executed which deliver customer satisfaction.

4.4 THE STRUCTURE OF KNOWLEDGE ABOUT CONSUMER BEHAVIOUR

Consumer behaviour is a developing science. Scientific method, that is the setting up and testing of hypotheses which confirm or refute existing theory, thereby strengthening or weakening the theory, is the formal and normal method of development in any science. Consumer behaviour conforms to this method of investigation.

There is no single, irrefutable body of knowledge about consumer behaviour for it is a dynamic, eclectic, changing area of investigation. Theorists and researchers have drawn upon psychology, sociology, social psychology, anthropology, economics and philosophy in their attempts to build a body of knowledge.

The main contributions of the social sciences are detailed below.

Psychology	needs and motivation
	learning
	perception
	information processing
	decision-making processes
	personality
Social psychology	attitudes
	values
Sociology	family influences
	organisational influences
	interpersonal communication
	group influences
	influence of social class
Anthropology	cultural and subcultural influences
Philosophy	motives
Economics	choice behaviour
	responsiveness to price

Several consumer behaviour theorists have attempted to integrate the findings of social science researchers and behavioural scientists into descriptive models. Most notable are the efforts of Howard and Sheth,[1] Nicosia,[2] Engel and Blackwell,[3] Andreason[4] and Howard.[5] The models attempt to map the mental processes through which consumers pass in making buying decisions and, further, attempt to relate marketing strategy and marketing mix decisions to purchasing behaviour.[6] This approach to the study of consumer behaviour is shown diagrammatically in Figure 4.1

These models take observed and measurable consumer behaviours such as restaurant choice, and draw inferences about what happens inside the consumer to cause these behaviours. Towards the end of this chapter a number of these models are presented; in the intervening pages we discuss some of the constructs built into them.

There is a growing body of researchers not schooled in the conventional sciences, but rather in marketing or business administration, who investigate consumer behaviour as

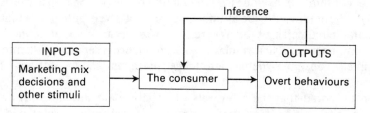

Figure 4.1 The inferential approach to the study of consumer behaviour.

a phenomenon in its own right. Their research is reported in publications such as the *Journal of Marketing, Journal of Advertising, Journal of Advertising Research, International Journal of Advertising, Journal of Marketing Research, Journal of the Market Research Society* and *Journal of Consumer Research.*

Just as there is no single body of consumer behaviour theory, there has been no concerted effort to investigate the hospitality consumer. What appears in this chapter is culled from the general literature, although where research findings are available about hospitality markets they have been incorporated.

4.5 KEY CONCEPTS IN CONSUMER BEHAVIOUR

There are a number of social science constructs which make important contributions to our understanding of consumer behaviour.

Personal characteristics (see section 4.6)
    Involvement
    Decision-making
    Information processing
    Learning
    Personality
    Needs
    Values
    Attitudes
Social influences on behaviour (see section 4.7)
    Reference groups
    Family
    Social class
    Organisation
Culture (see section 4.8)

Kurt Lewin has proposed that behaviour B is a function of two interdependent variables: the person p and the environment e, as shown in formula 4.1:[7]

$$B = f(p, e). \tag{4.1}$$

Lewin's approach can be developed to explain the nature of consumer behaviour. The formula

$$CB = f(p, s, e) \tag{4.2}$$

suggests that consumer behaviour *CB* is a function of the personal characteristics of the individual *p*, the immediate social influences in any given purchase situation *s* and environmental circumstances *e*. Whereas Lewin regards social influences as an important component of *e*, in formula 4.2 social influence is separately identified. This is because much consumer behaviour takes place in group settings—family or organisation.

It should be noted that the three sets of variables are interactive. For example, attitudes (*p* factor) may be developed as a result of family influence (*s*), and the values (*p*) of an individual are frequently those of the culture (*e*) in which he lives.

4.6 PERSONAL CHARACTERISTICS

Involvement

Not all products have equal significance to the consumer. Some have high personal importance or relevance, others score low on these dimensions. Involvement is the term which is used to describe this condition. High involvement purchases may be significant for a number of reasons, as outlined below.

(1) Risk
The higher the perceived risk in a purchase, the greater the level of involvement. Perceived risk exists either when the consumer is uncertain about the consequences of a purchase or about the decision itself. It arises when there is little information about the product category, when the consumer has little experience, when the product is new or complicated, when the consumer has low self-confidence, or when the price is high.[8]
Risk can take a number of forms: economic, social psychological, or physical:
Economic risk is felt with higher-priced products, when the purchase takes a large proportion of disposable income, or when the purchase has long-term financial repercussions.
Social risk is felt where the products have social significance. Some purchases (e.g. the consumption of fast food) imply group affiliations. This is especially significant with visibly consumed products.
Psychological risk is suffered when the self-image or self-esteem is threatened. A vegan forced by circumstances to eat a burger of uncertain ingredients would perceive risk.
Physical risk occurs when the body is exposed to potential damage.

(2) Social-group influence
Many products and brands are bought, directly or indirectly, as a result of group influence. A soldier, for example, is unlikely to eat in the mess if his peers eat elsewhere. Where this type of pressure to conform exists, involvement tends to be high.

(3) Product symbolism

Many products communicate information about the purchaser to others. The choice of venue for a dinner-for-two or a business meeting is symbolic. The more the product communicates—i.e. the greater its symbolic significance—the more involved is the purchaser.

Decision-making

The decision-making process gone through by an individual will vary according to whether the decision is about a high- or low-involvement product. High-involvement decisions are more complex; most conceptualisations are similar to the multi-stage processes shown in Figure 4.2.

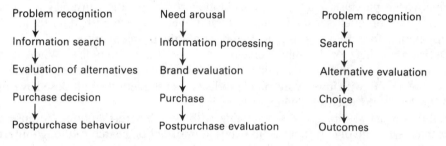

Figure 4.2 Complex decision-making process.
Note: Models proposed, left to right, by Kotler[9], Assael[10], Engel and Blackwell[11].

The process starts when the consumer recognises he has a need which is not currently being satisfied adequately. Recognition of this deficiency may stem from an *internal* state (e.g. hunger pangs) or from *external* stimuli (e.g. an advertisement which promises improved satisfaction). Not all deficiencies become problems, only those which are sufficiently important to the consumer. However, if an unsatisfied need does represent a problem, the consumer will proceed to search for ways of solving it. Search can be internal or external. Internal search involves calling up from memory previous experience or information. If this is insufficient, external search may occur.

Having searched for alternative ways of solving the problem, the consumer has a *choice set* from which to select. The evaluation process involves weighing the alternatives against a set of criteria. One American survey investigated the relative significance of 66 different criteria in hotel selection. Included were accommodations, ambience, cleanliness, location, parking, price, quality, quality of food, quiet, security, service and sports facilities. The researchers concluded that different criteria became important as the purpose of travel changed. Location is much more important for business travellers, and price is more important for pleasure travellers:[12]

> Individuals decide consciously or unconsciously, which attributes they must have in a hotel, which of those attributes are present in one hotel and absent in another, and finally which combination of those attributes is being best delivered by a particular hotel. This last combination is perceived as offering the best bundle of benefits available in a given situation.

Another survey showed that travel agencies use 5 main criteria when selecting hotels for clients: the hotel's reputation for honouring reservations, its general reputation, the attitude of the hotel (chain) towards travel agents, presence of direct reservation facilities and the hotel's commission policies.[13] A third survey, into the criteria used in the purchase of Chinese take-away food, showed that convenient location and gastronomic considerations such as taste, flavour and freshness were most important.[14]

A fourth survey has shown that the criteria used when selecting a place to eat varied by time of day: at lunchtime the most significant criteria were the type of food served, atmosphere and price; in the evening a liquor licence became more important as price became less important, and more care was exercised over selection.[15]

As a result of the evaluation, a purchasing intention is reached and the choice made. The actual choice is not invariably the intended choice. Situational factors such as inadequate money to pay for the intended purchase may intervene.

Finally, the purchase made and consumption complete, the consumer weighs up whether the product satisfied the need and met the established criteria. This information is forgotten or stored in memory until the problem arises again.

Decision-making for low-involvement products is less complex. Whereas the consumer of high-involvement products is an active information seeker and processor, he is more passive with low-involvement products. Consequently, as proposed by Engel and Blackwell, the decision-making process is shorter,

Figure 4.3 shows the process beginning with problem recognition. Because the consumer is less involved, there is no external information search (although internal search may occur) and the consumer immediately proceeds to choice. If there is any evaluation of the product, it occurs after product experience. Indeed, for many low-cost, low-risk and low-involvement items where there are no (or at best insignificant) differences between options, alternative evaluation might not take place at all. Could this be true of vending-machine coffee? If evaluation does take place, it is likely that the criteria are elementary and functional. In the coffee example the criteria might be: did it taste OK? Was it warm? Did it quench the thirst?

Problem recognition
↓
Choice
↓
Alternative evaluation

Figure 4.3   Low-involvement decision-making process.
Note: Modified from Engel and Blackwell[16].

Sometimes consumers, faced with a problem, will reach for a routine solution. A hungry student at 10.00 p.m. may habitually buy fish and chips from a nearby take-away outlet. This form of behaviour is one of three classes identified by Howard[17]—routine response behaviour (RRB).

Howard suggests that all consumer decisions can be categorised by the amount of information search and alternative evaluation that takes place. Where comprehensive search and evaluation occur, the decision is placed at the extensive problem-solving (EPS) end of the scale (see Figure 4.4). Between EPS and RRB lies limited problem-solving (LPS).

It may appear at first glance as if all high-involvement purchases are bought after careful consideration of the differences between alternatives. This need not be the case. Even routine purchases can reflect high involvement. A business traveller who always stays in a Holiday Inn may do so because his peers also stay there; this reflects a high degree of social-group influence.

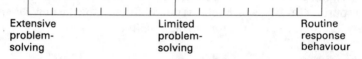

| Extensive problem-solving | Limited problem-solving | Routine response behaviour |

Figure 4.4 Howard's conceptualisation of consumer problem-solving.

The two variables—involvement and differences between alternatives—appear as the axes of the chart in Figure 4.5. Four types of buying behaviour are identified.

INVOLVEMENT

		High	Low
DIFFERENCES	High	Complex buying behaviour	Variety-seeking behaviour
BETWEEN ALTERNATIVES	Low	Dissonance-reducing buying behaviour	Inertia

Figure 4.5 Types of buying behaviour.
Note: Developed from Assael's original proposal.[18]

(1) Complex buying behaviour

Consumers expressing this pattern of behaviour are cautious but active learners. Because of the high involvement, they hunt out information, examine its source for credibility, learn the criteria to use in evaluation and carefully consider each alternative.

Travel agents have been shown to use 6 main criteria when evaluating alternative hotels for business travellers: prior client satisfaction, the hotel's reputation for honouring reservations, proximity to the traveller's destination, the hotel's policy on commission payments and the availability of toll-free or direct reservation.[19] Travel planners in the incentive travel market use different criteria.[20]

(2) Variety-seeking buying behaviour

Consumers in this mode of behaviour tend to be adventurous. There are significant differences between alternatives, but because of low involvement, the consumer is prepared to sample a number of alternatives. Choice may be random, or may reflect a desire in the consumer to experiment. This mode of behaviour is more likely to occur with low-cost, low-risk items.

(3) Inertia
This occurs when the consumer perceives few differences between brands and is not involved in the product. Assael comments that 'inertia is probably more common than most marketing managers would like to admit'.[21]

The implication here is that marketing management is less able to influence consumer purchasing than for higher-involvement products or those where significant differences between alternatives exist. This is because the consumer either chooses at random or develops a spurious loyalty, which reflects not preference, but an unwillingness to spend time, effort, or money searching for anything better.

(4) Dissonance-reducing buying behaviour
This type of buying behaviour occurs when there is high involvement in the product but few perceived differences between alternatives. Consider a middle-aged person taking his first winter skiing holiday. It is a high-risk product because it is expensive, novel and may result in damaged self-esteem! Having no experience on which to draw and no established criteria against which to judge the alternative products, he reads the brochures and makes his selection. On arrival at the resort he mixes with more experienced skiers, samples the slopes and begins to feel concern about the correctness of his decision. This dissonance he reduces by gathering reinforcing information, distorting, or ignoring the adverse opinions of others.

Dissonance theory was developed by Leon Festinger as a means of explaining how people handle inconsistency.[22] His basic proposition was that cognitive dissonance (i.e. inconsistencies between beliefs or bits of knowledge) is psychologically uncomfortable and that people will strive to achieve consonance.

Conventionally marketers have believed that all purchases are made following the complex buying behavioural model. The consumer has been regarded as active, concerned with products and the differences between them. The recent emergence of low-involvement theory has called this into question.

In the early 1960s a variety of models (detailed in Chapter 16), known collectively as hierarchies of effects, proposed that purchasers pass through 3 principal stages: they *learn* about alternatives; having evaluated them, they develop a *preference or liking* for one or more; and finally, they *purchase*—in effect a learn–feel–do process. This is at the heart of complex buying behaviour. However, the learn–feel–do model is an inadequate explanation for the other forms of decision-making shown in Figure 4.5.

In variety-seeking buying behaviour purchases are made without prior evaluation of alternatives. The appropriate model is learn–do–feel since evaluation takes place after the random or experimental purchase. The pattern for inertia is learn–do. The consumer learns that the product is in the general class from which he wishes to select, and makes his choice. In dissonance-reducing buying behaviour learning about the product principally occurs after product experience, as does the development of feelings or attitudes towards the product. Accordingly, the appropriate model is do–learn–feel.

Information processing

Marketers attempt to influence the purchasing of consumers through persuasive communication and are, therefore, concerned with how the consumer is exposed to, searches for, processes and uses information.

Information is obtained from many sources, both marketer controlled (advertising, salesmen and literature) and independent (editorial matter and word of mouth). There have been many attempts to model how the consumer obtains and handles the information. Figure 4.6 shows the Britt model.[23] Britt takes the viewpoint of a producer attempting to induce a particular behavioural response (e.g. favourable attitude or purchase) in his audience. The 6 stages of communication are exposing, attending, perceiving, learning and remembering, motivating and persuading.

If the consumer fails to attend to, perceive or learn and remember the information, or if he is neither motivated nor persuaded by the information, miscommunication has occurred. Britt views this process as taking place against a background of the audience's needs and wants, social and cultural setting, personality, mental set (i.e. state of readiness for a particular action or experience) and 'noise' from competing internal stimuli.

McGuire's model (see Figure 4.7) also views the consumer's handling of information as a multistage process. Day has commented on McGuire as follows (but it should be pointed out that most people do not expose themselves to information sources which are inconsistent with their present interests, beliefs and attitudes; this is called 'selective exposure'[24]):[25]

Before an individual can be persuaded by a communication he must have the message presented to him via informal or formal media; then the message must get and hold his attention. The ability of a message to hold attention depends on whether the receiver can comprehend the arguments and conclusions. Comprehension is influenced by the complexity and clarity of the message.

The likelihood of acceptance, or yielding to the comprehended mesage, is theorized to depend on the extent of incentives. The incentives in the message may be in the form of arguments or reasons why the advocated point of view should be accepted in favour of the old attitude, or the arousal of expectations that have reinforcing value. Suspicion of someone's manipulative intent is another expectation that will nullify the prospects of acceptance because it is seen as a threat to one's freedom to decide for oneself.

If the recipient has taken the fourth step of yielding or accepting the message, there is the further question of whether he will retain the new position until he has an opportunity to behave accordingly. As a rule, retention depends on the informational content of the message and the incentives for acceptance.

Each step in the chain is taken with only a certain probability, and its occurrence depends on the probabilities associated with the earlier steps in the chain. The model suggests that the probabilities are multiplicative; so if there were a probability of 0.5 at each step there would be a less than 0.02 probability that purchase behaviour would be influenced by the persuasive message.

Engel and Blackwell adopt the same process as McGuire, exposure, attention, comprehension, yielding/acceptance and retention, but stress that information processing is quite different for low-involvement products.[26] For low-involvement products:

- Attention is involuntary and occurs when the consumer is exposed to the information-carrying medium for other reasons. This is called 'passive learning'.[27]
- There is no cognitive learning. Detailed information is not stored in the brain and

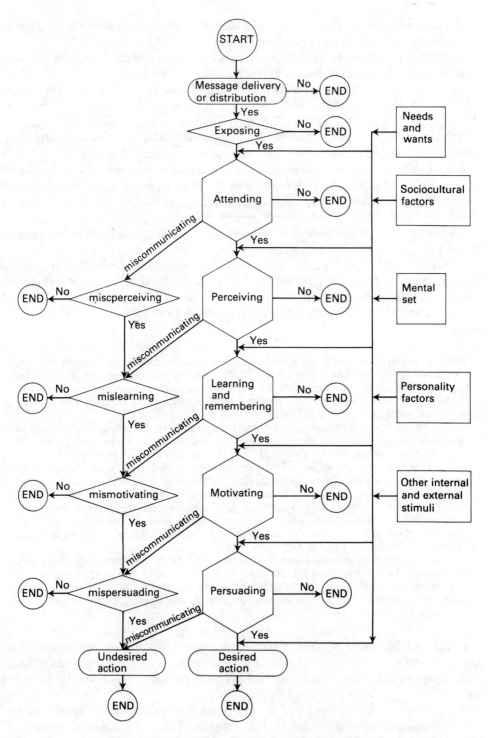

Figure 4.6   The Britt model of information processing.

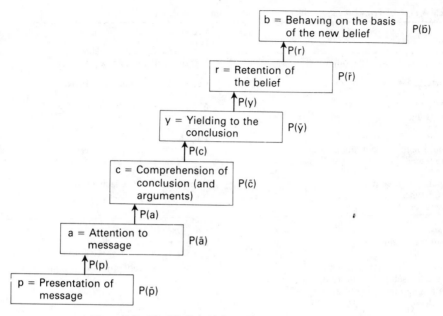

Figure 4.7 The McGuire information-processing model.

there is no attempt to integrate the new information with existing information in a way which is consistent and balanced. Dissonance does not occur.

- Visual images are retained in the brain although the yielding/acceptance stage is by-passed. As there is no cognitive learning, there can be no recall of cognitive information when the consumer searches his memory during future decision-making.[28]

The low-involvement information processing model proposed by Engel and Blackwell appears in Figure 4.8.

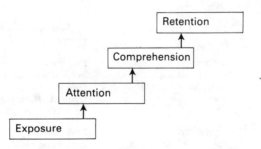

Figure 4.8 Engel and Blackwell's model of information processing under conditions of low involvement.

Table 4.1 summarises the principal decision-making and information processing differences between high- and low-involvement consumer behaviour. Table 4.2 lists how involvement can influence the decisions of marketing management. When the consumer has acquired information, how does he use it in alternative evaluation?

Table 4.1   *Differences between low- and high-involvement consumer behaviour.*

Level of involvement	
Low	High
Predominantly low-risk purchases	Predominantly high-risk purchases
Shorter decision-making process	Longer decision-making process
Less complex information processing	More complex information processing
Low level of information (or none) sought when making initial purchase	High level of information sought when making initial purchase
Repeat purchase may reflect unwillingness to search for a better product	Repeat purchase reflects preference for the purchased brand
Consumer learns passively about the product	Consumer learns actively about the product
Consumer does not selectively expose himself to, attend to or retain competing promotional stimuli	Consumer actively processes promotional stimuli
Weak attitude towards purchased brand	Strong attitude towards purchased brand
Consumer able to recognise product from visual images held in memory	Consumer able to recall product information

Table 4.2   *Managerial implications of involvement.*

	Level of involvement	
	Low	High
Product:	Product as a problem-solver Product as satisfactory solution	Product as a deliverer of benefits Product as optimal benefit package
Price:	Use price deals	Reduce economic risk through credit, guarantees, etc.
Advertising:	Awareness through repetition Aim for memorability Stimulation of purchase	Persuasive message Much information Aim for learning Content organisation important Develop favourable attitudes
Sales promotion:	More effective Sampling leads to adoption	Less effective Information leads to trial
Merchandising:	More productive	Less productive
Sales:	Salesman takes orders Immediate results	Salesman as educator Long-term relationship
Distribution:	Widespread availability Stockouts disastrous	Buyer seeks supplier Stockouts less important

Let us assume that 4 coastal hotels are under consideration by a holidaymaker. Each hotel is assessed against 3 criteria: proximity to beach, room rate and the range of in-house facilities such as lounge, bar, restaurants and games room. Rating is on a 7-point scale, where 7 indicates a high level of expected satisfaction and 1 indicates a low level of expected satisfaction. Table 4.3 summarises each hotel's performance on the 3 attributes.

Table 4.3 *Hotel attribute rating.*

	Suntrap Hotel	Seaview Hotel	Jacaranda Hotel	Homeleigh Hotel
1. Proximity to beach	2	7	7	4
2. Room rate	6	6	4	6
3. Facilities	7	5	2	7

Consumers use 2 approaches in handling this information: compensatory and non-compensatory. In the *compensatory* approach a poor rating on one attribute is compensated by a high rating on another attribute. A compensatory approach would assign cumulative ratings to the hotels (15, 18, 13 and 17 from left to right), with the Seaview Hotel being selected. In the *non-compensatory* approach a poor rating on one scale cannot be compensated by a higher rating elsewhere. There are 3 non-compensatory forms of alternative evaluation, known as the conjunctive model, the disjunctive model and the lexicographic model.[29]

(1) Conjunctive model
The holidaymaker considers only those hotels which meet minimum standards. If his requirements are for a minimum rating of 5 for 'proximity to beach', Suntrap and Homeleigh are eliminated from the choice set. If the minimum rating for 'facilities' is 4, Jacaranda is further eliminated. Seaview is selected. The choice is of the hotel which *conjunctively* satisfies all minimum standards.

(2) Disjunctive model
If a minimum rating is set for 1 or more attributes regarded as *essential* by the holidaymaker, the model is disjunctive. A minimum rating of 7 for the perceived key attribute 'facilities' would eliminate Seaview and Jacaranda. The final choice would be made from Suntrap and Homeleigh.

(3) Lexicographic model
If the holidaymaker first ranks the attributes in order of importance and then compares ratings on the attributes in order of importance, the model is lexicographic. Let us assume our holidaymaker ranks 'facilities' as most important, 'room rate' as second and 'proximity to beach' third. On the most important attribute Homeleigh and Suntrap are equally rated, so Sunview and Jacaranda are eliminated. Homeleigh and Suntrap tie on ratings for the second most important attribute, so the third attribute is brought into consideration. As Homeleigh is superior to Suntrap, it is selected. Had any hotel rated as best on the most important attribute, it would have been selected.

Learning

Behaviours are either innate or learned responses to stimuli. Consumer behaviour is entirely learned. Learning, which can be defined as 'a more or less permanent change in behaviour which occurs as a result of practice',[30] is the subject of much empirical research. There are 2 principal avenues of investigation,[31] one adopted by the behaviourist school, the other by the cognitive school. The main distinctions between them appear in table 4.4.[32] There have been attempts to integrate the apparently irreconcilable schools, the most notable being that of Gagné.[33]

Table 4.4 *Schools of learning.*

Criteria for comparison \ School of psychology	Behaviourist	Cognitive
Major contributors	Skinner, Thorndike, Pavlov, Guthrie, Tolman	Wertheimer, Köhler, Koffka
Major concepts	Stimulus, response, reinforcement, chaining, conditioning, shaping contiguity, repetition	Gestalt (wholeness) organisation, closure, proximity, similarity, trace, insight
Major period of development	1890–1940	1912–date

(1) The behaviourist school
Two theories of learning have evolved in the behaviourist school: classical conditioning and instrumental conditioning. The most famous experiments into *classical conditioning* were conducted by Pavlov. He knew that dogs salivated (response) when exposed to food (unconditioned stimulus). He repeatedly sounded a bell (conditioned stimulus) to coincide with the appearance of the food. The dogs eventually learned to associate the bell with food, and continued to salivate in subsequent replications, even in the absence of food. Key issues to marketers are contiguity and repetition:
- Contiguity. For classical conditioning to succeed the conditioned and unconditioned stimuli must be closely associated.
- Repetition. Association between conditioned stimulus and response only occurs through repetition.

This theory has implications for marketers. Advertisements attempt to perform the function of the conditioned stimulus.

Classical conditioning believes learners are passive subjects whose responses to conditioned stimuli can be formed through repetition, whereas *instrumental conditioning* holds that learning occurs when behaviour is reinforced either with a reward or punishment. Skinner's experiments are seminal. By rewarding certain behaviours with food he managed to shape the behaviour of pigeons to the extent that the birds learned to play ping-pong!

In marketing terms the reward is satisfaction. The greater the satisfaction experienced by the consumer, the stronger is the reinforcement and the more likely will be repurchase. Instrumental conditioning holds that the learner makes voluntary responses to stimuli but that the response is more likely to be repeated if the outcome is satisfactory. This appears to explain much about inertia and variety-seeking behaviour.

(2) The cognitive school

The cognitive school proposes that learning is essentially problem-solving behaviour in which new information is acquired and processed against a background of existing information. Clearly, the cognitive learning school's view parallels the information-processing activities undertaken during complex decision-making.

Hoteliers wishing to produce business from the corporate meetings market should realise that meetings planners take a problem-solving view of venue choice, in that the venue must be the optimal alternative for a given meeting. Information from alternatives is evaluated; according to one survey, the 3 most important criteria are comfortable meeting rooms, satisfactory price level compared to alternatives and the venue's willingness to assign a staff member to handle group problems.[34]

Personality

Research into the relationship between personality—which may be defined as an habitual mode of response to environmental stimuli—and consumption has been rather disappointing for those who believe that the consumer's personality is a major determinant of his product and brand choice. Kassarjian comments:[35]

> A review of . . . dozens of studies and papers can be summarised in the single word, equivocal. A few studies indicate a strong relationship between personality and aspects of consumer behaviour, a few indicate no relationship, and the great majority indicate that if correlations do exist they are so weak as to be questionable or perhaps meaningless.

Needs

The first stage in consumer decision-making for both low- and high-involvement products is problem recognition. This occurs when the person perceives some discrepancy between the ideal state of affairs and the actual situation. In effect, the consumer experiences discomfort because his needs, wants, or demands are not being satisfied.

The cause of this discomfort are stimuli which are either internal or external to the consumer. Internal stimuli—drives—tell the consumer he is, for example, hungry, thirsty, or sleepy. Marketers have no control over this, but they do over cues—external stimuli which arouse consumer wants, demands, or needs. Food displays, for instance, are cues which can arouse hunger.

A need can be defined as:

> a physical or psychological state which is tension creating.

Kotler distinguishes between needs, wants and demands.[36] He describes a want as a desire for some specific item which will satisfy a need—e.g. the need is for food but the want is for a hamburger. Demand is a want backed up by purchasing power. The marketing concept demands that organisations attempt to satisfy consumer needs. So what are these needs that are aroused by internal and external stimuli?

The physical needs for food, drink and sleep are innate. But not all needs are, for many needs are learnt, and much research effort has been diverted to discovering what these needs might be. Three efforts, by Murray, Maslow and followers of Sigmund Freud are particularly useful. Both Murray and Maslow suggest that when a need is aroused, the individual is put into an uncomfortable state of *tension*, which *motivates* the individual to find a way of reducing the tension thereby satisfying the need. In 1938 Henry Murray identified 11 needs said to be present in all human beings to a greater or lesser extent. They are listed and defined in Table 4.5. The demand for hotel accommodation derives from the demand for travel. The motives for travel, given Murray's interpretation, are as shown in the table. Maslow's work, published in 1954, has achieved a good deal of acceptance amongst psychologists and marketers.[37] Maslow suggests that man is a creature who behaves in a constantly need-satisfying manner. As one need is satisfied another need replaces it. Those needs can be hierarchically organised in order of 'prepetency' or importance to the individual.

Table 4.5   *Murray's need classification.*

- Business travel: an expression of the need for abasement, achievement, deference, dominance, exhibition, self-defence
- Pleasure travel: an expression of the need for affiliation, autonomy, exhibition, play, sex, understanding
- Emergency travel (e.g. to visit sick relative): an expression of the need for affiliation, deference, self-defence, understanding

Abasement	The need to accept blame, criticism, error, inferiority
Achievement	The need to master, manipulate, organise, surpass others
Affiliation	The need to win affection
Autonomy	The need to become free of restraint
Deference	The need to admire superiors, to yield to influence of others
Dominance	The need to control and direct the behaviour of others
Exhibition	The need to be seen and heard
Play	The need to act for fun without any other purpose
Self-defence	The need to defend the self against criticism, blame and assault
Sex	The need for an erotic relationship
Understanding	The need to ask or answer general questions

Maslow's 5-level hierarchy (from low to high level) is shown in Table 4.6. Demand for food and drink away from home occurs for 2 reasons: first, it can be a 'substitute domestic activity'; and second, it can be a source of pleasure and entertainment.[38] This implicitly recognises the basic physiological and the higher social, ego and self-fulfilment needs.

Axler's list of motives for eating out can largely be explained in terms of Murray and Maslow:[39]

- hunger
- mood change: entertainment and escapism
- social needs
- habit: security and routine
- reassurance: forget personal troubles
  assertion of individuality
  reward for personal achievement

Table 4.6 *Maslow's need hierarchy.*

1 *Physiological needs*   Physical/physiological needs such as food, clothing, rest, exercise, sex, liquid, shelter. Higher-level needs remain latent whilst these basic needs remain unsatisfied
2 *Security needs*   Needs for safety, security. These needs serve to protect the individual from danger and deprivation
3 *Social needs*   To belong, to live, to be loved, to be a valued part of a group. Man's needs for affiliation and love motivate him to seek fulfilling relationships with others. A feeling of insecurity arises when an individual is not 'needed' by others.
4 *Ego needs*.   The need for esteem. These needs are of 2 types: those that relate to the individual's *self-esteem*—e.g. the need to feel independent, accomplished in a field, or competent in an activity; and those that relate to the individual's *reputation*—e.g. the need to have the esteem of others, to enjoy a social status
5 *Self-actualising needs*   The need to realise one's full potential, to be creative, to make the fullest demands on one's intellect, talent, abilities. These highest-level needs do not become behaviour motivating until the more basic needs are satisfied; but: 'What man *can* be, he *must* be' (Maslow)

- role expectations: entertain visitors

According to the proponents of the Freudian approach to motivation, our behaviour is largely shaped by psychological conditions of which we are not consciously aware. Freud believed the psyche consisted of 3 basic parts—the id, the ego and the superego:

- the id is the basic reservoir of instincts and primitive drives
- the ego is a conscious planning centre which finds outlets for the expression of the id
- the superego channels drives into socially acceptable behaviour

Dichter is a Freudian psychologist who has researched consumer motivations. He comments on the reasons for drinking alcohol, motel selection and food preferences:[40]

Drinking permits the discovery of a different personality within oneself. The person who is drunk really says, 'Is this me? I did not know that I had these other sides, these other potentialities.' Thus, drinking has one major psychological function; it helps bring about changes.

In the selection of motels the following factors are important. The number of cars parked in front of the rooms of the motel often gives the motorist a measure as to the extent to which this is a popular or unpopular place. The way in which a motel has preserved the maximum amount of greenery and trees is to many people a sign of the concern the owners have for the overall welfare of their customers.

The name of the motel is very important. Does it convey a feeling of romance, of being sheltered, of being taken care of? Does it establish rapport on first sight?

Keeping the motel and its office and grounds lighted during the night is an important factor. Many people hesitate to stay in a motel if they cannot see a substantial part of it from the highway; this first impression is of great psychological importance. It must be love at first sight.

Some people reject all kinds of slimy and gelatinous foods. The reason is erotic associations. Foods which require licking, such as many sweets, are also like forbidden sexual pleasures. We are fairly uninhibited when we eat ice cream. But the expression of people enjoying it could be described as of an almost orgasmic nature. Like or dislike of strong-smelling cheese is often quite closely associated with the acceptance or rejection of body odours.

Values

Values have been defined as 'basic systems of generalized cognitive beliefs and affective evaluations that represent what is broadly held good, worthy and correct'.[41] Values, therefore, are relatively enduring core beliefs and feelings which guide behaviour. A person who values family life is likely to stay in hotels affording opportunities for family activities and eat in restaurants which welcome children.

Values have a number of characteristics in common:

- Values are *shared*. They are founded in culture. Many people value good health. This reflects in sales of health food and fitness equipment, and explains why many hoteliers have changed breakfast menus (bran cereals), issued jogging route maps and opened gymnasia
- Values are *learned*. Values are learned by children through the process of socialisation and developed in adulthood as a result of exposure to the values and behaviour of others
- Values direct *behaviour*
- Values are *stable but flexible*

Values, although passed from one generation to the next, tend to become modified as a result of social experience. Some values, such as truth and self-discipline tend to change little although some values find expression in different behaviours between generations. A teenager expresses the value 'friendship' in shared social behaviour, such as dancing and sports activities, whereas an older person helps share physical tasks around the home.

There have been a number of investigations into changing social values. Two of particular note are those of the Stanford Research Institute in the USA, and Taylor Nelson in the UK. The Stanford Research Institute identified 13 major trends in values in the 1980s (see Table 4.7).[42] The table has potential significance to marketers. For example, it explains the trend away from the formality of silver service and the demand for local flavour in international hotel-chain operations.

Table 4.7   *Stanford Research Institute's inventory of changing values.*

From	To
Quantity	Quality
Group	Individual
Abundance	Sufficiency
Formality	Flexibility
Fads	Fashion
Complexity	Simplicity
Spendthrift	Frugality
Waste	Conservation
Falseness	Authenticity
Tradition	Experimentation
Mechanical	Personal
Efficient	Pleasing
Impressive	Meaningful

The *Taylor Nelson Monitor*, published by the marketing research company of the same name, has identified 3 major groups of consumers with particular values:

- sustenance values
- outer-directed values
- inner-directed values

Consumers with sustenance values have little disposable income and value security and survival most highly. They largely buy on the basis of the perceived price–value relationship. Consumers with outer-directed values, the largest of the 3 segments, buy products which bring the approval of others. They are concerned with appearance and social status. Consumers with inner-directed values, the fastest growth segment, buy for reasons of personal gratification; self-expression and fulfilment are high on their list of values.

McNulty[43] suggests that there are 2 inner-directed groups, 2 outer-directed groups, 2 sustenance groups and 1 group bridging both the inner and outer groups. The characteristics of each group appear in Table 4.8, together with implications for their buying behaviour. A significant relationship between personal values and beverage consumption has been indicated experimentally.[44]

Attitudes

Marketers have long felt favourable attitudes towards a product or brand to be a worthy marketing and promotional objective. Indeed it is axiomatic in complex buying behaviour (see Figure 4.5) that a favourable attitude is a precondition for purchase. The learn–feel–do model presupposes the development of an attitude at the feel stage.

For many years marketers have believed that a favourable attitude was a necessary precondition for *all* purchases. However, with the evolution of low-involvement theory, this has been called into question. The term 'attitude' can be defined as:[45]

a learned predisposition to respond to an object or class of objects in a consistently favourable or unfavourable way.

This 'predisposition to respond' is manifest in 3 ways. First, in the beliefs consumers have about the attitudinal object. Attributes are ascribed to the object. This is the *cognitive* dimension of an attitude. Second, attitudes have an evaluative or *affective* dimension. Consumers develop a feeling towards the object which can be placed at a point on a 'like very much–dislike very much' scale. The third dimension of attitude is *behavioural*—the tendency to act. This is shown in positive or negative buying intentions.

Most marketing researchers employ a multi-attribute approach in their attempts to measure attitudes. Not only do they assess the 3 dimensions, but they also try to discover the full range of beliefs about the attitudinal object. A buyer of conference facilities may evaluate competing suppliers against a list of 20 criteria. His ratings are, in effect, his cognitions about the alternatives. Consistent with his cognitions, he forms a preference towards one of the alternatives (affective component) and makes an intention to buy (behavioural component). Of these 20 criteria, some may be more important than others. These beliefs are known as determinant or salient cognitions and they have a higher degree of influence upon intentions to buy. As might be expected, researchers have confirmed that a balance or consistency exists between the 3 attitude dimensions. Intention-to-act is consistent with evaluations and beliefs.

Attitudes vary in strength. Those which are strongly held and closely related to values are less easy to change. However, many attitudes are weak, particularly those towards low-involvement products. Since attitudes develop from family influence, personality traits, peer-group influence, information from mass media and personal experience, it is these sources which play an important role in attitude change. Marketers have little control over the first two sources, but through persuasive communication and product trial can induce change.

Table 4.8   Taylor Nelson Monitor's *classification of consumers*.

	Demographics	Values	Buying behaviour
Outer-directed consumers	*Conspicuous consumers* 20% of population Predominantly women Slightly more northerners All social classes Medium income	Work primarily for money Average level of leisure activity Expect conformity from children Not concerned with political/social issues Highly materialistic 'Successful' lifestyle Concern for future Less innovative	Want the 'right' product Heavy furnishing buyers Appearance over function Followers of trends
	Belongers 19% of population Mr and Mrs Average Middle income	Devotion to family, home, work Traditional views about work Family leisure activities Socially and politically unaware No concern for self-development Fairly materialistic Reject change Plan for future	Buy DIY products Tried/trusted products Savers Reject fads Plain, practical products
Sustenance groups	*Survivors* 14% of population Heavily C2DE social classes Predominantly male More northerners Grown rapidly recently Low incomes Indebted	If working, money over job satisfaction Few leisure activities Soccer, gambling, bingo Chauvinistic Traditional family views No concern for self-development Escapist 'Life has little to offer' Fear change	Heavy pub-users Heavy TV-watchers Price over quality Impulsive Day-to-day buying Buy known brands
	Aimless 5% of population Young and old Predominantly female Young unemployed Old solitary survivors Midland/north resident Worst off financially	Young dismiss work Old seek work Lack enthusiasm Young form cohesive groups—punks, skinheads Traditional family views Reactionary Chauvinistic Fear technology Not innovative Demoralised No concern for self-development	Heavy TV-watchers No disposable income

	Demographics	Values	Buying behaviour
Inner directed consumers	*Self-explorers* 17% of population Equally male and female All age groups Average age 34 40% reside in south-east Better educated 60% ABC1 social classes	Socially aware Supporters of single-issue groups Work brings satisfaction Less materialistic Highly active Women's rights supporters Individuals are important Innovative	Can afford to indulge themselves Pursue interests No wish to keep up with Joneses Buy leisure products Read a lot Less time for TV/ radio Buy health-care products Buy nutritional foods Open to new products Resistant to advertising Information-seekers
	Social resisters 13% of population Reasonably well-off	More traditional, conservative, work hard, sedentary leisure interests, family loyalty Duty is important Politically and socially aware Concern for environment Personal integrity vital Confident and concerned	Buy home-craft products Concern for quality Concern for durability Use informational media Save and invest
Inner/outer directed consumers	*Experimentalists* Mostly males, 12% of population 60% aged under 34 Mostly ABC social classes London resident Quite affluent	Work is important Ambitious Women's rights supporters Accept authority Highly active Enjoy experiential pursuits Less concerned with health Materialistic Pleasure/excitement Trend-setting	Social activities Car and DIY products Variety-seekers High-tech products

The primary reason for marketing's concern with attitudes is that there is an assumed relationship to purchasing behaviour. Researchers have investigated the attitude–behaviour link in a number of ways: first, they have looked for a cause–effect relationship between attitude and behaviour; second, they have investigated the relationship between attitude and intention-to-buy; thirdly they have looked into the relationship between intention-to-buy and actual purchase; and fourthly, they have investigated the existence of a cause–effect relationship between purchase behaviour and attitude. Broadly the conclusions are:

- For many purchases there is a relationship between attitudes and behaviour. However, this is not universally true
- There is generally a very high correlation between attitude and intention-to-buy as well as between intention-to-buy and actual purchase
- Purchase behaviour and product experience exert a strong influence on attitude development

As intimated, the attitude–behaviour relationship is not altogether clear-cut. Personal, social and environmental factors may intervene, preventing a favourable attitude being translated into a purchase, as indicated in Table 4.9. The table is illustrated with hospitality examples.[46]

Table 4.9   *Factors intervening between attitude and behaviour.*

1 **Personal factors**
   Conflicting attitudes
   Consumer has favourable attitude to restaurant X, but *more* favourable attitude to restaurant Y
   Variety-seeking behaviour
   Restaurant selection often reflects desire to experience something new, despite strong attitudes to other establishments
   Conflicting motives
   A favourable attitude towards taking a weekend break at hotel Z is not acted upon because the need for achievement motivates a working weekend
   Involvement
   The attitude–behaviour link is weaker for low-involvement products because evaluation does not necessarily take place
   Verbal, social, intellectual abilities
   Mr B. has a favourable attitude to 5-star hotels but does not stay in them because he feels he lacks the necessary social skills to mix with other guests
2 **Social factors**
   Preferences of others
   Father prefers steak-house but accedes to children's demand for a burger
   Presence of other people
   An unmarried couple have a favourable attitude towards spending a weekend in hotel P, but do not do so for fear of 'discovery' by other people
   Behavioural norms (standards of behaviour)
   A junior sales representative's unfavourable attitude to 2-star hotels is ignored because corporate norms require him to book into such hotels
3 **Environmental factors**
   Unavailability
   All rooms at the preferred hotel are booked
   Money restriction
   Young tourist prefers to stay in 3-star hotels but can only afford budget accommodation
   Time
   Elapsed time between attitude measurement and taking observations of behaviour accounts for poor correlation
   Unforeseen extraneous events
   Mrs T does not dine in her preferred restaurant because she has lost her credit card
   Alternative behaviours available
   Favourable attitude towards sea food may not result in patronage of a sea-food restaurant, but in purchase of fresh fish for preparation at home

We have noted that not only can attitudes influence behaviour, but behaviour can influence attitudes. This is particularly the case under 2 conditions:
   (a) *Cognitive dissonance*
       When consumer expectations about product performance are not confirmed by experience, evaluations and beliefs (and therefore attitudes) change. Post-purchase evaluation thus leads to modification of attitudes
   (b) *Passive learning*
       Protagonists of the low-involvement view believe that simple exposure and attention to a commercial stimulus may be sufficient to cause trial and that attitudes are only formed after experience
Attitude measurement is particularly difficult. Attitudes are intangible; they can only be inferred from behaviour and verbal or physiological responses to questions and other

stimuli; a measuring instrument has to be selected from the several that are available; salient cognitions much be distinguished from minor cognitions. Of the several approaches to attitude measurement that have been developed, the highest regard is reserved for the *multiattribute* model, which views attitudes as the outcome of the consumer's beliefs about each alternative in the choice set when they are judged against a number of attributes.[47]

Most widely applied is the Fishbein model which, as originally proposed, takes this form:

$$A_o = \sum_{i=1}^{N} B_i a_i \qquad (4.3)$$

where A_o = attitude towards the object
B_i = the ith belief about the object
a_i = the evaluation of the belief
N = the total number of beliefs

For example, the attitude towards a particular hotel is the outcome of beliefs about the hotel multiplied by evaluation of those beliefs. Some beliefs—e.g. that it is noisy—will be evaluated negatively; others—e.g. as to the standard of room service—will be evaluated positively. To achieve a single attitude score the products of the evaluated beliefs are summed.[48]

The model, proposed in 1963, has been subsequently refined. Fishbein concluded that a better predictor of behaviour than attitude to the object was attitude to the purchase of the object under any specifically defined set of circumstances. He also concluded in his revision that the subjective norms (standards) which govern behaviour and the individual's motivation to comply with those norms should be explicitly stated. In effect, he and his collaborator Ajzen, proposed the model expressed in formula 4.4:[49]

$$B \approx BI = W_1(A_B) + W_2(SN) \qquad (4.4)$$

where B = behaviour
BI = behavioural intention
A_B = attitude towards the purchase of (or consumption of) product B
SN = subjective norm
$W_1 W_2$ = empirically determined weights

According to this revision, A_B and SN jointly provide a sound predictor of a consumer's purchase (or consumption) intentions. For reasons tabled earlier (see Table 4.9) *BI* is not always the same as *B*.

Computational formulae for A_B and SN were proposed:

$$A_B = \sum_{i=1}^{n} b_i e_i \qquad (4.5)$$

where A_B = attitude towards purchasing (or consuming) product B
  b_i = belief that this act of purchase (consumption) will lead to consequence i
  e_i = evaluation of consequence i
  n = number of beliefs

In the hotel example the consumer believes that staying in the hotel (an act of consumption) carries with it the probability of certain consequences—that it is highly likely the noise will result in an interrupted night's rest, and that the quality of room service will be high. Each of these consequences is evaluated (e); our consumer may evaluate an interrupted night's sleep highly unfavourably (on the 7-point scale +3, +2, +1, 0, −1, −2, −3 it would be evaluated −3), whereas experiencing a very high standard of room service would be rated only moderately favourably (say, +1). The attitude A_B is the sum of the products of the evaluated beliefs:

$$SN = \sum_{j=1}^{n} NB_j MC_j \qquad (4.6)$$

where SN = subjective norm
  NB_j = normative belief (the consumer's belief that reference group or individual j endorse, or do not endorse, his purchase or consumption of the product)
  MC_j = the consumer's motivation to comply with this influence
  n = number of relevant reference groups or individuals

A reference group is a group of people against whom an individual sets and judges his own standards of behaviour. Our hotel guest may use his work colleagues, members of his family, or some abstract conception like 'middle management' as his reference groups. Normative beliefs and motivation to comply can both be measured on a 7-point scale between polar statements. Engel and Blackwell's review of Fishbein's work concludes that 'the expanded Fishbein model predicts both intentions and behaviour far better than the various A_o models'.[50]

4.7 SOCIAL INFLUENCE

The consumer of hospitality products is rarely, if ever, totally divorced from the influence of others. So far in this chapter we have discussed *p*-variables, the personal characteristics of the consumer; now we turn to *s*-variables, the social influences upon consumer behaviour.

A social group is simply a set of people which has at least one condition in common— tourists, families, and businessmen are all social groups. Sociologists have identified several forms of social group:
- the *primary group*—a group in which members meet face to face (e.g. the family or a card school)
- the *secondary group*—a group in which face-to-face interaction does not occur (e.g. a trade union, company, or a correspondence school)

- the *reference group*—a group to which an individual may or may not belong, but which influences his behaviour

We now discuss reference groups, the family, social class and formal organisations (the company).

(1) Reference groups

Reference groups are so called because they are used as referents for standards of behaviour. Those to which an individual belongs are called 'affiliative groups'; those to which the individual does not belong are called either 'aspiration groups' or 'dissociative groups', depending upon whether the individual would like to be a member or not. But whatever the type of reference group, they all have a strong effect on consumer behaviour because it is through reference groups that norms are learned and enforced. Deviance from the norm may, in an extreme case, result in exclusion from an affiliative group or ineligibility to join aspiration groups.

Ethnic reference groups have great impact upon food preferences. One survey of workforce attitudes to in-company food service revealed great dissatisfaction. The workforce was 52 per cent Asian, 12 per cent West Indian and 30 per cent Caucasian; each group had its own food preferences. The investigator concluded that 'a vastly different range of foods should be provided . . . should be cooked and presented in a different way'.[51]

Reference groups perform two main functions: the normative and the comparative.[52] The normative function is active when the group sets and enforces behavioural standards; the comparative function is active when an individual assesses himself or others against group norms. The normative function presumes the presence of some interaction between the individual and the group, so that norms can be enforced; the comparative function can operate when the individual is at a distance from the group. Marketers can attempt to exploit these functions by suggesting that non-purchasers of the product are comparatively less acceptable to the reference group than are purchasers.

The amount of influence a reference group has over the behaviour in question appears to be related to several factors:[53]

- the relevance of the group to the behaviour in question. We all have many reference groups but they are not equally relevant to any given behaviour. The up-and-coming young executive may find his superiors a relevant reference group in his choice of hotel but not in the purchase of brake linings for his car
- group cohesiveness. The more cohesive the reference group, the less likely is the group member to deviate from accepted group norms
- the positive and negative sanctions attributed to the group by the individual. Exclusion from the group would normally be regarded as a most severe negative sanction to apply in order to discourage deviant behaviour. Ridicule is a less powerful but more used sanction. Men may well be afraid to drink a 'feminine' drink such as port and lemon because of fear of ridicule
- the degree of attraction of the individual to the reference group. The more the individual wants to be a member of the reference group, the greater the likelihood that the group will influence his behaviour

- the degree of susceptibility of the individual to reference-group influence. Some people, particularly those low in self-esteem or self-confidence, are more susceptible to group influence

Additionally, some products appear to be consumed under greater reference-group influence than others; examples are given below:

- products which are consumed in the presence of others—e.g. food and drink
- products which are perceived as symbolically meaningful—does the purchase of a Buddies holiday say anything about the purchaser?
- products which are risky—the inexperienced purchaser may seek information from others more qualified

The norms of a reference group, or of any group, are collectively supported guides for behaviour which are enforced by the group. Individuals comply with them because they fear that sanctions will be applied for non-compliance, or because they genuinely believe in and support them. Evidently the more widely accepted a norm is amongst a marketer's target population, the better advised he generally is also to conform to it. If it is normal for consumers to buy on credit, then the marketer must provide credit facilities.

One test of the power of reference groups on purchasing behaviour was conducted by Bourne,[54] whose main conclusion was that the conspicuousness of a product was a major factor in determining the influence a reference group has on purchases. The reference group may have influence, first, upon whether a product category is bought, and second, upon the brand that is chosen from the product category.

(2) The family

Despite changing social conditions reflected by statistics on divorce, single-parent families, house-husbands, *de facto* relationships and older unmarried single people, the family is still the most common form of social organisation. Families are important to marketers for 2 main reasons:

(a) There is much joint consumption of items such as food and accommodation by family members.

(b) The relationships between family members largely determine what is bought.

A family is a primary reference group, a dynamic social institution in which individual members have accepted family-group levels of power and authority, and in which the roles of individual members are normally well established. Most families comply with cultural mores in the way that intrafamily relationships and roles are devised and maintained. Yet the nature of the family is changing. There is a trend towards greater equality of wives and husbands, a greater tolerance of the individual needs of family members and greater influence of children on family decisions.

Studies of group purchase decision-making have shown that there are various roles performed by group members:

Initiator   The initiator is the person who first suggests, or has the idea of, purchasing a product.

Influencer The influencer is any person who explicitly or implicitly carries some influence in the final decision.

Decider   The decider is the person who ultimately determines any part, or the whole, of the buying decision—whether to buy, what, when, how and where to buy.

Purchaser   The purchaser is the person who physically makes the transaction.

User   The user is the person who eventually consumes the product.

These roles vary between family members according to the purchase being made, and marketers should recognise that promotional efforts may need to be directed at one or more family members.

Family purchasing can be classified as expressive or instrumental. *Expressive* purchasing is concerned with system maintenance within the family whilst *instrumental* purchasing is concerned with interactions between the family and environment. Conventionally wives have dominated expressive purchasing, husbands instrumental purchasing.

Another approach to the study of family decision-making has been to concentrate on who makes the decisions. Four styles of decision-making have been identified:[55]

(a) autonomic—husband and wife make an equal number of decisions about purchasing the product in question but do so independently of each other.

(b) wife dominant.

(c) husband dominant.

(d) joint—husband and wife have equal influence in each decision.

According to Sheth, joint decision-making is more likely to be encountered:[56]

- when perceived risk is high
- when purchasing a high-involvement product
- when there are no time pressures
- in middle-income groups; high-income groups tend to be husband-dominant, low income groups are wife-dominant
- in younger families
- in childless families
- in families where only one parent is in the workforce.

It has been found that the family purchase of holidays and outside entertainments (including presumably dining out) is a joint decision between husband and wife.[57]

Another study of family travel decision-making showed that the destination decision was joint, the route decision was husband dominated (presumably because he was the driver) and the accommodation decision was joint in most cases, and husband dominated in most of the balance. The researchers noted that the accommodation decision has both instrumental and expressive elements, accounting for the shared decision-making.[58]

The power structure of the family changes throughout the family's life. Joint decision-making tends to occur in the early years of marriage; according to Cox, 'There is a great deal of both joint decision making and joint purchase activity in which special preferences and skills are revealed'. However, in later years:

'Individual roles tend to become highly stabilised and joint decision making and purchase activity is replaced by varying degrees of specialisation of labour.'[59]

A further complication is that the concept of 'decider' is oversimplified. The decision to buy a particular brand involves many subordinate and related decisions. The holidaymaker deciding to stay in a coastal hotel must decide how to travel there, how to pay, whether to dine in or out, and so on. Some American research into car purchasing has shown that husband and wife influence varied in importance in the different subordinate decisions.[60]

Finally, if we can reduce purchasing to the 3 main stages of recognition of need, search for information and final decision, how does husband/wife dominance vary at each stage? There are indications that there is more role specialisation at the information-search stage than at either of the other two stages.

One of the major family tasks of parents is the socialisation of children. As children are allowed more say in family decision-making, acquire purchasing power through the tradition of pocket-money and become more commonly targeted audiences for advertising, more attention has been given to understanding how children learn consumption-related skills, knowledge and attitudes. According to Ward,[61]

> Consumer socialization necessarily involves analysis of childen's influence on intra-family patterns. Moreover, what kinds of consumer or consumer behaviours are 'transmitted' across generations? Which are modified as a result of contemporaneous social trends and technological developments? And how do early learning experiences facilitate or inhibit these changes in consumption patterns?

Although there is little empirical evidence in support, one popular view is that children learn consumption necessities from parents but affective consumption (styles and modes of consumption) from peers.

Children appear to learn consumption in 4 principal ways:
(a) Through observation of parents (and others).
(b) Through participation in shopping and consumption experiences.
(c) Through their own shopping experience, using limited funds provided by family members.
(d) Through formal training such as lessons in budgeting or instruction in how to shop.

But not only do parents influence children's consumption behaviour, the reverse is also true. Research has shown that parents are more likely to yield to children's influence as the children grow older, but not to the same degree for all types of products. Also it is probable that where objective criteria for product selection are unknown or unimportant to the parent, children's preferences take on a degree of importance that they are not normally accorded.[62]

(3) Social class

Social classification systems categorise individuals or households according to criteria valued by society. The criteria include occupation, income, ownership of durables, educational attainment, capital ownership and type of home. One or more of these criteria may be used during classification. The resultant categories are also known as social strata or social grades.

Three approaches have been used for categorisation:
(a) The *subjective* approach in which individuals assign themselves to a group.
(b) The *reputational* approach in which people assign each other to strata—many prestige-ranking systems use this approach.

(c) The *objective* approach in which hard data are used about individuals, so that a researcher can assign them to groups.

Marketers generally use the third approach.

In the UK the most common classification system is that employed by the Joint Industry Committee for National Readership Surveys (JICNARS). As shown in Table 4.10, strata are based on the occupation of the head of the household. Monk comments that it is 'a reasonable "general purpose" classification in that it is useful for most product fields without necessarily being the most ideal'.[63] An investigation into the value of occupation as a predictor of purchasing behaviour, in comparison to other social-class variables such as income and educational level, concluded that occupational group was the best indicator.[64] The JICNARS social grading system has been widely used as a correlator of purchasing behaviour—e.g. in the holiday, car and banking markets.[65] Assael reports that purchasing behaviour, media use, patterns of communication, pricing behaviour and information search can be associated with social class.[66]

Table 4.10   *JICNARS social grading system.*

Social grade	Social status	Occupation of head of household	All adults over 15		Men		Women	
			000s	%	000s	%	000s	%
A	Upper-middle class	Higher managerial, administrative, or professional	1 220	3	613	3	606	3
B	Middle class	Intermediate managerial, administrative, or professional	6 253	14	3 021	14	3 232	14
C1	Lower-middle class	Supervisory or clerical and junior management, administrative, or professional	9 770	22	4 499	21	5 271	23
C2	Skilled working class	Skilled manual workers	12 834	29	6 842	32	5 993	26
D	Working class	Semi-skilled and unskilled manual workers	7 974	18	3 898	18	4 076	18
E	Lowest-income levels	State pensioners, widows, casual and lowest-grade workers	6 149	14	2 320	11	3 829	17

* Social grade of housewives is based on occupation of head of household.
Source: JICNARS (1985) *NRS* July–June

(4) The company

Marketers of industrial products (this also includes suppliers of accommodation to the business market) are especially interested in understanding how buying decisions are made within companies and other formal organisations. Similar buying roles to those enacted in family purchasing exist. Webster and Wind[67] identify 5 roles, each of which have a bearing upon organisational buying behaviour (OBB). Since it it possible to conceive of a family unit as an informal organisation, the categories are predictably similar to those above in section 2 (see pp. 100–101):

Users   In many cases users also initiate the buying process.

Influencers Influencers are organisational members who directly or indirectly influence buying or usage decisions.

Buyers   Buyers are those organisational members with formal authority for selecting the supplier and arranging the terms of the purchase.

Deciders　　Deciders are those members of the organisation who have either formal or informal power to determine the final selection of suppliers.

Gatekeepers　Gatekeepers are organisational members who control the flow of information to the decision-makers.

Organisational buying behaviour can be characterised thus:[68]

> Buying is a complex process, not an instantaneous act. Buying involves the determination of the need to purchase products or services, communications among those members of the organization who are involved in the purchase or will use the product or service, information-seeking activities, the evaluation of alternative purchasing actions, and the working out of necessary arrangements with supplying organizations. Organizational buying is therefore a complex process of decision making and communication, which takes place over time, involving several organizational members and relationships with other firms and institutions. It is much more than the simple act of placing an order with a supplier.

The act of placing an order with a supplier is normally the job of a specially appointed person—the purchasing agent—but as the quotation above makes clear, marketers wishing to become suppliers or retain their status as suppliers to companies will normally have to communicate with and persuade several members of the organisation. These several persons, identified by their role titles of user, influencer, buyer, decider and gatekeeper, are known collectively as the decision-making unit (DMU) or buying centre. Hotel choice for the travelling businessman has been shown to be predetermined by other than the user in over 40 per cent of cases.[69]

Historically attempts to understand OBB have emphasised the rational-economic nature of parties to the decision. It has been assumed that the DMU has a set of rational criteria against which an exhaustive list of suppliers and products are evaluated. But members of the DMU are human: they have preferences, predispositions and favourites; they may find the conduct of an exhaustive search for suppliers tiresome; they may disagree with the goals of the organisation and use their own standards as criteria; they may be neurotic or unable to handle risky situations; or they may be aggressive, ambitious people wanting to be noted as effective managers by their superiors. In short, the assumption that members of the DMU only apply an agreed, single and rational set of economic criteria in their purchasing decisions is invalid.[70]

A most useful aid to marketing managers was devised in the late 1960s, based on empirical study of industrial buying. Its developers concluded that there were 8 basic stages to OBB, which they called 'buyphases', and that the speed with which a particular purchaser passed through these phases was related to how new was the purchase. They identified 3 types of purchase: the new task when a company is confronted by a need or problem, the straight rebuy of a previously purchased product and the modified rebuy where some part of a previously made purchase is being reconsidered—e.g. following a price increase imposed by the current supplier. These purchase types they called 'buyclasses'. The resulting chart appears as the buygrid framework in Figure 4.9.[71] The buygrid draws attention to the 2 major decisions: what to buy (the product decision), and from whom to buy (the vendor or supplier decision).

Hospitality marketing management can use the buygrid to raise questions such as these:

- how can non-suppliers to a prospective customer turn a straight rebuy into a modified rebuy? Who needs to be persuaded and at what buyphases should this be

Buyphases	Buyclasses		
	New task	Modified rebuy	Straight rebuy
1 Anticipation or recognition of a problem and a general solution			
2 Determination of characteristics and quantity of needed item			
3 Description of characterisitcs and quantity of needed item			
4 Search for and qualification of potential sources			
5 Analysis and acquisition of proposals			
6 Evaluation of proposals and supplier selection			
7 Selection of order routine			
8 Performance feedback and evaluation			

Figure 4.9   The buygrid framework.

attempted? Should the non-supplier, for instance, get his name into the gatekeeper's files for use at buyphase 4 or should he direct-mail the decider at buyphase 5?

- how can a marketer identify when there is a new task purchase to be made in the near future? Does he keep in regular contact with the people most likely to initiate a new task, for example, the marketing manager, who may be planning a sales conference?
- how can a supplier retain its status by fighting off challenges from competitors trying to turn the customer's straight rebuy into a modified rebuy?

It is not possible in this book to fully investigate the relevance of the buygrid for marketers.

An attempt has been made to model the decision-making process used by travel planners in the incentive travel sector of the market. Hoteliers are offered advice on how to influence each stage in the process leading to venue selection.[72]

Both the product and supplier decision are the outcome of a set of interacting factors which are relatively easy to recognise but whose degree of influence upon the decisions is difficult to determine in practice. There are 4 sets of factors which appear to influence decisions:

Personal factors   Each member of the DMU has his own sources of information, his own values and attitudes, his own ability to understand technical detail and his own particular task to perform in the buying process.

Interpersonal factors   The relationships, both formal and informal, within the DMU, and between the DMU and potential suppliers, can have significant influence upon the final decisions. For example, one DMU member with a dominating personality or a senior member may be able to lead the DMU to his own preferred decision. The gatekeeper may have especially good relationships with some suppliers or may be unwilling to share information with some members of the DMU.

Formal organisational factors   The company may have established procedures and rules requiring minimum acceptable product quality, long-term contacts and centralised purchasing or credit requirements. The company's directors may evaluate members of the DMU according to the technical quality of their decision-making.

Environmental factors   Confidence in the economy, beliefs about future price stability, expectations of competitive developments may all influence what is bought and from whom.

4.8 CULTURE

More pervasive than the influence of social groupings on consumer behaviour is that of culture. Within our culture we accept many activities as normal parts of everyday life; dining out, taking holidays, purchasing entertainment and making business trips are all unquestionably part of our culture.

Culture can be defined as:[73]

> the way of life common to a group of people, a collection of beliefs and attitudes, shared understandings and patterns of behaviour that allow these people to live together in relative harmony, but set them apart from other peoples.

A culture is integrative of its subparts—i.e. morals, attitudes and behavioural standards lock together into a coherent whole. By definition, it is shared and it is learned through the process of socialisation, which is a broad term for the process through which an individual develops his specific patterns of socially relevant behaviours and experience.[74]

Culture has many influences on consumer behaviour. Some examples are given below:

- Cultural values and mores determine that parents should provide nutritious and safe food for their children. Family restaurant operators obviously realise this.
- Gift-giving is an expected behaviour at Christmas, birthdays, weddings and certain other festive occasions. Belk comments: 'The pre-eminent theoretical analysis of the gift-giving process is an essay by French anthropologist-sociologist Marcel Mauss. Mauss concluded that gift-giving is a self-perpetuating system of reciprocity. More specifically, Mauss outlined three types of obligation which perpetuate gift-giving: 1. The obligation to give. 2. The obligation to receive. 3. The obligation to repay.'[75] (Restaurants catering for business entertainment, please note!)
- Parents are expected to bring up children, so that they can lead full adult lives within society. The socialisation of children into consuming members of society appears to occur 'more through subtle interpersonal processes than through direct purposive consumer training in families or schools'.[76] Children tend to mimic and imitate parents following observation, and 'learning no doubt occurs as a function of patterns of intrafamily influence which emerge as children attempt to acquire goods and services for themselves by requesting them of parents'.[77]

Within a larger culture abound smaller subcultures. Within the UK are the Pakistani, Indian, Ukrainian and West Indian subcultures all with their own forms of social institutions and behavioural standards. These subcultures also exert an influence on consumption behaviour.

Cultural differences are particularly important in international marketing; for instance:

- literacy levels vary quite considerably, therefore, print media cannot always be used for promotion
- the target for communication in some cases should not be the actual consumer of the product, but senior tribal members who approve the product

Marketers engaged in international marketing need to possess some cultural empathy in order to be effective and profitable.

4.9 MODELS OF CONSUMER BEHAVIOUR

In section 4.4 of this chapter we wrote that a number of comprehensive models of consumer behaviour had been developed. In this section the Howard–Sheth,[78] Nicosia[79] and Engel–Blackwell[80] models are presented and discussed.

The Howard-Sheth model was first proposed in 1969 and revised in 1974, taking the form shown in Figure 4.10. The model is a flowchart of implicitly high-involvement, in that purchase is subsequent to attitude formation. The model explicitly incorporates an information-processing subsystem, motivational subsystem, perceptual subsystem and other decision process variables.

The *Nicosia* model was published in 1966. As shown in Figure 4.11, it hinges on the proposition that attitudes which develop as a result of exposure to a firm's messages determine subsequent behaviour.

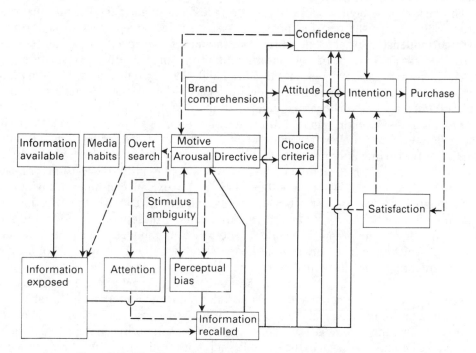

Figure 4.10   The Howard–Sheth model of consumer behaviour (1974).

Field One: From the source of a message to the consumer's attitude

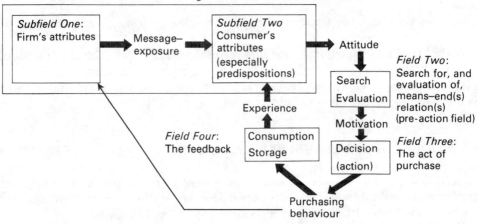

Figure 4.11 The Nicosia model of consumer behaviour.

Of all the major contributors, Engel and Blackwell are unique in distinguishing between high and low involvement. Consequently two models are proposed—one for high-involvement purchases (see Figure 4.12) and the other for low-involvement purchases (see Figure 4.13).

The high-involvement model comprises 5 fields: information inputs, information-processing system, the decision process, associated decision process variables and external influences. Social-group and cultural influences are explicitly stated and choice is regarded as an outcome of prior information processing and attitude formation.

The low-involvement model, on the other hand, features only 3 fields: information inputs, information processing and decision-making processes. Social-group and cultural influences are disregarded other than their implicit functioning as sources of information. As noted in Figure 4.3, the decision process allows for choice to occur immediately after problem recognition, with alternative evaluation (and attitude formation) occurring after product experience.

All of the models which attempt to describe what happens inside the consumer's head can be labelled 'inferential' because they all purport to explain consumer behaviour in terms of non-observable constructs which are assumed to be related to the behaviour in question. The only observable and measurable parts of these types of model are the input stimuli and the output behaviours. The rest of the models are simply inferred variables which intervene between these inputs and outputs. They have no objective reality and are largely developed as a matter of personal opinion.

As Engel, Blackwell and Kollat say: 'Many schools of thought have arisen, each of which views the same phenomenon and postulates different intervening variables.'[81] Given that the intervening variables selected by different consumer behaviour theorists may vary and that there is little consensus between theorists as to a universally acceptable definition of each of the variables, it is not surprising that these models have come under criticism.

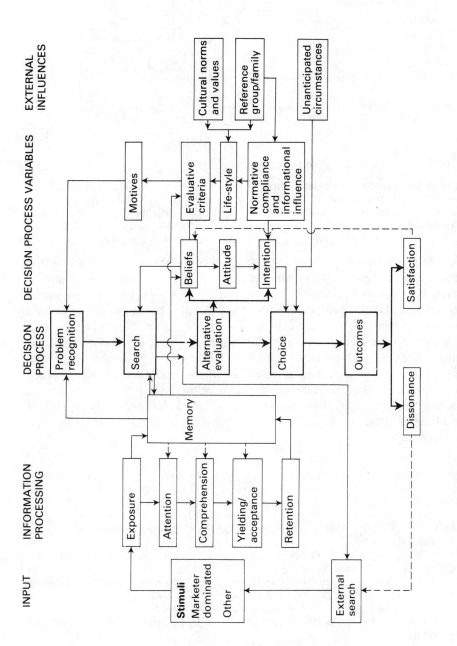

Figure 4.12 The Engel–Blackwell model of high-involvement consumer behaviour.

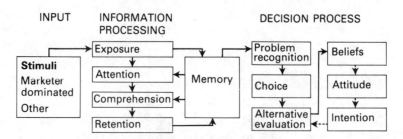

Figure 4.13   The Engel–Blackwell model of low-involvement consumer behaviour.

Jacob Jacoby had this to say about such models:[82]

> Several of our most respected scholars seem to belong to a theory of the month club which somehow requires that periodically they burst forth with new theories and rarely, if ever, provide any data collected specifically to support their theories. Perhaps those with a new theory or model should treat it like a new product, either stand behind it and give it the support it needs (i.e. test and refine it as necessary), or take it off the market.

Opponents of the inferential approach to the study of consumer behaviour believe that consideration should be given solely to measurable and observable inputs and outputs. Leading proponents of this approach are the behaviourists. They believe that consumer behaviour is modified and developed as a result of rewarding behaviour that is desired and punishing behaviour that is not desired. Such reinforcement, both positive and negative, eventually establishes a pattern of behaviour. The behaviourist avoids the complications faced by the inferential modeller. He has a much simpler model: he examines external, observable and measurable stimuli and the behaviour which follows, looking for regularities in the relationships between them.

The relevance of these criticisms to marketers is that marketers need only to discover which stimuli result in the desired behaviour, and provide reinforcement to ensure that the behaviour is repeated.

4.10 CHAPTER REVIEW

1. The study of consumer behaviour provides marketers with some insights into how to influence demand.
2. Consumer behaviour theory draws on psychology, social psychology, sociology, anthropology, economics and philosophy.
3. There have been a number of attempts to model consumer behaviour—notably by Howard and Sheth, Nicosia, Engel and Blackwell, Andreason and Howard.
4. There is no single, unified body of consumer behaviour knowledge.
5. Behaviour is influenced by personal characteristics, social relationships, culture and environmental factors.
6. A key variable in understanding consumer behaviour is involvement—the degree of personal importance that a product has for a consumer.
7. Involvement is higher when risk, social-group influence and product symbolism are significant.

8. Risk can be economic, social, psychological, or physical.
9. The high-involvement decision-making process is problem recognition, search, alternative evaluation, choice, outcomes.
10. The low-involvement decision-making process is problem recognition, choice, alternative evaluation.
11. Consumer problem-solving can be categorised as extensive problem-solving, limited problem-solving and routine response behaviour.
12. Four types of buying behaviour can be identified: complex buying behaviour, variety-seeking buying behaviour, inertia and dissonance-reducing buying behaviour.
13. Marketers have conventionally believed that consumers follow a learn–feel–do process in decision-making.
14. Other models of decision-making are learn–do, learn–do–feel and do–learn–feel.
15. Consumers process information actively or passively.
16. A typical view of the active model of information processing is: exposure, attention, comprehension, yielding, retention, behaving.
17. For low-involvement products a preferred model of information processing is: exposure, attention, comprehension, retention.
18. The low–high involvement dichotomy should influence marketing decision-making.
19. Consumers use one of 2 approaches to handle information about competing products: a compensatory approach or a non-compensatory approach.
20. Consumer behaviour is learned.
21. There are two principal theories of learning: the behaviourist and the cognitive.
22. The behaviourist school has proposed 2 forms of learning: classical conditioning and instrumental conditioning.
23. The cognitive school regards learning as problem-solving behaviour.
24. Research into the personality–behaviour relationship has been inconclusive.
25. Maslow, Murray and Freud have contributed to our understanding of the relationship of behaviour to needs.
26. Maslow's hierarchy of needs—physiological, security, social, ego and self-actualising—is widely accepted in marketing circles.
27. Freud sees behaviour as the outcome of a largely subconscious struggle between the id, ego and superego.
28. Values, being relatively enduring core beliefs, exert a strong guiding influence on behaviour.
29. In the UK the *Taylor Nelson Monitor* tracks changing values. Three main categories of consumer have been identified: sustenance driven, inner directed and outer directed.
30. The relationship between attitudes and behaviour is not always one to one.
31. Attitudes can be measured using the Fishbein multiattribute model.
32. Attitudes have 3 dimensions: cognitive, affective and behavioural.
33. Social influences on consumer behaviour are reference groups, the family, social class and the organisation.
34. Reference groups can influence both product and brand choice.
35. Family roles in consumer behaviour are initiator, influencer, decider, purchaser and user.
36. Four styles of family decision-making have been identified: autonomic, wife dominant, husband dominant and joint.
37. Patterns of influence vary by product and by stage of the family life cycle.
38. Children learn consumption behaviour in the family.
39. Social class has been widely used as a correlate of buyer behaviour.
40. The most widely used social-class schema in the UK is that of JICNARS.
41. Organisational buying behaviour (OBB) is complex.
42. The roles of members of the decision-making unit (DMU) are those of user, influencer, buyer, decider and gatekeeper.
43. OBB can be viewed as an 8-stage process.
44. Personal, interpersonal, formal organisational and environmental factors influence OBB.
45. Culture is the most fundamental influence on consumer behaviour.
46. Models of consumer behaviour have been criticised.

4.11 QUESTIONS

1. Sort the following list cf influences upon consumer behaviour into *p* (personal characteristics), *s* (social influences) and *e* (environmental factors):
    personality, family, attitudes, public transport, values, culture, workmates, the boss, previous experience, social class.
2. What arguments would you use to convince a welfare catering manager that it was worth while to study consumer behaviour?
3. Draw up a list of hospitality products and divide them into groups according to the type of buying involved: learn–feel–do, learn–do–feel, learn–do, and do–learn–feel.
4. How relevant is the issue of involvement in captive catering markets such as hospital or prisons?
5. In a small group list group-member cognitions about the following products: college catering, motorway service-station catering, budget hotels and 5-star city-centre hotels.
6. What evaluative criteria would you use to select between Indian, Chinese and French restaurants for the celebration of the birth of a child? Would different criteria be used when different motives apply?
7. Use the buygrid framework to describe the behaviour of a decision-making unit when buying hotel accommodation as a reward for high-achievement salesmen (incentive travel).
8. Use one of the models in section 4.9 to describe your most recent purchase of a hospitality product. How helpful is the model?

REFERENCES

[1] Howard, J. A. and Sheth, J. N. (1969) *The Theory of Buyer Behaviour*. New York: Wiley; revised in 1974 as Farley, J. U., Howard, J. A., and Ring, L. W. (eds) *Consumer Behaviour Theory and Application*. Boston, MA: Allyn & Bacon.
[2] Nicosia, F. M. (1966) *Consumer Decision Processes*. Englewood Cliffs, NJ: Prentice-Hall.
[3] Engel, J. F. and Blackwell, R. D. (1982) (4th edn) *Consumer Behaviour*. London: Dryden Press.
[4] Andreason, A. R. (1965) Attitudes and customer behaviour: a decision model, in Preston, L. E. (ed.) *New Research in Marketing*. Berkeley, CA: University of California Institute of Business and Economics Research, 1–16.
[5] Howard, J. A. (1977) *Consumer Behaviour: Application of Theory*. London: McGraw-Hill.
[6] See particularly Assael, H. J. (1984), (2nd edn) *Consumer Behaviour and Marketing Action*. Kent.
[7] See Marrow, A. J. (1969) *The Practical Theorist: The Life and Work of Kurt Lewin*. New York: Basic Books.
[8] Bettman, J. R. (1973) Perceived risk and its components: a model and empirical test. *Journal of Marketing Research*, **10**(5), May, 184–90.
[9] Kotler, P. (1984) (5th edn) *Marketing Management: Analysis, Planning and Control*. Englewood Cliffs, NJ: Prentice-Hall, 148.
[10] Assael, H. J. (1984) op. cit., 28.
[11] Engel, J. F. and Blackwell, R. D. (1982) op. cit.
[12] Lewis, R. C. (1984) The basis of hotel selection. *Cornell Hotel and Restaurant Administration Quarterly*, **25**(1), May, 54–69.
[13] *Travel Weekly*'s Harris Poll reported in Bush, M. (1976) The sales inter-relationship between hotels and travel agencies. *Cornell Hotel and Restaurant Administration Quarterly*, **18**(4), February, 35–43.
[14] Meidan, A. (1979) Buyers' behaviour and preferences for Chinese take-away food. *HCIMA Journal*, August, 13–16.
[15] Graham, J. J. and MacPherson, N. C. (1977) Food preferences with particular reference to wholefood, *HCIMA Journal*, October, 17–21.
[16] Engel, J. F. and Blackwell, R. D. (1982) op. cit., 38.
[17] Howard, J. A. (1977) op. cit.

[18] Assael, H. J. (1984) op. cit., 13.

[19] Bush, M. (1982) Capturing business travellers; the travel agency connection. *Cornell Hotel and Restaurant Administration Quarterly*, **23**(2), August, 58–61.

[20] Lewis, R. C. (1983), The incentive travel market: how to reap your share. *Cornell Hotel and Restaurant Administration Quarterly*, **24**(1), May, 19 ff.

[21] Assael, H. J. (1984) op cit., 83.

[22] Festinger, L. (1957) *A Theory of Cognitive Dissonance*. London: Harper & Row.

[23] Britt, S. H. (1977) *Psychological Principles of Marketing and Consumer Behaviour*. Lexington, MA: D.C. Heath (Lexington Books).

[24] See literature review in Cox, D. F. (1961) Clues for advertising strategies. Pt 2. *Harvard Business Review*, 39, November–December, 160–82.

[25] Day, G. S. (1973), (rev. edn) Attitudes and attitude change, in Kassarjian, H. H. and Robertson, T. S. (eds.) *Perspectives in Consumer Behaviour*. Chicago: Scott, Foresman, 188–209.

[26] Engel, J. F. and Blackwell, R. D. (1982) op. cit., 289–94.

[27] Krugman, H. E. (1965) The impact of television: learning without involvement. *Public Opinion Quarterly*, **29**, 349–56; and Robertson, T. S. (1976) Low commitment consumer behaviour. *Journal of Advertising Research*, **16**, April, 19–24.

[28] Krugman, H.E. (1977) Memory without recall, exposure with perception. *Journal of Advertising Research*, **17**, August, 7–12.

[29] See discussion in Wilkie, W. L. and Pessemier, E. A. (1983) Issues in marketing's use of multi-attribute models. *Journal of Marketing Research*, **10**, November, 428–41.

[30] Hilgard, E. R. and Marquis, D. G. (1966) Conditioning and learning, in Britt, S. H. (ed.) *Consumer Behaviour and the Behavioural Sciences*. London: Wiley, 123.

[31] See Hill, W. F. (1972) (2nd edn) *Learning*. University Paperbacks, for a review of theories of learning.

[32] Buttle, F. (1980) Learning theory and marketing. *Quarterly Review of Marketing*, **6**(1), Autumn, 1–7.

[33] Gagné, R. M. (1965) *The Conditions of Learning*. London: Holt, Rinehart & Winston.

[34] McCleary, K. W. (1978) The corporate meetings market: components of success in attracting group business. *Cornell Hotel and Restaurant Administration Quarterly*, **19**(2), August.

[35] Kassarjian, H. H. (1968) (rev. edn) Personality and consumer behaviour: a review, in Kassarjian, H. H. and Robertson, T. S. (eds.) *Perspectives in Consumer Behavior*. Chicago: Scott, Foresman.

[36] Kotler, P. (1984) op. cit., 4–5.

[37] Maslow, A. H. (1954) *Motivation and Personality*. London: Harper & Row.

[38] Medlik, S. and Airey, D. W. (1978) (2nd edn) *Profile of the Hotel and Catering Industry*. London: Heinemann.

[39] Axler, B. H. (1979) *Foodservice: A Managerial Approach*. Lexington, MA: D. C. Heath.

[40] Dichter, E. (1964) *Handbook of Consumer Motivations*. New York: McGraw-Hill.

[41] Granzin, K. L. and Bahn, K. D. (1982) Personal values as an explanation of food usage habits. *Home Economics Research Journal*, June, **10**(4), 401–10.

[42] Mitchell, A. (1981), *Changing Values and Lifestyles*. Stanford, CA: Stanford Research Institute.

[43] McNulty, C. (1984) Social change and its implications for retailing. Paper presented at Management Horizons Conference, March. See also Nelson, E. and Corry, C. (1983), Social change and the marketing function. *Survey*, June, 18–19; and Shay, P. (1978) A consumer revolution is coming. *Marketing*, September, 37–42.

[44] See Granzin, K. L. and Bahn, K. D. (1982) op. cit.

[45] See Allport, G. (1935) 'Attitudes', in Murchison, C. A. (ed.) *A Handbook of Social Psychology*. Clark University Press, 798–844.

[46] Table 4.8 is based partly on Wicker, A. W. (1969) 'Attitudes vs actions'. *Journal of Social Issues*, **25**(41), 41–78.

[47] For a review of multiattribute models refer to Lutz, R. J. and Bettman, J. R. (1977) 'Multi-attribute models in marketing. A bicentennial review', in Woodside, A. G., Sheth, J. N., and

Bennett, P. D. (eds) *Consumer and Industrial Buying Behaviour*. Elsevier: North-Holland, 137–49.

[48] Fishbein, M. (1963) 'An investigation of the relationships between beliefs about an object and the attitude towards that object'. *Human Relations*, **16**, 233–40.

[49] Fishbein, M. and Ajzen, I. (1975) *Belief, Attitude, Intention and Behaviour: An Introduction to Theory and Research*. London: Addison-Wesley.

[50] Engel, J. F. and Blackwell, R. D. (1982) op. cit., 455.

[51] Bareham, J. (1980) The needs of ethnic groups at work. *Hospitality*, June, 15–19.

[52] Kelly, H. H. (1965) Two functions of reference groups, in Proshansky, H. and Siedenberg, B. (eds) *Basic Studies in Social Psychology*. London: Holt, Rinehart & Winston, 210–14.

[53] See Witt, R. E. (1969) Informal social group influence on consumer brand choice. *Journal of Marketing Research*, **6**, November, 473–6.

[54] Bourne, F. S. (1959) Group influence in marketing and public relations. Foundation for Research on Human Behaviour, Ann Arbor, Michigan.

[55] Davis, H. L. and Rigaux, B. P. (1974) Perception of marital roles in decision processes. *Journal of Consumer Research*, **1**, June, 51–60.

[56] Sheth, J. N. (1974) A theory of family buying decisions, in Sheth, J. N. (ed.) *Models of Buyer Behaviour*. London: Harper & Row, 17–33.

[57] Davis, H. L. and Rigaux, B. P. (1974) op. cit.

[58] Myers, P. B. and Moncrief, L. W. (1978) Differential leisure travel decision making between spouses. *Annals of Tourism Research*, **5**(1), January–March, 157–65.

[59] See Cox, E. P. III (1975) Family purchase decision making and the process of adjustment, *Journal of Marketing Research*, **12**, May, 189–95.

[60] Davis, H. L. (1970) Dimensions of marital roles in consumer decision making. *Journal of Marketing Research*, **7**, May, 168–77.

[61] See Ward, S. (1974) Consumer socialization. *Journal of Consumer Research*, **1**, September, 7–13.

[62] Ward, S. and Wackman, D. (1971) Family and media influences on adolescent consumer learning. *American Behavioural Scientist*, **14**, January–February, 415–27.

[63] Monk, D. R. (1967) (3rd edn) *Social grading on the national readership survey*. London: JICNARS.

[64] Lunn, J. A. (1965) Exploratory work on social class, *Commentary*, **7**(3), 195–7.

[65] Monk, D. R. (1967) op. cit., 16.

[66] Assael, H. J. (1984) op. cit., 348–51.

[67] Webster, F. E. and Wind, Y. (1972) *Organisational Buyer Behaviour* (Foundations of Marketing series). Englewood Cliffs, NJ: Prentice-Hall, 77–80.

[68] ibid, 1.

[69] Lewis, R. C. (1984) op. cit.

[70] Fletcher, W. (1978) The diversity within the DMU. *Marketing*, December, 46–8.

[71] Robinson, P. J., Faris, C. W., and Wind, Y. (1967) *Industrial Buying and Creative Marketing*. Boston, MA: Allyn & Bacon.

[72] Lewis, R. C. (1983), op. cit.

[73] Friedl, J. (1976) *Cultural Anthropology*. Harpers College Press, 41.

[74] Zigler, E. and Child, I. L. (1969) (2nd edn) Socialisation, in Lindsay, G. and Aronson, E. (eds) *The Handbook of Social Psychology*, Vol. 2. London: Addison-Wesley.

[75] Belk, R. W. (1976) It's the thought that counts: a signed digraph analysis of gift giving. *Journal of Consumer Research*, **3**, December 155–6.

[76] Ward, S. (1974) op. cit.

[77] ibid., 8.

[78] See Howard, J. A. and Sheth, J. N. (1969) op. cit.

[79] See Nicosia, F. M. (1966) op. cit.

[80] See Engel. J. F. and Blackwell, R. D. (1982) op. cit.

[81] Engel, J. F., Blackwell, R. D., and Kollat, D. T. (1982) (3rd edn) *Consumer Behaviour*. London: Dryden Press, 19.

[82] Jacoby, J. (1978) Consumer research: a state of the art review. *Journal of Marketing*, April, 89.

—5————————————————

Identifying Target Markets

5.1 CHAPTER PREVIEW

There are an infinite variety of decision choices about product, price, promotion and distribution.

If the manager considers the nature of his target market in making these decisions, the choice becomes reduced and the probability of making better decisions is enhanced. Consequently the selection of target markets is a vital prerequisite to successful marketing.

In this chapter we discuss 2 approaches to market targeting: the first regards all prospective customers as a single mass market whilst the second attempts to pick out subsets of potential customers from the mass market.

5.2 LEARNING OBJECTIVES

By the end of the chapter you should be able to:
1. Define the difference between market targeting and market segmentation.
2. Using Figure 5.1 (a 5-stage approach to market segmentation), analyse the segmentation characteristics of hospitality markets.
3. List and define the criteria which are used to identify worthwhile segmentation opportunities.

5.3 THE BASICS OF MARKET TARGETING

The identification of target markets is fundamental to marketing management. All subsequent decisions about product, pricing, distribution and promotion depend upon prior identification of, and empathy with, the market.

Market targeting can be defined as:

> the identification of a group of consumers, so that a marketing mix can be devised specifically to satisfy its demand.

There are 2 basic approaches, one of which can be further subdivided:
  (a) mass marketing
  (b) segmented marketing
    • single segment
    • multiple segments

The basic choice facing a company is to pursue either a mass marketing strategy or a segmented strategy. In mass marketing, also known as 'aggregated marketing' and 'undifferentiated marketing', a single marketing mix is used to reach all geographic or customer markets. Segmented marketing requires the selection of one (single) or more (multiple) segments of demand. The basic requirements of segmented marketing are that:

- a homogeneous segment of demand is found
- a marketing mix is devised specifically for the segment

The type of market targeted is heavily constrained by resources, relative inexperience of the markets, company image and by the strength of competitors.

Most products which have traditionally been regarded as undifferentiated are now marketed to selected target markets. For instance, the market for salt can be divided into 2 major segments—domestic and institutional, each of which can be treated with a specially devised marketing mix. It is not so many years ago that both markets could buy salt only in block form. However, a company which treats its markets as unsegmented places itself in grave danger. Aggressive competitors, prepared to produce marketing mixes to meet the needs of specific target markets, can undermine demand.

5.4 MARKET SEGMENTATION

Market segmentation can be defined as the

> identification of a subset of consumers, so that a marketing mix can be devised specifically to satisfy its demand.

This definition varies from that of market targeting only in emphasis. Here the target is a subset of consumers. The smallest subset is the individual person. London 5-star hotels will treat visiting aristocracy, celebrities and major politicians as unique target markets. Each individual is attracted and retained through a marketing mix designed specifically for the task. The opposite case, where the population is not divided into segments but treated as if demand were homogeneous, is not market segmentation at all—it is mass marketing. Most marketers, either consciously or subconsciously, pursue a middle road by dividing the entire market into groups with relatively homogeneous demand.

A distinction can be made between imposed, elected and acquired market segmentation. *Imposed* segmentation occurs when a higher authority determines that some groups of consumers should not be exposed to a given marketing mix. Licensed or registered premises may exclude groups on the basis of age (public houses), sex (private men's clubs), or occupational status (professional associations). *Elected* segmentation occurs when, following analysis of segmentation alternatives, a marketing mix is subsequently designed. In *acquired* segmentation the marketing mix is first designed and its market appeal subsequently analysed. In turn, the mix may be refined so as to be more cost effective. Many businesses evolve a marketing orientation despite having started as a product idea in an entrepreneur's mind.

A second distinction can be made between *macro- and microsegmentation*. Macrosegmentation is used to analyse large-scale consumer behaviour—national or international travel patterns, for example. Microsegmentation, which is unit or enterprise specific, is the focus of this chapter.

A further distinction is made between consumer, organisational and channel segmentation. *Consumer* segmentation divides the user market into subsets. *Organisational* segmentation divides the corporate or group sector into subsets. *Channel* segmentation divides distributors of hospitality products into subsets—travel agents, tour operators, and so on. Finally, market segments can be classified as *free* or *captive*—free being those where choice is available. The catering function in a charitable rest-home has a captive market; a city-centre lunch bar competes in a free market.

5.5 SEGMENTATION PROCEDURE

One procedure for segmenting a market is the 5-stage process shown in Figure 5.1 At the first stage, the segmentation problem would be defined. For instance, the problem may be 'to segment the market for accommodation'. Second, a list of variables used for market segmentation is produced. Figure 5.2 shows a number of examples. The figure gives 2 classes of segmentation criteria, relating either to customer characteristics or customer behaviour. The former is subdivided into demographic/geographic criteria and psychological/sociological criteria.

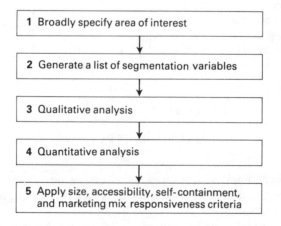

Figure 5.1 A procedure for segmenting markets.

Demographic criteria are the most widely used, being simple to understand and obtain—yet how could it help a restaurant manager if the only information he has about his target market is that they are singles aged 18–25? He will need to assume much about the eating behaviour, values, attitudes and media habits of this group before designing a marketing mix. One noted researcher has commented: 'Analyses of market segments by age, sex, geography and income level are not likely to provide as much direction·for marketing strategy as management requires.'[1] These variables are then considered

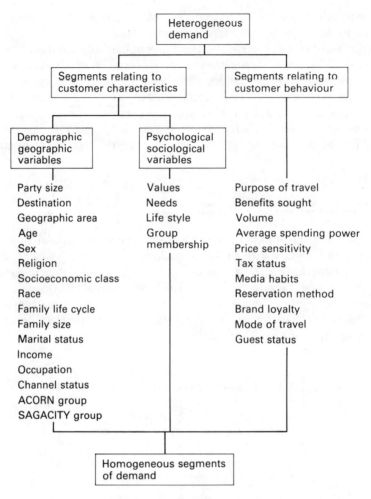

Figure 5.2 Segmentation variables.

individually and in combination, at stage 3, until one or more segmentation alternatives are described. The actual size of each segment is then calculated, making assumptions where hard data are absent.

A food-service operator investigating the wedding reception market segment could proceed as follows:

1. Define market area (20 minutes' drive maximum from churches and register office).
2. Calculate number of marriages per annum (refer to Registrar of Births, Marriages and Deaths).
3. Estimate proportion holding wedding receptions (telephone interview or consult with church/registry officials).
4. Estimate party size (telephone interview or consult with church officials).
5. Estimate revenue per cover (past records).
6. Calculate total market expenditure per annum ($3 \times 4 \times 5$).

A shift from mass marketing to market segmentation can be expensive as it often necessitates changes not only in the marketing function, but also in finance, administration and production functions both in the long and short term. Some of these are charted in Table 5.1. Because of the costs, stage 5 in the process of market segmentation proposes that each potential segment is evaluated against a set of criteria; the following 4 criteria are especially relevant.

Table 5.1 *Organisational consequences of segmentation.*

Function	Long-term changes	Short-term changes
Finance	1 New capital investment 2 New expenditure patterns 3 New sources of funds 4 Staff segment specialisation 5 Provision of information for marketing 6 New screening policy for new product ideas 7 Long-term financial planning redefined	1 New budgets and controls 2 Increases in cash/credit availability required 3 Writing off some assets before fully depreciated 4 Cash-flow changes
Administration	1 Company reorganisation 2 Retraining 3 Marketing planning	1 New specialist staff, retraining old 2 Invoicing procedures change 3 Staff segment specialisation 4 More and different records maintained
Production including product development and buying	1 Replacement of old products 2 New production systems 3 More flexibility 4 Shorter production runs and leadtimes 5 Investment in new product development (NPD)	1 Adaptation of current products 2 Costs/unit increase, low volume/high cost 3 Spare capacity 4 Specialist staff 5 High costs of new equipment 6 New raw materials 7 New buying contacts 8 Buying costs increase because of smaller quantities

(a) Profitable size
A large segment may not be worth entering if it is widespread. Size alone is no criterion; profitability also should be considered. The relative profit potential in a segment is directly related to the competitive strength and cost effectiveness of the marketer. Even a small segment can be highly profitable if the profit on each unit sold, or the repeat purchase frequency, is high.

(b) Accessibility
A segment must be accessible through advertising and the other promotional media. Accessibility through channels of distribution serving the geographic area in which the segment is located is also vital.

(c) Self-containment

The most valuable segment is one which is distinct from others served by a business; generally a product newly launched into a segment should not take demand from another product in a company's range. Demand substitution can be self-defeating unless the company is (1) deliberately pursuing a multiple-branding strategy, where the individual sales of the competing brands are of no importance but where their combined volume is; or (2) phasing out the product whose sales are being undermined. When Holiday Inns launched its 4-star Crowne Plaza hotel product in the USA, it found that there was no cannibalisation of its core brand, a 2-star product.

(d) Marketing mix response

Of major importance in selecting a target market is the sensitivity of the segment to a particular marketing mix. The ideal segment responds to a particular advertising claim and price level; has identifiable product preferences and media usage habits; and buys through known channels of distribution.

5.6 SEGMENTATION VARIABLES

This section examines the variables used to segment hospitality markets. *Purpose of visit* is the most common variable used to segment accommodation markets. Medlik[2] identifies 3 purposes: *business, holiday* and *other*. Business travellers vary in status from lorry drivers to managing directors; they may be delivering goods, visiting exhibitions or trade fairs, calling on customers, or attending seminars or conferences. Their usage is typically short term, city-oriented, frequent, less price sensitive and unseasonal. The holiday traveller, on the other hand, stays longer, is resort-oriented, infrequent, price sensitive and seasonal. Other accommodation users are extremely varied—family members attending a wedding, visiting a hospital patient, or belonging to common interest groups. A number of hotel chains have courted business travellers. Hyatt Hotels has a programme called the Regency Club in which one or more floors are reserved for executive use and a number of special benefits are conferred. Sheraton Hotels and Inns run the Sheraton Towers Club. In the UK Thistle Hotels have targeted the business executive with a number of corporate and contract rates, special promotions and enhancement of the basic accommodation product.[3]

The distinction between business and holiday travel is blurred in the incentive travel sector. Incentive travel is a motivational device used by companies to reward sales staff, distributors, customers, or employees, often for reaching or exceeding sales and other performance criteria. The blurring occurs because the buyer is a business customer, but the user is a holidaymaker. The needs of both must be satisfied. A growing proportion (about 75 per cent in the USA) is programmed by full-time incentive travel planners.[4]

The British Tourist Authority reports that of the 11.6 million overseas visitors to the UK in 1982, 46 per cent were holidaymakers, 21 per cent were business travellers, 20 per cent were visiting friends and relatives whilst the balance had a variety of other purposes.[5]

A second segmentation variable, often used in conjunction with purpose of visit, is *party size*. A basic distinction is made between *independent* and *group* travel. Group travellers have business, holiday, or other purposes. Of the 11.6 million overseas visitors, about 14 per cent were holidaymakers on inclusive tours. Hospitality marketers sell accommodation and other products to tour operators and organisers at discounted rates and they, in turn, build them into packages for resale to holidaymakers.

Other group markets for hospitality products are congresses, associations (national and international, local and regional), businesses (meetings, seminars, conferences, incentive travel, exhibitions and fairs), families, special-interest groups and clubs (athletics, culture and hobbies) and trade unions.

The international congress averages 500 delegates, frequently holding simultaneous exhibitions and assembling in purpose-built centres.[6] Examples are the General Assembly of the International Union of Radio Science (700–1,000 delegates) and the Congress of the International Federation of Gynaecology and Obstetrics (6,000 delegates).

The conventions held by associations such as the World Health Organisation and Unesco are also large-scale events, lasting on average 3 days, and comprise both regular and periodic programmes. Regular programmes tend to be held near headquarters whilst periodic conventions use varied locations.[7]

Business meetings are estimated to account for about 75 per cent of group accommodation sales.[8] The majority of such meetings have less than 50 participants, meet more frequently than most other group hospitality customers and are not of a seasonal character.[9]

A recent survey of the provision of accommodation for business-group customers revealed oversupply. Some 535,000 spaces were available in hotels and an additional 400,000 in town hotels, civic centres, pavilions, theatres, cinemas and winter gardens.[10]

A third variable used in combination with purpose of visit and party size is *destination*. The conventional division is into *transient* and *terminal* customers. The transient is en route to another destination. Airport and ferry locations have many hotels catering for transients. The terminal customer stays longer, regards the hotel as a place of residence and thus has different expectations of the product and is more price sensitive. Furthermore, since a much higher percentage of the terminal customers' hotel selections is planned in advance, different promotional vehicles are required.

Geographic area is a variable used to segment both accommodation and food service markets. Such segments may be local, regional, or national. When sterling is weak against the dollar, UK hotel groups target the American tourist. Between 1980 and 1984 the dollar acquired 50 per cent more purchasing power in the UK. Consequently London became an attractive destination. Hoteliers in the Avon area tend to target West Midlands holidaymakers. Historically the association between the 2 areas has been strong. Blackpool's hoteliers likewise target Lancashire. Fast-food operators target the local area. Two-thirds of sales are generally to people living within a radius of 2 miles. In comparison, a gourmet restaurant may draw the bulk of its custom from a radius of 30 miles.

Age is a more common variable in food service segmentation than accommodation; however, some hoteliers do target the over 60s particularly in the shoulder months, offering products augmented with social and welfare benefits such as organised sing-songs and health care. The UK has 9 million elderly, most of whom feed themselves, although some 43 million meals are prepared and delivered to them each year, largely by the meals-on-wheels services.[11] Tour operators such as SAGA, who specialise in meeting the needs of older holidaymakers, take care to design appropriate packages of travel, food, accommodation, transfer, excursions, evening entertainment and courier availability whilst also making discreet contingency plans to deal with ill-health and death.[12] Club 18–30 also assembles age-oriented holiday packages.

The relationship of age to domestic tourist behaviour, shown in Table 5.2, points to younger people being much more active in making business trips than they are in domestic holiday trips. Eating out is also a younger person's activity, although some locations and styles of operation lend themselves to older customers.[13]

Table 5.2   *Age and domestic tourist behaviour.*

Age	Adult British population* (%)		Domestic holiday trips (%)		Business and conference trips (%)	
16–24	17	} 51	19	} 56	11	} 71
25–34	17		19		26	
35–44	17		18		34	
45–54	14	} 48	13	} 44	16	} 29
55–64	15		15		12	
65+	19		16		1	

* Based on sample structure for BHTS survey
Source: BHTS *British Home Tourism Survey* (1983)

Consumer behaviour may also be related to *sex*. A number of products are deliberately targeted at a single sex, others attempt to meet the needs of both sexes, whereas a third group becomes strongly associated over time with either male or female consumers.

Researchers have found that whilst foods may be perceived as 'masculine' (heavy, solid-looking foods), or 'feminine' (pretty, dainty, decoratively garnished, rounder and smaller foods), these perceptions 'do not automatically indicate differential appeal' and are 'not necessarily related to eating satisfactions'. Men differentiate between 'male appeal' and 'female appeal' in food dishes but women do not feel that their own food tastes are radically different from those of men.[14] Breweries are coming to realise that they have to develop new forms of public house to attract female customers, whose wants have been inadequately met in the past.

The hotel industry is also learning the value of female customers. In the UK about 20 per cent of business travellers are women;[15] an American survey found that nearly 50 per cent of hotel guests were female.[16] A conference on the special hospitality requirements of businesswomen found the following: that women spend longer in their rooms than men, making comfort, good design and in-room services more important; women do not like to be treated as 'special', but rather as the equals of male guests; women want rooms designed with a work area away from the bed; women guests feel more secure with sound locks and peepholes as standard room equipment; women may feel that the attitude of staff towards them is condescending, and training is needed; women's business travel is largely to conventions but there are few appropriate entertainment programmes for accompanying husbands; and women feel awkward dining alone—well lit or communal tables satisfy many—but food portions are too large, cocktail lounges intimidating and room service is more important than for men.[17] To meet the needs of female guests Crest Hotels have introduced a new product—Lady Crest—whilst Hyatt and Marriott Hotels have begun retraining staff.

Socioeconomic class (SEC), which we examined in Chapter 4, is widely used to classify macromarket segments. Although 16 per cent of the population is group AB, 28 per cent of holidays abroad were taken by this group, whereas the 30 per cent who are in group DE bought only 20 per cent.[18] ABs also account for 43 per cent of business and conference travel,[19] eat out more often than other groups[20] and are heavier users of licensed accommodation.[21]

At unit level it is difficult to apply successfully socioeconomic class as the sole segmentation variable. Its principal value occurs when purchasing space in the advertising media; many print and broadcast vehicles classify their audiences by SEC, so that marketers are able to reach a specific target audience. However, in designing other elements of the marketing mix SEC affords little assistance. The marketer either has to assume much or use other segmentation variables in conjunction with SEC. Many hospitality marketers assume that the higher the SEC, the more refined and elaborate are food preferences, the more sophisticated are accommodation requirements and the less price sensitive is the consumer.

Race is a segmentation variable which has to be used with sensitivity because of provisions within the Race Relations Act 1976. Its prime applications are for hospitality properties located in neighbourhoods with particular racial characteristics. A hotel in a West Indian neighbourhood might design a product offering and promotional plan to attract West Indian guests visiting friends and relatives. A restaurant in a Pakistani neighbourhood would adapt its product mix accordingly, print its menu in Urdu and advertise in minority print vehicles.

Religion is similarly applied. Restaurants might be designed to appeal to the Hindu or Jew.

The *family life cycle* (FLC) is a concept borrowed from sociology which traces the ascent, maturity and decline of a family. The 9-stage FLC is shown in Table 5.3. However, FLC omits large numbers of the population: long-term singles, single-parent families, extended families, childless couples and unmarried couples. Even so, FLC is often a better predictor of buying behaviour than age because changes in family structure have a greater influence on purchasing power and product requirements than

Table 5.3 *The family life cycle.*

Stage	Description
1 Bachelor	Young, single, living away from home
2 Newlyweds	Young, no children
3 Full nest I	Youngest child aged under 6
4 Full nest II	Youngest child aged 6 or over
5 Full nest III	Older couples, dependent children
6 Empty nest I	Older couples, no children at home, family head working
7 Empty nest II	Older couples, no children at home, family head retired
8 Solitary I	One survivor, working
9 Solitary II	One survivor, retired

the mere passage of time. American researchers have found that FLC is an important determinant of leisure activity and deserves 'equal significance as social class, sex and religion.'[22]

A number of food service operations have targeted various FLC stages: Courage have introduced a number of new formats; and Harvester Inns aim particularly at stages 3 and 4. Wine bars often aim at stage 1. Many resort hotels are designed to appeal to stage 3—babysitting and baby-care services augment the basic product. Stage 6 holidaymakers are big spenders.

Family size correlates well with eating out. Single-parent families eat out more often than any other family group. As two-parent families acquire more children, the incidence declines.[23] Whilst not universally true, larger families tend to have less disposable income and are, therefore, likely to holiday less frequently and in less lavish surroundings. They are more likely to be price sensitive and to forward-plan holidays with care.

Segmenting markets by *marital status* is common. Singles, who spend heavily on entertainment, are prime targets for food service and accommodation marketers in the leisure sector. We have already seen how newly-weds are targeted by caterers and honeymoon hotels. Special products are frequently designed for divorced or widowed adults attempting to rebuild their social lives.

Income is closely associated with eating-out behaviour. Higher-income people eat out more often and tend to spend more per meal experience. A distinction should be made between net income and disposable income. Some high-earners have little disposable income because of other financial commitments. It is disposable income which is the important variable in hospitality market segmentation. Income is closely linked to socioeconomic class. ABs have more disposable income than DEs. However, skilled manual workers (C2) often earn more than clerical workers (C1). Even though individuals from classes C2 and B may have similar disposable incomes, patterns of expenditure can vary considerably due to different family circumstances and lifestyles. Widespread availability of credit has reduced the significance of income as a major segmentation variable.

Occupation is used to segment markets in 2 ways: first, in terms of whether a person is employed or not; and second, in terms of the type of job, if employed. Women in paid employment spend considerably more on eating out than do their housebound counterparts. Furthermore, because of their higher disposable income, they are more likely to take holidays. Patterns of expenditure are likely to vary according to the type of occupation a person holds (see socioeconomic class, above).

Most of the variables we have mentioned so far are used to segment user markets. *Channel status* is used when segmenting distributor markets. A hotel group might decide to sell 40 per cent of its rooms through its own reservation system (direct sell), 20 per cent through travel agents and 40 per cent in block bookings to tour operators. Greater precision is possible; a hotel aiming at the business traveller is more likely to target the top-4 UK travel agency multiples—Thomas Cook, Pickfords, Lunn Poly and Hogg-Robinson—since they generate 30 per cent of all business travel booked through travel agencies, despite operating only 14 per cent of travel agency offices.[24]

SAGACITY and ACORN are two commercially developed segmentation variables. SAGACITY combines a number of demographic variables to produce 12 segments of

consumers 'at a similar stage of their [family] life cycle, and with similar disposable income and cultural characteristics'.[25] SAGACITY uses a 4-stage family life cyle: dependent (10 per cent of adults aged 15+), pre-family (8 per cent), family (36 per cent) and late (40 per cent). Each stage is defined as below:
- the *dependent* stage is where an individual is still living in the parental household, or studying full time if living away from home
- the *pre-family* stage consists of adults under age 35 who have already established their own households but as yet have no children
- the *family* stage consists of all housewives and heads of household under 65 with one or more children (under 21) in the household
- the *late* stage includes all other adults whose children have already left home or who are 35 or over and childless

Family and late stages are classified as either 'better off' or 'worse off' (these classifications take into account disposable income and spouses at work) and all groups are further classified into socioeconomic classes—ABC1s appearing as 'white collar' and C2DE as 'blue collar'. Figure 5.3 portrays the segments schematically, and Table 5.4 describes each segment. SAGACITY has been used to segment the package holiday market and to classify audiences for the print and broadcast media.

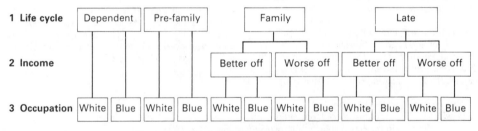

Figure 5.3 SAGACITY classification scheme.

ACORN, which stands for 'A classification of residential neighbourhoods', segments consumers according to the type of area in which they live. Developed by CACI, it has been widely applied by all sectors, including the hospitality industry. Berni Inns and the Host Group are users.

ACORN classifies neighbourhoods into 12 major groups (see Table 5.5), which are further refined into 39 types. ACORN can help management to choose restaurant sites, set sales targets, select advertising media and create direct-mail shots.

So far we have examined only demographic and geographic segmentation variables. Figure 5.2 also lists four psychological/sociological variables—values, needs, life style and group membership. (We gave detail about *values* in Chapter 4, so there is no need to discuss their significance here.)

Food service and accommodation product offerings can be designed to satisfy groups of customers with specific *needs*. Meals out can satisfy physiological, security, social, ego or self-actualisation needs. Similarly, accommodation can meet all five needs. Some hotels sell rooms to local authorities who house the homeless. Homes for the elderly provide a convivial atmosphere which meets social needs; yet other hotels confer status on their guests.

Table 5.4   *SAGACITY market segments.*

Dependent, white (DW) 6%
Mainly under-24s, living at home or full-time student, where head of household is in an ABC1 occupation group

Dependent, blue (DB) 9%
Mainly under-24s, living at home or full-time student; where head of household is in a C2DE occupation group

Pre-family, white (PFW) 4%
Under-35s, who have established their own household but have no children and where the head of household is in an ABC1 occupation group

Pre-family, blue (PFB) 4%
Under-35s, who have established their own household but have no children and where the head of household is in a C2DE occupation group

Family, better off, white (FW+) 6%
Housewives and heads of household, under 65, with 1 or more children in the household, in the 'better-off' income group and where the head of household is in an ABC1 occupation group (65% are AB)

Family, better off, blue (FB+) 9%
Housewives and heads of household, under 65, with 1 or more children in the household, in the 'better-off' income group and where the head of household is in a C2DE occupation group (72% are C2)

Family, worse off, white (FW−) 8%
Housewives and heads of household, under 65, with 1 or more children in the household, in the 'worse-off' income group and where the head of household is in an ABC1 occupation group (72% are C1)

Family, worse off, blue (FB−) 14%
Housewives and heads of household, under 65, with 1 or more children in the household, in the 'worse-off' income group and where the head of household is in a C2DE occupation group (47% are DE)

Late, better off, white (LW+) 5%
Includes all adults whose children have left home or who are over 35 and childless, are in the 'better-off' income group and where the head of household is in an ABC1 occupation group (60% are AB)

Late, better off, blue (LB+) 7%
Includes all adults whose children have left home or who are over 35 and childless, are in the 'better-off' income group and where the head of household is in a C2DE occupation group (69% are C2)

Late, worse off, white (LW−) 9%
Includes all adults whose children have left home or who are over 35 and childless, are in the worse-off' income group and where the head of household is in an ABC1 occupation group (71% are C1)

Late, worse off, blue (LB−) 19%
Includes all adults whose children have left home or who are over 35 and childless, are in the 'worse-off' income group and where the head of household is in a C2DE occupation group (70% are DE)

Table 5.5   *ACORN groups.*

ACORN groups		%	1981 population (million)
A	Agricultural areas	3.4	1.8
B	Modern family housing, higher incomes	16.2	8.7
C	Older housing of intermediate status	17.6	9.4
D	Poor-quality older terraced housing	4.3	2.3
E	Better-off council estates	13.0	7.0
F	Less well-off council estates	9.4	5.0
G	Poorest council estates	7.6	4.0
H	Multiracial areas	3.9	2.1
I	High-status non-family areas	4.2	2.2
J	Affluent suburban housing	15.9	8.6
K	Better-off retirement areas	3.8	2.0
U	Unclassified	0.7	0.4
		100.0	53.5

Source: CACI *ACORN Profile: Great Britain (1981)*

The main benefit of using *lifestyle* segmentation techniques is that a much fuller picture is obtained of the target market. It tells the marketer about the sort of lifestyle his customer leads, the beliefs and opinions he holds, the types of interests he has and the background he is from whilst the more common demographic techniques tell little about these matters, which can be very important in all aspects of marketing strategy.

The types of information collected about the consumer by lifestyle researchers are shown in Table 5.6.[26] Not surprisingly, this type of study has also been called AIO (activities, interests, opinions) research and psychographics, which is a term valuable for contrasting lifestyle studies with demographics. There is no agreement as to what constitutes lifestyle or psychographics. Wells reports that 'twenty-four articles on psychographics contain no less than 32 definitions, all somewhat different'.[27]

Table 5.6 *Dimensions of lifestyle.*

Activities	Interests	Opinions	Demography
Work	Family	Selves	Age
Hobbies	Home	Social issues	Education
Social events	Job	Politics	Income
Vacation	Community	Business	Occupation
Entertainments	Recreation	Economics	Family size
Club membership	Fashion	Education	Dwelling
Community	Food	Products	Geography
Shopping	Media	Future	City size
Sports	Achievements	Culture	Family life cycle

Lifestyle research is extremely expensive to conduct. It generally consists of a large number of personal interviews with up to 600 questions being asked and the application of advanced multivariate statistical techniques to the collected data. The outputs are profiles such as those listed in Table 5.7, which outlines 8 UK female psychographic groups.[28]

Lifestyle research has had little application in the hospitality industry. MacPherson has attempted to segment the winter weekend-break market by lifestyle.[29] Noting that demographically the top third of socioeconomic classes provide the demand for such products, he proposed 6 lifestyle segments: the peace-and-quiet seeker; the quality-service seeker; the sportsperson; the specialist-activity seeker; the city-life seeker; and the entertainment seeker.

Both primary and secondary groups can be selected as target markets. *Group membership* implies segments of consumers with at least one characteristic in common: businesswomen, members of the British Institute of Management, Diners' Club card carriers, stamp collectors, fell walkers, residents of Leeds, commercial travellers and employees in the footwear industry are all examples of groups which have been targeted by commercial hospitality establishments

Figure 5.2 shows 12 segmentation variables relating to customer behaviour. Amongst the more frequently used is *benefits sought*. It is axiomatic in marketing that customers buy benefits, not features. Therefore, the physical product, service and environment created by hospitality marketers is only the means by which benefits are delivered. Research has indicated that 'consumers simultaneously process a total benefit bundle in deciding whether or not to go to a particular restaurant'.[30] Not all people seek the same benefits. To use a consumer goods analogy: some toothpaste users want white teeth, others fresh breath and others protection from dental decay. One examination of 270

Table 5.7   *Eight female psychographic market segments.*

1 '*Young sophisticates*' (15%) Extravagant; experimental; non-traditional; young; A, B and C1 social classes; educated; affluent; sociable; cultural interests; owner-occupiers; in full-time employment; interested in new products

2 '*Cabbages*' (12%) Conservative; less quality-conscious; demographically average but more full-time housewives; middle class; average income and education; lowest level of interest in new products; home-centred; indulging in little entertaining

3 '*Traditional working class*' (12%) Traditional; quality-conscious; seldom experimenting with food; enjoying cooking; middle-aged; D and E social groups; less educated; lower incomes; council house tenants; sociable; husband and wife share activities; betting

4 '*Middle-aged sophisticates*' (14%) Experimental; non-traditional; less extravagant; middle-aged; A, B and C1 social classes; educated; affluent; full-time housewives; owner-occupiers; interested in new products; sociable; cultural interests

5 'Coronation Street *housewives*' (14%) Quality-conscious; conservative; traditional and obsessional; D and E social classes; live relatively more in the Lancashire and Yorkshire ITV areas; less educated; lower incomes; part-time employment; low level of interest in new products; not sociable

6 '*Self-confident*' (13%) Self-confident; quality-conscious; not extravagant; young and well educated, owner-occupiers; average income

7 '*Homely*' (10%) Bargain-seekers; not self-confident; houseproud; C1 and C2 social classes; Tyne Tees and Scotland ITV areas; left school at an early age; part-time employed: average level of entertaining .

8 '*Pennypinchers*' (10%) Self-confident; houseproud; traditional; not quality-conscious, aged 25–34; C2, D and E social classes; part-time employed; less education; average income, betting; saving; husband and wife share activities; sociable

restaurant advertisements found that 5 major benefit appeals were used to attract custom: food quality, menu variety, attractive price, pleasant/interesting atmosphere and convenient location.[31] It was also found that these benefits had different significance for patrons of gourmet, family/popular and atmosphere restaurants, although food quality 'is the predominant benefit appeal as a basis for consumer choice.'[32]

Benefit segments are often also analysed for demographic variables with which they can be closely associated. If an hotel operator's major benefit appeal, 'escape from pressures of everyday family life', appeals to married couples at stage 4 of the FLC, resident in the West Midlands and with relatively low disposable income, then considerable assistance is offered to the creation of an effective marketing strategy.

The above paragraph suggests that the heavy users of a hospitality product can be identified. This is the basis of *volume segmentation*. Marketers using this approach to segmentation try to distinguish heavy from medium and light users. Heavy users of a product can be defined in terms of frequency of purchase or size of purchase. Other segmentation variables are used to 'escribe the heavy users. A sandwich bar is used heavily by female office workers aged 16–24. A traditional pub is used most frequently by males, C2D socioeconomic classes and aged 18–30.

Marketers must decide whether to target heavy, medium, or light users. If a homogeneous group can be isolated as the heavy users, then there may be considerable marketing economies in targeting that segment. However, the marketing strategy of competitors may suggest that medium or light users offer better potential. Within the light-user sector it may be possible to identify a number of alternative target markets. Females and families at stages 3 and 4 of the FLC are infrequent users of pubs, yet brewers are increasingly designing marketing mixes to attract these light users. The aim, of course, is to identify the causes of light use, remedy them and convert the light user into a medium or heavy user. Hoteliers who promote to past customers are attempting to generate a group of more frequent users. It may be possible to discriminate between heavy and light users on the basis of the benefits they seek.[33]

Food service operators frequently use *average spending power* (ASP) as a variable in their segmentation strategies. When London's Grosvenor House Hotel restyled its food and beverage operations, it developed 3 products:
1. Pasta, Vino and Fantasia, where customers spend on average £6–£7 per head.
2. Pavilion, which offered a fixed-price lunch/dinner at £12 per head.
3. Ninety Park Ave, with an ASP on food and liquor of £22 at lunchtime and £26 in the evening.[34]

In other words, ASP is simply the average per capita expenditure. Clearly, it is lower for fast-food operations than for a gourmet restaurant; it also has applications in the accommodation sector. Travelling salesmen frequently have a per diem subsistence allowance which determines their ASP. Customers whose expenditure is constrained by the policies of their employers, or their own low personal disposable income, tend to be highly *price sensitive*. Marketers of any commercial hospitality product have to make judgements about the price sensitivity of their target market. Consumers often have thresholds below which (or ceilings above which) they will not spend! Products must compete between these levels. A product outside the acceptable price bands does not become part of the choice set. As long as products fit into the acceptable price band relative price level is not a major determinant of product choice. Business travellers tend to be less price sensitive than holidaymakers.

A related variable is the *tax status* of the customer. Commenting on the American travel market, a Sheraton Hotels executive noted:[35]

> The Federal income tax has divided travellers into 'pre-tax' and 'post-tax' travellers, and I insist that it is not possible to cater to both groups. At least 80% of guests should be in one of the two categories. One group is more interested in price first, and the other is interested in quality and service first and price second.

When customers are segmented according to their *media habits*, the marketer produces a marketing mix to appeal to the audience of a specific medium or advertising vehicle within a medium. Many vehicles are able to describe their audiences in intimate detail, particularly in terms of their demographics and marketers need only devise an appropriate marketing mix to satisfy the audience which the vehicle can deliver. A hotel near a salmon river could target readers of a fishing magazine. A resort hotel could target readers of a boating magazine.

Just as segmentation by media habits attempts to take advantage of the accessibility of a group of consumers, so do segmentation by *reservation method* and *brand loyalty*. Hoteliers can target guests who book through travel agents or those who prefer to use a toll-free, computerised reservation system. In the former case the marketer creates a product designed to satisfy both the travel agent and his customer. Computerised reservation systems are designed to simplify the purchase and administration of hotel space. The main advantages offered to the user are convenience, speed and economy. These are the sorts of benefit which encourage loyalty to a hotel chain or independent hotels in a referral system.

Mode of travel is an important variable in the segmentation of accommodation markets. Hotel location is a vital consideration: is it located near motorway access-points; airport; sea, rail, or coach terminals? Even in food service, mode of travel can be applied. Specific products are designed for air, rail, sea and coach travellers.

A final variable used to segment the market for a hotel's food and beverage operations is *guest status*. Is a customer *resident* or *non-resident*? In the Grosvenor House Hotel case only 30 per cent of the Pavilion's customers were hotel residents whereas 60 per cent of Pasta, Vino and Fantasia customers were residents. One national hotel chain has combined guest status with party size to produce the grid shown in Figure 5.4.[36] The grid identifies all major customer groups. Each group has specific requirements in terms of atmosphere, type of food and method of payment.

Individuals or couples	Groups	
Salesmen Vacationers Family visits Moving through, in or out	Tour groups Military Conventions Sports groups	Resident
'Night out' 'Special occasion' Regular buffet Transients	Tour groups Business meetings Wedding receptions Receptions Religious groups	Non-resident

Figure 5.4   Guest status and party size.

Medlik prefers to specify 3 categories of customer for a hotel's food and beverage operations: hotel residents, non-residents and organised groups.[37] Residents commonly take breakfast at their hotel and are more likely to be evening than lunchtime guests. Non-residents, individually or in small groups, are important lunchtime and weekend evening customers. Organised groups often make advance arrangements for functions and comprise local clubs, societies, business and professional groups as well as participants in meetings and conferences originating from outside the area.

5.7 BENEFITS OF MARKET TARGETING

Many of the examples in this chapter have hinted at the beneficial effects of market targeting and market segmentation. Let us now identify them specifically:
- it leads to a sharper definition in setting marketing objectives. A company selling into a £3 million market segment will be able to set its market share objectives at 5 per cent in year 1, 7.5 per cent in year 2, 12 per cent in year 3, and so on.
- it enables marketing mix decisions to be tailored to the unique characteristics and requirements of the target market. This leads to greater cost effectiveness of marketing resources.
- it enables better identification of competitors. Competitors are those individuals or organisations which deliver the same benefits to the same target market.
- it causes a heightened awareness of new opportunities. The characteristics of a market can change rapidly in response to technological advances in products or processes, marketing activities of competition, or changes in consumer tastes.
Skilled marketers can both initiate or respond to shifts in segmentation opportunities as the characteristics of the market-place change.

5.8 CHAPTER REVIEW

1. There are 2 approaches to market targeting: mass marketing and segmented marketing.
2. Market segmentation i the identification of a subset of consumers for which a marketing mix can be devised specifically to satisfy its demands.
3. Distinctions can be made between:
   - imposed, elected and acquired segmentation.
   - macro- and microsegmentation.
   - consumer, organisational and channel segmentation.
4. A simple 5-stage segmentation procedure comprises:
   (a) specification of area of interest.
   (b) generation of a list of segmentation variables.
   (c) qualitative analysis.
   (d) quantitative analysis.
   (e) application of criteria to detect worthwhile segmentation opportunities.
5. There are 4 main criteria used to detect worthwhile segmentation opportunities: size; accessibility; self containment; and marketing mix responsiveness.
6. The 2 main classes of segmentation variables are those which are based upon customer characteristics (demographic, geographic, psychological and sociological) and those based on customer behaviour.
7. A corporate shift from mass marketing to segmented marketing may have serious organisational consequences.
8. The main demographic/geographic segmentation variables are party size; geographic area; age; sex; religion; socioeconomic class; race; family life cycle; family size; marital status; income; occupation; channel status; and ACORN and SAGACITY groups.
9. The main psychological/sociological segmentation variables are values; needs; lifestyle; and group membership.
10. The main behavioural segmentation variables are purpose of travel; benefits sought; volume; average spending power; price sensitivity; tax status; media habits; reservation method; brand loyalty; mode of travel, and guest status.
11. Segmentation variables can be used singly or in combination.
12. Market targeting brings about a number of benefits: sharper definition in objective-setting; improved cost effectiveness in marketing expenditure; clearer identification of competitors; and heightened awareness of new opportunities.

5.9 QUESTIONS

1. What segmentation criteria would you consider in choosing a target market for:
   - a private convalescent home?
   - a sandwich bar?
   - a hotel coffee shop?
   - an ice-cream parlour?
2. What advantages and disadvantages accompany the use of demographic segmentation variables?
3. Is any catering product mass-marketed?
4. 'The process of segmentation leads to the identification of ever smaller groups of consumers as target markets. Since high sales volumes are essential for high profits, segmentation is counterproductive.' Discuss.
5. Would you expect socioeconomic class or income to be the better predictor of overseas holidaymaking?
6. What benefits might attract customers to:
   - a camp-site operator?
   - a department store restaurant?

- a contract catering operation for bank employees?
- a small business offering a mobile catering service for children's parties?

REFERENCES

[1] Yankelovich, D. (1964) New criteria for market segmentation. *Harvard Business Review*, **42**, March–April, 83–90.

[2] Medlik, S. (1980) *The Business of Hotels*. London: Heinemann, 15–16.

[3] See: Thistle £100,000 bid for businessmen. *Caterer and Hotelkeeper*, (1983) 8 September, 13.

[4] Lewis, R. C. (1983) The incentive travel market: how to reap your share? *Cornell Hotel and Restaurant Administration Quarterly*, **24**(1), May, 19ff.

[5] British Tourist Authority (1983) *Digest of Tourist Statistics*, No. 11.

[6] Gray-Forton, G. (1977) The conference business and the travel trade. *International Tourism Quarterly*, 4, 49–63.

[7] Lawson, F. R. (1980) Congresses, conventions and conferences. *International Journal of Tourism Management*, **1**(3), September, 184–8.

[8] Gray-Forton, G. (1977) op. cit.

[9] McCleary, K. W. (1978) The corporate meetings market: components of success in attracting group business. *Cornell Hotel and Restaurant Administration Quarterly*, **19**(2), August, 30–35.

[10] Lawson, F. R. (1980) op. cit.

[11] Lawson, F. R. and Thomson, J. (1981) *The Meals on Wheels Service in the U.K.* University of Surrey.

[12] Braham, B. (1983) Catering for senior citizens. *Hospitality*, February, 12–13.

[13] Hotel and Catering Economic Development Committee (1976) *Trends in Catering*, Quarterly Report No. 8.

[14] See Dickens, J. and Chappell, B. (1977) Food for Freud? A study of the sexual polarization of food and food products. *Journal of the Market Research Society*, **19**(2). 76–92.

[15] Moore, C. (1984) Businesswomen—finding it tough on the road, *Signature*, November–December, 13–14.

[16] Chesanow, N. (1983) How hotels can make women more welcome. *Caterer and Hotelkeeper*, 27 October, 77–8.

[17] See: Women business travellers: satisfying the needs of a growing new market. *Cornell Hotel and Restaurant Administration Quarterly*, **19**(4), February, 67–9.

[18] British Tourist Authority (1982) *British National Travel Survey*.

[19] *British Home Tourism Survey*, 1982.

[20] Ministry of Agriculture, Fisheries and Food (1981), *Household Food Consumption and Expenditure*. London: HMSO.

[21] *British Home Tourism Survey*, op. cit.

[22] Rapoport, R., Rapoport, R. N., and Strelitz, Z. (1975) *Leisure and the family life cycle*. Boston, MA: Routledge & Kegan Paul.

[23] *Household Food Consumption and Expenditure*, op. cit.

[24] See: UK travel agents: who they are and their market. Pt 2, The agents. *International Tourism Quarterly*, 3, 1984, 40–56.

[25] Research Services Ltd (1981) SAGACITY: a special analysis of JICNARS NRS 1980 undertaken by Research Services Ltd. Research Services, London.

[26] Plummer, J. T. (1974) Applications of life style research to the creation of advertising campaigns, in Wells, W. D. (ed.) *Life Style and Psychographics*. AMA.

[27] See Wells, W. D. (1975) Psychographics: a critical review. *Journal of Marketing Research*, **12**, May, 196–213.

[28] Lunn, T. (1972) Monitoring consumer life styles. *Admap*, November.

[29] MacPherson, N. C. (1978) Winter weekend. *HCIMA Journal*, January, 43–9.

[30] See Lewis, R. C. (1981) Restaurant advertising: appeals and consumers' intentions. *Journal of Advertising Research*, **21**(5), October, 69–74.

[31] Lewis, R. C. (1980) Benefit segmentation for restaurant advertising that works. *Cornell Hotel and Restaurant Administration Quarterly,* **21**(3), November, 6–12.

[32] See Lewis, R. C. (1981) op. cit.

[33] Swinyard, W. R. (1977) A research approach to restaurant marketing. *Cornell Hotel and Restaurant Administration Quarterly,* **17**(4), February, 62–5.

[34] Hyam, J. (1984) How Grosvenor House restyle its F & B operation. *Caterer and Hotelkeeper,* 5 January, 31–3.

[35] Quoted in Vallen, J. J., Abbey, J. R., and Sapienza, D. L. (1978) *The Art and Science of Managing Hotels, Restaurants, Institutions.* New Jersey, NJ: Hayden, 212.

[36] Stevens, R. E. (1977) Careful analysis first step to successful hotel and catering marketing, in Brymer, R. A. (ed.) *Introduction to Hotel and Restaurant Management.* Des Moines, IA: Kendall-Hunt, 177–83.

[37] Medlik, S. (1980) op. cit., 17.

—PART II—

Planning Marketing Strategy

Part II comprises two chapters, the first of which examines the planning process whilst the second looks at the development of marketing strategy. Together they form a framework which integrates the subsequent chapters in Part III.

—6—

Company and Marketing Planning

6.1 CHAPTER PREVIEW

If a marketing plan is to succeed, it must be integrated into the overall corporate planning system. Consequently this chapter investigates the relationship between the two. Common skills such as analysis, prognosis and objective setting are discussed, and the implications of corporate objectives such as profitability and growth for marketing strategy are explored.

A model of the corporate planning process is proposed. It shows that objectives are set and subsequently refined following the conduct of internal and external audits. Forecasting and profit gap analysis also feature in the process. A discussion of management by objectives (MBO) shows the importance of people in planning.

6.2 LEARNING OBJECTIVES

By the end of this chapter you should be able to:
1. Identify the main benefits of planning.
2. Describe the process of corporate planning.
3. Explain the relationship between corporate and marketing planning.
4. Distinguish between direct and indirect methods of sales forecasting.
5. Describe the four essential elements of MBO.
However, you should not expect to be able immediately to apply any of the material in this chapter.

6.3 WHY PLAN?

All hospitality organisations are founded with some purpose in mind—whether the purpose is achieved is a different matter! The job of planning is to improve the odds of successful achievement; it is, however, no guarantee.

Planners in large organisations (and small ones) sometimes fail to identify the factors which cause underachievement. Movements in exchange rates, interest rates and taxation levels can all undermine the achievement of even the most carefully considered plans. However, planners still persist, often because their organisations have experienced benefits of the sort specified by American Airlines, where:
1. The planning procedure has helped executives step out of the restricting confines of day-to-day problems.

2. The planning procedure has illustrated the interrelationships between key decisions in different functional departments.
3. The planning procedure has highlighted the cumulative effect of individual day-to-day decisions, and has demonstrated that short-term actions must be closely tied to specific long-term objectives.
4. The planning procedure has improved forecasting techniques and procedures for evaluating alternative courses of action.
5. Planning activities have assisted in sharpening the decision-making processes on a broad front.

Large organisations have responsibilities towards shareholders, employees and customers.

Some, like Whitbread, even believe they have a 'social responsibility to invest in the community, and thereby strengthen the future social fabric of the country'.[1] The meeting of such responsibilities is jeopardised by inadequate planning. Smaller organisations with ambitions for growth also plan; often their financiers insist prior to funding ventures.

Planning exists in a number of forms:

- Corporate plans specify the major objectives and strategies for an entire organisation or a major division
- Functional plans such as financial, manpower, or marketing plans detail objectives and strategies within each function or department. Functional plans are interdependent with corporate plans, deriving objectives and strategies from the corporate plan whilst also helping to create them
- Special ad hoc plans are for activities beyond the normal scope of the organisation. Venture plans, new product plans, or market development plans may be created, funded and executed quite separately from other business activities

Plans also vary by their time scale:

- Long-term plans have a 5–10-year horizon
- Medium-term plans deal in objectives and strategies for 1 to 5 years ahead
- Short-term plans consider the coming 12 months, and unlike medium- and long-term plans, tend to be more detailed and concerned with tactical issues

It has been noted that 'as marketing considerations increasingly tend to influence the short-term and long-range policies in a company, then total company planning and marketing planning tend to merge'.[2] Certainly, the major parameters used by many companies to define their future plans are products and markets. These are also the building-blocks for marketing plans.

6.4 CORPORATE PLANNING

Planning has been defined by Ackoff as:[3]

> the design of a desired future and of effective ways of bringing it about.

Corporate planning, therefore, defines the desirable future state of a company and specifies means for its achievement. Because the fundamental task of a for-profit hospitality organisation is to convert resources into profit, the 'desirable future state' is usually quoted in financial terms.

The development of a corporate plan is a costly, time-consuming process requiring analytical, diagnostic, forecasting and strategic skills. Furthermore, its implementation requires sensitive man management since success depends upon the commitment of people who often are not party to its development. Whilst the details of individual corporate planning processes may vary, Figure 6.1 shows what is common to most. The process is explained in sections 6.5–6.11 below.

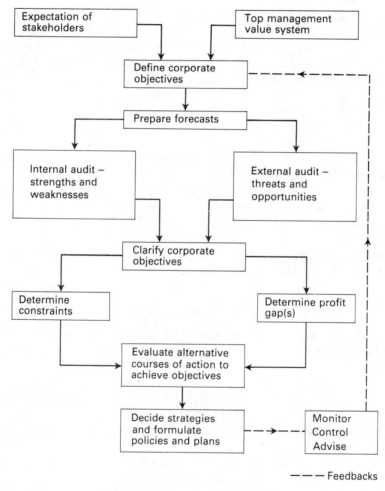

Figure 6.1   Corporate planning process.

6.5 CORPORATE PLANNING: OBJECTIVES

The starting-point in corporate planning is the formulation of objectives. Two sets of factors bear upon this: the expectations of stakeholders, and the values of the top management who are writing the plan.

The term 'stakeholder' encompasses all those individuals, groups, or organisations who have a financial, or other, interest in the activities of the company, including:

- shareholders wanting capital growth or income from their investment
- employees and trade unions wanting high wages, job security and satisfactory working conditions
- customers wanting uninterrupted supply of products
- the local community wanting employment prospects and a healthy and clean environment
- creditors wanting assured debt settlement

Top management balances the interests of these stakeholders against their own personal values. Typically the top management resolves a number of dilemmas whilst corporate planning; they decide to what extent the plan will reflect their preference for:

- employee participation or management control
- growth or stability
- risk-taking or security
- short-term profit-taking or long-term profit-making
- market followship or innovation

The larger and longer-established a company is, the greater the number of stakeholders and the less able is top management to express its own values. Compromise becomes more significant. Where top management and major shareholders are one and the same, as is often the case in private limited companies, the corporate plan is a purer reflection of management values.

Ansoff identifies 8 major corporate objectives:[4]

1. Maximisation of company's present net worth.
2. Maximisation of company's market value.
3. Survival.
4. Satisfactory profit.
5. Profit-constrained growth.
6. Maintenance of equitable and working relationships amongst the claims of the various interest groups.
7. Maximised sales volume.
8. High return on capital employed.

At any one time a company may express several of these in its statement of objectives; furthermore, unless the company is extraordinarily unified, it is probable that interest groups will be pursuing their own objectives, thus suboptimising corporate performance.

If objectives are to be used as benchmarks against which corporate managerial or departmental performance is to be evaluated, they must be:

- quantifiable, measurable and specific
- set to a time scale
- achievable

Of the 8 objectives listed by Ansoff, 2 are particularly important for marketing management: return on investment, and growth.

Return on investment

Return on investment (ROI) is a measure of the profit-earning performance of the capital invested in a business. It is calculated thus:

$$\text{ROI} = \frac{\text{Profits} \times 100}{\text{Capital employed}} \qquad (6.1)$$

Management strives to produce ROI figures more favourable than those of comparable companies in the same industry. To do so it has 3 options, as follows.
1. Improve profits.
2. Reduce capital employed.
3. Do both of the above.
Reduction of capital employed is not usually in the domain of the marketing manager, although he is able to influence profit levels.

Profit is calculated thus:
$$Z = TR - TC \qquad (6.2)$$
where Z = profit
TR = total revenue
TC = total costs

Increases in profit come about by raising total revenues, decreasing total costs, or favourably adjusting the balance between the two, so that productivity improves. The 2 main avenues for increasing total revenues, which are shown in Figure 6.2, are expansion of market size (achievable in 3 ways) and improvements in market share (achievable in two ways).

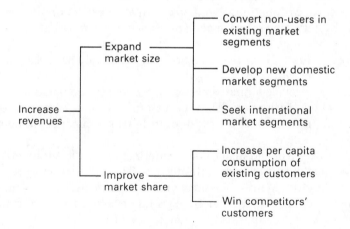

Figure 6.2 How to increase revenues.

Costs may be classified as fixed (independent of volume sold) or variable (tied to volume sold). Cost control is a major element in the thrust for profitability in many companies. Allied-Lyons, for instance, report that pre-tax profits rose by 32 per cent, largely as a result of cost cutting.[5] Marketing costs which are fixed include salaries of sales management, advertising production costs, depreciation of vehicles; variable costs include commissions to salespeople and discounts to an hotel's corporate users. Analysis will reveal whether there is scope for cost cutting.

Price adjustments and alterations to the sales mix are 2 further ways of influencing the relationship between costs and revenues, so that productivity improves. The raising of price will improve profitability, provided that it does not have too great an effect on sales volume.

The degree of freedom to manipulate price is determined by a number of factors:

- the elasticity of demand for the product; the more elastic the demand, the more sales will decline given a price rise
- the likelihood of other competitors in the market following the price increase
- whether the rest of the marketing mix can be used to offset a decline in sales volume
- whether the product can be repositioned in a different market segment willing to pay a higher price (see Chapter 7 for detail on positioning)
- the interpretation consumers have of a price increase; it may be taken to mean an improvement in quality, a response to profit margins being eroded, a signal that the item is moving quickly and may soon be sold out, or that the operator is avaricious

Adjustment of the sales mix would involve the company in pushing the sale of products which make a greater than average contribution towards profit. The key factor considered is unit contribution—i.e. the difference between the selling price of a product and the direct costs of producing it. Promotional efforts would support these preferred items, but this is clearly an option only for a multiproduct company.

An investigation by the Hotels and Catering Economic Development Committee pinpointed 4 principal ways to improve hotel profitability:[6]

1. Increase occupancy (only possible if spare capacity exists) or alter the pattern of occupancy by deflecting overdemand at seasonal peaks to weekend, off-season, or shoulder periods.
2. Raise prices at a rate faster than inflation. This can 'only be successful in a period when real incomes are rising'.
3. Price cutting, provided that improved occupancy compensates more than adequately for the lower price. (The report estimated that to compensate for a 10 per cent reduction in room rates a typical resort hotel's occupancy would need to rise from 65 to 70 per cent.)
4. Improved cost control and management information: 'Efficient hotel-keeping . . . requires adequate management information. The industry in general is poorly served in this respect. Many hotels do not keep departmentalized accounts and some establishments do not analyse guest registration and occupancy statistics. Such information is essential for effective planning and control.'

Growth

The term growth can be interpreted in a number of ways: growth in net present value, turnover, employment, profit, the number of products marketed, or the number of markets served. Comfort Hotels International measures its growth by the number of hotel units acquired.[7] De Vere Hotels & Restaurants look to both organic growth and acquisition.[8]

Figure 6.3 shows how product and market development combine in a growth vector matrix. Growth in the range of products currently marketed demands product improvement or new product launches; growth in markets served comes from finding new domestic geographic, customer, or international segments to enter.

NEW PRODUCTS ⟶

		NEW PRODUCT MIX		
		No product change	Improve or adapt product	Introduce new product
	Existing markets	No change	Product improvement	Product replacement or product line extension
New market segments	New regional markets	Market expansion – geographic	Market expansion – geographic and improved product	Market expansion – geographic and new product
New market segments	New customer markets	Market expansion – customers	Market expansion – customers and new product	*Diversification* Market expansion – customers and new product
New market segments	New international markets	Market expansion – international	Market expansion – international and improved product	*Super diversification* Market expansion – international and new product

NEW MARKETS (left vertical axis)

Figure 6.3   Growth vector matrix.

The most ambitious and risky form of growth is a diagonal shift from top left towards bottom right. The more conservative company will tend to plan for growth *either* by altering the product mix *or* by seeking new markets. The most appropriate route across the matrix is determined by competitive strengths and market opportunities.

The dynamics of corporate growth are shown in Figure 6.4.[9] The most common path is shown by the heavier arrows. The simple one-product company looks for new markets to enter with the aim of increasing turnover. It then moves into related spheres of business (e.g. an airline moving into hotel operation). Eventually each related sphere of business is accorded the status of a division with profit responsibility—and they, in turn, seek international opportunities for expansion. The result is a global multinational business. It is shown in the figure that as companies expand in products, markets, functions and technologies, so must the structure of the organisation change.

At each stage of the growth process the nature of the company changes and the need for company and marketing planning becomes more important. One attempt[10] to diagnose these changes in organisational style and planning needs has led to the proposal of typical organisation stereotypes. Demonstrated in Table 6.1, they show that as the mix of markets and products becomes more complex, so the need for integrated planning and control systems becomes more important and the company becomes

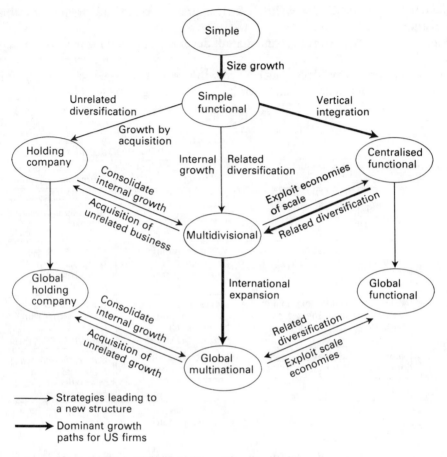

Figure 6.4   How companies develop.

increasingly concerned with the formal statement and achievement of objectives. The price of growth for the owner/manager is loss of control and increasing institutionalisation of decision-making.

Like profitability, the objective of growth has clear implications for marketing planning, involving, as they both do, decisions about market development, market segmentation, market share, marketing costs, pricing, the sales mix, product improvement and new product development.

6.6 CORPORATE PLANNING: FORECASTING

Sales, profits and profitability forecasts are made so that the company will know whether it will achieve its objectives given no change in trading conditions. The starting-point is the sales forecast, which can be made for products or markets, or for the company as a whole. Profit and profitability forecasts can then be derived. Forecasting methods are both quantitative and qualitative.

Table 6.1   *Three stages of organisational development.*

Company characteristics	Stages in development of growing companies		
	I	II	III
1 Product line	Single product or single line	Single product line	Multiple product lines
2 Distribution	One channel or set of channels	One set of channels	Multiple channels
3 Organisation structure	Little or no formal structure, 'one-man-show'	Specialisation based on function	Specialisation based on product–market relationships
4 R&D	Not institutionalised; directed by owner/manager	Increasingly institutionalised search for product or process improvements	Institutionalised search for *new* products as well as for improvements
5 Performance measurement	Personal contact and subjective criteria	Increasingly impersonal, using technical and/or cost criteria	Increasingly impersonal, using *market* criteria (return on investment and market share)
6 Rewards	Unsystematic and often paternalistic	Increasingly systematic	Increasingly systematic, with variability related to performance
7 Control system	Personal control of both strategic and operating decisions	Personal control of strategic decisions, with increasing delegation of operating decisions based on control by policies	Delegation of product–market decisions within existing businesses, with indirect control based on analysis of 'results'
8 Strategic choices	Needs of owner vs needs of firm	Degree of integration; market share objective; breadth of product line	Entry and exit industries; allocation of resources by industry; rate of growth

The 8-step process shown in the diagram in Figure 6.5 attempts to provide a structured approach to the forecasting of sales.[11] The main point behind the early establishment of forecasting objectives is to clarify the purposes to which the forecasts will be put. The corporate planner's reasons for forecasting include the following:

- to identify whether the company can achieve its objectives with no change to either products or markets
- to help allocate resources more effectively
- to provide guidance to departmental/functional planners.

The forecast should enable departmental budgets to be set; help identify marketing opportunities; enable marketing and sales strategies to be devised; help finance and capital funding requirements to be established; and enable labour requirements to be calculated.

Before starting calculations, the forecaster needs to consider such issues as the following:

1. The degree of aggregation of the sales forecasts: is a separate forecast necessary for each sales territory, market segment, product and product group or will one grand, all-encompassing sales forecast suffice?

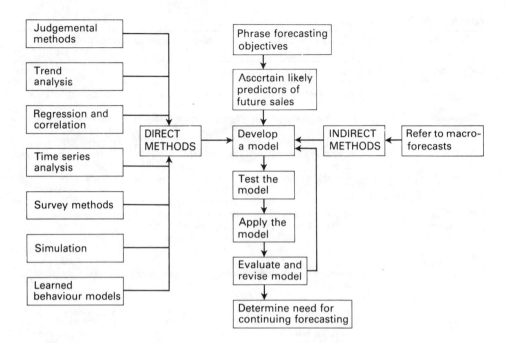

Figure 6.5 The forecasting process.

2. The ability of management to interpret and use the forecasts.
3. The period of time for which forecasts are required: long term or short term—six months, 1 year, or 5 years.
4. The accuracy of the forecast; if large-scale investment decisions are to be based upon the forecast, then a high level of accuracy is required.

The development of an appropriate model is critical in forecasting. The main function of such a model is to 'provide a simplified and understandable representation of systems'.[12] The system that we are particularly interested in representing is the business/environment system which creates sales. Two simple examples which are frequently used in sales forecasting will illustrate the nature of modelling:

$$S_{t+1} = f(S_t, S_{t-1}, S_{t-2} \ldots S_{t-n}) \tag{6.3}$$
$$S_{t+1} = f(A_t, A_{t-1}, D, P) \tag{6.4}$$

where S = sales volume
 t = the present time period
 A = advertising expenditure
 D = distribution
 P = relative price level

Equation 6.3 suggests that sales next year can be directly computed from sales in previous years (time periods $t, t - 1$, going back n-years). This is a simple model of sales forecasting, known as time-series analysis. Equation 6.4 relates next year's sales volume to a history of advertising expenditure (A_t, A_{t-1}), distribution (D) and relative price level (*P*). Models vary in their complexity from specifying a single deterministic cause of sales to the proposal of multiple probabilistic causes.

Any model which is developed as a predictor of sales should be pre-tested, preferably inexpensively on past sales data to test for reliability and validity. If it meets these criteria acceptably, it can be used, then subsequently evaluated and revised.

Two types of models were identified in Figure 6.5—macro- and micromodels. Macroforecasts normally relate to some aggregate measure such as the forecasting of industry demand. Microforecasts are used more widely to forecast company, market or product sales.

Direct methods of sales forecasting

Judgemental methods

Some planners rely heavily on the value judgements or opinions of various experts. These include executives, sales persons, customers, specialists and a host of other technical experts. Various methods of acquiring and manipulating experts' opinions are available. The programme evaluation review technique (PERT), for instance, involves computing a weighted mean of optimistic, pessimistic and most likely estimates.

The judgements-from-the-extremes (or Delphi) method involves initial specification of a wide range of potential sales, followed by sequential steps that narrow the range. This method uses the ability of the expert to move from a general range of sales possibilities to a specific one.

Decision theory requires that a weighted probability of possible sales levels be specified. The weights for the various levels are subjective probabilities provided by the expert. The output is an expected value of sales that reflects these probabilities.

Judgemental models are sometimes criticised as being too subjective or non-scientific in nature. Experience in the use of these techniques has shown that they are capable of producing highly accurate forecasts, provided that their particular assumptions and limitations are fully understood.

Trend analysis

Trend analysis involves the mathematical determination of the trend or overall tendency of the forecast variable (sales) over the historical period under examination. The trend is then projected into the future. Trend analysis can proceed through free-hand smoothing, where the planner plots past sales levels on a graph, visually estimates their line of central tendency and extends this estimated trend line. This method is subject to error on the part of the planner, but is applicable in cases where the analyst wants a rough estimation of future sales in a short period of time, pending the usage of more refined methods.

A more refined method of trend analysis is the method of least-squares. Here the planner, with a set of mathematical manipulations, develops a function which describes the behaviour of the historical data over time. This function, when plotted on a graph of past sales data, forms a line which minimises the vertical deviations of historical data points to the line. The function can be applied to future periods in order to generate forecasts for these periods.

Trends may also be analysed through the computation of a moving average, where the forecast variable's values over a fixed number of time periods are transformed into an arithmetic mean. The mean is computed repeatedly for successive periods of time, so that trends in the means of the variable might be made evident. The planner may choose to weight later years' sales by some factor, on the assumption that later years are more accurate predictors, thus producing a weighted moving average.

Linear trend analysis is sometimes not appropriate. This occurs when the data are distributed in a curvilinear fashion. In this case curve-fitting techniques may be appropriate. Here the planner attempts to find a curve superior to others, in that the deviations from the curve are minimised. Various kinds of curvilinear functions may be used, including parabolas and growth curves. The problem confronting the planner is to find a function that will accurately predict future sales levels.

Regression and correlation

Two widely used forecasting tools are regression and correlation. In the former a function is developed mathematically which expresses the relationship between a dependent variable (sales) and one or more independent variables (as shown earlier in equation 6.4). Correlation, on the other hand, is designed to measure the direction and intensity of this relationship. Normally only those variables manifesting a significant level of correlation are subjected to regression analysis.

Regression may be linear or non-linear, depending on the nature of the regression equation. It may be simple where only one independent variable is considered, or multiple where more than one is subjected to study. Computations for curvilinear and multiple regression usually require a computer.

Regression and correlation analyses are extremely useful to the planner. They generate forecasts based on relationships between logically connected variables, rather than on arbitrary relationships, such as is the case in time series where sales are related to the passage of time. Forecasts developed through regression and correlation possess potential for a substantial degree of causal validity.

Time-series analysis

Time-series methods assume that sales are a function of time; 4 components of time-series analysis are recognised:
- general trend
- cyclical variation
- seasonal variation
- random variation

The time-series technique sometimes requires separate forecasts of each of the 4 elements, based on past patterns. Each element is extracted from the historical data and projected into the future. The sum of the projections constitutes the sales forecast. A number of methods are available for making these projections.

Time-series techniques are appropriate for forecast variables having values that fluctuate in a stable pattern over time. They are less appropriate for variables having values that fluctuate widely as a result of movements in the industry and economy.

Surveys

Some forecasts use surveys on the premiss that buyers are in a position to estimate their future behaviour—often a questionable assumption. Nevertheless, well-conceived and implemented studies are capable of providing numerous insights into future sales fluctuations. (Survey procedures have been examined earlier in this book.)

Akin to surveys are test markets, during which a product is launched into a limited geographic area and its sales results grossed into national equivalents. (This is covered later in the book.)

Simulation
Simulation employs a mathematical model designed to copy the behaviour of the firm in the market-place. Simulation models, of course, require input data. Where possible, the planner seeks objective data which cannot be biased by subjective judgement. In many cases, however, hard data for all of the variables included in the model are not available and the use of judgemental data is necessary.

Learning models
Several forecasting methods are based on learning theory. Their premiss is that purchase behaviour is learned and future sales estimated through an analysis of purchasing patterns currently existing in the market-place.

An important learning-theory technique deals with consumer loyalty and brand switching. Models used for the analysis of these variables attempt to predict the share of the relevant market which various firms will enjoy in future periods. The underlying assumption is that past brand loyalty and brand switching are indicative of future purchase behaviour.

Indirect methods of sales forecasting

Indirect methods of forecasting derive their estimates from macroforecasts. Nandola, Koshal and Koshal have formulated and tested a model designed to forecast national expenditure on restaurant food. The model, detailed below, inputs data about price, income, family size and age to produce the forecast:[13]

$$F = a + bP + cY + dS + ePOP + u \qquad (6.5)$$

where F = family expenditure on restaurant food at 1967 prices
P = price index for food taken away from home (1967 = 100)
Y = median family income
S = average size of family
POP = population aged 16+, as a percentage of the total
u = random error
a, b, c, d, e = coefficients

An individual restaurant proprietor could derive his own forecast from the national estimates.

6.7 CORPORATE PLANNING: INTERNAL AND EXTERNAL AUDIT

These forecasts are made on the assumption that there will be no significant changes in trading conditions. One of the reasons for auditing the company's internal and external environments is to identify potential causes of under- or overachievement.

The external environment's threats and opportunities were discussed in Chapter 2 (see Figure 2.1, p. 32). Here we shall concentrate on the internal audit of corporate strengths and weaknesses.[14] A comprehensive audit will examine finance, sales, management, structure, employees, products, resource allocation and company image.

Finance

The ability of a company to take advantage of future opportunities is based largely upon its financial stability and liquidity position. If the company is pursuing a return on investment objective, the pyramid of ratios shown in Figure 6.6 should enable the planner to provide useful information to management. The pyramid helps in locating areas of financial strength and weakness and enables the planner to initiate remedial action where necessary. For example, if it is noticed a company has annual sales of £250,000 and accounts receivable (debtors) of £100,000, this indicates that 40 per cent of the firm's sales are on credit. This might suggest to the planner that the credit control policy of the firm requires revision. Some of these ratios are more frequently used than others.

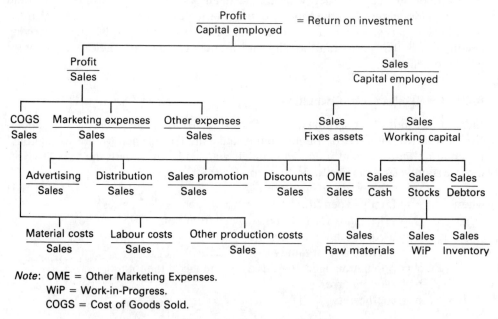

Note: OME = Other Marketing Expenses.
    WiP = Work-in-Progress.
    COGS = Cost of Goods Sold.

Figure 6.6   Ratio pyramid.

The profitability ratio (ROI) can be repeatedly decomposed until weaknesses or the causes of underperformance are identified. Ratios are only meaningful if they are used to compare actual to budgeted performance or to external standards regarded as normal for the industry. Liquidity ratios which indicate a company's ability to meet current financial obligations—and, therefore, its solvency—are also extremely useful. The 2 key liquidity ratios are:

- current ratio—
  current assets/current liabilities
- acid test—
  current assets less stock/current liabilities

The hospitality industry uses a number of sales and financial criteria to judge its performance. The most common statistics are:

- rooms available—not the total number of guestrooms, but the number actually available for use; some rooms are unusable because of broken windows, leaking plumbing, etc.
- rooms occupied—individual, group, or complimentary, expressed as a percentage of rooms available (known as the occupancy level)
- rooms for house use
- out-of-order rooms
- vacant rooms
- double-occupancy rooms
- average room rate—calculated by dividing rooms revenue by rooms occupied
- house count—the total number of guests
- average guest rate—calculated by dividing rooms revenue by house count[15]
- covers—the number of diners at any meal
- average spending power (ASP)

There have been a number of attempts to isolate the key ratios which predict restaurant failure.[16] Critical are:

Liquidity ratios
  current assets/current liability
  working capital/total assets
Profitability ratios
  earnings before interest and taxes/total assets
  earnings before interest and taxes/revenue
  total assets/revenue
Asset utilisation ratio
  working capital/revenue

As with all financial ratio analysis, it is helpful to make intraindustry comparisons. The annual report of consultants Horwath & Horwath, entitled *United Kingdom Lodging Industry*, provides such data for first-class and de luxe hotels.[17] The key statistics in Figure 6.7 show rooms as the major source of revenue. The report shows that regional variations exist. Rooms are a larger part of the London hotel's revenue than that of the provincial hotel. The major expense is payroll. Gross operating profit averages 28 per cent of sales. Marketing expenses are estimated at 2.5 per cent of sales. The terminology is that of the Uniform System of Accounts for Hotels, of which details appear in Chapter 7. The Horwath & Horwath report also includes a host of other useful indicators, including: occupancy levels; average room rate; average guest rate; percentage of repeat business; use of advance reservations; analysis of guest types; details of account settlement; employee statistics; food sales through restaurant; room service; banqueting or bar/lounge; average spending power; beverage sales by facility; sources of cost; and so on.

In 1979 Drury and Murphy undertook a study of the financial performance of the

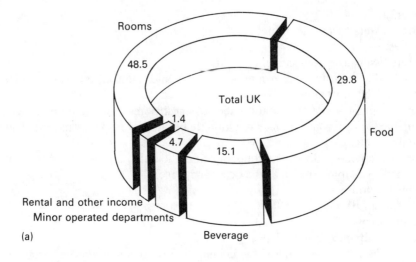

(a)

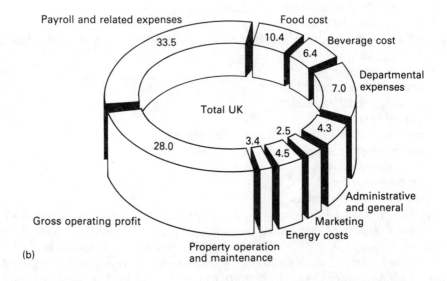

(b)

Figure 6.7 Key hotel statistics: (a) sources of hotel revenue; (b) sources of hotel expense as a percentage of sales revenue.

hotel industry.[18] They observe that averages are misleading because they give no measure of dispersion. Table 6.2 shows the hotel industry's performance on ROI and acid test ratios. The data show a relatively low ROI in the hotel industry compared to all other UK firms, the hotel average being 11.7 per cent. Similarly, hotels are much less liquid. The authors remark that a ratio of less than 0.4 gives cause for concern since the hotel could not easily meet its current financial obligations.

Table 6.2 *ROI and acid test ratios in hotels (1979).*

Return on investment (%):	0–9.9	10–19.9	20–29.9	30–39.9	40+
Hotel industry (%)	50	36	14	0	0
All UK firms (%)	13	40	35	9	3
Acid test	<0.4	0.4–0.59	0.6–0.79	0.8–0.99	1+
Hotel industry (%)	45	9	23	9	14
All UK firms (%)	9	11	20	23	34

Planners should be aware of the limitations of using static ratio analysis to determine the company's financial position. Static ratios reflect the position only for one given point or period of time, whereas the planner is usually endeavouring to gauge a trend.

Management

The management audit should consist of an appraisal of the skills, experience, strengths, weaknesses, aptitudes, flexibility, training needs, job satisfaction, workloads, competence, effectiveness, organisation and efficiency of management. This will serve to identify areas where the company is particularly strong which, in turn, can be used as a basis for future company development.

Employees

A similar audit is here directed at more junior employees than the manager. Once again, it should enable the planner to find areas of strength—and areas in need of strengthening.

Products

The planner will need to know what plans exist for product deletion, addition, or modification.

Hotel products comprise 5 major elements—location, facilities, service, image and price—but customers tend to accept or reject the hotel as a whole.[19] Product-deletion decisions have to be cautiously considered since modification of one or more of the elements (except, in many cases, location) could revive hotel fortunes.

Resource allocation

This part of the internal audit should reveal areas in which the company is either overspending or underspending. Examination can be made of:
- departments
- functions
- budgets
- products
- managers

Resource allocation studies also attempt to make judgements about the relative effectiveness and efficiency of resource use, and to identify any improved distribution of resources.

Company image

The image acquired by a company is developed over time and is difficult to change. It can be an asset or a liability. Certainly, the way in which customers, employees, competition and distributors behave towards the company will, to some extent, be based upon its image. An image is developed from information and experience. It may be accurate or inaccurate, but it is certainly a determinant of consumer purchasing.

6.8 CORPORATE PLANNING: DETERMINING CONSTRAINTS

The audits will have highlighted factors which constrain objective achievement—e.g. forthcoming legislation, new products from competitors, trends in unemployment, exchange rate movements, poorly trained sales management, or low advertising budget. Some of these problems can be resolved by the company, but constraints imposed by the external environment are usually insurmountable.

6.9 CORPORATE PLANNING: DETERMINING PROFIT GAPS

Having revised sales estimates and objectives in the light of internal and external audits, it is now possible to produce a profit gap analysis. This process involves plotting forecast profits for the planning period against profit objectives for the same time period. The graph in Figure 6.8 shows how a least-squares extrapolation of past and present profit

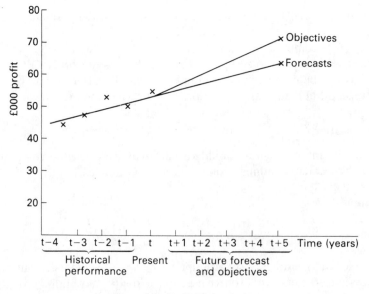

Figure 6.8 Profit gap analysis.

performances produces a forecast profit of £62,000 in year $t + 5$. The objective for $t + 5$ is £70,000; the profit gap is, therefore, £8,000.

Profit gap analysis (PGA) can be approached in 2 main ways, which are largely predetermined by the manner in which the sales forecasts were compiled:

(a) If the sales forecasts were made for the company as a whole, then PGA will refer to the company's overall operations.

(b) If the sales forecasts were originally made for each product or market, or for each sales territory, or for company divisions, then the overall profit forecast will be a compilation of these individual forecasts. This is a highly valued approach to PGA because it more readily allows the planner to identify those products which will be tomorrow's breadwinners or failures, respectively the prime candidates for exploitation or deletion.

6.10 CORPORATE PLANNING: EVALUATE COURSES OF ACTION

The profit gap is now identified as being the amount of profit that needs to be earned by the company from *new* activities—i.e. new products, new markets and new sources of earnings. It identifies a time period over which the earnings should occur and enables criteria for new ventures to be established. New proposals can be subjected to these profit-creation criteria, building upon corporate strengths and marketing opportunities.

6.11 CORPORATE PLANNING: PRODUCE STRATEGIES AND FORMULATE POLICIES AND PLANS

Now that the planner knows what has to be done to fill the profit gap, products and markets are selected for exploitation. We shall examine in Chapter 7 how such marketing strategy develops.

Simultaneously, financial and manpower strategic plans are developed. Together with the marketing plan, they implement the corporate plan in a unified, integrated manner.

6.12 PEOPLE IN PLANNING

People implement plans—a fact which is ignored by most planning systems proposed in the literature. Management by objectives (MBO) enthusiasts have adopted planning systems which recognise the vital role of the manager in the setting and subsequent achievement of objectives.

The MBO process is a multistage set of procedures resulting in the output of a set of action requirements. It is illustrated diagrammatically in Figure 6.9. The figure complements that of the corporate planning process (see Figure 6.1) by showing how career and manpower plans join with other internal and external inputs for objective formulation; MBO suggests that departmental and personal objectives should be

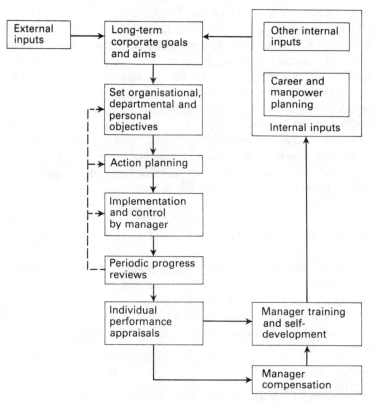

Figure 6.9   A system of management by objectives.

devolved from organisational objectives. Since departmental plans are implemented and controlled by managers, the causes of underachievement (inadequate training, staff development, or career planning; and insufficient compensation) can be identified and rectified. It is fundamental to MBO that only committed and motivated management will successfully create and execute plans. Management involvement in the planning process is detailed in Table 6.3.

Table 6.3   *The major components of MBO.*

The 4 essential elements	The major steps
1 Goal setting	Formulate long-range goals and aims
	Define specific overall organisational objectives
	Establish departmental objectives
	Set individual job objectives
2 Action planning	Formulate action plans
3 Self-control	Implement corrective action
4 Periodic reviews	Review progress towards objectives
	Appraise overall performance, reinforce behaviour and strengthen motivation via:
	manager training and self-development
	compensation
	career and manpower planning

6.13 CHAPTER REVIEW

1. Planning brings about a number of benefits; as well as integrating departmental decisions, it places short-term decisions in the context of long-term objectives and stimulates improvement in forecasting technique.
2. Plans may be corporate/functional/ad hoc and long/medium/short term.
3. Marketing considerations have a formative influence on corporate plans and vice versa.
4. Corporate plans specify the desirable future state for an organisation and the means for its achievement.
5. The main steps in corporate planning are as follows: specify objectives, prepare forecasts, conduct internal and external audit, refine the objectives, determine constraints, determine profit gap, evaluate alternative courses of action and devise strategies/policies/plans.
6. Objectives are formed when top management considers the interests of stakeholders against their own values.
7. Two major corporate objectives of significance to marketers are growth and profitability.
8. Sound objectives are quantitative, measurable, specific, achievable and set to a time scale.
9. Profitability is improved by lifting profits, reducing capital employed, or favourably adjusting the balance between them.
10. Profit increases derive from raising revenues, decreasing costs, or otherwise improving productivity, especially through price adjustments or alterations to the sales mix.
11. Growth is achieved in 2 ways: by entering new markets (segments) or by developing a new product mix.
12. As companies grow, planning and control systems become more formalised.
13. Sales forecasting precedes profit and profitability forecasting.
14. Sales forecasters use 2 methods: direct and indirect.
15. Direct methods include judgement, trend analysis, regression and correlation, time-series analysis, surveys, simulation and learning models.
16. Internal audits investigate strengths and weaknesses; and external audits opportunities and threats.
17. Internal audits examine finance, management, employees, products, resource allocation and corporate image.
18. The profit gap is the difference between forecast and objective profits.
19. The 4 essential elements of MBO are goal setting, action planning, self-control and periodic reviews.

6.14 QUESTIONS

1. What significance have growth and profitability objectives for marketing management?
2. Should marketing issues be the focal point of corporate plans?
3. What objectives can you find mentioned in the annual reports of hospitality companies?
4. Are the aims and objectives of a welfare industrial catering unit likely to be different from those of a major food service company such as Kentucky Fried Chicken?
5. Figure 6.6 (sources of hotel expense) identifies 8 different sources of expense. Are marketing costs fully represented in the 2.5 per cent identified as marketing expense or are some costs of creating and maintaining customer satisfaction concealed elsewhere?

REFERENCES

[1] Whitbread & Co. (1984) *1983–84 Annual Report*.
[2] Stanton, W. J., (1978) (5th edn) *Fundamentals of Marketing*. London: McGraw-Hill, 536.
[3] Ackoff, R. L. (1970) *A Concept of Corporate Planning*. New York: Wiley/Interscience.

[4] See Ansoff, H. I. (1968) *Corporate Strategy*. Harmondsworth: Penguin.

[5] Allied-Lyons Plc (1983) *Annual Accounts, 1982–83*.

[6] See Hotels and Catering Economic Development Committee (1976) *Hotel Prospects to 1985*. London: NEDO.

[7] Comfort Hotels International (1984) *Annual Accounts 1983–84*.

[8] De Vere Hotels & Restaurants Plc (1983). *Annual Accounts 1982–83*.

[9] Galbraith, J. R. and Nathanson, D. A. (1978) *Strategy Implementation: The Role of Structure and Process*. St Paul, MN, West.

[10] Scott, B. R. (1971) Stages of corporate development. Case No. 9–371–291, BP 998, Intercollegiate Case Clearing House, Harvard Business School, Harvard, MA.

[11] Adapted from Gross, C. W., and Peterson, R. T. (1976) *Business Forecasting*. New York: Houghton Mifflin.

[12] Encel, S. (1975) *The Art of Anticipation*. London: Martin Robertson.

[13] Nandola, K., Koshal, M., and Koshal, R. K. (1982) Forecasting restaurant food sales. *Cornell Hotel and Restaurant Administration Quarterly*, 23(2), August, 92–6.

[14] For more detail refer to Stevenson, H. H. (1984) Defining corporate strengths and weaknesses, in Weitz, B. A. and Wensley, R. (eds) *Strategic Marketing: Planning, Implementation and Control*. Boston, MA Kent 68–86.

[15] Brymer, R. A. (1977) Basic lodging computations, in Brymer, R. A. *Introduction to Hotel and Restaurant Management*. Des Moines, IA: Kendall-Hunt, 213-16.

[16] Olsen, M., Bellas, C., and Kish, L. V. (1983) Improving the prediction of restaurant failure through ratio analysis. *International Journal of Hospitality Management*, 2(4), 187–93.

[17] Horwath & Horwath (UK) Ltd (1984) *UK Lodging Industry 1984*.

[18] Drury, J. C. and Murphy, B. (1979) A study of the financial performance of the hotel industry. *HCIMA Journal*, September, 38–41.

[19] Medlik, S. (1980) *The Business of Hotels* London: Heinemann.

—7————————————

Creating Marketing Strategy

7.1 CHAPTER PREVIEW

Chapter 6 reviewed company planning and ended with a promise to examine how a sound marketing strategy can be built. This is the aim of the present chapter. We discuss the differences between policy, strategy and tactics before presenting a review of the process of strategic marketing planning, which includes selection of strategic business units; writing marketing objectives consistent with corporate objectives; deploying resources; constructing a strategic marketing mix; and detailing how the plan is to be implemented, controlled, organised and evaluated.

7.2 LEARNING OBJECTIVES

By the end of this chapter you should be able to:
1. Define these terms: strategy, policy, tactics, marketing strategy, strategic business unit, budget and product positioning.
2. Write marketing objectives.
3. Identify the key components of marketing strategy.
4. Construct a marketing budget.
5. Explain how to organise for, and control the execution of, a marketing plan.
6. Use the criteria inherent in the Boston Consulting Group model and the directional policy matrix to identify strategic business units worthy of future support.

7.3 STRATEGY, POLICY AND TACTICS

A dictionary definition of strategy is:[1]

Generalship, or the art of conducting a campaign.

Strategy, in a business sense, can be defined as:[2]

the fundamental pattern of present and planned resource deployments and environmental interactions that indicates how the organization will achieve its objectives.

One view of the role of strategic planning in the food service business has been expressed thus:[3]

Strategic planning is the managerial process of developing and maintaining an optimal fit between the deployment of an organization's resources and the opportunities of its changing environment.

Strategy is, therefore, the general plan of action for achievement of objectives. The basic corporate strategy decisions are (1) how to use resources, and (2) how to interact effectively with the business environment.

The element of the business environment of prime concern to marketing is the customer. Therefore, marketing strategy is concerned with the selection of target markets and the deployment of marketing resources, so that marketing objectives are achieved.

Strategy differs from both policy and tactics. Policy refers to those more or less permanent constraints or conditions which impinge upon decision-making. For instance, it may be policy to spend no more than 4 per cent of last year's sales revenue on this year's advertising or to review prices twice a year. These are decision rules in which no flexibility is allowed.

Tactics differ from policy and strategy. Tactics are short-term decisions made when implementing strategy for marketing objectives to be achieved within a given timeframe. Eight distinctions have been drawn between strategic and tactical decisions. Strategic decisions are:[4]

- more important to the organisation; inadequate strategy has more damaging effects than inadequate tactics
- made at a higher level
- have a longer time horizon
- formulated continuously and irregularly; tactics are normally fixed to an annual planning cycle
- responses to unstructured problems; tactical decisions such as when to buy advertising space are structured and repetitive
- made following greater information input; strategy is concerned with changing the company to match the environment; environmental data are essential
- broader; strategy is the 'big picture'; tactics are details
- more difficult to evaluate; the outcomes of tactical decisions are evident within the short-term, whereas strategic outcomes may not be felt for several years

7.4 MARKETING STRATEGY

Sirkis and Race identify 5 principles which govern strategic planning:[5]
1. Strategy centres in an organisation can be identified (we call them strategic business units, or SBUs).
2. Planning is data based. Facts are required.
3. Business is not random. Success may be a reflection of the status of the market. If market demand is growing, product demand often follows.
4. Strategic alternatives are limited. The focus may be on marketing, production, or distribution.
5. Business is condition driven more than ambition driven. Environmental factors are significant.

Marketing strategy is developed as a logical extension of the corporate plan, and involves taking a number of related decisions.
1. Confirm corporate objectives.

2. Identify which SBUs to support.
3. Write marketing objectives.
4. Construct strategic marketing mix.
5. Implement, control, organise and evaluate.

This process is:

- disciplined—it is an orderly, sequential flow of analysis and decisions which leads to the production of a sound strategic plan
- flexible—it can be used by hospitality marketers in profit or welfare sectors, in accommodation or food service
- achievement-oriented—it encourages the user to consider alternative marketing objectives and various means of reaching them
- integrated—it ensures that marketing strategy is consistent with the corporate plan and that all marketing mix decisions are designed to achieve chosen objectives

Hospitality marketers adopt a number of approaches to strategic marketing planning.

Yesawich, for example, suggests a 7-step planning sequence for the hotel marketer:[6]

1. Know your property profile.
2. Know your prime prospects.
3. Know your competitors.
4. Establish realistic objectives.
5. Formulate a marketing plan.
6. Implement the plan.
7. Evaluate the plan's effectiveness and adjust as required.

The analysis which takes place at Yesawich's steps 1–3 enables the planner to identify which SBUs to support. Otherwise the planning process develops in much the same way as recommended in this chapter. However, Yesawich fails to relate marketing strategy to corporate objectives.

7.5 RELATIONSHIP TO CORPORATE OBJECTIVES

The first stage in planning marketing strategy is to confirm corporate objectives. As noted in Chapter 6, two corporate objectives of major interest to marketers are growth and profitability.

Growth occurs through adjustments to the product mix—adding new products and dropping or modifying existing products—or increasing the numbers of markets served—domestic or international. Both of these can occur simultaneously.

When the corporate plan demands improvements in profitability, marketers consider the following alternative means for its achievement:

- increase sales by expanding market size
- increase sales by raising market share
- improve productivity by reducing costs or adjusting the sales mix

7.6 SELECTING STRATEGIC BUSINESS UNITS

As businesses grow their products and markets are acquired or developed. The strategist has to decide which to support. Resources are invariably limited, so allocations must be carefully considered. Products or markets likely to contribute most towards objective achievement are better supported.

First, the marketing strategist must identify all strategic business units (SBUs). The SBU is the planning unit. Allied-Lyons is organised into 3 major divisions—the Beer Division, Wines, Spirits and Soft Drinks Division and Food Division. Each of these is an SBU at *group corporate planning level*. Within the Foods Division are over 20 limited companies headquartered in the UK, Republic of Ireland, USA, Europe and Africa. Each is an SBU at *divisional planning level*. Embassy Hotels Ltd and J. L. Catering Ltd are two member companies of the Foods Division. Within J. L. Catering are a number of SBUs, including outdoor catering, Lyons Grills and Fisherman's Wharf speciality restaurants. Strategic marketing plans have been developed for all of these. Embassy Hotels' management must decide whether to regard each hotel property as an SBU. If it does, then individual strategic marketing plans must be created. What is perceived as an SBU will alter from time to time, according to environmental change—as competitors enter or quit markets, introduce or remove products and as technological, social, legal, political and economic changes occur—and the relative strengths and weaknesses of the company.

At *marketing planning level* the SBU is an existing or forthcoming product, a market, or more commonly, a cell of a product–market mix. Figure 7.1 demonstrates this concept for an independent city-centre hotel. The figure shows a 5 × 6 matrix of products against markets. The cells marked with an asterisk (*) are those in which the hotel is already active; the hotel presently allocates resources to 16 of the 30 cells. Over the next planning period this number may contract or expand. The hotel might plan for 6 market SBUs, 5 product SBUs, the 16 current product–market SBUs, or developing SBUs such as the independent pleasure traveller, which does not yet feature in the product–market mix.

PRODUCTS

MARKETS	Overnight accommodation	Exhibition area	Coffee shop	Restaurant	Meetings room
Independent business traveller	*		*	*	
Group business traveller	*	*	*	*	*
Local companies		*			*
Shoppers			*		
Private functions			*	*	*
Loving couples	*			*	

Figure 7.1   Product–market mix.

Medlik comments that 'in most hotels room sales are the largest single source of hotel revenue, and in many of them more sales are generated by rooms than by all the other services combined. Room sales are invariably also the most profitable source of hotel revenue, which yield the highest profit margins and contribute the main share of hotel operating profit'.[7] Horwath & Horwath report that 59 per cent of the revenue of first-class and de luxe hotels in London is from room sales (48.5 per cent, UK-wide). Over 70 per cent of room sales revenue is profit, whereas from food and beverage sales the profit–sales ratio varies between 15 and 30 per cent.[8] Obviously profit-oriented hoteliers will regard rooms as a more attractive SBU than food and beverage.

There are a number of ways of evaluating the relative merits of SBUs. Typically a profit-oriented business will look for indications of:

- long-term competitive advantage
- building on corporate strengths
- prospects for high ROI
- positive cash flow
- market growth
- growth in market share

Clearly information from internal and external audits, and sales forecasts, as explained in Chapter 6, is used to produce a prognosis for each SBU.

It is particularly important to examine the marketing mixes of competitors when conducting the external audit. Figure 7.2 shows a partial audit form, which when completed would identify the relative strengths and weaknesses of competitors. Some of the judgements entered $(-,?,0,+$ indicate whether the competitor is worse, 'don't know', equal, or better) are objective, others are subjective.[9]

In recent years a number of models which aim to assist marketing management to make better decisions about the allocation of resources between SBUs have been developed. Most notable are the profit impact of management strategies (PIMS) model and the business portfolio models used by the Boston Consulting Group and others.[10]

The PIMS model derives from research into the causes of superior profitability and cash flow. Nine influences appear to account for higher performance as follows:

1. Investment intensity. Business requiring heavy investment in plant or stock show lower ROI.
2. Productivity. Business with higher value added (difference between selling price and material costs) per employee are more profitable.
3. Market share. Higher-share companies earn more profit and have better cash flows.
4. Market growth. Businesses in high growth markets produce more profit but have poorer cash flow.
5. Quality. The better the perceived quality of product (by customer), the more profitable the business.
6. Innovation. The more innovative companies are better financial performers.
7. Manufacturing. Companies in stable, mature markets earn more profit by manufacturing, rather than buying in, products for resale. In other markets the opposite is true.
8. Cost push. Wage, salary and material cost increases have a complex effect on profitability depending upon the business' ability to absorb or pass on costs.
9. Current strategy. The costs of striving to achieve a satisfactory level of performance

PRODUCT	Comp. A				Comp. B				Comp. C			
	−	?	○	+	−	?	○	+	−	?	○	+
1 Customer acceptance												
2 Customer satisfaction in use												
3 Product quality level(s)												
4 Adequacy of offerings												
5 Services provided												
a Extent												
b Quality												
PLACE												
1 Customer accessibility												
2 Suitability of site for:												
a Services offered												
b Attracting customers												
3 Customer traffic potential												
4 Appearance of facility												
a Outside												
b Inside												
5 Selling areas												
a Adequacy of space (capacity)												
b Attractiveness												
c Layout												
6 Parking facilities												
a Adequacy												
b Customer convenience												
7 Drawing power of neighbouring firms												
8 Customer image of facilities												

Figure 7.2   Partial marketing audit form (omitting promotion and price).

in any of the above factors can be high. For example, whereas high market share produces strong positive cash flows, the push to obtain high market actually drains the company of cash.

Two business portfolio models are the market growth/market share model developed by the Boston Consulting Group (the BCG model) and the market attractiveness/competitive capabilities model (the directional policy matrix). The BCG model assesses SBU alternatives against 2 criteria: market growth, and relative market share. Market growth determines the ease, and cost, with which improvements in market share can be gained. In low-growth, declining, or static markets the market share gains are generally at the expense of competitors, whereas in high-growth markets gains can be made as competitors' sales volume remains undisturbed. Growth markets also 'provide the ideal vehicles for investment, for ploughing cash into a business in order to see it compound'.[11]

Relative market share (the company's market share divided by that of the largest other competitor) is a measure of the cash-generating power of the SBU. The higher the relative market share, the higher should be a company's margins. The experience, or learning, curve effect suggests that the total cost of producing and marketing an item reduces as experience and volume rise. The causes are:[12]

- productivity improvement due to technological change at higher levels of output
- economies of scale and specialisation
- product modification to achieve lower unit costs
- displacement of less efficient factors of production

The two criteria—market growth and relative market share—form the axes of the graph in Figure 7.3. Each SBU falls into one of 4 categories: stars, cash cows, dogs and question-marks. The main characteristics of each are detailed below.

Stars	Need large amounts of cash to maintain share
	Generate large amounts of cash
	Balanced cash flow
	Turns into cash cow if share maintained when growth slows, otherwise eventually becomes a dog
Cash cows	Strong market share, low unit costs
	Profits and cash generation high
	Fund investments elsewhere
Dogs	Poor competitive position
	Low volume, low margins, low profits
	Negative cash flows
Question marks	Cash needs high because of market growth
	Cannot recover cash unless becomes star and eventually a cash cow, otherwise turns into dog

According to Hedley, the appropriate strategy for a business involves 'striking a balance in the portfolio such that the cash generated by the cash cows, and by those questionmarks and dogs which are being liquidated, is sufficient to support the company's stars and to fund the selected questionmarks through to dominance'.[13]

The directional policy matrix (DPM), as illustrated in Figure 7.4, uses the company's competitive capabilities and the business sector's prospects as axes. The competitive

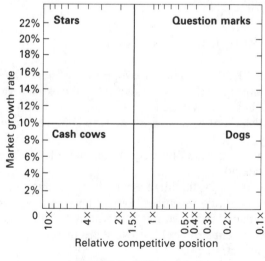

Figure 7.3 BCG model.

capabilities of a company can be judged as strong, average, or weak by reference to its market share, production capabilities and product development practices. The prospects of a business sector can be rated as attractive, average, or unattractive by reference to its growth rate, record of profit earning, availability of factors of production and environmental constraints such as legislation.[14]

Nine matrix positions are identified. Every SBU is allocated to one of the positions and the appropriate strategy selected. An SBU in the leader position will aim to maintain market share and develop extra capacity to cope with market growth; SBUs in the double-or-quit position could be tomorrow's high-fliers. Some should be supported and others dropped. The limitations and applications of these approaches have been analysed elsewhere.[15]

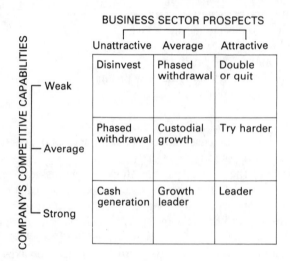

Figure 7.4   Directional policy matrix.

7.7 WRITING MARKETING OBJECTIVES

Having picked some SBUs worthy of more support, the marketing strategist must now specify what his company wishes to achieve. Objectives may vary according to the prospects for the SBU as follows:

1. Maintain market share of *cash cows* in order to generate strong positive cash flow (milking strategy).
2. Hold market share of *stars* in order to create the cash cows of the future (maintenance strategy).
3. Lose market share of *dogs*; liquidate assets (harvest strategy).
4. Since *question-marks* drain resources in the longer term unless their market share can be improved, there are two strategic alternatives: build market share to become a future star (investment strategy), or lose share by selling off or discontinuing the product (divestment strategy).

It has been argued that not all dogs need be unprofitable. An independent hotelier with very little share of the total business travel market can be very successful, provided that occupancy levels are high: 'We have found that a small market share is not necessarily a handicap; it can be a significant advantage that enables a company to compete in ways that are unavailable to its larger rivals.'[16]

Marketing objectives for the hospitality industry are phrased in a number of ways:

- *market growth*—in the early stages of market development (e.g. the development of drive-in fast-food outlets in the UK) operators are often more interested in expanding the total market than competing for share. Co-operatively operators can share the costs of promoting the product and educating prospective customers. Their aim is to stimulate primary demand (for the category) rather than secondary demand (for the brand)
- *market share*—which is defined as the proportion of demand obtained in a product category, market or product-market cell, is widely used by national companies
- *sales volume* (covers or guests) and *sales value* (covers × ASP or guest × average guest rate)—Comfort Hotels International report the objectives of higher occupancy levels and higher average room rate.[17] Jointly they would substantially improve sales volume, and because the company was already in profit, would enhance the bottom line. Similarly, De Vere Hotels & Restaurants note that even modest increases in turnover can have a 'disproportionate beneficial effect . . . on our net profits'[18]
- *market penetration*—which is defined as the percentage of prospective customers in the target market, who have tried the product at least once, is used by companies who have particular reasons for wanting to sell to a specified group of customers. For example, a new public house concept, specifically designed for the 18–25-year-old would set its objectives this way
- *trial purchases*—these are the numbers of first-time purchases made by the target market
- *repeat purchases*—these are the numbers of customers making a second, third, or further purchase. A company may aim to stimulate a 20 per cent trial level in a target market, followed by a 50 per cent repurchase level (i.e. 10 per cent of the target market will buy at least twice) in order to achieve a desirable ROI.

Condominium hotels and timeshare hotels have more complicated objectives.

A condominium hotel is one in which some or all of the rooms or suites are owned by individuals or organisations. The hotel provides food and beverage, and other common areas and facilities. In such situations the primary marketing objective is often to sell rooms; failing this, the secondary objective is to let rooms to a high occupancy level. A timeshare hotel is one in which rooms or suites are owned for a defined period of time (normally in multiples of one week). The owner uses his rooms for this period, and if he decides he has no future requirement for them in coming years, can either attempt to resell or let them. The developer keeps a week or so for maintenance.

There are a number of timeshare practices in the UK:

1. The purchaser receives a lease for a specified time of the year in a particular property.
2. The purchaser joins a club which holds the lease.
3. The purchaser is licensed to use the property.
4. The purchaser is given an interest in the freehold of the building.

5. The purchaser buys shares in a company which owns the building and receives
   dividends in the form of occupancy rights.

For a hotelier the costs of marketing can be extremely high (a 30-room property sold off
in two-week periods requires 780 sales to be made before the entire building is
timeshare owned) but benefits are gained by freeing capital for use elsewhere or
obtaining guaranteed income from management charges.[19]

It is quite possible for a specific room or suite to be timeshare owned for only part of
the year. The hotel manager would retain the right to let the suite whilst it is not owned.
Such hotels also have dual objectives—to sell timeshare units, and failing that, to let the
rooms in conventional hotel style. Management, as in condominium hotels, continues
to provide food and beverage and other services. A number of hotel properties operate
in conventional, timeshare and condominium styles.

7.8   THE STRATEGIC MARKETING MIX

A planned strategic marketing mix should:
- enable objectives to be achieved and should, therefore, be budgeted and
  controlled. It should have a time duration over which its effect is to be measured
- ideally be product–market cell specific, although it is quite satisfactory to produce
  product plans or market plans
- be integrated. Each element of the marketing mix—product, price, promotion and
  place—should complement the others
- be built upon sound principles of marketing and knowledge of consumer
  behaviour

Prior to evolving the marketing mix, 3 preliminary decisions have to be made:
1. Selection of target market.
2. Positioning of the product.
3. Determination of the means of market entry.

Whilst specifying target markets, decisions are made about whether to mass-market or
segment; and if segmenting, is one or more than one segment to be targeted? Finally,
what sort of person or organisation is the target and what benefits do they seek? What
are their buying motives and how many are there?

Product positioning underpins the development of the marketing mix. The marketer
decides how he wants his product to be perceived (in comparison with competitors) by
his target markets, be they consumers or intermediaries. Lewis comments that hotel
positioning statements must[20]
- be related to the needs and wants of the customer
- create an image
- promise the delivery of benefits
- differentiate the property from competitors

Many things could happen to influence the target markets' perception of the product.
New competitors might enter above, below, or alongside the product; a poorly
executed advertising campaign may create an inappropriate image; consumer tastes
may change; and legislation may be introduced which, for instance, makes food appear
less nutritious and, therefore, less attractive to the consumer.

The marketer's response to these changes could be to
- do nothing
- attempt to reposition his product through redesigning the marketing mix
- remove the product from the market

The position which is optimal for the product is the one which offers sales and profit potential in a relatively free competitive environment. The job of the marketing mix is to give an image to the product which is consistent with the desired product position.

One way in which consumers often compare products is in terms of quality and price. This too can be a useful approach for marketers, who can calculate if there is room for another product positioned somewhat differently in terms of these two variables, within an existing market or market segment. The main alternative strategies are identified in Figure 7.5.[21]

		PRICE		
		High	Medium	Low
QUALITY	High	Premium strategy	Penetration strategy	Superbargain strategy
	Medium	Overpricing strategy	Average quality strategy	Bargain strategy
	Low	Hit and run strategy	Shoddy-goods strategy	Cheap goods strategy

Figure 7.5 Positioning strategies.

When developing strategy for an SBU in which the company is not yet active, an early decision has to be made about the means of market entry. There are a number of options available to hospitality marketers
1. Acquire a going concern, retaining management.
2. Build/purchase and operate independently.
3. Build/purchase and offer a contract to a management company (hotels).
4. Acquire a management contract (Marriott, Hilton, Sheraton and Intercontinental all operate hotels under contract; in a similar way the pub manager in a tied house operates under contract).
5. Acquire a franchise.
6. Establish a joint venture (Whitbread-Pepsico launched Pizza Hut (UK) in this way).

Each of these has particular merits and they are discussed in greater detail in subsequent chapters on distribution. At this point, we simply note that both franchising and contracting impose major constraints on the marketing mix. For example, Kentucky Fried Chicken franchisees are tied in to a product, price, promotion and retailing system which offers no scope for self-expression. Where freedom exists, several key strategic decisions have to be made for each of the Four Ps—product, price, promotion and place.

(a) Product
1. *Quality.* What is to be the perceived quality of the product? Consistency with product position and suitability for the target market are essential.

2. *Life cycle*. For how long is the product to be marketed? Is it a replacement for, or modification of, another product? What is its planned commercial life?
3. *Single-product item/multiple-product line*. Management must decide whether to market a single product or several. Whereas Spud-u-like, the fast-food chain, has a single style of food retailing, Berni Inns have 3—Burgundy Room, Berni and Eleven Eleven. Trusthouse Forte (THF) recognises 5 styles of hotel operation in its organisation.
4. *Branding*. Most hospitality products are branded. The main question for the multiproduct business is whether to use individual brandnames, a generic family brand for all products; or individual brands associated with the company name. A subsidiary issue is whether to launch 2 or more brands into the same market. This is known as multiple branding and it is popular amongst operators hoping to capture brand-switching customers. At Heathrow Airport, for example, THF has several hotel properties.
5. *Augmentation*. How is the core product to be augmented, so that its competitive edge is enhanced? (See Chapter 8.)

(b) Price
1. *Level*. What is to be rack rate (hotel), ASP, or price of major items on the menu? Consistency with product position and suitability for target market are essential.
2. *Discounts*. Are these to be offered? Group rates, business rates, contract rates for heavy users; settlement seasonal and cash discounts; and commissions to intermediaries: what is to be the overall price structure?

(c) Promotion
1. *Emphasis*. Is the emphasis to be on selling, sales promotion, public relations, or advertising? (This is treated in subsequent chapters.)
2. *Communication theme*. The communication theme (also known as copy strategy or basic copy platform) is the core element or basic message of marketing communication. The theme is generally reflected in all communication materials— advertising, sales promotions, sales aids, price lists, brandname, brochures, livery, letterheads, and so on. It should be consistent with the quality and price of the product.
3. *Push or pull strategy*. Pull strategy is usually typified by heavy consumer advertising. The primary aim is to pull the consumer towards the product. The alternative push strategy occurs when a marketer tries to push the product into and through channels of distribution. This normally involves the use of advertising and personal selling to obtain the co-operation and involvement of distributors.

(d) Place
1. *Form of distribution*. Direct sell or availability through intermediaries? Which intermediaries? Which forms of reservation system?
2. *Location*. How many units are to be operated? There is only one Dorchester Hotel in the UK (exclusive distribution), but there are dozens of Happy Eaters (extensive distribution).

Budgets for each of the Four Ps are compiled. Allocated between the Four Ps are the costs of: (1) registering and protecting trademarks or designs; (2) new product development; (3) product research; (4) discounts off rack rate or normal menu prices, and commissions to intermediaries; (5) production costs for all print or broadcast materials; (6) fees to sales promotion, advertising, or public relations agents; (7) costs of buying space/time in various media; and (8) sales staff remuneration.

On to these costs of marketing are added salaries of marketing/sales management, a proportion of rent, rates and other overheads, secretarial staff wages and a contingency allowance for emergencies.

Naturally budgeting practices vary from company to company. It has been noted that marketing strategy varies according to the status of the hospitality company; 4 levels of status exist as follows:

1. Market leaders hold the largest market share in the relevant product-market and strive to increase the market size, protect their market share and, if feasible, expand share.
2. Market challengers are companies with major but not leading market shares, who strive aggressively for further market share through innovation and risk-taking.
3. Market followers may be major or minor companies. Essentially they follow the successful strategies of the market leader, but instead of chasing market share emphasise profitability.
4. Market nichers are specialist companies who operate in product markets overlooked or consciously ignored by the bigger companies. Profitability is often high because of market monopoly.[22]

Meidan and Lee point out that hotel market leaders expand through acquisition and retain or enhance market share through powerful referral or reservation systems and heavy advertising and promotion.[23]

7.9 IMPLEMENTATION, CONTROL AND ORGANISATION

Implementation

The overall strategy now must be developed into an action plan. The detailed implications of strategic decisions must be considered. For example, if strategy dictates that advertising dominates promotion, then decisions must be made upon: (1) advertising objectives; (2) which of the media to use; (3) which advertising vehicles within the medium; (4) how the basic copy strategy is to be executed; (5) who is to manage the advertising budget; (6) the timing; and (7) how to measure its effect. (These and all other detailed marketing mix decisions are investigated in subsequent chapters.) In addition, the action plan would specify how the plan is to be controlled, the appropriate form of marketing organisation for achievement of the objectives and the management responsible for its implementation, control and evaluation.

Implementation requires resource deployment. Resources which are known collectively as the Four Ms—manpower, materials, money and machinery—are deployed, so that SBU marketing objectives are achievable.

Control

As we have seen, the marketing plan specifies objectives and allocates resources. The task of evaluation is to assess whether (and how) objectives have been achieved; in doing so it deals with the issues of effectiveness (has achievement occurred?) and efficiency (how economically have the resources been used to achieve objectives?).

Control is required to keep the marketing plan on a trajectory which will achieve objectives. It is concerned with detecting, correcting and preventing unacceptable variances from the trajectory.[24] Variance is of 2 forms: overachievement and underachievement. Although substantial underachievement is invariably unacceptable, this may also be true of overachievement. A holiday resort positioned as quiet and peaceful could receive damaging long-term publicity if it became too popular. Control involves comparing budgeted to actual performance. If no variance exists, monitoring continues. If variance occurs, the causes are identified and corrective action taken as necessary.

Several control techniques have evolved and are widely used:
- budgeting
- marketing cost analysis
- ratio analysis
- the marketing audit
- experimentation
- reporting systems
- management-by-exception

For *budgeting* to be successful a number of requirements must be met:
- there must be an approved and agreed marketing plan
- the plan should specify measurable objectives and a timeframe for achievement
- top management should support the plan; if they don't, why should subordinates be reprimanded for producing unacceptable variance?
- costing and budgeting expertise
- pertinent, accurate, timely and usable marketing and costing data
- managerial decisiveness; and willingness to introduce corrective tactics
- marketing expertise to ensure that the true causes of variance are identified and that the corrective tactics chosen are effective

A budget is a quantitative revenue and cost plan to achieve stated objectives. Budgets may be compiled for any planning period, but perhaps most useful for control purposes is the rolling budget. Typically this is a monthly breakdown of revenues and costs into which the effects of seasonality can be built. Month-by-month and year-to-date data are normally listed.

Nykiel recommends zero-based budgeting be applied to the annual planning cycle. This approach starts from the basic premiss that no expenditure is justified simply because it was spent last year.[25] The main disadvantage of this approach is that it precludes the establishment of a long-term perspective. Not all marketing objectives can be achieved in a 1-year cycle and development of a planned marketing strategy is better viewed as a long-term investment. Zero-based budgeting is better applied to tactical expenditure.

American hoteliers have made widespread use of a uniform system of accounting which aims to be 'a manual of instructions for preparing standard financial statements and schedules of the various operating and productive units which make up a hotel'.[26] A British equivalent has been proposed but is very rarely applied.[27] The American system defines marketing as the efforts of a hotel to obtain and retain customers. Not all associated costs are included in the marketing budget. For example, travel agency and tour operators' fees and the expenses of a reservation system are charged to rooms, not marketing. However, the marketing budget includes sales, advertising, merchandising, public relations and publicity, research, and fees, commissions and other selling and promotional expenses, as shown in Figure 7.6.

Travel agency commissions vary by location of hotel and by source of bookings. A Caribbean operator would expect to lose nearly 10 per cent of sales revenue to travel agents because the majority of bookings are received through this channel. However, a provincial city hotel catering for business travellers would pay very little commission. First-class hotels in the UK lose up to 2.5 per cent of room sales to commissions.[28]

Marketing cost analysis aims to establish which SBUs are most profitable. Each type of marketing cost is allocated between products or markets on an agreed basis. Direct selling expenses, such as hotel salesforce salaries, commissions and expenses, can be apportioned between products (conference facilities, banqueting, etc.) on the basis of call reports which indicate time spent selling each product; the same expenses can be allocated between markets (e.g. travel agents and incentive travel planners) on the basis of time spent making sales calls on each type. Indirect selling costs, such as supervision, training and administration, can be allocated in proportion to direct selling time.

Where marketing management is charged with achieving profitability rather than sales, a closer understanding of the costs–revenue–profit relationship is essential. Consequently variances between budgeted and actual covers, guests, ASP and average guest rate are studied on a monthly or, in some cases, weekly or daily basis. Figure 7.7 is a typical example of marketing cost analysis documentation.[29]

Ratio analysis is used as described in Chapter 6. Standards are set and performance is judged against them. Advertising costs are commonly calculated as a percentage of sales.

The marketing audit is an annual review of the internal marketing system and external marketing environment which checks whether the chosen strategy is still appropriate and whether the marketing system is operating effectively and efficiently. The external marketing audit provides environmental data in much the same way as described in Chapter 2. The internal audit checks

- the application and soundness of existing control devices
- managerial compliance with corporate policies and plans
- security of marketing assets such as literature, customer files, sales records and research information
- the quality of information supplied to and by marketing management
- managerial control of subordinates
- systems of delegation, communication, authority, responsibility and planning

Experimentation, as described in Chapter 3, brings caution into marketing expenditure. Few marketers are able to claim that they know with certainty the sales effect of a particular marketing mix. Experimentation permits trial without large-scale

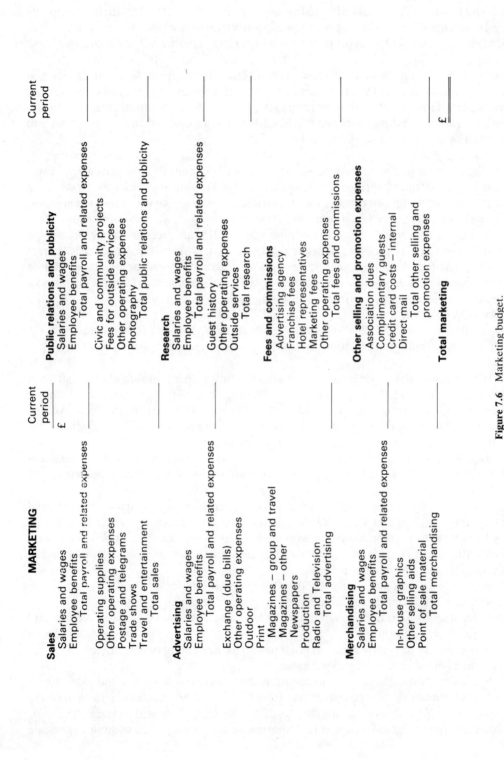

Figure 7.6   Marketing budget.

Period – four weeks ending

Bedrooms	Budget	Actual	Remarks
1 Percentage of rooms occupied			
2 Percentage of beds occupied			
3 Average room rate			
4 Average spend per guest			
5 Average length of stay			
Function rooms			
1 Occupancy percentage			
2 Number of functions			
3 Average spend on food			
4 Average spend on drink			
Food			
1 No. of covers – lunch			
2 No. of covers – evening			
3 Average spend			
4 Percentage food cost to sales			
5 Percentage gross profit			
6 Drink sales per cover			
Beverages			
Sales of spirits – £s			
Sales of wine – £s			
Sales of beer – £s			
Sales of other – £s			
%drink cost of sales			
%gross profit			
Stock turnover on wine			
Stock turnover on spirits			

Figure 7.7   Marketing cost analysis documentation.

expenditure and risk. Allied-Lyons, for example, report that they experiment with different catering concepts prior to widespread introduction.[30]

Reporting systems allow management to evaluate the performance of sales staff and others. Sales staff are widely expected to provide written or oral reports on calls made, results of calls (bookings received), prospecting (identification of prospective new customers) and information about competitors or customer reaction to the implementation of the marketing plan. Reporting systems are very important in the hotel business where sales-staff turnover is high; they ensure continuity of customer service. *Management-by-exception* is a reporting system, often computer based, which reports only when unacceptable levels of variance have been recorded.

Although control is desirable in marketing, it is far from being simple to achieve; there are 5 reasons which can be identified as follows.

1. *Creativity*. Prior to the implementation, marketers are frequently called on to judge the relative merits (and probable sales effects) of creative proposals for advertising and sales promotion. Unfortunately no universal laws govern the creativity–sales relationship and there is scope for considerable ineffective resource use.
2. *Interrelationships with other functions*. The success of a marketing plan can be hampered by sloppy housekeeping standards and inadequate credit control.
3. *Third parties*. Hospitality marketers rely heavily on external third parties—

advertising agents, public relations agents, travel agents, reservation bureaux and airlines. Their inadequacies could spell the plan's failure.
4. *Environment.* The marketing mix gives incomplete control over consumer purchasing. A host of uncontrollable environmental factors also play an influential role.
5. Ad hoc *activities.* Many hospitality activities, especially in hotel and outdoor catering, are one-offs. Whilst each can be costed and controlled individually, seeking to make a profit on each event, be it a conference or a tennis tournament, is short-sighted. The long-term view might permit short-term losses in order to build a continuing future relationship with an important customer.

Organisation

In the hospitality business organisations range from the sole trader to the multinational corporation. No one organisational structure of the marketing function is appropriate for all.

The marketing organisation can be defined as the relationship of functions and authority arranged to accomplish efficiently marketing objectives. As originally remarked by Chandler, structure follows strategy![31] The right structure facilitates the achievement of objectives. Accordingly organisational structures should change as objectives and strategy change. Unfortunately, in many cases, strategy is imprisoned by structure.

The hospitality industry, with some major exceptions such as MacDonalds, is not noted for its marketing orientation. Consequently responsibility for the various components of strategy are spread wide or may not be recognised at all. It has been noted that:[32]

> Depending on the size and structure of the organization, the marketing manager may be dependent on a half-dozen or more executives. Reservation, reception and registration are traditionally the responsibility of the front office. Baggage, exhibits, freight and elevator service depend on the service chief. The steward must be relied on to buy, the chef to prepare and the banquet department to serve. The problems of credit, spotlights and microphones, housekeeping and public safety bring still others onto the scene. Without line authority, the marketing manager finds it difficult organizationally to demand performance at the time, place and manner he has promised.

Where identifiable marketing organisations exist, they fall into 5 major categories, being arranged around:
1. Functions.
2. Products.
3. Customers/markets.
4. Geographic areas.
5. A mixture of the above.
In a functional marketing organisation the sales or marketing director/manager/vice-president has reporting to him specialists who have responsibility for sales, advertising/promotions and marketing research. One such plan suggests that the marketing manager should be of the same status as the operations manager (see Figure 7.8).[33]
In larger, multiproduct companies marketing is frequently organised around

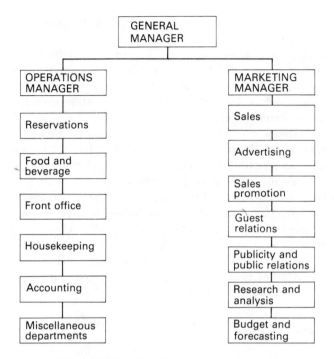

Figure 7.8 Functional marketing organisation.

products, with a product or brand manager taking responsibility for the sales of one or more. The banqueting manager and conference manager are product managers. Companies serving several identifiable customer groups sometimes organise around markets, using the title market manager. The travel trade sales manager is a market manager.

International hotel companies generally have 3 tiers of marketing organisation—i.e. the head office, region and unit.[34] Corporate marketing executives at head office co-ordinate marketing planning, develop and buy advertising, and offer public relations and promotional assistance to unit managers. Marriott Hotels, for example, runs product planning, market development and marketing services from its Washington, DC, head office. Regional sales offices prospect for new business and liaise with incentive travel planners and travel agents. Sales directors of individual hotels follow up sales leads from the regional offices and are responsible for developing local trade. Organisations of this international kind are both functionally and geographically structured.

7.10 PLANNING IN PRACTICE

A review of marketing planning in international hotel firms shows variation in practice. Each Hilton hotel produces its own marketing plan which includes an assessment of its competitive position, a market segmentation study, positioning statement and budget. This is prepared by the general manager. Intercontinental's practice is to prepare individual marketing plans for each hotel and integrate them to provide an aggregate marketing goal for the firm.

Sheraton's marketing plans are produced at unit level by the general manager. He analyses past and present business by market segment (individual business travellers, aircrew and groups) to discover the causes of changing patterns of demand, and then attempts to forecast future demand. Corporate marketing staff refine and assist in developing unit marketing plans.[35]

Best Western Hotels, an international consortium of independent hotels, has a marketing committee which produces a budgeted plan. The budget is inspected by each hotel member and a meeting convened to obtain approval. Overall the marketing objectives are to 'sustain and increase profitable occupancy of all member hotels'. The target markets are hotel users and recommenders whilst members are positioned as 'dependable hotels of character, with high standards, giving value for money'. The main elements of strategy are national advertising, public relations, installation of a reservation system, face-to-face selling to the travel trade and conference buyers, special promotions (normally with a tactical, short-term aim) and effective print material. In 1970 Best Western appointed its first director of marketing.[36]

7.11 CHAPTER REVIEW

1. Strategy differs from policy and tactics.
2. Marketing strategy is concerned with the selection of target markets and the deployment of marketing resources, so that marketing objectives are achieved.
3. Marketing strategy is developed from the corporate plan.
4. The main components of marketing strategy are: confirmation of corporate objectives, selection of SBUs, writing marketing objectives and construction of a strategic marketing mix; and then implementing, controlling, organising and evaluating the plan.
5. At marketing planning level the SBU is a product, market, or product–market.
6. In choosing which SBUs to support a profit-oriented business would look for indications of long-term competitive advantage, building on corporate strengths, prospects for high ROI, positive cash flow, market growth and growth in market share.
7. The PIMS model has identified a number of correlates of high profitability.
8. The criteria used by the Boston Consulting Group to compare between SBUs are market growth and relative market share; SBUs are subsequently classified as stars, cash cows, question-marks and dogs.
9. The criteria used in the directional policy matrix to compare between SBUs are the company's competitive capabilities and the business sector's prospects.
10. Marketing objectives generally stress market growth, market share, sales volume, market penetration, trial purchases and repeat purchases.
11. Prior to constructing a strategic marketing mix, decisions must be made about target markets, product positioning and means of market entry.
12. Product positioning refers to the way a product is perceived by customers or intermediaries *vis-à-vis* competitors.
13. Products are often positioned in terms of price and quality.
14. Key strategic marketing decisions are made about: product (quality, life cycle, item or line, branding and augmentation); price (level and discounts); promotion (emphasis, push or pull and communication theme); and place (form of distribution and location).
15. Marketing strategies vary according to the status of the marketer—leader, challenger, follower, or nicher.

16. Marketing control is applied to keep the SBU on target for objective achievement. Control requires comparison of actual to budgeted performance.
17. Control techniques include budgeting, marketing cost analysis, ratio analysis, the marketing audit, experimentation, reporting systems and management-by-exception.
18. Structure follows strategy.
19. Marketing organisation is functional, product-oriented, market-oriented, or a mix of 2 or more of these forms.
20. Planning practice in the hospitality industry is varied.

7.12 QUESTIONS

1. To what extent does marketing strategy derive from corporate strategy?
2. How might the strategic marketing planning process be applied to:
    (a) catering on a cross-channel ferry?
    (b) catering for schoolchildren?
    (c) a hot and cold croissant retailer at a major city bus terminus?
3. What marketing objectives are most appropriate for:
    (a) an independent 5-star capital-city hotel?
    (b) a budget hotel which is part of a national group?
    (c) a food and beverage department operated as a service (rather than as a profit centre) to guests of a 3-star business traveller's hotel?
    (d) an international chain of fast-food retailers?
4. How does a product positioning statement influence strategic marketing mix decisions?
5. Obtain the recent annual report of a multiproduct hospitality company. To what extent can the BCG and DPM models be applied when selecting SBUs to support?
6. Distinguish between push and pull promotional strategy? Give hospitality examples.
7. What marketing control techniques could be effectively applied by an independent family restaurant proprietor?
8. Why should structure follow strategy?

REFERENCES

[1] *Chambers 20th Century Dictionary* (1983 edn).
[2] Hofer, C. W. and Schendel, D. (1981) *Strategy Formulation: Analytical Concepts.* West.
[3] Lawless, M. J. and Hart, C. W. (1983) Forces that shape restaurant demand. *Cornell Hotel and Restaurant Administration Quarterly*, 24(3), November, 7–17.
[4] Steiner, G. A. and Miner, J. B. (1977) *Management Policy and Strategy: Text, Readings and Cases.* London: Macmillan.
[5] Sirkis, R. L. and Race, S. M. (1981) Principles of strategic planning for the food service firm, *Cornell Hotel and Restaurant Administration Quarterly*, 22(1), May, 35–41.
[6] Yesawich, P. C. (1977) Know your prime prospects. *Cornell Hotel and Restaurant Administration Quarterly*, 17(4), February, 11–16.
[7] Medlik, S. (1980) *The Business of Hotels* London: Heinemann, 35.
[8] Horwath & Horwath International (1984) *UK Lodging Industry*.
[9] Stevens, R. E. (1977) Careful analysis first step to successful hotel and motel marketing, in Brymer, R. A. (ed.) *'Introduction to Hotel and Restaurant Management.* Des Moines, IA Kendall-Hunt, 177–83.
[10] For an excellent review of these models see Weitz, B. A. and Wensley, R. (1984) *Strategic Marketing: Planning, Implementation and Control.* Kent; references 11, 12, 13, 14, 15 and 16, and the articles in reference 23, are cited in this volume.
[11] See Hedley, B. (1977) Strategy and the business portfolio. *Long Range Planning*, 10, February, 9–15.

[12] Hedley, B. (1976) A fundamental approach to strategy development. *Long Range Planning*, **9**, December, 2–11.
[13] Hedley, B. (1977) op. cit.
[14] Robinson, S. J. Q., Hichens, R. E., and Wade, D. P. (1978) The directional policy matrix—tool for strategic planning. *Long Range Planning*, **11**, June, 8–15.
[15] Wensley, R. (1981) Strategic marketing: betas, boxes or basics. *Journal of Marketing*, Summer, 173–83.
[16] See Hamermesh, R. G., Anderson, M. J., and Harris, J. E. (1978) Strategies for low market share businesses. *Harvard Business Review*, May–June, 95–102.
[17] Comfort Hotels International (1984) *Annual Report 1983–4*.
[18] De Vere Hotels and Restaurants Plc (1983) *Annual Accounts, 1982–83*.
[19] Konopka, C. (1982) Great potential for hoteliers in timeshare market. *Caterer and Hotelkeeper*, 28 October, 50 ff.
[20] Lewis, R. C. (1981) The positioning statement for hotels. *Cornell Hotel and Restaurant Administration Quarterly*, **22**(1), May, 51–61. See also Lewis, R. C. (1982) Positioning analysis for hospitality firms. *International Journal of Hospitality Management*, **1**(2), 115–18.
[21] Kotler, P. (1980) (4th edn) *Marketing Management: Analysis, Planning and Control*. Englewood Cliffs, NJ: Prentice–Hall, 86.
[22] ibid., 383–414.
[23] Meidan, A., and Lee, B. (1982) Marketing strategies for hotels. *International Journal of Hospitality Management*, **1**(3), 169–77.
[24] For more detail on control refer to Wilson, R. M. S. (1979) *Management Controls and Marketing Planning*. London: Heinemann; Hulbert, J. M. and Toy, N. E. (1977) A strategic framework for marketing control. *Journal of Marketing*, April, 12–20; and Kotler, P., Gregor, W., and Rogers, W. (1977) The marketing audit comes of age. *Sloan Management Review*, Winter, 25–44.
[25] Nykiel, R. A. (1983) *Marketing in the Hospitality Industry*. London: CBI.
[26] See Hotel Association of New York City (7th edn) *Uniform System of Accounts for Hotels*.
[27] Hotel and Catering Economic Development Committee (1969) *A Standard System of Hotel Accounting*; a different version exists for catering establishments.
[28] See Horwath & Horwath (1984) op. cit.
[29] Shepherd, J. W. (1982) *Marketing Practice in the Hotel and Catering Industry*. London: Batsford.
[30] Allied-Lyons Plc (1983) *Annual Report 1983–4*.
[31] See Chandler, A. Jr. (1967) *Strategy and Structure*. Cambridge, MA: MIT Press.
[32] Vallen, J. J., Abbey, J. R., and Sapienza, D. J. (1978) *The Art and Science of Managing Hotels, Restaurants, Institutions*, Hayden.
[33] ibid., 229.
[34] ibid.
[35] See: Marketing today: a survey of the marketing function in international firms. *Cornell Hotel and Restaurant Administration Quarterly*, **19**(4), February 1979, 39–47.
[36] See Bird, C. (1980) Marketing: never perfect but essential. *Hospitality*, May, 37–40.

—PART III———————————————

The Marketing Mix

Part III contains 4 major sections, one for each of the Four Ps of the marketing mix. Each section is further divided into chapters, the first of which presents basic issues and principles. Further chapters develop managerial considerations.

SECTION 1
The Product

—8—
The Product

8.1 CHAPTER PREVIEW

This chapter introduces some fundamental concepts. We ask—and answer—the question: what is a product? We distinguish between various forms of product:
core/tangible/augmented
primary/secondary
hospitality/hotel/food service/function
mix/class/line/type/brand/item
The chapter then reviews the product life-cycle concept, which is used to describe the sales and profit behaviour of a product from its launch to its demise. Finally, we examine a number of key product decisions faced by marketers.

8.2 LEARNING OBJECTIVES

By the end of this chapter you should be able to:
1. Define these terms: product, meal experience, product mix and product life cycle.
2. Distinguish between core, tangible and augmented products.
3. Classify hotel and food service products and identify their main components.
4. Distinguish between primary and secondary/derivative products.
5. Draw the 3 major forms of product life cycle (PLC) and discriminate between them.
6. Describe marketing strategy at each stage of the normal PLC.
7. Identify the major product decisions.

8.3 WHAT IS A PRODUCT?

Ask a food scientist to describe a product, such as a wholewheat burger bun, and he'll probably tell you its material composition. If you ask a marketer, you will receive a quite different answer.

To every product there are 2 dimensions: features and benefits. Marketers stress benefits because they realise that consumers buy a product for the satisfactions it delivers to them. Features are the physical characteristics designed into a product, so that it is capable of satisfaction delivery.

The hospitality product can be defined as the set of satisfactions and dissatisfactions which a customer receives from a hospitality experience. The satisfactions may be physiological, economic, social, or psychological, as follows:

1. Physiological satisfactions—full stomach, quenched thirst, comfortable bed, warm and subdued environment.
2. Economic satisfactions—good value for money, rapid service, convenient location and credit facilities.
3. Social satisfactions—enjoyable company, attentive service and sound advice on wines.
4. Psychological satisfactions—enhancement of self-esteem, status and security.
   The dissatisfactions may or may not be under the control of management.
1. Controllable. Dirty uniforms, unhelpful staff, greasy spoons, or cramped conditions.
2. Uncontrollable. Road works, behaviour of other customers, or seasonality of some menu items.

The product which the marketer means to create and deliver may be quite different from that received by the customer.

An important distinction can be drawn between the core, tangible and augmented conceptions of a product.[1] The core product is the fundamental benefit which the customer receives. Hospitality products are problem-solvers: hotels deliver a place to sleep or meet whilst restaurants quell hunger pangs or provide opportunities to socialise.

The tangible product is the way the fundamental benefit is translated physically—e.g. a certain sized room equipped to a specified standard and marketed under a given brand. A budget hotel, for example, could define its tangible product as a 180-ft^2 room with colour television, telephone and small (40 ft^2) bathroom costing £14 per night.[2]

The augmented product is the complete product offering. Every hotel offers the same core product but this is modified and enhanced in cost-effective ways to make it more attractive to its target markets. Competition takes place largely at the augmented level. Table 8.1 lists ways in which accommodation and food service products are augmented.

Table 8.1 *Hospitality augmentation.*

Accommodation	Food and beverage
Reservation system convenience	Speed of food service
Reservation system simplicity	Ordering convenience
Acknowledgement of reservations	telephone
Lift attendants	advance orders
Room service	order-taking table staff
Standard of housekeeping	Complaints procedures
Courtesy	Advance reservations
Procedures for handling overbooking	Reliability of food/beverage quality
Information services	Customer advice on wines
Customer recognition	Provision of special foods
Credit provision	Cooking to order—e.g. steaks
Baggage handling	Acceptance of credit cards
Pet/child care	Variations in portions
Provision for disabled	Home deliveries
Group accommodation	Extent of non-available menu items
Discounts on club referrals, etc.	Fibre/calorie information
Cleaning/laundry	Provision of 'doggy-bags'
Courtesy care	Function-catering facilities
Willingness to bill later	Quality of table appointments
	Entertainment
	Privacy/discretion

Distinctions can also be drawn between product mix, product class and product line; and between product type, brand and item. A product mix is the complete assortment of products made available by a marketer. The product mix of Comfort Hotels International includes hotels, motels, a banqueting/exhibition centre, restaurants and ice-cream. A product class is a group of products delivering the same core benefits— e.g. restaurants. A product line is a major subdivision of a product class in which the products are closely related, for instance, by type of customer, price, or style—e.g. speciality restaurants. A product type is a subdivision of a product line, closely related by form—e.g. seafood restaurants or steak houses. A brand is a symbol, consisting of word(s) and/or device, used to identify the products of a specific marketer—e.g. Strikes Restaurants. An item is a specific unit offered to the market—e.g. every Strikes Restaurant is a different product unit.

Very often, hospitality products are the raw materials of a larger product. A tour operator will bring together a number of raw materials—such as rooms, food, service and flight—and offer them as a package. Tourists buying such a package regard these hospitality products as components, not as independent products. As Medlik notes, 'What the tourist buys is a composite product, an amalgam of attractions, transportation, accommodation, entertainments, and other activities.'[3]

The most prevalent manifestation of packaging is the inclusive tour. It is important to realise that the hotel or food service outlet is simply a part of the total tourism product—i.e. the satisfactions and dissatisfactions experienced by the traveller when away from home—and because of this, co-operative marketing between the various components may be more cost-effective than independent marketing.

There are 3 types of co-ordination required for effective marketing.[4]

1. At the destination it is the role of the official tourist organisation to formulate and develop tourist products based on the destination and to promote them in appropriate markets.
2. At the generating end it is the role of the tour operator to assemble component services into packages and to promote them and sell them as single products.
3. It is the role of individual operators to formulate, develop and supply their product as parts of a total tourist product.

8.4 THE HOTEL PRODUCT

There are several lines and types of product in the class accommodation. Brymer discriminates between them on the basis of form; there is the hotel, motor-hotel or motel, condominium, residential hotel, campsite/trailer park and institutional housing.[5]

Not all of these terms have been explained before. The motor-hotel, or motel, generally provides similar services to those in a hotel, but here they are distinguished by the provision of free parking facilities for the vehicles of their car-driving customers. Most motels are located on out-of-town or edge-of-town sites adjacent to major roads. In the USA demand for the subsector budget motels has grown rapidly. The product is essentially 'no frills'; food and beverage facilities are largely eliminated, rooms are functional and standardised, and public areas minimised. Most operators use prefabrication to reduce construction costs. The residential hotel is a peculiarly American phenomenon, where the guests are long-term residents, normally enjoying the full range of hotel amenities—i.e. housekeeping, room service, concierge, bar, restaurant and swimming-pool.

Brymer's list is not exhaustive; timeshare accommodation, private clubs, bed-and-breakfast, holiday camps and digs or lodgings are other forms. All offer the same core benefit but appeal through tangible and augmented dimensions to different markets.

Medlik identifies 5 components of the hotel product, all of which contribute to guest satisfaction or dissatisfaction.[6] Its *location* places the hotel geographically in or near a particular city, town, or village; within a given area location denotes accessibility and convenience, attractiveness of surroundings, freedom from noise and other nuisances, or otherwise. Its *facilities* which include bedrooms, restaurants, bars, function rooms, meeting rooms and recreation facilities such as tennis-courts and swimming-pools, represent a repertoire of facilities for the use of its customers, and these may be differentiated in type, size and in other ways. Its *service* comprises the availability and extent of particular hotel services provided through its facilities; and the style and quality of these facilities in terms of formality/informality, degree of personal attention, and speed and efficiency. Its *image* may be defined as the way in which the hotel is perceived by an individual or group; it is a by-product of its location, facilities and service, but is enhanced by such factors as its name, appearance, atmosphere and its associations—by who stays there and who eats there, by what it says about itself and what other people say about it. Its *price* expresses the value given by the hotel through its location, facilities, service and image, and the satisfaction derived by its users from these elements of the hotel concept. The individual elements assume greater or lesser importance for different people.

Doswell and Gamble adopt a slightly different view. They suggest that the total hotel product comprises *physical products*—i.e. foods, beverages and accommodation—and *services* and the *emotional satisfactions* of image and atmosphere. Atmosphere has to do with 'what people expect to take place in the hotel and what they think of these expectations'.[7]

This interpretation of the 'hotel product' includes core, tangible and augmented dimensions. It has also been suggested that the true hotel product is:[8]

> hospitality . . . cordial, generous and gracious reception of strangers . . . the comfort of a good bed, the pleasure of a hot shower and the delight of a well prepared breakfast unobtrusively served. Above all, the hospitality of the hotel is the personality of management . . . the guest feels the attitude of its owners and operators.

Because of the diversity of hotels—particularly in their facilities, service and price—a number of classification or grading schemes have been introduced.

In those countries where hotels are required by law to register classification occurs simultaneously. The principal benefits of such a scheme are the establishment/maintenance of standards of safety and public health, protection of the consumer and simplification of marketing. There is no system of compulsory registration in the UK. Consequently, classification schemes are voluntary.

Amongst the most widely used are those of the motoring organisations—the Automobile Association and the Royal Automobile Club—and those of the English, Welsh and Scottish Tourist Boards.

The AA/RAC schemes are very similar. They classify hotels by type, not by merit and award a star-rating. The higher-rated hotels incorporate the facilities of those lower-rated.

1 star   Simple in furnishing or menus or service. May well be managed by the proprietor personally, with few employed senior staff. Usually few, if any private bathrooms.

2 star   Formal reception arrangements and more employed staff. More accommodation usually of a higher standard. Greater provision for non-resident diners, including separate toilet arrangements. Lounge service available to residents.

3 star   Small luxury hotels or larger well-appointed hotels offering a high degree of comfort. Some room service. Telephones in bedrooms. A good proportion of bedrooms with private bathrooms. Full meal facilities for residents and non-residents including chance callers, on every day of the week.

4 star   Large hotels with a full brigade of professional staff. Reception, porterage and room service at all hours. Post Office telephones in all bedrooms. A high proportion of private bathrooms. Some bedrooms with private lounges, conference and/or banqueting facilities, or recreational facilities.

5 star   Large luxury hotels offering the highest standard of accommodation, service and comfort.

At the time of writing the English, Welsh and Scottish Tourist Boards have agreed to implement a common voluntary serviced accommodation classification scheme. The scheme identifies six standards—listed or allocated from one to five crowns. To be 'listed' a hotel must maintain certain standards in room security, room size, room furnishings, housekeeping, heating, bathroom and WC provision and food service. Crown ratings establish progressively higher standards. The five-crown standard, for example, requires that all the facilities of lower rated hotels be offered, plus provision of bath/fixed shower/WC in every bedroom, direct-dial telephone, writing table and seat, trouser press (or valet service), one or more suites, room service, all night lounge service, 24 hour laundry return service and night porterage.

8.5 FOOD SERVICE

Food service is a class of product comprising many lines and types. Commentators have applied many different criteria to discriminate between food service operations, as shown in Table 8.2. Hotel restaurants can be regarded as a class of food service products in their own right since they provide the same core benefit, hunger and thirst drive reduction, to a selected target market. We find 4 major types of hotel restaurant when the criterion of style of operation is applied.[9] These are the classical restaurant, the speciality restaurant, the coffee shop and the fast-food restaurant or snackbar. Each of these provides different meal experiences. The speciality restaurant, for instance, generally builds its tangible product around a certain theme, such as personality or food, and has a limited menu, distinctive simple style of service, interesting china and glassware, reasonable prices but no music or entertainment. The classical restaurant serves fine food in elegant surroundings at a high price. Sheraton's Kon Tiki restaurants and Sonesta Hotels' Rib Room have been notably successful speciality operations.

Table 8.2 *Food service variants.*

Basis of comparison	Food service operations
Location*[1]	1 Commercial/high street 2 Hotel/motel 3 Institutional 4 Industrial
Motive*[2]	1 Profit: retail operations, leisure operations, business/industry operations, hotels 2 Welfare
Extent of menu‡	1 Limited (less than 15 items) 2 Full (15–40 items) 3 Extensive (over 40 items)
Menu style	1 Table d'hôte 2 à la carte
Service style	1 Eat in 2 Take away
Seating style‡[3]	1 No seating 2 Counter and stools 3 Booth (fixed tables and chairs) 4 Table (free-standing tables and chairs)
Level of personal service‡	1 No (or self) service 2 Minimal service 3 Moderately attentive service 4 Very attentive service 5 Extremely attentive service
Specialisation	1 Pizza (Pizza Hut) 2 Steak (Aberdeen Steak Houses) 3 Burgers (Burger King) 4 Fish (Hungry Fisherman) 5 Ice-cream (Dayvilles) 6 Roasts (Roast Inns), etc.
Method of food delivery	1 Table service: plate service, wagon (gueridon) service, platter (silver) service, family service 2 Stand-up service: counter service, attended line service 3 Machine service: vending machine, automat, conveyors and turntables, fixed and mobile vehicles

[1] See Brymer, R. A. *Introduction to Hotel and Catering Management*, Des Moines, IA, Kendall-Hunt (1977)
[2] See Seltz, D. D. *Food Service Marketing and Promotion*, Lebhar-Friedman (1977)
[3] See Axler, B. H. *Food Service: A Managerial Approach*, Lexington, MA, D. C. Heath (1979)

The coffee shop is equipped with counter and tables, and menu features simple, low-priced cook-to-order or convenience foods; service is normally by waitress. The fast-food restaurant generally features systematised counter service, eat-in and take-away options, process manufactured food and low prices.

Some hotels provide a single, multipurpose restaurant, normally offering table service in an informal atmosphere. If the numbers of customers warrant, several food and beverage products may be offered—e.g. coffee shop and speciality restaurant. Customers obtain satisfaction or dissatisfacion from the entire meal experience, not from the food and drink alone.

Three components of the meal experience have been identified as food and drink, service and atmosphere.[10] As Axler remarks, food service products 'are more than just food. They also include service, decor, table appointments, credit policies and the operation's prestige as well as other characteristics designed to produce consumer satisfaction'.[11] Axler classifies food service products (and, therefore, benefits) into primary and secondary (or derivative). The primary product is food and drink, which satisfies the customers' physiological need for sustenance. However, the derivative product satisfies quite different requirements: convenience, sociability, or entertainment/novelty/fun.[12]

Convenience is an important issue in food-outlet patronage; the 3 dimensions of convenience are ·location, time and speed. Marketers strive to add locational convenience to their products. Vending-machine technology has developed to such an extent that tasty, hot fast food can be sold at locations previously regarded as unsuitable for food production. Food kiosks at railway and bus termini and coffee-shop operations in airports which stay open 24 hours a day offer time convenience. Many fast-food operators aim to provide instant gratification (maximum waiting-period 3 minutes, average wait 1 minute) of food demands. Speed of service is important to many customers.

Where sociability is an important derivative product, food service operators stress customer–staff relations, atmosphere and privacy. Some operators emphasise the entertainment/novelty/fun derivative product to such an extent that it becomes a more important motivator of patronage than the food—e.g. dinner–theatre packages, dinner–disco river cruises and lunch/stag club parties. Operators may use exotic stage settings, liveried waiters, historical characters, *flambé* presentations and silver service to deliver derivative product satisfactions. The aim of the secondary product is to enhance profitability by using low-cost, high-value derivatives.

The style, level and quality of *service* can contribute significantly towards customer satisfaction. Marketers are advised to identify what role service has in creating customer satisfaction, develop an instrument to measure satisfaction and feed back the findings to service workers, so that behaviour can be modified and satisfaction improved.[13]

Atmosphere can be classified in many ways—e.g. contemporary, Dickensian, Victorian, avant-garde, high-tech, or sporty. Each derives from the cumulative and combined effects of a large number of variables (see Table 8.3). Hotel bars can vary considerably. Smaller hotels usually have a single bar for both residents and non-residents. Larger hotels may have a residents' bar, television lounge, restaurant bar and cocktail bar, all featuring different atmosphere, price, drinks and level of service.

Table 8.3 *The components of atmosphere.*

Noise level	Age, sex, dress, appearance of staff
Table appointments	Cleanliness
Nationality of restaurant	Other customers
Layout of seating	Temperature
Type of seating	Colour
Number of vistas from different seats	Illumination
Size/shape of room	Comfort

8.6 FUNCTIONS

Functions are products which usually combine elements of both food service and accommodation—e.g. banquets, parties, conferences, conventions and weddings.

Functions are distinguishable from other hotel products because of the following:
1. The customers are groups such as families, clubs, societies and other organisations.
2. The organised groups make arrangements for dates and times, numbers attending, menus and other requirements in advance.
3. Each function can be treated as a separate operation.
4. Normally the same agreed menu is served to all participants.
5. The operation usually takes place in separate rooms and is served by staff who are distinct from those serving others in restaurants and bars, although they may be interchangeable between the facilities.

Larger hotels are more likely to have a banqueting or functions manager.

Because each function is a separate occasion, with its own price, menu and staffing, it can be closely controlled, especially when food production takes place in a separate kitchen and when the function is provided with its own bar. The revenue and the direct costs can be ascertained with accuracy. Moreover, the volume of identical meals prepared and served together enables higher profit margins to be achieved from functions than from other food and beverage activities; functions often represent the second most profitable hotel product, after rooms.[14]

8.7 PRODUCT CLASSIFICATION SCHEMES

Services, like goods, can be classified. Rathmell[15] suggests that service products can be split into 2 groups: shopping and convenience products such as banqueting and fast food respectively. The distinctions between these and a third group, speciality products, hinge on differences in consumer behaviour, as shown in Table 8.4. The speciality product is an infrequently bought, high-risk, high-priced item for which the buying process is lengthy and slow. The convenience product is the opposite.

Table 8.4 *Comparing convenience, shopping and speciality products.*

Comparison criteria	Type of product Convenience	Shopping	Speciality
1 Frequency of purchase	Frequently	Occasionally	Rarely
2 Level of perceived risk	Low	Medium	High
3 Unit value	Low	Low–medium	High
4 Amount of comparison shopping	Little	Some	Plenty
5 Speed of purchase decision	Fast	Medium	Slow
6 Routine buying?	Often	Sometimes	Hardly ever

Hospitality products can also be classified as durable or non-durable, where durability is defined by the period of time over which benefits are experienced by the consumer. A 2-week period of residence at a health farm could have benefits lasting for a year or longer, whereas the benefits from a lunch-time drink in a public house are experienced over a much shorter period.

8.8 PRODUCT LIFE CYCLE

Sales

The product mix of most hospitality companies contains well-established products, newly launched products and candidates for deletion. New products face an uncertain life: consumer acceptance may be below expectation and commercial death may be premature. On the other hand, management hopes that each new product will lead a long, profitable life.

The concept of the product life cycle (PLC) has been devised to describe what happens during the market life of a product from its introduction to its withdrawal. Additionally, the PLC acts in a prescriptive way; it helps management formulate appropriate marketing strategies. There is a general agreement that the PLC adopts an 'S'-shaped pattern and comprises 4 stages: introduction, growth, maturity and decline. Sales and profits vary between stages (see Figure 8.1).

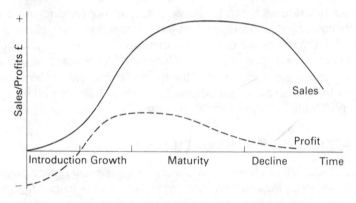

Figure 8.1   Product life cycle.

PLCs are used to describe the sales behaviour of items, brands, types, lines, or classes of products. The product class, hotels, is enjoying a long life cycle, whereas the product line, budget hotels, is in its early infancy. It is quite conceivable—indeed likely—that within a single hotel room sales, restaurant sales, coffee-shop sales and function sales are at different stages in their PLCs. Taking the case of an item or brand, let us see what happens to sales at each stage.

Stage 1   Introduction
Some hospitality establishments make a point of publicising the operation for a period of time before opening. For food service outlets, in particular, early sales may be at a very high level, as innovators try the product. However, for accommodation marketers the sales level generally builds up more slowly. Exceptions do occur. Hotel developments in growing holiday resorts where demand exceeds supply may be able to sell blocks of rooms to tour operators prior to opening, with the result that occupancy levels are high from the first week of operation.

Most purchases are trial, as opposed to repeat, purchases during the introductory period. During this stage marketers try to stimulate word-of-mouth promotion, commence advertising, obtain publicity and establish distribution.

Stage 2   Growth
Eventually the cumulative effects of distribution and promotion take effect and sales literally take off. A large proportion of consumers in the target market become aware of

the product. More and more try the product and some—the early adopters—make repeat purchases. Hence the product is now benefitting from both types of purchases, though trial purchases still probably account for the majority of sales.

Depending on several factors, competitors may begin entering the market at this stage. Some companies have a policy of always being a follower rather than innovator. Whilst the follower will often realise a lower reward than the innovator, he also has a much lower level of commercial risk. The innovator normally bears the heavier costs attendant upon the introduction of new products—i.e. marketing research, new product development, advertising, promotion, and so forth. In some cases the innovator may even welcome competition entering the field. One such example is when a product is totally new and requires considerable consumer education.

Stage 3 *Maturity*

Sales growth now starts to slow down considerably and, at the conclusion of this phase, levels off completely. What is happening is that the last few members of the target market who have not previously tried the product finally do make their first purchase. Sales volume, therefore, has shifted to a greater proportion of repeat purchases which tend to follow a fairly stable pattern.

Depending on several factors, including the shape of the sales curve in the growth phase and the type of product, more competitors enter the market with imitations of, or improvements upon, the innovator's product. Many companies look for growth opportunities, thus growth markets become fair game for 'me too' products. Quite frequently, more competitors enter a market than the market can profitably sustain.

In the introduction stage the innovator normally has the market to himself as competitors wait to see what will happen. When its pioneering effort starts to reap dividends, that is when sales take off in the growth stage of the life cycle, competitors enter the market. Then, in the mature phase, slower (or perhaps more cautious) competitors launch their answer to the innovator's product.

Stage 4 *Decline*

Eventually, and inevitably, consumers lose interest in the product (perhaps because the product is superseded or consumer tastes change) and sales decline as fewer and fewer people repurchase. This is usually a gradual process, thereby providing marketers with time to liquidate their assets.

Profits

What of profits during these sales stages? Let us once again examine this stage by stage.

Stage 1 *Introduction*

Normally a loss is sustained throughout this stage for 3 reasons. First, substantial marketing research and new product development costs are usually incurred before a final decision is made to market the product. Second, once that decision is made, the company has to make substantial investments in buildings and plant, fixtures and fittings, advertising (creative and production), and so on. All of these costs are committed prior to the first sale. Third, a sizeable proportion of the first year's advertising and promotion budget may be spent during the launch period of the product in order to achieve the objective of trial purchase.

The costs are somewhat offset during the introduction stage by sales to distributors (in the hotel market) or to innovators. However, the various investment costs normally exceed the first round of sales by a substantial margin, thereby resulting in a loss.

Stage 2   Growth

Profits start to be realised during the growth phase, thanks to 2 phenomena which operate to the marketer's benefit. On the one hand, marketing expenditures are substantially reduced—in both variety and amounts (start-up costs in research, development and advertising are completed; advertising is reduced as it is less costly to maintain consumer awareness than it is to create it in the first place). On the other hand, sales revenue is increased dramatically.

Stage 3   Maturity

In the early maturity stages profits may still be increasing, but later this is not so. At that stage the best that can be hoped for is stabilisation of profits. More realistically, however, it is likely that profits will begin declining in view of the following set of circumstances:

- total market demand has stabilised
- competition becomes fierce, probably resulting in a lower share of the market for the innovator
- the innovator is probably forced to increase his marketing expenditures in order to maintain his market share
- the market has become highly segmented

This was precisely the situation in the American fast-food market. The profits of Kentucky Fried Chicken fell after they had been stable for a 5-year period.[16]

Stage 4   Decline

Reduced sales confer the status of 'question-mark' or 'dog', in the Boston Consulting Group terms, on the product. Both classes of product return poor profits. If the market is growing, the question-mark can perhaps be remarketed, so that it gains 'star' status, recovers the market share and transforms into a 'cash cow' in the longer term. However, if poor sales accompany a slow growth or declining market, there is no opportunity for improved profits. Divestment becomes essential.

8.9 PLC VARIATIONS

Not all products have sales curves such as those above. Researchers have discovered up to 17 variants.[17] However, there are 2 *major* variations: the fad product life cycle (FPLC), and the extended product life cycle (EPLC).

The FPLC (shown in Figure 8.2) has 2 main stages—a rapid growth stage, matched by an equally dramatic collapse. The life cycle for skateboard parks, for instance, followed this pattern; discos often enjoy fad status.

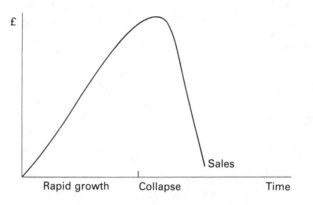

Figure 8.2 Fad product life cycle.

Most fads appear to have these characteristics in common:
- a lot of media time and space is devoted to the product. Skateboarding, for instance, featured heavily in television magazine programmes and in the press, this being editorial matter rather than paid advertising
- fads are often accompanied by a lot of pre-launch publicity. For this reason there is no identifiable slow introductory sales stage in the cycle
- fads are normally adopted only by a very delimited market, frequently identifiable as a specific age-group
- most fads are items which are consumed visibly. Conspicuous consumption enables the consumer to identify himself with significant others. A product which is consumed privately cannot offer this benefit
- within the target market there are no identifiable adoption stages (innovators, early adopters, early majority, later majority and laggards). The entire market adopts the product within a short period of its launch
- the fad's marketing mix is organised to achieve rapid market penetration
- most fads are non-necessaries

A major difficulty in planning marketing strategy for the fad market is knowing when to divest. The market can change rapidly and unpredictably, leaving the market with valueless products. Park operators and skateboard component manufacturers lost heavily following their investments in this sport because they assumed that there would be a maturity stage, as in a normal PLC.

The second major variant of the PLC, the extended product life cycle (EPLC), is shown in Figure 8.3. The EPLC, has an extended maturity stage which we have entitled saturation. During saturation repeat purchases are high, giving a stable volume of sales. Products which exhibit this sales pattern eventually find a permanent place (or at least a 'less temporary' place than most products) within the purchasing repertoire of the market. The extended maturity stage implies high consumer repurchase levels with little loss of sales to other competitors.

There are a number of products which exhibit the EPLC sales pattern:
- staple products. Demand for a number of staple classes of product follows this pattern—e.g. potatoes, bread and beds

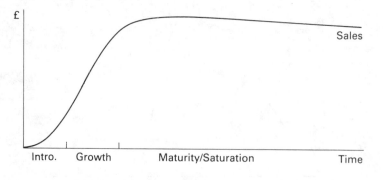

Figure 8.3   Extended product life cycle.

- fashion/style classics. Demand for London's ever-fashionable 5-star hotels remains solid
- functional products. Performance of an essential function guarantees a long commercial life—e.g. food service outlets
- multiple-use products. Architects attempt to build multifunctional use into new hotel developments
- cultural necessities. Many Western European people regard a holiday as an annual essential
- relaunched/remarketed products. A number of food service operators revamp their products at intervals in order to extend their commerical life

The normal PLC is proposed as the most common form of PLC. But what empirical evidence is there to support or refute the hypothesised cycle? A survey of published research into the PLC reveals these findings:[18]

- the majority of products do pass through a sales pattern similar to the 'S'-shaped PLC
- profits do tend to be at their highest during the growth stage, but competition, market segmentation and product proliferation cause profits to decay in the maturity stage
- the normal PLC is tending to become shorter because of the rapidity of change in social, economic and technical systems
- the length of time spent in each stage varies between products. Indeed it is often possible to recycle the PLC through a second or further growth stage by increased promotional expenditure, sales promotion, product redesign, or development of new markets and users

Cox suggests that the application of promotional strategies can extend the life cycle into a cycle–recycle pattern (see Figure 8.4). Says Cox: 'The promotional effort . . . almost invariably results in increased sales of the product.'[19] Whilst the profits in the late maturity and decline stages are typically declining or even negative, such an extension does allow a company to introduce a replacement product to the product mix before dropping the declining product. Companies which plan their product mix carefully tend to introduce new products timed to make their own existing products obsolescent as—or before—sales and profits start to fall as a result of competitive forces. Their adopted strategy is to make their own product obsolescent before competitors do so. Not only does this mean that sales volume and profits can be maintained at satisfactory levels, but also that competitors' investment in product development largely may be wasted as a result of pre-emptive product replacement. The effect is to create a series of PLCs each designed to maintain or increase sales volumes and profits, as shown in Figure 8.4.

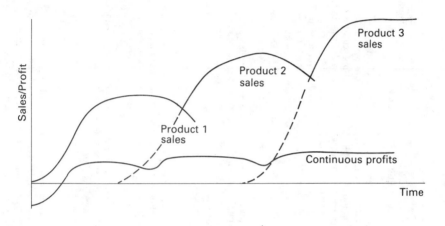

Figure 8.4   Sales and profits from new product introductions.

8.10 USING THE PLC

PLCs not only can be determined; they are particularly useful as marketing models.[20]

Rather than discuss shifts in marketing strategy stage by stage, Table 8.5 presents a tabulated summary for quick reference, including what happens during the final phases before launch. The table shows how marketing strategy changes from stage to stage of the PLC. Yet this is only of value if 3 conditions are met. First, the marketer must determine whether the product will follow the normal PLC, the fad PLC, or the extended PLC. Second, he must be able to locate his product's position in the PLC. Third, he must find out when to expect turning-points, for instance, from growth into maturity stage. The first issue is relatively simply solved. He must assume a normal PLC unless he can identify some of the conditions specified earlier.

Determining where the product lies in its PLC is more difficult, but one way is to investigate the number of competing companies, the number of competing products, the proportion of sales that are first-time trials as opposed to repeat sales, the degree to which competing products offer significant advantages or are merely 'me too' products, and the level of market penetration. These environmental factors are detailed in Table 8.6.

Table 8.5 *Marketing decisions during the PLC.*

Marketing decisions	Pre-commercialisation (final phases only)	Introduction	Growth	Maturity	Decline
Product	Positioning decision; branding decision	Narrow line	Focus on best-selling product and a few related additions	Proliferation of items, flavours; augmentation and differentiation	Rationalise product mix or plan for relaunch
Advertising	Set objectives, media schedules, copy pre-tests	Separate campaigns for distributors and customers; develop product awareness, understanding, interest; foster favourable word-of-mouth amongst end-users; high per unit expenditure	Nurture brand preference; encourage adoption via sampling; high level of industry and brand advertising	Brand claims; co-operative advertising; cultivate brand loyalty amongst users; support new product versions; use reminder ads for established item; expenditure per item stable	Eliminate
Personal selling	Training	Obtain trial orders through salespersons on commission; hire commando salesforce	Repeat business through salaried personnel; system of sales reports	Selective selling; service of existing accounts and development of new segments; salary and bonus	Revert to commission basis where possible
Sales promotion	Generate ideas; cultivate suppliers of sales promotion materials	Explanatory literature; outlet/unit promotions; free samples; coupons; incentives to salesforce, trade, users	Continue literature; promotions to build repeat business	Literature; heavy incentives programme, merchandising; many short-term promotions, deals, contests	Eliminate all except literature
Publicity	Identification of relevant publics; cultivation of editors; planning of staged events	Introductory splash; topical tie-ins; human interest: employees, struggles of inventor	Product-use studies and human interest, naming locations, distributors, customers	Focus on new versions; trade publicity	Token efforts
Channels	Plan and build distribution structure	Use own reps to penetrate market; introductory deals; special promotions; often few distributors, one type	Move towards direct distribution; reservation system; eliminate reps except in sparse areas or market segments; expand number of locations	Widest feasible distribution; battle to retain distribution; some forward integration; many trade deals, speciality advertising	Increasing in number of own representatives; selective distribution

	Planning				
Pricing		Introductory specials; high price for radical new products or low price to deter competitors	Beginning of price erosion	Heavy competitive pressure on price	Temporary price like to increase profit, or decrease to lift volume
Marketing research	Product development; site location, target market research; test marketing	News of buyer reactions, especially complaints	Comprehensive exploration of opportunities and problems; segmentation studies	Panels, audits, other routine intelligence	Focus on laggards for clues on product deletion
Type of product-oriented executive	Champion of evolving product; combination of entrepreneur and expediter	Analytical marketer	Smooth co-ordinator for fast-changing internal and external factors	Routine administrator	Controller type
Sales forecasting	Delphi; historical analogies; panel; experiments; test marketing	Consumer surveys; repeat ratio analysis; identify and appraise critical events upon which the onset of growth depends; identify PLC turning-points	Intentions-to-buy; compilation of causal variables; learning models	Salesmen's estimates; time series; econometric models; regression and correlation	Same as maturity, with new data base; regression analysis; accurate sales forecast very important
Behavioural observations	Resistance against change	Diffusion of innovations	Bandwagon effect	Desire for variety	Various factors: boredom, technological obsolescence, government regulation
Customers	Panels and other test respondents	Innovators and some early adopters	Early adopters and early majority	Early adopters, early and late majority, some laggards; first discontinued by late majority	Mainly laggards
Typical duration	More than twice as long as expected	Brief if product-line extension; long if risks perceived by prospects	Short; reduced if market potential is small or competitive products enter	Longest	In many companies longer than commercially justified

Table 8.6 *Market conditions during the PLC.*

Condition	Introduction	Growth	Maturity	Decline
			Stage of PLC	
Market growth	Slow	Fast acceleration	Levelling	Decline
Market penetration	Low	High	Higher	Highest
Market segmentation	Aimed at risk-takers	Mass market; some segmentation	Segmentation at highest; some unprofitably small segments	Least profitable segments no longer targeted
Differentiation (for a radical new product)	Unique product, highly favourable differentiation	Competitors entering; decreased differentiation	Revised, improved versions being marketed; higher but often unfavourable differentiation of original product	With exit of some competition and new versions on market, high differentiation, but often unfavourable
Number of brands; product proliferation	Few	Increasing	Highest	High dropout rate
Number of competitors	If radically new product, none; if a copy or 'me too' product, several	Growing	Highest	High dropout rate
Industry capacity	Low	High and rapidly increasing as profit opportunity noted	Optimal	Overcapacity, although some operators leave market

Finally, there is the anticipation of turning-points. Turning-points occur as a result of the interaction of 4 factors, as follows.

1. The product's marketing mix.
2. Competitors' marketing mixes.
3. Natural diffusion of the innovation in the market-place (partly influenced by factors 1 and 2). See chapter 9 for detail.
4. Environmental changes such as shift in business confidence, or the introduction of new legislation such as the imposition of value added tax.

If the marketer has access to information in these 4 areas and is alert to the changes shown in Table 8.6, he will be in a better position to judge turning-points, though not with absolute certainty. Occasionally there are early warning signs which mark a turn in the PLC, for example:

1. Government statements about future policies.
2. Lagged correlations. The introduction of the Hotel Development Incentive Scheme

in 1969 correlated with a dramatic rise in the number of hotel rooms available in later years.

3. Activities of trade associations to influence demand or supply.
4. Consumer advocates' attacks upon nutritional value of foods, safety, or hygiene standards.

The PLC concept has met with considerable criticism. Most vocal have been Dhalla and Yuspeh, who claim that 'The PLC is a *dependent* variable which is determined by marketing actions; it is not an *independent* variable to which companies should adapt their marketing programmes', and that attempts to identify variants of the PLC 'S'-shaped curve are 'sterile exercises in taxonomy'.[21] Other criticisms have been temporary plateaus in sales which are misinterpreted as the beginnings of maturity, the difficulty of distinguishing between PLC stages and the wisdom of pursuing a standardised marketing strategy at each stage.

8.11 PRODUCT DECISIONS

Hospitality marketers have to make a number of product decisions:
- what satisfactions to deliver through the product. This will be reflected in both its tangible and intangible dimensions—e.g. quality of beds and standard of service
- what tangible form the product should take—e.g. room size, amenities, restaurant format (coffee shop, speciality restaurant), etc.
- whether to market a single item as do Cavalier Steak Houses or a line of related products like Berni Inns
- whether to market the product independently or as part of a package of travel-related products, or both. If both, it is probable that different target markets will be selected for each form of product
- how to augment the product, so that it acquires the desired 'product position' in the customer's mind and is differentiated from competitors
- how to define, develop and promote the image and atmosphere dictated by the product-positioning statement
- what style, form and standard of service to build into the product
- whether to brand the product. Most hospitality products are branded. Exceptions are machine-vending systems, in-company catering and institutional catering. Some products are branded—e.g. Gardner Merchant's contract catering operations—but consumers may be totally unaware of the brand. Branding options are (1) individual brandnames—e.g. Beefeater; (2) a family brand—e.g. Holiday Inns, which is used to identify 2 quite different products in the USA and UK; and (3) company and brandnames combined—e.g. THF Posthouse Hotels.

Brand names should convey the product's benefits (Comfort Hotels) or qualities (Pizza Express); and be memorable, pronounceable, recognisable and distinctive. The Trade Marks Act 1938 requires that a trademark—defined as a symbol (whether word, device, or a combination of the two) which a person uses in the course of trade in order that his goods may be readily distinguished from similar goods by the purchasing public—be distinctive. A trademark confers a statutory monopoly in the use of the mark in relation to the products for which it is registered.

8.12 CHAPTER REVIEW

1. A hospitality product is the set of satisfactions and dissatisfactions received from a hospitality experience.
2. Satisfactions are classified as physiological, economic, social and psychological.
3. Dissatisfactions may or may not be under the control of management.
4. An important distinction can be drawn between core, tangible and augmented products.
5. Food service products are classed as primary (food and drink) or secondary/derivative (convenience, psychological satisfaction and a place to consume the food).
6. Convenience, sociability and entertainment are 3 important derivative products.
7. Distinctions can be made between the product mix, product class and product line; and the product type, brand and item.
8. Sometimes hospitality products are part of a packaged tourism product.
9. Accommodation is a class of product which can be subdivided into lines on the basis of form—hotel, motel, residential hotel, etc.
10. Five components of the hotel product are location, facilities, service, image and price.
11. Food service products can be classified by location, motive, style of operation, menu style, extent of menu, level of personal service, service style, seating style, speciality and method of food delivery.
12. The complete set of satisfactions and dissatisfactions from a food service product is called the 'meal experience'.
13. Food service benefits are gained from both primary (food and drink) and secondary/derivative products.
14. Important derivative food service products are convenience, sociability and entertainment/novelty/fun.
15. Functions are one-off products which often combine food service and accommodation elements.
16. Hospitality products are convenience, shopping, or speciality products and may be either durable or non-durable.
17. The product life cycle (PLC) tracks the sales and profit performance of products from their launch to their demise.
18. The 'S'-shaped, normal PLC has 4 sales stages: introduction, growth, maturity and decline.
19. Profits are normally highest in the growth stage.
20. Two major exceptions to the 'S'-shape are the fad PLC and the extended PLC.
21. Some normal PLCs exhibit a secondary growth stage, commencing during the late maturity/decline stages.
22. PLCs are useful models for developing marketing strategy.
23. To be able to use the PLC a marketer must know: (1) which shape of PLC his product follows; (2) which stage it is in; and (3) when to expect turning-points.
24. Some critics believe the PLC to be a dependent, rather than independent, variable.
25. Marketers make decisions about: (1) whether to market the product as part of a package or independently; (2) what satisfactions to build into the product; (3) how to augment the product; (4) whether to market a single item or a line; (5) what tangible form the product should take; (6) what atmosphere and service components to build into the product; and (7) whether and how to brand the product.

8.13 QUESTIONS

1. How would you measure the atmosphere and service elements of a meal experience?
2. What assistance does the PLC concept afford the marketing strategist:
   - when opening a new themed restaurant?
   - when managing a well-established motor-hotel (mature stage) at a major road junction?
3. Examine the class of products 'food service' and break down into lines and types. Find branded examples of each type you identify.

4. What physiological, economic, social and psychological satisfactions might be planned into:
   - a budget hotel?
   - a restaurant themed around Charles Dickens?
   - the school meals service?
5. What are the core products of hotels and restaurants?
6. Select a food service operation you know. Define its core product, detail the tangible product and list ways in which the product is, or could be, augmented.
7. Are other customers part of the hotel product?
8. Draw up a list of occasions on which customers make use of food service operations, including lunch during shopping trip; romantic evening out; and as a means of killing time. Then decide whether the consumer's purchase behaviour indicates that it is a convenience, shopping, or speciality product.

REFERENCES

[1] Kotler, P. (1984) (5th edn) *Marketing Management: Analysis, Planning and Control.* Englewood Cliffs, NJ: Prentice-Hall, 463–4.

[2] Quest, M. (1983) Is there a future for low-tariff UK hotels. *Caterer and Hotelkeeper*, 29 September, 55 ff.

[3] Medlik, S. (1980) *The Business of Hotels*. London: Heinemann, 115.

[4] ibid., 116.

[5] Brymer, R. A. (1977) *Introduction to Hotel and Catering Management*. Des Moines, IA: Kendall-Hunt, 1.

[6] Medlik, S. (1980) op. cit. 13–14.

[7] Doswell, R. and Gamble, P. R. (1979) *Marketing and Planning Hotels and Tourism Projects*. London: Hutchinson, 19–20.

[8] Vallen, J. J., Abbey, J. R., Sapienza, D. L. (1978) *The Art and Science of Managing Hotels, Restaurants, Institutions*. Hayden.

[9] Lattin, G. W. (1977) (3rd edn) *Modern Hotel and Restaurant Management*. Reading: W. H. Freeman.

[10] Campbell-Smith, G. (1967) *Marketing of the Meal Experience: A Fundamental Approach*. Guildford: University of Surrey Press.

[11] Axler, B. H. (1979) *Food Service: a Managerial Approach*, Lexington, MA: DC Heath.

[12] ibid.

[13] McCleary, K. W. and Weaver, P. A. (1982) Improving employee service levels through identifying sources of customer satisfaction. *International Journal of Hospitality Management*, **1**(2), 85–9.

[14] Based on Medlik, S. (1980) op. cit., 55.

[15] Rathmell, J. M. (1974) *Marketing in the Service Sector*. Cambridge, MA: Winthrop.

[16] Gillespie, B. (1979) Fast food formula; time for a taste a class. *National Business Review*, 28 February, 18 ff.

[17] Tellis, G. J. and Crawford, C. M. (1981) An evolutionary approach to product growth theory. *Journal of Marketing*, Fall, 125–34.

[18] Sources include Buzzell, R. D. (1966) Competitive behaviour and product life cycles. *Proceedings of American Marketing Association*, Spring Conference, New York; Polli, R. and Cook, V. (1969) Validity of the PLC. *Journal of Business*, October; Dhalla, N. K. and Yuspeh, S. (1976) Forget the PLC concept. *Harvard Business Review*, January–February, 102–12; Doyle, P. (1976) The realities of the PLC. *Quarterly Review of Marketing*, Summer; Cox, W. E. (1969) PLCs as marketing models. *Journal of Marketing*, Spring.

[19] Cox, W. E. (1969) op. cit.

[20] ibid.

[21] Dhalla, M. K. and Yuspeh, S. (1976) op. cit.

9

Marketing New Products

9.1 CHAPTER PREVIEW

This chapter is about new products, their development and marketing. We mention several types of new product from the original innovation to minor modifications, and discuss the motives for new product development.

New product development (NPD) is a process which involves 7 steps, starting with the specification of a strategic or tactical role for new products and ending with their commercialisation. This process is presented and elaborated.

We then turn to the new product adoption process, and ask why some innovations are adopted quickly by their target markets whilst others fail. The distinguishing characteristics of successful innovators (companies) and innovations (products) are identified. The chapter closes with an introduction to new product launch strategy.

9.2 LEARNING OBJECTIVES

By the end of this chapter you should be able to:
1. Explain why new products are developed.
2. Outline the new product development process.
3. List and describe the main sources of new product ideas.
4. Draw up a list of criteria for use in screening.
5. Specify the data that should be collected in a feasibility study.
6. Select the appropriate marketing strategy for the launch of a new product.
7. Identify factors which are associated with corporate success in new product development.

9.3 WHAT IS NEW?

What is a new product? Newness, novelty, or innovation is measured by divergence from what is current. However, a number of products marketed as new are in fact very similar to existing products, whereas others are dramatically different. Any product which is perceived as different by consumers can be called new; although the degree of difference or originality may be major or minor.

In a survey of 700 American companies responsible for 13,000 new product introductions over 5 years management consultants Booz Allen & Hamilton identified 6 categories of new products, as follows.[1]

1. New-to-the-world products—i.e. new products that create an entirely new market (10 per cent of introductions).
2. New product lines—i.e. new products which allow a company to enter a market for the first time (20 per cent).
3. Line extensions—i.e. new products which supplement a company's existing product lines (26 per cent).
4. Improvements/revisions to existing products—i.e. new products that provide improved performance or greater perceived value, and replace existing products (26 per cent).
5. Repositionings—i.e. existing products which are targeted to new markets or segments (7 per cent).
6. Cost reductions—i.e. new products which provide similar performance at lower cost (11 per cent).

The figures show that most new products are evolutionary, not revolutionary. The degree of difference tends to be minor.

9.4 WHY DEVELOP NEW PRODUCTS?

New products can be very costly to develop and there is no guarantee that they will capture the consumers' imagination and succeed. Booz Allen & Hamilton estimate that despite sophisticated new product development processes and cautious management, only 65 per cent of new products are successful.[2] A number of other studies undertaken into new product failure rates indicate a much lower rate of success[3] whilst one examination of the service sector estimated a success rate of 82 per cent.[4]

New products are introduced for a number of strategic and tactical reasons. Strategic reasons are concerned with the long term and include the following.
1. Profit maintenance. The product life cycle (PLC) shows how profits decay during the maturity and decline stages. Maintenance of satisfactory profit performance requires new products to replace old. The growth stage is the most profitable position in the PLC.
2. Profit growth. Growth in profit normally involves enlarging the product portfolio through successive new product introductions.
3. Defence of market share. As competition hots up in the growth/maturity stages of the PLC market share is eroded. Competitors can be pre-empted through line extensions and product improvements, in particular—thus retaining market share.
4. Entry of new market. Some innovations are introduced to establish a presence in a developing market or market segment.
5. Maintenance of status as product innovator. Companies develop self-images which over time become significant influences on policy and strategy. The status of innovator is one such self-image.
6. Cash generation. New products absorb large amounts of cash in development, and during the early stages of the PLC, but as high-share products of the low-growth markets become the 'cash cows' which support further product development.
7. Exploitation of technology. It has been noted that in the food service industry 'the successful firms are the innovators, and their efforts have not been confined to

products and services. They have adapted systems originally developed by manufacturing firms to their own environment'.[5] McDonalds' production systems, production control systems, production floor layout and inventory control systems are based on manufacturing models.

8. Capitalisation on competitive strengths, especially distribution. An effective computerised reservation system lends itself to other applications.

Tactical short-term motives for new product development include the following:

1. Use of excess or off-season capacity. Fixed costs have to be paid whether or not a hotel is occupied. New products, such as weekend breaks, conferences and functions, can help recover these costs.
2. Avoidance of labour lay-offs. It can be more costly to lay-off labour because of high redundancy payments than it is to develop new products.
3. Undermining of competitor's test market or new product launch. A 'fighting brand' or new product may be developed specifically to strike at a competitor's innovation and force its premature withdrawal.

Some companies establish very specific roles for each new product launched. One product may aim to absorb excess capacity, whereas another may aim to produce profit growth. Clearly, the standards against which performance is measured must vary according to the role—there is no single definition of success. Booz Allen & Hamilton found that two-thirds of their surveyed companies formally measured new product performance, using on the average more than a single performance criterion.[6] Details appear in Table 9.1. Further criteria used in hospitality are occupancy level, average guest expenditure on rooms and other products, and cash flow.[7]

Table 9.1   *New product performance criteria.*

Profit contribution (80% of respondents used this criterion)
Sales volume (70%)
Return on investment (70%)
Payback period (65%)
Internal rate of return (30%)
Net present value (20%)

9.5 NEW PRODUCT DEVELOPMENT (NPD)

New products emerge in many ways. Sometimes an idea germinates, is developed and a market is sought. In other cases a new product proposal is developed as a consequence of market analysis. The latter approach is clearly more 'correct' for marketing-oriented companies but there are numerous examples of creative spark and entrepreneurial flair leading to successful new products—e.g. Bob Payton's Chicago Rib Shack.

Booz Allen & Hamilton reckon that successful NPD should follow the 7-step process shown in Table 9.2. Rathmell comments that the 'conventional steps of exploration, screening, business analysis, development, testing and commercialisation apply to services as well as goods'.[8] We shall follow this process in sections 9.6–9.12, below.

Table 9.2 *The NPD process.*

Step	Process component
1	New product strategy development
2	Idea generation
3	Screening and evaluation
4	Business analysis
5	Development
6	Testing
7	Commercialisation

9.6 NPD: NEW PRODUCT STRATEGY DEVELOPMENT

Booz Allen & Hamilton remark that this stage provides a focus for idea generation and helps to develop the criteria that are used during screening and exploration. It involves clearly defining the roles and objectives for new products; the role of the new product is often tied to the type of new product. Innovations intended to exploit technology in a new way tend to be more original, whereas defence of market share generally implies line extensions or product modifications. Performance criteria are also tied to the strategic role of the new product: a high ROI is expected of new-to-the-world products because risk and development costs are normally higher, whereas the profit maintenance role implies using the profit contribution criterion.

This new product strategy links NPD to corporate and marketing objectives. This is partly responsible for the improved mortality rate for new product ideas. In 1968 Booz Allen & Hamilton estimated that the ratio between commercially successful new product launches and new product ideas was 1:58; by 1981 this ratio had improved to 1:7. Most of the 7 ideas are eliminated by a process of progressive rejection. The major expenditures in NPD occur during the development and testing stages, so it is wise to weed out the feebler ideas earlier in the process. Consequently limited NPD resources can be spent where they are likely to bear most fruit.

9.7 NPD: IDEA GENERATION

Ideas can be generated from a number of sources using several collection methods and stimulants to creativity.

Sources can be classified as internal and external to the company:
(a) *Internal*. Marketing management, product management, R&D and sales representatives
(b) *External*. Competitors, patent office, inventors, customers, distributors, suppliers, universities, new product consultants, advertising and marketing research agencies, the government and franchisors

Marketers, particularly product management, are ideally placed to spot trends and developments in consumer tastes. Consequently line extensions and product modifications are more prone to occur this way. Research and development (R&D) is more likely to create new-to-the-world ideas. The relationship between R&D and marketing determines the originality of ideas. A review of the R&D/marketing interface has concluded:[9]

> So close is the integration of R & D and marketing activity (in the Food & Drink Industry) that the weakness of the system appears to be in the apparent difficulty of producing true innovations. Concern with the near term, a prevailing attitude among many marketing managers, is a disincentive to look for innovation that will carry the firm into the future, ahead of its competitors.

Marketing is capable of both directing and restraining R & D effort. There are few R & D teams in the service sector.[10]

Sales representatives are adept at solving customers' problems with existing products. Where a problem is suboptimally resolved, there is an indication for a new product. Representatives must be encouraged to feed back pertinent information to management.

Competitors' products can be copied (product cloning), or adapted or improved. Ideas can be sought from existing or potential competitors at home and abroad. Patents offer a 16-year protection to an innovation. Frequently patented innovations are never produced because the idea is quickly superseded, because of lack of resources, or because the patent holder's attention is diverted elsewhere. Some companies regularly search patent files for ideas and then either buy the patent from the holder or start production regardless—16 years being a long time to wait!

Customers, actual or potential, are often the starting-point for new product idea generation. Suggestions and complaints act as stimulants. Distributors and suppliers can spawn ideas, but for different reasons—distributors because they are normally closer to the customer than the product marketer, and suppliers because of their efforts to reduce costs and provide improved service.

Universities undertake research, both pure and applied, but often without a commercial application in mind. Specialist new product consultants, such as KAE, exist to help develop and launch innovations. Market research and advertising agencies, in particular, employ creative people whose innovative output can be harnessed.

Government legislation, particularly on safety and health, spurs NPD. Many existing hospitality products have been introduced to new markets under franchise arrangements.

Having identified sources of ideas, the next stage is to access them through collection methods such as formal marketing research (involving surveys, group discussions and observation) or less formal and structured marketing intelligence. Marketing intelligence is taking place when the manager scans the trade press, business press and new product press—e.g. *European New Product Report*—or when talking informally to customers, suppliers, distributors and sales representatives.

Companies may also buy new product ideas through acquisition of more innovative businesses. Acquisition is a multistage process (see Figure 9.1). There are a number of problems which are likely to hinder the successful application of an acquisition strategy.[11]

1. Failing to place responsibility for the decision at a sufficiently high level in the organisation.
2. Failing to establish a real unanimity of opinion as to what should be the acquisition objectives.

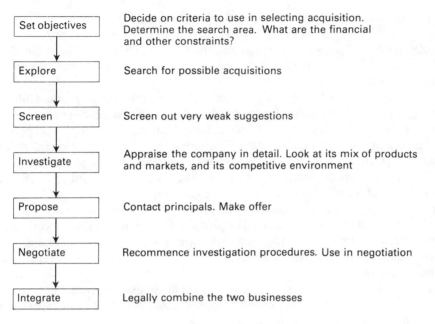

Figure 9.1   The acquisition process.

3. Searching only amongst companies for sale.
4. Failing to recognise the time required for a successful acquisition programme.
5. Failing to focus the search correctly.
6. Failing to investigate prior to actual negotiations.
7. Overlooking opportunities by using mechanical screening procedures.
8. Failure to obtain qualified outside assistance when needed.
9. Too much analysis and too little action, or vice versa.

Ideas are sometimes stimulated by applying techniques such as creativity tests, climate measurement, morphological analysis, brainstorming, forced relationships, synectics, work simplification and suggestion schemes.[12]

Creativity tests help management to identify idea-producing individuals capable of a creative approach to problem-solving. Climate measurement is a method for assessing the internal climate of an organisation, especially as it affects creativity. Morphological analysis ensures that all possible solutions to a problem are enumerated through a systematic breakdown of the problem into its constituent parts. The parameters of the problem are established and the different values of each parameter listed. Then a 'morphological box' is constructed in which every combination of the different values of the different parameters is considered as a potential solution to the problem. For example, a food service operator might be considering what sort of product to develop. The parameters are food, service, extent of menu and the production system. Each of the parameters has a number of variables:

- food: roast, burger, chicken, pizza, kebab (5)
- service: take-away, eat-in, both (3)
- extent of menu: limited, moderate, extensive (3)

- production system: cook-serve, cook–chill, cook–freeze,
  cook–freeze–thaw, convenience (5)

The total number of potential new products, then, is 225 (5 × 5 × 3 × 5). Some of them will be excluded for a variety of technical or competitive reasons. The balance products are then considered on merit.

The forced relationship technique attempts to develop new product ideas by imposing relationships between 2 or more elements or objects which are not normally associated with each other—e.g. holiday accommodation, blind people and pets.

Brainstorming is a method of creative thinking based on free association and deferred judgement. A group of 6 to 12 people assemble, agree to investigate a new product problem and to suspend criticism until later. They then tape-record proceedings. A large quantity of ideas is generated for later evaluation.

Synectics is an approach similar to brainstorming but in which the specific problem is initially concealed from participants. The problem is approached from several angles, so that different perspectives and viewpoints are investigated.[13] Chairmanship of a synectic group is a skilled task for which a week of formal training and several months' practice is advised.

Work simplification and suggestion schemes are in-company devices which stimulate cost reduction and new product ideas. Some schemes reward all participants, others reward only those whose ideas are used.

9.8   NPD: SCREENING AND EVALUATION

Screening is the first step in idea elimination. What is needed is a cheap and quick method of identifying weak ideas.[14] Most screening systems consist of a set of criteria against which ideas are evaluated. One such screen listing 44 criteria (see Table 9.3) assesses the fit between the idea and the company. Each idea is rated from 'excellent' to 'bad' on a 5-point scale. An important issue is how to manipulate the results. Several approaches are feasible.

1. Calculate the grand total. If it reaches a predetermined acceptance score (min. = 44, max. = 220), say, 180, then the idea is allowed to proceed.
2. Weighting. Some criteria are thought to be more important than others and are weighted accordingly. Again, a cut-off point is established and the total score calculated.
3. Essentials first. Ideas are allowed to proceed if minimum ratings are achieved on key criteria, say, a score of 4 or 5 on contribution to profit and availability of finance.

There are a number of problems that even this simple form of screening can encounter:

- who does the screening? Different people are likely to evaluate the same idea differently. One solution is to have several staff members, including the idea originator, appraise the idea and then average the results
- assumption of knowledge. The method assumes the raters know enough about the product idea to give fair ratings, even though at this stage the idea may not be fully conceptualised
- meaning of the summation. The total rating could have been achieved in various

Table 9.3 *New product screen.*

CRITERIA	RATING				
	Excellent	Good	Fair	Poor	Bad
Financial Availability of finance Effect on overall company profitability Effect on overall company volume Effect on breakeven point Effect on overall working capital Rate of return on investment Fits present terms of trading Contribution to profit					
New product Unique characteristics Difficulty of imitation Expected life (for marketing) Absence of seasonal effect Few variations Complementary to present products Compliance with legal requirements Price advantage over competitors' products Technical advantage over competitors' products					
Marketing Size of market Growth prospects of market Stability of market Excess of demand over supply Company familiar with market Strength of competition Impact on present products Impact on relations with customers Suitability of present channels Suitability of present locations Time between launch and saturation Speed of launch and developing sales Stability of input costs Comparative promotion cost					
Production Suitability of buildings and services Suitability of present technology Availability of suitable staff Availability of suitable materials Value added Fuller utilisation of spare capacity Maintenance of balanced workload Ability to meet service requirements Ability to hold requisite stocks Minimum re-layout and re-equipment required					
Summary Compatibility with New Product Strategy Overall business prospects of product Low risk of failure					

ways (scoring heavily on low-weighted dimensions or scoring low on high-weighted dimensions). The pattern by which the score has been achieved should also be considered.

- interpretation. A major difficulty is setting a cut-off point above which ideas progress and below which they are dropped.

9.9 NPD: BUSINESS ANALYSIS

This is a much finer and more detailed screen which will further reduce the number of ideas progressing towards commercialisation. However, for the business analysis to be truly meaningful, the idea needs to be fleshed out into a full product concept. For example, if the idea is to open a high-street food service outlet, decisions must be made about type (coffee shop, fast food, speciality, etc.), extent of menu, service level, size, seating and atmosphere.

In effect, the product concept is a *fully working mental prototype* specifying all three product components—i.e. core, tangible and augmented. However, before this can be tested for acceptability in the market-place, further preliminary decisions must be made about marketing strategy—i.e. target market, product concept positioning, marketing objectives, key promotional price and place decisions (as outlined in Chapter 7).

For any single product there may be several product concepts. These can be tested on their prospective target markets with a view to establishing which is most likely to achieve new product objectives. Not all product concepts are understood by, or are perceived to offer significant additional benefits to, consumers, so these do not undergo the detailed business analysis which in the hospitality industry is more often known as the *feasibility study*.

The feasibility study is defined as:[15]

> a systematic study of the potential of an idea from a technical, marketing, economic, financial, social, ecological, resource and legal point of view.

Clearly, feasibility studies extend far beyond simple marketing and operational considerations. Feasibility studies can be undertaken internally or externally. Most large hoteliers prefer to use external consultants; the American hospitality consultants Laventhol & Horwath have developed a computer program to assist in project evaluation. The hotel group Ramada has developed such in-house expertise that it sells its feasibility study capability to third parties.

Many investors will not even discuss projects with hotel developers without a professionally prepared feasibility study:[16]

> Feasibility studies that merely predict a project's gross operating profit no longer suffice. Lenders wants to see actual cash flows, usually from a five year period out. Therefore, a feasibility study must include analysis of the initial requirements of a project, projected advertising and promotion and other pre-opening expenses and a prediction of the time involved to achieve a sufficient volume of occupancy.

Feasibility studies are becoming more sophisticated and using better data-collection and analytical methods. Beals and Troy identify 4 reasons for this trend, as follows.[17]
1. Heightened competition between hotel developers for sites, funds and custom leads to demand for more accurate studies.
2. Greater consumer sensitivity to the price–value relationship. Hoteliers believe feasibility studies can improve the fit between market and product.
3. The greater number of participants in hotel investment—i.e. management companies, lenders, developers and equity investors—creates demand for feasibility studies by independent third parties.
4. The impact of inflation upon construction costs can reduce profitability.

Figure 9.2 shows the data collection and analysis that takes place in a feasibility study.[18]

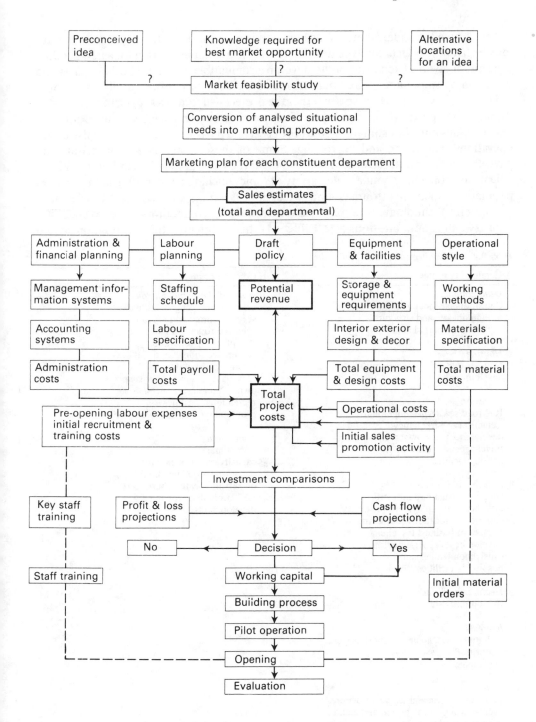

Figure 9.2   Feasibility study.

The motive for undertaking a feasibility study may be to identify gaps in the market for which new products could be developed, to find a suitable location for a new product concept, or given a fixed location, to develop a compatible product. In other words, the study can be stimulated by external demand conditions or internal supply conditions.

The aim, however, is to assess whether the project will return a satisfactory reward to the interested parties—i.e. developers, financiers, owners and management. Both costs and revenues must be estimated. Sources of cost and payroll, materials, administration, operations, marketing and borrowing. Some of these costs, notably materials and payroll, are related to sales, so most studies start by estimating demand potential.

Data are collected about a wide variety of topics, including the trading area, resident population, incoming tourists and excursionists, transport, sources of demand, legislation, technology, the physical environment, competitors, site availability, industry and communications (see Table 9.4). In combination this information should

Table 9.4 *Data collected in feasibility studies.*

A Community profile	B Competitor profile
1 *Demographics* Education/age/income/social class/ race/family size and structure/ employment/marital status	1 *Hotels and accommodation* Beds/rooms/occupancies/market segments targeted/rack rates/ achieved room rates/length of stay/property condition/
2 *Housing* Number/type/prices/ownership/ developments	conference rooms/food and beverage/ location/accessibility/ seasonality/reservation system/ ownership/guest services/
3 *Transport* Rail/road/sea/air/passenger and freight/service frequency/ developments/car ownership/ travel agents/ accessibility/ parking facilities	recreational facilities/ profitability/planned developments 2 *Food service* Target markets/types/seating capacity/service standard/ decor/prices/opening hours/
4 *Industry and commerce* Employers/standard industrial classification/employment/prospects/ conferences/locations/source and number of business travellers/ developments/general health/ satisfaction with existing hospitality facilities	ownership/locations/turnover/ ASP/profitability/planned developments
5 *Health and education* Institutions/visitors/developments	
6 *Recreation* Facilities/amusement and sport/usage/ visitor traffic/seasonality/ developments	
7 *Other* Festivals/historic and scenic attractions/ events/local government/planning and licensing restrictions/local associations/ agricultural markets/military establishments/ physical environment	

identify the strength of competition and demand potential for the product concept. In practice, hotel feasibility studies are much more comprehensive than those of food service operations because the level of investment is higher and the geographical market from which custom is obtained much wider.

Sources of information about the community include tourist information offices, trade directories, Yellow Pages, Chambers of Commerce, local newspapers and radio stations. Whilst it is relatively easy to 'case' a competitor's hotel or restaurant, gaining access to confidential records is more difficult.

Demand for a new product concept may be judged at 3 levels: pessimistic, normal, or optimistic, and a weighted average is taken. Against these revenue estimates are set costs for profit calculation.

Some feasibility studies attempt to estimate the full economic life of a property and its eventual disposal. These reports try to predict the commercial value of the property or site at the end of its life cycle. Laventhol & Horwath produce cash-flow projections for a 10-year period, adding in inflationary effects.[19]

If at the end of the business analysis or feasibility stage the product concept does not meet a pre-set criterion of minimum profit, then the idea should be abandoned. Otherwise it should proceed to the next stage. But just how much profit should be the acceptable criterion? Normally profits need to satisfy at least 4 conditions, as follows.

1. Profit as a percentage of capital employed should be related to:
   - any necessary increase in capital needed to develop and market the new product
   - the risk involved; the less the company's previous experience with the product or market, the higher the risk
   - the size and growth level of the product's intended market
   - the performance of other companies in the same industry
   - the expectations of stakeholders in the company
2. The profits earned should provide for:
   - future new product development
   - dividends to shareholders
   - satisfactory emoluments to directors
   - tax demands
3. The profit should enable the 'real' value of the assets to be maintained.
4. The profit should contribute towards the maintenance of a satisfactory profit record.

9.10 NPD: DEVELOPMENT

During this stage the mental prototype is transformed into a marketable product. Finance is secured and property design and construction, installation of equipment and recruitment of staff take place. For example, in developing a restaurant diagrams are produced which integrate the 4 basic flows of any food service system, as follows.[20]

1. Product flow, from delivery through storage, preparation and service to customer.
2. Employee flow, from dressing-rooms to work stations and through their various duties.
3. Hardware flow, of crockery, cutlery and glassware from storeroom, to table and sink and back.

4. Guest flow, from parking and entrance to table, cashier, toilet and exit.

Marketing's influence does not falter. Marketers ensure that the product is developed in line with the approved concept and finalise a marketing plan based on the strategy outlined earlier.

9.11 NPD: TESTING

The fully developed product is now ready to be marketed. Some companies elect to trial their product on a small scale prior to going to wider or national introduction. This is known as 'test marketing', or 'market testing', and is defined as a live marketing situation analogous to an intended large-scale or national launch. It is the final risk-reduction opportunity before commitment of further resources. The main objectives for test marketing are to:

1. Establish what sales volume or market share a product will obtain nationally.
2. Test particular components of the marketing mix.
3. More clearly identify the product's prime prospects and customer mix.
4. Estimate effect of the new product launch on total market size.

However, there are excellent reasons why the hospitality industry does not always test market.

1. Many hospitality marketers only own/manage a single site, so it is not possible to construct an experiment involving interunit comparisons.
2. Entrepreneurs opening their first unit cannot experiment on a small scale. They either open for business with the approved product concept or do not open at all.
3. Evidence that the product concept has succeeded elsewhere—many franchises have been imported to the UK following success in the USA.
4. The nature of costs—a very high proportion of hospitality costs are fixed such as rent, rates, insurance, and interest; some are semi-fixed such as lighting, heating and labour; and others are variable such as food and drink and laundry. Consequently the costs of withdrawing an unsuccessful new product and developing a replacement are low—as are the risks.
5. Change is endemic in some catering operations—gourmet restaurants change menus frequently, unlike speciality restaurants. Change or experimentation is sometimes a competitive strength.
6. The tangible dimension of the hospitality product is easy to duplicate. Large-scale marketing pre-empts competitors who may be quick to copy.
7. Many new hospitality products are line extensions or product improvements developed in response to consumer demand. Market testing may be superfluous.

Despite this, a number of hospitality marketers do opt for experimental test markets. The recent repositioning strategy of Kentucky Fried Chicken, which incorporated changes to the menu, was tested experimentally.[21] Over a 10-month period sales in the 2 test regions, the south-west and East Anglia, rose by 43 and 45 per cent respectively, and the distribution of sales throughout the day changed.

The process of test marketing is a multistage procedure (see Figure 9.3).

Step 1   Devise test market objectives
We have already discussed the main objectives for undertaking a test market.

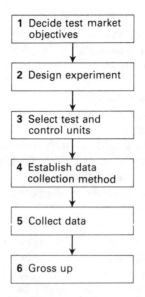

Figure 9.3   The process of test marketing.

Step 2   Design experiment
A test market is basically an applied experiment in which data are collected from a test unit (hotel or restaurant) and compared to similar data collected from a unit where the new product is not available. The most frequently used form of test market experiment is the pre-test/post-test control group design (as discussed in Chapter 3). The experimental design has to be more sophisticated when attempting to gauge the overall effect of different marketing mixes. However, in a country of only 55 million people, finding matched test and control units for each of the marketing mix combinations can be difficult. One valuable extension of the experimental design is to lengthen the period over which pre- and post-launch measurements are taken. This enables an analysis of market trends to be made and permits estimations of the shape of the product life cycle.

This leads us to consider the duration of the tests. The length of time over which measurements are taken should relate to the objectives for the test. If, for instance, a company is trying to measure the percentage of first-time buyers that become repeat buyers, then the period should be appropriately extended. A. C. Nielsen Ltd believe that an 8-month test market is necessary before a confident prediction can be made about the success of a national roll-out.[22] However, such a lengthy period invites the national launch of a competitive product.

Step 3   Select test and control areas
At least 3 sets of criteria should be considered in selecting the areas:
  • *demographic criteria*   The demographic structure of the country as a whole should be reflected accurately in the trading areas of both units
  • *product-specific demographics*   The intended target market for the product should be reflected in the test and control areas in the same proportion that it occurs in the national market

- *media and distribution*   If the intended advertising media schedule for the national launch includes, say, radio and local newspapers, then these media should be present—and used in the test market. Similarly, the intended form of national distribution should be reflected in test and control areas

Step 4   Establish data-collection method

The most common forms of data collection are:
- *sales audit*   Comparisons are made between the recorded sales of test and control units. If data are available, further comparisons are made with competitors
- *consumer panels*   A panel is a group of consumers which keeps records of its purchasing and consumption behaviour
- *omnibus surveys*   Questions are placed in commercial omnibus surveys

Step 5   Collect data

The company launching the new product has a choice of either using its own staff to undertake the research or using market research agencies to gather the data. The cost of specially commissioned research may be prohibitive, but some market research companies perform regular omnibus surveys in which it is possible to place questions; there are also established panels which may mean that it is unnecessary to commission special research.

Step 6   Gross up

If the objective of the test market is to estimate the market share or sales that would be achieved during a national launch, the marketer must consider how to develop national estimates from the experimental data. The most common method is a direct translation of the test. If the new product results in a 10 per cent increase in sales in the test area, it is assumed that it will have this effect nationally. Similarly, if market share in the test area rises by 3 per cent, this is taken as an indication of what will happen to national market share. A. C. Neilsen Ltd believe that there is a 50–50 chance that national sales will be within plus or minus 10 per cent of the test area results, given a 12-month test market.[23] However, there are several other ways of grossing up test market results, which can produce dramatically different estimates.[24]

9.12 NPD: COMMERCIALISATION

The final stage of the NPD process is the wider commercial launch of the product. Assuming that the product meets the success criteria of the test market, it can now, with the necessary adjustments to the marketing mix, be launched nationally. The test market will have indicated likely national sales volume, so tentative first-year trial purchase and repurchase objectives can be set consistent with expected sales volume and market share. The launch normally follows a planned market-by-market penetration pattern because the company has a number of time-consuming organisation development and marketing tasks to complete and cash-flow constraints. Figure 9.4 lists several recent new hospitality product introductions.

The prime target market for the initial launch consists of heavy buying early adopters

Product/brand	Introduced by:
Accommodation	
Comfort Inns	Comfort Hotels
Crowne Plaza (4 star)	Holiday Inns
Hampton Inns (budget)	Holiday Inns
Courtyard	Marriott
Park Hyatt	Hyatt
Food service	
Eleven Eleven (winebar)	Grand Metropolitan
Burgundy Room (restaurant)	Grand Metropolitan
Family Inns	Allied-Lyons
Barnaby's	Host Group
Drummond's (café bar)	Charrington
CK's (drive-thru restaurant)	Campbells Kitchens

Figure 9.4   New hospitality product introductions.

who are likely, at little cost, to influence other people to buy.[25] In notation form the target market can be defined thus:

$$V = A(Q + I) - C \qquad (9.1)$$

where V = the value of a prospect
A = the probability of the prospect being an early adopter
Q = the quantity an average early adopter buys in year 1
I = the quantity of purchases generated in others by the early adopter as a result of his influence
C = the cost of an effective communication exposure to this person

If we compare 2 target prospects, one of whom (y) has a higher probability of being an early adopter, but who buys little and has little influence on others, and another (z), who is a high-consuming, influential person less likely to be an early adopter, we can see how the first prospect is of greater value to the marketer:

prospect	value as target market
y	$V = 0.10 \, (£5.00 + £5.00) - £0.20 = £0.80$
z	$V = 0.02 \, (£10.00 + £10.00) - £0.20 = £0.20$

Prospect y is of greater value to the company.

9.13 NEW PRODUCT ADOPTION

The pattern and speed of adoption of a new product by its target market are related to 2 factors:
  (a) the nature of the new product
  (b) the nature of the target market
      • personally
      • socially

Five attributes of new products appear to influence the adoption process.[26]
1. *Relative advantage*   A product which is perceived as superior to competitors will spread more quickly. Superiority may be reflected in an improved relationship between price and quality.
2. *Compatibility*   If an innovation fits into the target market's lifestyle and value system, it will more readily be accepted.
3. *Complexity*   The simpler the product, and the quicker the consumer understands what the product can do for him, the faster will be the speed of adoption.
4. *Divisibility*   If the product can be tried on a limited scale without risk to the consumer, adoption is more speedy.
5. *Communicability*   Where the benefits of the product can be communicated to the target market, adoption will be quicker.

Certain types of people also seem to adopt new products earlier than others. Rogers[27] has assigned arbitrary labels to each of these groups of consumers, as shown in Table 9.5. Because of the assistance which would be given to new product marketers if they

Table 9.5   *Categories of adopters.*

Title	Time of adoption
Innovators	The first 2.5% of adopters
Early adopters	The next 13.5% of adopters
Early majority	The next 34% of adopters
Late majority	The next 34% of adopters
Laggards	The last 16% of adopters

were able to identify the early target markets (innovators and early adopters) demographically, much effort has been put into trying to isolate them. The general findings, which have tended to be confirmed by further research, are presented as Table 9.6. The table points to the need to aim communication about new products at early adopters and innovators. Many members of these 2 categories, but particularly the

Table 9.6   *Personal and social characteristics of adopter categories.*

	Personal characteristics	Social charactistics
Innovators	Risk-takers, venturesome, like new ideas, cosmopolite	Socially aggressive, communicative
Early adopters	Enjoy prestige as competent, knowledgeable early adopters; less venturesome than innovators; respectable, enjoy leadership; tend to reinforce opinion leadership position through seeking objective product information	Socially well-integrated; gregarious; influential of others' buying
Early majority	Tend to conform to social trends and follow opinions of early adopters; more traditional outlook; upper social classes	Well-integrated socially
Late majority	Orientated towards local or family events; not responsive to change; sceptical; follow the majority	Less gregarious than early majority
Laggards	Suspicious of change, cautious, conservative, cost-conscious, impervious to social pressure	Socially isolated

former, are opinion-leaders and socially gregarious people who enjoy the respect of others for their competence and expertise in certain areas. It is through opinion-leaders that word-of-mouth social influence is exerted; they tend to seek objective information which reinforces their social status as opinion-leaders before passing it on to others, who may either actively seek or be voluntarily offered advice. The process by which this occurs has become known as the 'two-step flow of communication'. It was first proposed in the 1940s by Lazarsfeld, Berelson and Gaudet, who having studied the pattern of social influence in an American presidential election, concluded: 'Ideas often flow from radio and print to the opinion leaders and from them to less active members of the community.'[28]

All this, of course, was in pre-television days, but nonetheless, the general conclusion is still supported. Opinion-leaders do legitimate product use, and others do follow the opinion-leader's purchasing behaviour. Studies have tended to support the view that personal influence from opinion-leaders is more persuasive at inducing changes in purchasing behaviour than mass-media influence, because it is perceived as more personal, flexible, non-purposive, independent and trustworthy. Opinion-leaders influence other members of their own social group. There is very little support for the view that influence trickles down from the upper social classes to the lower groups. Current theory holds that 'trickle-across' influence is the norm and that opinion-leaders, who exist within every stratum of society, only influence members of their own social class normally.

9.14 NEW PRODUCT SUCCESS

Why are some companies more successful at NPD, and what factors contribute towards the successful launch of a new product? Booz Allen & Hamilton's research shows that successful companies, in which 90 per cent of all new-product introductions meet company-set performance criteria, differ from the unsuccessful, in which less than 50 per cent of introductions satisfy the pre-set criteria in several important ways, as follows.[29]

1. A commitment to growth from internally developed new products which is reflected in a specific role for new products in the strategic corporate plan.
2. Screening procedures are more thorough.
3. Responsibility for NPD is more likely to be vested in R&D. Marketing and R&D functions are likely to have a greater degree of influence on the NPD process.
4. Stability—senior NPD executives are less likely to be replaced or moved on.
5. Experience with increased new-product experience, profitability is improved through cost reductions.
6. Flexible management style—3 styles have been identified: entrepreneurial, collegial and managerial. The entrepreneurial approach is more suited to new-to-the-world products and features an autonomous interdisciplinary new-product group. There is a positive environment for risk-taking. The collegial approach, which is associated with companies adding to existing product lines, is characterised by senior-management participation in NPD and a formalised process to ensure discipline and guide effort. The managerial approach is characterised by a top–down direction in

what is often a formalised and inflexible NPD process, and is associated with products with are closely linked to existing business.

Commenting specifically on the hospitality industry, Bellas and Olsen identify 4 key characteristics of successful innovators.[30]

1. A management commitment to innovation.
2. A means of directing NPD effort to achieve organisational goals. Successful innovators do less 'pure' research.
3. Application of a system for testing alternatives and making decisions. Major criteria are ROI and market share. The screening process is simultaneously undertaken by several individuals.
4. A means of implementation including an organisational climate conducive to change. There is a willingness to drop the old, add new, retrain staff and alter processes.

A. C. Nielsen Ltd have investigated the characteristics of successful, new fast-moving consumer goods distributed through retail channels.[31] Accepting that some hospitality products such as fast food are of this type, there are lessons to be learned by hospitality marketers (see Table 9.7).

Table 9.7   *Factors which influence product success.*

Potential	Excellent	Very good	Good	Poor
1 Originality	Patents afford complete protection	Resistant to patent infringement	Product difficult to imitate	Product easy to copy
2 Market position	Supplies unfilled need	Definite improvement over existing products	Some features that have consumer appeal	Barely distinguishable characteristics
3 Future customers	Customers should increase substantially	Customers should increase moderately	Customers should increase slightly	Customers will remain the same or decrease
Demand				
4 Durability	Constant basic demand	Product demand expected to return investment, plus many years of additional profits	Product demand expected to return investment and several years of profit	Product should return investment but profit returns highly speculative
5 Market dimensions	Wide range of customers nationally, plus export potential	Wide range of customers nationally, little foreign potential	Nationwide appeal, narrow range of customers	Limited customers and area appeal
6 Dependence on economic climate	Sold regardless of general economic conditions	Strongly resistant to economic change	Average sensitivity to economic change	Highly sensitive to economic change
7 Seasonal stability	Demand unchanged throughout entire year	Very minor seasonal variations	Predictable seasonal fluctuations	Strong seasonal fluctuations of varying intensities

	Excellent	Very good	Good	Poor
Marketing characteristics				
8 Distribution	Prime markets via present channels	Present channels for majority of prime markets	New and present channels required	Many or all new channels required
9 Relationship to present products	Reinforces present product line	Fits current line	Can be introduced to current line	A rather poor fit
10 Price/quality comparison with competition	Equal quality, priced below competition	Priced below majority of competitors	Equal in price, same quality	Higher priced than most competition, no better quality
11 Promotion potential	Characteristics superior to competition, suitable for promotion	Demonstration shows superiority over competition	Potential equal to competitors	Promotable characteristics do not measure up to competition
12 Effect on present products	Complements sales of present products	May aid sales of present products	No effect	May hinder

9.15 NEW PRODUCT MARKETING STRATEGY

There have been numerous studies of the reasons for new product failure.[32] A variety of inadequacies, most of them in marketing, have been identified, including: mistimed introduction, poorly defined NPD objectives, faulty product, unacceptable price-value relationship, inadequate advertising support, product not perceived as different from competitors, unsatisfactory positioning, inadequate product performance and distributor unwillingness to sell the product. Clearly, there is a need to create an effective marketing strategy. Much of the planning should have been completed during the business-analysis stage for small-scale implementation during the test market.

Considering 2 marketing mix variables only, price and promotion, there are 4 main strategic options (see Figure 9.5).[33] Rapid skimming strategy, which aims to produce high profit contribution per unit, combines a high price with heavy promotional expenditure, and is suitable when product awareness is low and innovators or early

		PROMOTION	
		Heavy	Light
PRICE	High	Rapid Skimming Strategy	Slow Skimming Strategy
	Low	Rapid Penetration Strategy	Slow Penetration Strategy

Figure 9.5   Four introductory marketing strategies.

adopters are willing to pay a high price and where the marketer is aiming to build brand preference prior to competitors entering the market. Slow skimming (high price/light promotion), which also is suitable for profit objectives, is suitable when product awareness is already high and little consumer education is required, and price sensitivity is low and leadtime over competitors is high.

Rapid penetration (low price/heavy promotion) aims to develop high market share and penetration whilst keeping unit contribution to profit low in order to inhibit competitors. This makes sense when the market is large, and product awareness is low and buyers are price-sensitive, and where economies of scale can be achieved and competitors are waiting in the wings. Slow penetration (low price/light promotion) is used to achieve high market shares in price-sensitive markets. Suitable conditions for this strategy are price sensitivity, large demand potential and high product awareness.

New-to-the-world product marketers have greater freedom to select from these options, but marketers of products less differentiated from competition have less discretion over prices which are more or less determined by competitors. Only pioneers can opt for very high prices.

Distribution is being slowly developed in the early stages of the product life cycle. Food service independents are transformed into multiples as more units are opened; hotels often start by opting for one or few of the many channels of distribution open to them—e.g. direct sale and travel agents.

9.16 CHAPTER REVIEW

1. A new product is one which is *perceived* as different by consumers.
2. New products may be new-to-the-world, new product lines, line extensions, improvements/ revisions, repositionings, or cost reductions.
3. New products are developed for strategic and tactical reasons.
4. Strategic reasons for NPD are profit maintenance, profit growth and defence of market share, to gain entry to a new market, maintain status as innovator, generate cash, exploit technology, or to capitalise on competitive strength.
5. Tactical reasons for NPD include the use of off-season capacity, avoidance of labour lay-offs and destruction of competitors' test markets or new product launches.
6. New product introductions are normally evaluated against a set of financial and marketing criteria, including sales volume, ROI and profit contribution.
7. The NPD process comprises 7 steps: new product strategy development; idea generation; screening and evaluation; business analysis and feasibility study; development; testing; and commercialisation.
8. New product strategy clearly defines the roles for new products, establishes screening/ evaluation criteria and provides a focus for idea generation.
9. Sources of new ideas can be internal or external to the company.
10. Ideas are collected through formalised marketing research or informal marketing intelligence.
11. Stimulants to creative output are creativity tests; climate measurement; morphological analysis; brainstorming; forced relationships; synectics and work simplification; and suggestion schemes.
12. Screening is a quick, cheap and effective method of eliminating weak ideas. Most screens follow a checklist format.
13. The business-analysis stage is better known as the 'feasibility study' in hospitality marketing.
14. Prior to the feasibility study, the idea must be converted into a full product concept together with an outline marketing strategy.

15. Feasibility studies aim to assess whether the product concept, if launched, will return a satisfactory reward to the interested parties—e.g. developers, financiers, owners and management. Data are collected about likely demand and costs, and a satisfactory level of profit is established.
16. During development those concepts which have passed through business analysis are transformed into marketable products.
17. Testing is a trial stage during which the product and associated marketing strategy are tested for an experimental period on a small scale.
18. Many hospitality companies do not test-market.
19. The test marketing process comprises 6 stages: set objectives; devise experimental design; select, test and control units; establish data-collection method; and collect data and gross up results.
20. The prime prospects for the launch of a new product are heavy-buying early adopters who are likely, at little cost, to influence others to buy.
21. The speed and pattern of a new product adoption is dependent upon 2 factors: the product and the target market.
22. Products which display relative advantage, compatibility, simplicity, divisibility and communicability are more readily adopted.
23. Five 'adopter categories' have been identified: innovators; early adopters; early majority; late majority; and laggards.
24. Opinion-leaders play an influential role in the adoption process.
25. Successful innovating companies have a sophisticated operating philosophy towards new products, house NPD in the R&D function, have a history of NPD experience, and select and revise a style of NPD management appropriate to existing and changing new product opportunities.
26. Conditions which imply a successful future for the new product are constant basic demand, independence of economic climate, distribution through existing channels, compatibility with existing product mix and superiority over competitors.
27. There are many causes of new product failure, most of them in marketing.
28. Opening marketing strategies for newly launched products can be defined in terms of price (high or low) and promotional expenditure (heavy or light).

9.17 QUESTIONS AND EXERCISES

1. What new hospitality products are, or would have been, suitable for launch by rapid skimming, slow skimming, rapid penetration and slow penetration strategies?
2. You are an entrepreneur considering opening your first Burmese speciality restaurant in London. What criteria would you use for your initial screening?
3. A restaurant site has become available in a town of your choice. Detail the information you would collect in a feasibility study and the sources of information.
4. The mortality rate for independent restaurants is very high. What are likely to be the major causes?
5. If you were the marketing manager for a national fast-food chain and wanted to test the acceptability of a new menu, how would you design your test market? Use Figure 9.3 to guide your thinking.
6. List new hospitality products recently introduced into an area of your choice. Are they new-to-the-world, new product lines, line extensions, improvements/revisions, repositionings, or cost reductions?
7. Brainstorm ideas for a new fast-food operation at a specific site of your choice. Meet as a group of 6–10 people for 40 minutes, record proceedings on cassette tape and do not criticise or evaluate. Transcribe ideas on paper.
8. How much do relative advantage, compatibility, complexity, divisibility and communicability account for successful recent hospitality innovations such as doner kebab outlets, city-centre

sandwich bars and budget hotels? Do these factors have different significance for high-priced products such as gourmet restaurants, long-haul holidays and 5-star hotels?

REFERENCES

[1] Booz Allen & Hamilton Inc. (1982) *New Products Management for the 1980s.*
[2] ibid., p. 15.
[3] For a review of the literature see Crawford, C. M. (1977) Marketing research and the new product failure rate. *Journal of Marketing*, April, 51–61.
[4] Hopkins, D. S. and Bailey, E. L. (1971) New product pressures. *Conference Board Record*, June, 16–24.
[5] See Bellas, C. J. and Olsen, M. (1978) Managing innovation. *Cornell Hotel and Restaurant Administration Quarterly*, **19**(2), August, 26–9.
[6] Booz Allen & Hamilton Inc. (1982) op. cit., 11.
[7] Cornwell, R. and Greene, M. (1968) *Improving Hotel Profitability*. London: Northwood. 14.
[8] Rathmell, J. M. (1974) *Marketing in the Service Sector*. Cambridge. Mass. Winthrop, 63.
[9] Thomas, M. and Goodwin, J. (1976) An examination of the management of the research and development—marketing interface in several British companies. *Quarterly Review of Marketing*, Autumn,
[10] Rathmell, J. M. (1974) op. cit., 62.
[11] See Booz Allen & Hamilton Inc. (1968) *Management of New Products.*
[12] Holt, K. (1977) *Product Innovation*. London: Newnes-Butterworth, 79–89.
[13] Gordon, W. J. J. (1961) *Synectics*. London: Harper & Row.
[14] See, for example, Berridge, T. (1977) *Product Innovation and Development*. London: Business Books, 52–6.
[15] Holt, K. (1977) op. cit., 90.
[16] Keiner, R. (1977) Feasibility studies; still feasible?, in Brymer, R. A. (ed.) *Introduction to Hotel and Restaurant Management*. Des Moines, IA: Kendall-Hunt, 187.
[17] See Beals, P. and Troy, D. A. (1982) Hotel feasibility analysis: 1. *Cornell Hotel and Restaurant Administration Quarterly*, **23**(1), May, 11–17.
[18] See Davies, E. J. G. (1975) Market feasibility studies for hotels and restaurants, in Kotas, R. (ed.) *Market Orientation in the Hotel and Catering Industry*. Guildford: Surrey University Press.
[19] Keiner, R. (1977) op. cit.
[20] ibid.
[21] See: How KFC plan to fly back up the pecking order. *The Times*, 21 June 1983.
[22] A. C. Nielsen Ltd (1972) The odds in test marketing. *Nielsen Researcher*, 4.
[23] ibid.
[24] Buttle, F. (1976) Test marketing: go national or go broke. *Management Decision*, **14**(1).
[25] Kotler, P. and Zaltman, G. (1976) Targeting for a new product. *Journal of Advertising Research*, February.
[26] Rogers, E. M. (1962) *The Diffusion of Innovations*. New York: The Free Press.
[27] ibid.
[28] Lazarsfeld, P. F., Berelson, B. R., and Gaudet, H. (1948) *The People's Choice*. New York: Columbia University Press.
[29] Booz Allen & Hamilton Inc. (1982), op. cit.
[30] Bellas, C. J. and Olsen, M. (1978) op. cit.
[31] A. C. Nielsen Ltd (1970) The realities of new product marketing. *Nielsen Researcher*, 1.
[32] See, for example, Marvin, P. (1963) Why new products fail, in Berg, T. and Shuchman, A. (eds.) *Product Strategy and Management*. New York: Rinehart & Winston; A. C. Nielsen Ltd (1973) Test marketing reduces risks. *Nielsen Researcher*, 1; Angelus, T. L. (1969) Why do most new products fail? *Advertising Age*, **24**, March; and Berridge, T. (1977) op. cit., 14–15.
[33] Based on Kotler, P. (1984) (5th edn) *Marketing Management: Analysis, Planning and Control*. Englewood Cliffs, NJ: Prentice-Hall, 363.

Marketing Mature Products

10.1 CHAPTER PREVIEW

The majority of hospitality products on sale today are mature. This chapter gives guidelines which can be used, first, to identify when a product has entered the maturity stage of its life cycle; and second, profitably to extend its commercial life. We end with a discussion of the product deletion decision.

10.2 LEARNING OBJECTIVES

By the end of this chapter you should be able to:
1. Identify when a product is in the maturity stage of the product life cycle (PLC).
2. Describe 4 strategic options for mature products.
3. Construct a list of key questions to be answered when appraising candidate products for deletion.

10.3 THE MATURE PRODUCT SCENE

Many hospitality products have long and successful maturity periods. Kardomah (established in the UK in 1844), Wimpy (1954), Little Chef (1959) and Berni Inns (1961) have all seen their fortunes rise and fall, often to rise again through innovative marketing.[1]

Whilst these *brand* life cycles have experienced long maturities, many innovations to (and variations on) the basic product have been more short-lived. Each change to the core, tangible, or augmented product that is perceived as different by the consumer could conceivably be regarded as a new product, the sales and profit performance of which could be tracked by a separate PLC.

Let us briefly review what is happening in the market-place during a product's maturity. The review will help marketers to identify when a product has reached this stage of the PLC.

Heavy competition

Both the number of competing companies and their combined capacity (rooms or seats) reach their maximum during the maturity stage, although towards the end of this stage some competitors may drop out. Mature competition takes various forms as follows:

1. Product improvements or modifications introduced by competitors begin to undermine demand.[2]
2. Price competition is commonplace. Discount structures are developed for different hotel users. Price deals are frequent in food service.
3. Small-scale marketers meet the needs of the smaller market segments.
4. Hoteliers and food service operators integrate with suppliers or distributors for added competitive strength.
5. Promotional expenditure aims to build brand preference in order to reduce brand switching but claims may become less effective as purchase patterns become entrenched.

Market segmentation

The market is typically subdivided into very small subsets of demand.

Product proliferation

The number of competing products has never been greater, nor will be any greater in the future. Competition may use multiple-branding strategies. Under these sorts of conditions brands can lose their distinctiveness and consumers may become disenchanted.

Market penetration

Most mature products will never achieve deeper market penetration and market share than they do in the early maturity stage. Although sales volume might remain static because of market growth, market share normally falls in the later maturity period as the market diminishes.

10.4 MARKETING STRATEGIES FOR MATURE PRODUCTS

As sales and profits are eroded management may be tempted to divest. Indeed this makes sense if the product is a 'dog' (low relative market share in a low-growth market). However, mature products may also be 'question-marks' (low share, high growth), 'stars' (high share, high growth), or 'cash cows' (high share, low growth) in which there is considerable market potential. (See Chapter 7.)

In multiproduct firms a selection of mature question-marks could be chosen to *build* market share in order to become tomorrow's stars. Today's stars and cash cows should aim to *maintain* market share. The effect of this is to ensure that: (1) the star transforms into an income-generating cash cow as market growth slows down; and (2) the cash cow does not become transformed into a dog due to erosion of market share.

There are 4 basic forms of marketing strategy during the maturity stage:

1. Seek out new target markets.
2. Increase per capita consumption.

3. Repositioning.
4. Adjust the marketing mix.

It is important to emphasise that the chosen strategy should be *profitable*. It can be a relatively simple affair to maintain a high level of sales through sales promotions, advertising, new market entries, product modifications and improvements and use of new distribution channels. Profitable sales volume requires the marketing manager to keep guard over costs. During the maturity stage costs tend to rise as a result of the loss of scale economies following the introduction of modified products to suit specific market segments. This is often accompanied by segment-directed advertising and promotion, and higher inventory costs say for an increased variety of menu items. The emphasis in the maturity stage should be to lift or maintain sales volume, but not at the expense of profits.

Seek out new target markets

The new target market is usually defined geographically or demographically. International hotel groups have established new units in key locations around the world. American hoteliers have generally looked to Europe, the Middle East and Asia. There are signs that Asian hotel groups, particularly those in Singapore and Hong Kong, want to expand westwards.

Sometimes the geographical shift is accompanied by identification of a new demographic target market. Holiday Inns in the USA aims at travellers of a lower socioeconomic status than does Holiday Inns in the UK.

Targeting the product at a new demographic market can, of course, occur quite independently of any geographical shift. A city-centre restaurant appealing to lunchtime businessmen might target young couples in the evening. There is a danger that the two segments may be incompatible. Some resort hoteliers are loath to house groups of young people and families simultaneously. Other hoteliers, targeting the female business traveller, have introduced 'women-only' floors.

A second way of defining new target markets is in terms of brand choice. A deliberate attempt could be made to poach customers from a competing operation.

A third form of new target market is the non-user; these are prospects who do not currently buy from the product category, line, or type. Fast-food outlets could target older customers. Hotel coffee-shops could target shoppers.

Increase per capita consumption

Consumption can be increased among existing customers in a number of ways. First, by encouraging more frequent purchase: instead of taking 1 short-break holiday in a year, why not take 2? Participation in Let's Go, a weekend-break promotion scheme, has had dramatic effects. Small hotels significantly gain, particularly in seaside and rural areas. One group reports occupancy up 28 per cent, and revenue up 20 per cent.[3] Second, by developing new uses for the product: instead of private club members only using the facilities for lunchtime business meetings, they could be encouraged to book functions or stay overnight. Third, by increasing ASP or average guest expenditure: ASP can be raised through encouraging diners to buy desserts, wine and liqueurs; average guest expenditure can be raised through selling in-hotel amenities such as room service, the sauna and cocktail lounge.

Repositioning

As we noted in Chapter 9, repositionings are a way of revitalising sales of an existing product. This is normally done by promoting secondary benefits.

A spa hotel could reposition as a conference centre. A baked-potato operation might shift from offering convenience food to high-fibre health food. In both cases the tangible product does not change, but the core and augmented products do.

Adjust the marketing mix

Sometimes repositioning is accompanied by a major overhaul of the marketing mix. Imperial Inns, for example, have mapped out 12 different food service concepts to revitalise flagging sales and profits from their public houses—an investment of some £50 million over 5 years.[4] On other occasions modifications to 1 or more elements of the marketing mix may be sufficient to postpone entry to the decline stage of the PLC.

Product
Modifications can be made to the core product, the tangible product (e.g. hotel refurbishment), or to the augmented product (e.g. improved staff training). For example, the Cavalier restaurant chain have recently introduced new menu items and decor in order to distance themselves from the conventional steak house. Profits and meal numbers have risen in consequence.[5]

Price
Discount structures can be introduced to stimulate further demand and promote loyalty. Improved credit can take the form of acceptance of foreign currency and credit cards.

Place
Investigation of new sites or exploration of franchising, licensing and management contracts. New channels of distribution may be pursued.

Promotion
New advertising campaigns can involve greater expenditure or new copy strategy, together with sales promotion to stimulate repeat purchase (e.g. executive clubs); the overhaul of salesforce remuneration; salesforce refresher training; and improved merchandising and publicity.

10.5 PRODUCT DELETION

Eventually all products come to the end of their PLCs. Decline sets in due to technological obsolescence, competitive activity, government legislation, or changing consumer tastes. To these environmental forces there may be no suitable marketing response, but management often clings on to old products.

Sentiment and self-preservation are 2 disincentives to product deletion. Sentiment because management can develop an unreasoned affection and defensive attitude towards long-established items, and self-preservation because jobs are often axed when products are dropped; and particularly at risk are product or brand managers.

Weak products, especially those with small shares of static or declining markets, can be millstones around corporate necks. They drain resources, exhaust reserves which could be used for new product development and absorb unwarranted management time and effort. For this reason it is recommended that the internal audit of the annual marketing plan contains a product-appraisal component where rigorous criteria are applied to all products and candidates for deletion are identified. The questions to be asked include the following.

1. Is the product experiencing a drop in its share of company turnover?
2. Is the total market in decline?
3. Is the product a 'cash cow', 'star', 'dog' or 'question-mark'?
4. Are prices being eroded through competition?
5. Is there a decline in the product's turnover?
6. Is the product's market share falling?
7. Is the profit contribution of the product less than satisfactory?
8. Is management time spent on this product disproportionately high when compared to its profit contribution?
9. Are sales representatives and distributors having more difficulty selling the product this year than last?
10. Can it be proven that if the product were retained, there would be an adverse effect on overall company profitability?
11. Can it be shown that the sales of other products in the product mix are not dependent upon the sales of this product?
12. Can the capital investment in the product be put to more productive use?
13. If the product were dropped, what would be the effect on the costings of other products?
14. Does the product fit into the desired product portfolio?

There have been several attempts to devise systematic procedures for identifying and deleting weak products.[6] What is happening, in effect, is a reversal of the new product screening procedure recommended in Chapter 9, the results of which may be either rapid divestment or a slower market-by-market exit.

In the hospitality industry occasionally it can be very difficult to divest. Hotel and restaurant properties which are badly located for current market demand can be hard to sell. On the other hand, London hotels are exchanged for enormous sums because both properties and development sites are scarce.

10.6 CHAPTER REVIEW

1. Most hospitality products are mature.
2. Characteristics of the mature market are its intense competition, extreme segmentation, product proliferation and the depth of the product's market penetration.

3. The principal marketing objectives for mature products are the profitable maintenance or growth of market share.
4. Four strategic options are: (1) seek out new target markets: (2) increase per capita consumption; (3) repositioning; and (4) adjustment of the marketing mix.
5. Product deletion decisions are sometimes postponed for reasons of sentiment or self-preservation.
6. Deletion decisions should be made following appraisal of the product's true revenue, cost and profit contribution to corporate performance.

10.7 QUESTIONS

1. You are a catering manager at a college. Demand has been static for 2 years, although you still have unused productive capacity and empty seats. You are not yet breaking even. What strategic options do you have?
2. Draw up a checklist of questions to be asked during product appraisal, with a view to identifying candidates for deletion. Put yourself in the position of a small hotelier, with 50 bedrooms, 1 function room/dining-room with 35 covers, a licensed bar and gamesroom.
3. Drawing on your general knowledge, which of the following catering operations are in the maturity or decline stages? Beefeater, Casey Jones, MacDonald's, Pizza Hut and Wendy Hamburgers.
4. Would you ever launch a new product into a declining market? Give reasons for your answer.

REFERENCES

[1] *Popular Foodservice*, December 1983, 55 ff.
[2] For example, see: Cut throat competition shifts menu emphasis in steak houses. *Caterer and Hotelkeeper*, 19 January 1984, 51 ff.
[3] Ryan, C. (1980) The success of weekend promotions. *Hospitality*, January, 60.
[4] Hyam, J. (1984) Courage's bold plans to transform pub catering. *Caterer and Hotelkeeper*, 2 February.
[5] See: Families and themes feature in Tetley Walker restaurant plans. *Caterer and Hotelkeeper*, 5 April 1984.
[6] Hamelman, P. W. and Mazze, E. M. (1972) Improving product abandonment decisions. *Journal of Marketing*, April, 20–6; and Kotler, P. (1965) Phasing out weak products. *Harvard Business Review*, March–April, 107–18.

SECTION 2
Price

—11—

Principles of Pricing

11.1 CHAPTER PREVIEW

In this chapter we define price and discuss its significance to marketers. The bulk of the chapter, however, describes 10 influences upon the price decision—over 4 of which the marketer normally has a good deal of control, but in 6 of which the company is powerless to manipulate.

11.2 LEARNING OBJECTIVES

By the end of this chapter you should be able to:
1. Distinguish between price, worth and value.
2. Identify the main controllable and uncontrollable influences upon the pricing decision.
3. Explain the importance of costs in pricing.

11.3 INTRODUCTION

Pricing is the second of the 4 marketing mix components—product, price, place and promotion—that we are examining in Part III of this book. It could be expected, when considering the importance attached to price by economists, that a similar value would be attached to it by marketers. This is not the case. The economist's view of man's motivation has been that man is a rational and economic creature. He is seen as a calculating, cautious purchaser who carefully and systematically evaluates alternatives against price.

The marketing view of consumer motivation has absorbed this rational-economic model. Marketers are quite prepared to accept that economic motives do influence purchasing behaviour, but not in every circumstance. The marketing view also incorporates the belief that man is a social creature, motivated by social needs, deriving his behaviours and values from social contact and responsive to group influence. Marketers have also adopted the point of view that man is motivated by a need to fulfil himself creatively, to make maximum use of his personal resources.

However, the point of view which best describes the marketers' view of human behaviour is that man is a complex, multimotivated creature, acting according to motives both innate and learned, and capable of learning new motives and of behaving in a way which appears inconsistent with his expressed motivation.

In other words, price is not always a prime motivator; in fact occasionally a high-price item sells better than a lower-priced item possessing the same economic utilities. An expensive discothèque is often more attractive for a special night out than its cheaper competitor.

11.4 WHAT IS PRICE?

Price is:

> the summation of all sacrifices made by a consumer in order to experience the benefits of a product.

This definition includes both financial and other sacrifices such as time and energy expenditure; it is deliberately wide because the marketer has to realise that given an acceptable monetary price, the consumer may still not buy the product if the other sacrifices are too great. This chapter and Chapter 12 will primarily concentrate on the monetary dimension of the price.

An additional confusion is created by the careless and misleading use of the words 'worth', 'value' and 'cost'. A free gift of half a carafe of house wine may be given to the purchaser of a meal, the restaurant claiming it is worth £2, when what in fact is true is that the normal price for the wine is £2. Let us now clarify these terms. The value of the wine would vary from customer to customer. For the customer who holds the wine in low esteem it is of little value. An object which is highly valued is, therefore, one which is held in high esteem. Because highly esteemed products are often those of better quality, the relationship between value and price has been defined thus:[1]

$$\text{Value} = \frac{\text{quality}}{\text{price}} \qquad (11.1)$$

The worth of that object is also a subjective matter. A highly valued object has great worth—'worth' being sacrifice that the purchaser is *prepared* to make; the cost of the object is the sacrifice which the purchaser *actually* does make.

Despite these adverse remarks about its significance, price is important for a number of reasons.

1. Price is sometimes said to be the only means by which a company directly earns income. All other marketing mix components are cost creating or expense producing.
2. The price level at which a product sells can be a major contributor to brand image. Certainly, a major strategic price decision concerns whether to meet, or to price above or below, the competition; this is fundamental to the product positioning decision.
3. Other things being equal, price can act as a deciding factor in the allocation of household resources. Many households budget formally.
4. In times of inflation price becomes of critical importance to business. Costs of creating and delivering a service may increase quite significantly. Without an appropriate increase in prices, margins will be eroded.
5. Price sensitivity is an important criterion in market segmentation. Some segments—e.g. the pleasure traveller—are more price sensitive than others.

6. Many new product failures have been attributed to consumer dissatisfaction with value and pricing.
7. In markets where products are not well differentiated by non-price variables, an increase in price can cause a significant drop in demand, and a drop in price can cause competitive retaliation. Price changes can, therefore, be particularly difficult decisions for products such as bed-and-breakfast establishments.
8. Price partly determines the speed of new product adoption. A low price, which is regarded as a relative advantage over competitors, accelerates the adoption process.
9. Consumers vary considerably with respect to price:
   - in general, consumers lack awareness of price and find it difficult to recall even recently paid prices;[2] without price awareness, price sensitivity is inconceivable
   - consumers habitually patronise different price brackets[3]
   - consumers vary in the number of price comparisons made before and after purchases
   - consumers vary in their confidence to negotiate price, and in their concern for extended payment methods

11.5 INFLUENCES UPON PRICING DECISION-MAKING

The process of price decision-making involves consideration of a number of factors, which can be sorted into 2 major categories:
1. *Controllable factors*   Factors over which the marketer has a large amount of control.
2. *Uncontrollable factors*   Factors in the company's trading environment over which there is little control, but which still influence the pricing decision.
The influences are shown diagrammatically in Figure 11.1. The figure suggests that the

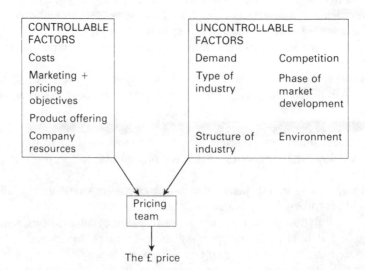

Figure 11.1   Influences upon the price decision.

pricing decision is made by a team; whereas it may not be formally made in committee, the pricing decision is of interest to accountants and marketers, sales and purchasing staff, engineers and trade unions for various reasons. It may affect their working environment, job content, or their departmental objectives or rate of pay. Many parties have an interest in the pricing decision and it is rare that the marketer has complete freedom to set price. The implication of the word 'team' is that there should be some integrated effort to set pricing objectives and work towards their achievement. Let us now examine each of these influences in detail.

Controllable factors

(1) Costs

A major input to the price decision is the cost of producing and marketing the product. Assuming the presence of a profit objective, during the course of a financial year all costs must be recovered and a profit made, although a company may suffer short-term losses in order that long-term profitability is enhanced.

In order to appreciate the cost-oriented pricing techniques presented in Chapter 12 we need to fully understand the nature of costs, of which there are several types:

Fixed costs do not vary with changes in sales volume. Examples are rent, rates, salaries, insurances and depreciation

Variable costs vary in proportion to sales. Examples are foods, beverages and laundry

Semi-fixed costs vary in sympathy with, but not in proportion to, sales volume. Examples are power, telephone and wages

Total costs are the aggregated fixed, variable and semi-fixed costs in a specified budgetary period

Average cost is total cost divided by number of units sold—rooms, guest-nights or covers; also known as 'unit cost' or 'average total cost'

Marginal cost is the increase in total cost caused by one more unit of output—i.e. accommodating 1 more guest

Direct costs are those which are traceable to a department or unit. Examples are food and kitchen labour

Indirect costs, also known as 'common' or 'joint' costs, are not traceable to particular units or departments. An example is general management

Controllable costs are those which management has the capacity to restrain. Examples are casual labour and food

Uncontrollable costs, such as rates and insurances, cannot be restrained by management

Discretionary costs are those which are incurred at the discretion of a particular person, normally of elevated status, such as the general manager. Examples are landscaping of grounds and refurbishment of rooms

Relevant costs are those which are pertinent to a given decision

Opportunity costs are the costs of *not* taking a particular course of action. If a restaurant is deciding whether to invest in refurbishment of existing premises or opening a second unit, the opportunity cost of pursuing one course of action is loss of the other

Standard costs are accepted or model costs for a given product or sales volume. The true costs of producing a meal vary from day to day according to input prices paid for meat, vegetables and other ingredients. Management prefers to use standard costs to calculate profit margins rather than make daily computations

In hospitality businesses a very high proportion of costs are fixed or semi-fixed.

Fixed costs partly result from the high level of capital intensity. Over 90 per cent of hotel capital is invested in fixed assets such as plant and buildings and fixtures and fittings. In catering establishments total investment is usually smaller, but the predominance of fixed assets is again the pattern. Variable assets, such as goods for sale, stock, cash-in-hand and debtors, account for the remaining 10 per cent. The dominance of fixed assets gives rise to high fixed costs of depreciation, insurance, rates and high semi-fixed costs of heating, lighting, labour, repairs and maintenance. Because of this, there is a significant dependence upon demand to generate profit.

Kotas demonstrates the relationship between cost structure, revenue and profit by comparing 2 hypothetical businesses of equal turnover (see Table 11.1).[4] Business A has a high proportion of fixed costs whilst business B has a high proportion of variable costs. Each suffers a 10 per cent loss of turnover. Because business A has a high proportion of fixed costs, total costs vary little but net profit drops by 40 per cent. Business B, the high variable cost business, sees total costs fall further, with the effect that net profits fall only by 20 per cent. Hence Kotas's comment that 'the hotel and catering manager must concern himself with the revenue side of the business at least as much as with the cost side'.[5]

Table 11.1   *Effects of turnover on profitability.*

| | Business A | | Business B | |
	Normal results £	Decreased sales £	Normal results £	Decreased sales £
Sales	10 000	9 000	10 000	9 000
Fixed costs	6 000	6 000	2 000	2 000
Variable costs	2 000	1 800	6 000	5 400
Total cost	8 000	7 800	8 000	7 400
Net profit	2 000	1 200	2 000	1 600

Medlik and Airey observe that:[6]

fixed costs [in hotels] remain static irrespective of occupancy and total variable costs rise more or less proportionately with occupancy. When unit costs are examined, the variable unit cost remains static but the fixed unit cost falls as occupancy increases. As each hotel bed has to bear its share of operating costs, it follows that with decreased occupancy the income from each occupied bed must meet a higher proportion of fixed costs.

In catering, fixed costs commonly are a smaller proportion of total costs—being between 45 and 55 per cent—than in hotels; the direct material costs of food and drink are normally between one-fifth and one-third of revenue. Consequently direct costs are a more important influence on food and beverage pricing than they are on room pricing.

The high proportion of fixed costs affords much discretion to the price-setter. If the variable costs of a single room sale in a 3-star hotel are estimated at £4 and competitors are charging £35 for similar accommodation, then there is a £31 discretionary price range. On the other hand, if the food costs for a meal total £1.00 and competitors retail a similar product at £4.00, then the range of price discretion is proportionately and monetarily much reduced. The relationship between fixed, variable and total costs is shown in Figure 11.2

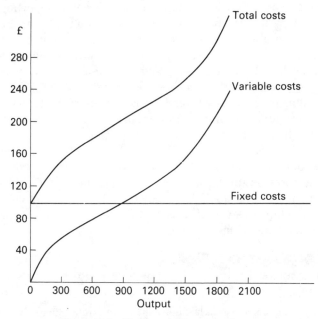

Figure 11.2   Fixed, variable and total costs.

The inclusion of cost considerations in the pricing decision abounds with difficulties.[7]
(a) Most costing techniques are retrospective. That is, they examine and record past expenses and expenditures. The pricing decision needs to be primarily prospective in orientation; the price set needs to recover not only past costs, such as those incurred during product development and testing, but also the future costs of producing and marketing the product. Frequently these costs are not known with any certainty and, to some degree, are uncontrollable.
(b) Depreciation of fixed assets is a major cost element in hospitality. Conventional accounting practice depreciates assets over their useful life, which may be 2 years for a piece of kitchen equipment or 40 years for a hotel. The process is one of allocating cost, not of revaluing the asset. However, prices must produce earnings which can be used to renew these capital items at their replacement cost.[8]
(c) A difficult accounting decision has to be made on how to apportion indirect costs between departments; this can have a significant effect upon apparent profits. Such costs include administration and general; advertising and promotion; heat, light and power; repairs and maintenance; and rent, rates, insurances, depreciation and interest.

Some of these costs can be apportioned logically. The cost of an advertising campaign to generate overnight guests would be charged to rooms (even though the food and beverage department may have benefited indirectly as a result). Other rules are to apportion administration and general expenses in line with departmental payroll; heat, light, power, rent, repairs and maintenance in proportion to departmental floor area; insurance in line with departmental sums assured; and depreciation on the basis of the department's or their cost or value relative to total cost or value. Common practice is not to apportion indirect costs, but to assess departmental performance on gross profit or contribution.

(d) Opportunity costs also need to be considered. The question is: should a company price to recover some of the interest it would have obtained had it invested resources elsewhere? The common practice is not to do so.

(e) The inclusion of costs in the pricing decision requires the company to establish policy on costing procedures. In some circumstances it is better to consider average costs; in others marginal costs are more important. Average costs tend to be used in long-term strategic pricing decisions and marginal costs in short-term tactical decisions. If a hotel is already making profit, then it will be profitable for a manager to accept a booking at below rack rate, provided that variable costs are recovered. For such a decision the appropriate concept is marginal cost. On the other hand, the rack rate will have been established following calculation of the total costs of hotel operation at a given level of occupancy; clearly, average cost is the more appropriate concept for this decision.

(2) Marketing and pricing objectives

Pricing objectives relate directly to marketing objectives which, in turn, depend upon company objectives:[9]

> In some instances, the objectives as laid down in the corporate plan can be translated more or less directly into pricing objectives. For example, a corporate objective of short-run profit-maximization leads to an objective of setting a price designed to maximise total contribution, or perhaps total cash flow.

More often it is the marketing objective which is the major influence on the pricing objective. The objective of high market share, for example, is normally inconsistent with above-average price whilst a marketing objective to acquire competitors' customers does not match a price which is perceived as offering poorer value for money than the competition.

Pricing objectives fall into 4 categories: profit-oriented, sales-oriented, competition-oriented and, for welfare organisations, cost-oriented objectives.

(a) Profit-oriented:

- maximisation of profit
- optimum profit
- satisfactory profit (known as 'satisficing')
- maximum positive cash flow
- maximum total contribution (calculated as total revenue less total variable costs)
- target return on investment (profitability)
- rapid payback—i.e. early recovery of capital investment
- harvesting i.e. reap cash for use in other ventures.

(b) Sales oriented:
- maximisation of sales volume
- satisfactory sales volume
- market share gain or maintenance
- target trial purchase level
- target repeat purchase level
- market penetration

(c) Competition-oriented:
- maintenance of price differentials
- matching competitors

(d) Cost-oriented:
- break even
- meet costs

Pricing objectives can be set for each department or product, each strategic business unit, or on any other basis appropriate to the company. The type of pricing objective has a bearing upon the techniques by which the price is calculated. For example, if the pricing objective is 'maximum profit', the marketer needs to calculate costs and demand for the product and perform a marginal analysis. Marginal analysis shows that maximum profit occurs at the sales volume where marginal cost equals marginal revenue (the income received from the sale of that last unit of output). We shall return to this in Chapter 12.

Pricing objectives may well vary between the short and long term. A new venture aiming for long term profitability may quote a target repeat purchase level as a short-term objective. Curiously, whilst the former is an 'end'-objective, the latter is a 'means'-objective.

(3) Product

The product can itself influence the price set by the marketer. Some product considerations which influence the price decision are listed below.

(a) *Novelty.* The newer the product, the more freedom there is in price setting. In new-to-the-world products the discretion in pricing is very high. The closer a new product becomes to being a copy or modification, the less discretion there is.

(b) *Product differentiation.* The more highly differentiated a product is from competitors, the more discretion there is in pricing. Hospitality products are differentiated through their tangible and augmented dimensions. Differentiation limits the substitutability between products. A high price is consistent with a well-differentiated product.

(c) *Prestige.* The more prestigious the product, the more freedom that is afforded the manager in setting a higher price. High occupancy levels at London's five-star hotels suggest that customers seeking prestigious accommodation are insensitive to price. However, 1- and 2-star hotels have to stay close to the going rate for similar establishments—too low and quality becomes suspect, too high and occupancy falls.

Many consumers perceive a relationship between the price of a product and its quality. Price tends to be used as an indicator of quality where:[10]

- the consumer has inadequate knowledge about either the company or the product; a holidaymaker uses price if he is unfamiliar with a resort's restaurants
- the consumer is uncertain of the criteria most suitable to assess quality; when purchasing spirits, a customer makes use of brandname to judge quality, but how does he judge a barman-prepared cocktail unless by price?
- the consumer knows how to assess product quality, but is not able to apply the criteria because of uncertainty about the accuracy of product information
- the consumer possesses product knowledge but is unsure as to its predictive validity as an indicator of quality

(d) The extent to which the *product is independent of other products in a line*. If a product is introduced as a line extension, then the price must be consistent with the others in that line. The more independent the product, the more discretion has the price-setter.

(e) *Product positioning*. The fundamental strategic decision which influences every element of the marketing mix, including price.

(f) *Perishability*. The more perishable the product, the greater is the need for flexibility in pricing decisions. As noted earlier, an unoccupied hotel room is a sale lost forever. Rigidity in negotiating room rates may result in lost profits, whereas it may be more advantageous for a room to be occupied, even if at a much discounted price.

(g) *Atmosphere*. The costs of producing the atmosphere component of the meal experience are largely fixed, labour and depreciation of fixtures and fittings being the 2 major elements. As ASP rises secondary products tend to become more important, and primary products less important. Consumer perceptions of the value of atmosphere become a more important consideration in pricing than material costs.

(4) Company resources

The fourth controllable factor which influences pricing decisions is company resources:

- generally speaking, the wealthier a company, the more able it is to support an unprofitable product or a loss leader—i.e. a product with a deliberately low (loss-making) price which attracts customers. Similarly, larger companies have a higher tolerance of short-term losses which can be incurred during the low-priced introduction of a new product
- working capital resources have an effect on costings. Old, inefficient plant generally produces higher unit costs than more modern investments. This will also influence price

Uncontrollable factors

We discuss 6 factors over which a company can exert little control, but which none the less do influence pricing decisions.

(1) Demand

At best, any one company can only partially influence total industry demand. Microdemand—i.e. demand for one company's products—is indeed controlled to a large degree by that company's own marketing, but unless the company is extremely powerful, it has little chance to influence the size of the total market. Price and demand are inextricably interlinked:

- Demand instability is the norm in hospitality. Demand fluctuations occur in a daily (coffee bar), weekly (business hotel) and seasonal (holiday-camp) cycle. Demand instability and fixed supply combine to present price decision-makers with an enormous challenge: how to use price (and other marketing mix components) to stimulate new demand, or deflect peak-time overdemand to quiet periods
- Different segments of demand have different price elasticities of demand. That is, as price increases consumer response varies between customer groups. Where a small change in price results in substantial change in demand, demand is said to be price elastic. Price inelasticity is the opposite condition. Marketers will drop price if they believe total revenue and profits will rise in consequence. For instance, in the hotel business the first group to drop out as prices rise are holidaymakers. Business travellers are normally less price sensitive. Kotas observes that, in many sectors of the industry, the higher the price level, the less elastic is the demand. Hence high-ASP establishments compete on non-price variables such as food quality and atmosphere, whereas low-ASP establishments favour price competition: 'In popular catering, therefore, unless sufficient emphasis is placed on acceptable food quality standards at an acceptable price, the achievement of long-term profitability, and indeed survival of the business, will prove extremely difficult.'[11] Banqueting, in comparison, is relatively price inelastic
- The more loyal a group of customers, the more discretion is afforded the price-setter, provided that loyal demand does not reflect the consumer's attitude towards low price

(2) Type of industry

Compared to hospitality, management in some industries has relatively little discretion in price setting.

- Capital goods are often bought following protracted negotiations in which price is one of the items for negotiation. Ships, machinery and armaments are typical examples
- Industrial goods are also frequently the subject of long-term negotiated contracts in which payment terms are debated. Hotels wholesale accommodation to tour operators and other major corporate users, negotiating price in the process
- The more fundamental in importance an industry is to the economic performance of a country, the more likely there is to be government control or influence over prices. There has been recent recognition of the significance of services and tourism, in particular, to the UK's economy but there is no direct control over prices and margins

(3) Structure of the industry

Economists have helped marketers to understand how price decision-making varies according to the type of economic structure within an industry. Four industrial structures have been proposed and modelled:

- pure (or perfect) competition
- monopoly
- monopolistic competition
- oligopoly

The relationship between price and demand varies between these 4 types because of differences in the number of competitors, their size and the nature of their output. The shape of the demand curve for each is shown in Figure 11.3.

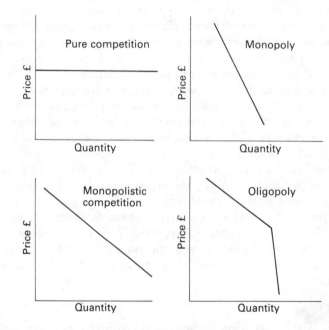

Figure 11.3   Demand curves in four differently structured industries.

(a) *Pure competition*. Pure competition is an economic condition in which there are many buyers and sellers, all of whom sell the same homogeneous product and all of whom know one another's prices. This gives rise to the horizontal straight line in Figure 11.3. There is no discretion in price setting; the nearest hospitality equivalent to perfect competition is found in the city-centre sandwich-bar sector. The marketing response is generally to differentiate the product in some way—e.g. by wrapping the sandwiches in branded paper-bags—in order to become more distinctive and command a higher price.

(b) *Monopoly*. A monopoly exists where there is a single supplier of a product for which there are no close substitutes. In these circumstances there is almost total discretion in price setting. Marketers of similar products may band together to form a price controlling group known as a 'price cartel', thereby constituting an artificial monopoly. Yet no firm has complete market power. There are always others competing for the same consumer expenditure. For example, the first hotel in a developing resort may have a local geographical monopoly, but its extent of discretion in price setting is limited because the resort competes with other destinations. The original motorway service stations felt that they were in a monopoly position; consequently their prices were high and their concern for customers low. As demand fell they learned that off-motorway facilities had competed. The product has since been remarketed with a new, more competitive pricing structure.

In hospitality markets, competitive substitutes nearly always exist either at a class level (hotels) or line level (3-star hotels), or at brand level.

(c) *Monopolistic competition.* In monopolistic competition there is a fairly large number of suppliers selling differentiated products. The range of prices from which a company in this type of industry can choose is limited by the degree of differentiation; competitors offer fairly close, but not perfect, substitutes. Hence the shallower curve.

(d) *Oligopoly.* The term which best describes the structure of many sectors of the hospitality industry is oligopoly, which is typified by competition between a few close competitors. However, price in these circumstances is not a matter of simple mathematical calculation. As Lipsey phrases it: 'Competitors' real and imagined reactions to each other contribute to the determination of price.'[12] This mutual uncertainty about competitors' reactions to pricing decisions results in non-price competition through forms of product differentiation, advertising and promotion, and in attempts tacitly to agree prices.

The demand curve is kinked at the going market price. If an oligopolist lowers his price, rivals will probably match the new price. If it is increased, the probability is that competitors will not immediately follow for fear of losing their new competitive advantage. However, where demand is relatively price inelastic, rises in the market leader's rates are likely to be followed. Kotas notes that: 'There is some evidence of price leadership in the British hotel industry, particularly in the large cities'.[13]

(4) *Competitive factors*

As we have seen, in the oligopoly there is a high degree of conjectural interdependence between competitors. No price change can be initiated without considering likely competitive reactions. However, competitors can influence a company's pricing decisions in a number of other ways:

- Interfirm competition on a basis other than price tends to devalue the potency of price as a determinant of purchasing behaviour, thus leading to price stability, or if price decreases occur, to price followership in order that competitive differentials are maintained. Price increases are less likely to be followed.
- Competitive new product launches, where if a competitor launches a lower-priced, improved product into the same segment, price changes are likely to be initiated, perhaps with a view to repositioning the product in a less competitive segment.
- Competition may have already established price brackets in which any newly launched products should be sold. This is sometimes known as 'price lining'.

(5) Phase of market development

The process of market development consists of the same stages as the product life cycle. Markets experience initially slow growth, then take off rapidly, level off and finally fall into decline. Pricing decisions vary at each stage in the development of the market. When a new product is introduced in order to create a new market, there are a number of alternative pricing strategies, as noted in Chapter 9.

If a product is introduced to a market during the early growth stage of market development, it is common practice to match the competitor's quality but to have a lower price, so that the product establishes a competitive advantage in the market. In the late growth stage of market development new entrants tend to be devised specifically for target groups which are not served by the product offerings currently available. The pricing strategy during these stages of market development is known as 'price discrimination'. The conditions necessary for price discrimination are:

- the market must be segmentable
- there must be no chance for segments who pay an advantageous price to resell at a higher price
- there should be little chance that competition will enter the higher priced segments and undercut the price
- the costs of segmenting and policing the market should not be greater than the extra revenue to be derived from price discrimination

The basic feature of price discrimination is that the product is priced according to the elasticity of demand of the segment at which it is aimed. Price discrimination can be based upon:

- time of purchase. Restaurants sometimes have 2 menus, a low-ASP version for lunchtime and a higher-ASP version for evening meals
- place of consumption. A hot day on the coast means that there is inelastic demand for ice-cream and liquid refreshments. Higher prices can be charged
- geographical location. Prices sometimes vary by geographical location—a multinational hotel group will invariably adjust prices to suit local conditions in the host country. It is not unknown for national hotel chains to adjust rack rates according to the nature of demand at each hotel location. This is an unusual practice for branded national food service chains
- sex. Admission to clubs often favours women with lower prices
- age. Young children are offered cheaper meals and accommodation

A particular form of price discrimination is discounting. In discounting a lower price is offered to customers where certain criteria are met. For instance:

- seasonal discounts. Prices vary according to season—normal season, high season and low season. High-season hotel prices may be inflated by 20 per cent, and discounted by up to 60 per cent in the low season. The winter weekend break attempts to offer low-season value for money
- volume discounts. These are offered to 2 types of customer—the regular patron, and the bulk buyer who may or may not be a previous purchaser. Business travellers may obtain special corporate rates of up to 20 per cent off rack rate, whereas the bulk-buying inclusive tour operator negotiates from 25 to 60 per cent discount according to season. To qualify for the corporate rates, Best Western customers must sign up for a minimum of 500 bed-nights over 6 months. Some

hotel groups have tiered discount systems, where the depth of discount increases as patronage increases
• trade discounts. These are offered to wholesalers and retailers of hotel products. Travel agents make a 10 per cent commission on room sales
• cash discounts. These are offered to customers who pay cash rather than buy on credit. This reflects the lower administration costs for cash transactions. Prompt payers are also offered discounts. Cash flows are improved as a result.

A product newly launched into a declining market is usually marketed for one of two reasons. Either it is an attempt to regenerate demand and start a secondary growth phase or it is an attempt to fill a still profitable gap which has been abandoned by others.

The pattern of market development is actually the combined sales volumes of all products sold into a market—i.e. the aggregated product life cycles of all items in the market-place. If, for instance, three products service a particular market, their combined sales represent the state of development of that market, as in the example in Table 11.2.

Table 11.2 *Market development and the PLC.*

Year	Product 1 Sales (000s)	Product 1 Stage of PLC	Product 2 Sales (000s)	Product 2 Stage of PLC	Product 3 Sales (000s)	Product 3 Stage of PLC	Market development Sales (000s)	Market development Stage of MD
1983	—	Not on market	30	Introduction	30	Introduction	60	Introduction
1984	17	Introduction	40	Introduction	60	Growth	117	Growth
1985	35	Growth	90	Growth	70	Maturity	195	Growth
1986	75	Maturity	150	Growth	30	Decline	255	Maturity
1987	85	Maturity	170	Maturity	—	Withdrawn	255	Maturity
1988	83	Maturity	165	Maturity	—	n.a.	248	Maturity
1989	70	Decline	110	Decline	—	n.a.	180	Decline

(6) Environmental factors
The final uncontrollable influence upon pricing decisions has been attributed to the catch-all heading—environmental factors. This refers to any type of pricing influence in the company's trading environment, including the current business climate, inflation, trade union pressure, consumer influence, and public opinion.

From time to time governments have introduced price controls or other legislation which influences the pricing decision. At the time of writing no such controls exist in the U.K. However, the Price Marking (Drinks on Premises) Order (1975) and Tourism (Sleeping Accommodation Price Display) Order (1977) do legislate for the display of value added tax-inclusive prices at the point of sale.

11.6 CHAPTER REVIEW

1. Price is the summation of all sacrifices made by a consumer in order to experience the benefits of a product.
2. Value, price and worth are not synonymous.

3. Although purchasing decisions are not often motivated by price alone, price is of great strategic significance in the marketing mix.

4. The influences upon price decision-making can be divided into 2 groups; controllable factors over which the marketer has a considerable amount of power, and uncontrollable factors over which the marketer has little power.

5. Controllable factors include costs, marketing and pricing objectives, the product itself and company resources.

6. Uncontrollable factors include demand, type of industry, structure of the industry, competition, phase of market development and other environmental factors.

7. It is not only marketers who have an interest in the pricing decision.

8. Costs of various types—total, fixed, semi-fixed, variable, direct, indirect, average, marginal, controllable, uncontrollable, discretionary, relevant, opportunity and standard—can have a bearing upon the price decision.

9. Hospitality businesses suffer from high fixed and semi-fixed costs.

10. Pricing objectives may be divided into 4 categories: profit-oriented, sales-oriented, competition-oriented and cost-oriented.

11. The novelty of a product, its differentiation from rivals, its prestige, its independence from other products in the product mix and its positioning, perishability and atmosphere all influence the price decision.

12. Demand for hospitality products is unstable and varies in price elasticity.

13. Economists have helped marketers to understand the significance of different types of industrial structure for pricing decisions; 4 such structures can be readily identified: pure (or perfect) competition, monopoly, monopolistic competition and oligopoly.

14. Non-price competition tends to devalue the potency of price as a competitive weapon.

15. The main pricing alternatives in the introductory phase of market development are skimming, penetration, or price promotion. During market growth the alternatives are lowered price if previously skimming; price maintenance if previously penetrating and price increase if previously promoting. The only strategy in a mature market is price differentiation.

16. Price discrimination can be based upon time of purchases, place of consumption, geographical location, sex, or age.

17. Discounts are of various types: seasonal, volume, trade and cash.

18. Environmental factors such as legislation, trade union, or consumer pressure, together with the current business climate, influence the price decision.

11.7 QUESTIONS

1. Does perfect competition, monopoly, monopolistic competition, or oligopoly best describe the competitive position of:
   - British Rail's on-train catering?
   - boarding-houses at a seaside resort?
   - in-flight catering?
   - the London Hilton?

2. If value = $\dfrac{\text{quality}}{\text{price}}$, does this mean that price = $\dfrac{\text{quality}}{\text{value}}$, or that quality = value × price?

3. 'In general, the higher the percentage of fixed costs, the greater is the degree of market orientation.' What is the significance of Kotas's remark for the pricing decision?

4. Distinguish between these costs:
   - fixed, semi-fixed and variable.
   - direct and indirect.
   - controllable and uncontrollable.

5. The apportionment of joint costs is a headache for pricing staff. What logic can be applied to

the apportionment of the following indirect costs in a hotel with 4 departments—rooms, bar, restaurant/room service and functions:
- insurance?
- reception staff wages?
- general manager's salary?
- electricity?
- telephone/postage?
- advertising?

6. Do hospitality consumers use price as an indicator of quality?
7. You run a small boarding-house in a popular seaside resort and your price discretion is highly constrained by the prices of competitors. You feel that prices could rise at the high season whilst still retaining 100 per cent occupancy. What arguments would you use to persuade competitors that it is in their interests to increase price?

REFERENCES

[1] Orkin, E. (1978) An integrated menu pricing system. *Cornell Hotel and Restaurant Administration Quarterly*, **19**(2), August, 8–13.
[2] Gabor, A. and Grainger, C. W. J. (1961) On the price consciousness of consumers. *Applied Statistics*, **10**.
[3] Marting, E. (1968) *Creative Pricing*. New York: AMA.
[4] Kotas, R. (1975) *Market Orientation in the Hotel and Catering Industry*. Guildford: Surrey University Press, 3.
[5] ibid.
[6] Medlik, S. and Airey, D. W. (1978) (2nd edn) *Profile of the Hotel and Catering Industry*. London: Heinemann.
[7] See also Bacher, M. (1968) The importance of costs in pricing decisions, in Marting, E., op cit.
[8] For a review of depreciation techniques refer to Coltman, M. M. (1978) *Hospitality Management Accounting*. London: CBI, 10–14.
[9] See Livesey, F. (1978) Why every company needs a pricing plan. *Marketing*, February, 29–34.
[10] Mason, R. S. (1974) Price and product quality assessment. *European Journal of Marketing*, **8**(1), Spring.
[11] Kotas, R. (1975) op. cit., 15.
[12] Lipsey, R. G. (1971) (3rd edn) *Positive Economics*. London: Weidenfeld & Nicolson, 270.
[13] Kotas, R. (1977) *Management Accounting for Hotels and Restaurants*. Guildford: Surrey University Press 100–1.

—12—

Mechanics of Pricing

12.1 CHAPTER PREVIEW

This chapter has 2 main purposes. First, to explain the many methods of calculating price. Second, to explore some difficult areas of price decision-making.

The 14 price-setting techniques we explore are as follows: cost-plus pricing; factor pricing; breakeven pricing; actual cost pricing; rate of return pricing; base pricing; IMPS; marginal pricing; pound-per-thousand pricing; price followership; marketing-oriented pricing; prestige pricing; leader pricing; and psychological pricing.

We also explore 5 particularly tricky pricing problems: when and how to use price promotions; transfer pricing; pricing of products whose costs and demands are interrelated; predicting trade and consumer response to price changes; and bidding for contracts.

12.2 LEARNING OBJECTIVES

By the end of this chapter you should be able to:
1. Identify any given pricing technique as cost-oriented, profitability-oriented, competitor-oriented, or marketing-oriented.
2. Given appropriate cost, demand, profit and competitive data, to calculate price.
3. Explain the pros and cons of using cost or market price to determine transfer price.
4. Identify the main issues in planning a price promotion and calculate the required increase in covers/guests in order to remain as profitable as before the cut.
5. Explain why interrelated costs and demands make pricing tricky.
6. Explain how probability theory can be used to help win sealed bids.

12.3 PRICING TECHNIQUES

Some companies pluck their prices out of the ether, despite the fact that there are a number of techniques used for calculating price in the hospitality industry. Some, particularly the cost-oriented methods, are more widespread in food service than in accommodation, but each has its merits and demerits.

In general, the techniques can be classified as cost-oriented, profitability-oriented, competitor-oriented and marketing-oriented, as shown in Table 12.1.

Table 12.1 *Pricing techniques.*

Cost-oriented	Profitability-oriented
• Cost plus pricing • Factor pricing • Break-even pricing • Actual cost approach	• Target rate of return pricing • Base pricing • IMPS • Marginal pricing • Pound-per-thousand pricing
Competitor-oriented	Marketing-oriented
• Price followership	• Marketing oriented pricing (MOP) • Prestige pricing • Loss leader pricing • Psychological pricing

12.4 COST-ORIENTED PRICING TECHNIQUES

Because costs in food service commonly are a higher proportion of total revenue than in accommodation, they play a more significant role in price determination. Horwath & Horwath Ltd report that in London hotels, 85 per cent of food and beverage revenue is lost to costs, whereas only 27 per cent of rooms revenue is so lost. In the UK as a whole the figures are 76 and 29 per cent respectively.[1] Most of the cost-oriented pricing examples, therefore, have a food and beverage bias.

Cost-plus pricing

This technique is in widespread use and follows the approach in formula 12.1, which shows how a percentage profit margin is added to costs to give a price:

$$C + f(C) = P \qquad (12.1)$$

where C = costs

f = the percentage mark-up

P = price

(For example: £1.00 + 80% (£1.00) = £1.80.)

The major question is this: what costs are to be used in the calculation? The options are to use variable costs, total costs, or marginal costs.

In the first approach the variable costs of creating a menu item are aggregated and a percentage added to provide for gross profit. Over the course of a trading-year the gross margins earned on each sale are used, first, to pay fixed costs, and then to return a net profit.

The variable cost approach requires the price-setter to estimate fixed costs and the likely annual sales of each menu item. Only then can he forecast whether the gross margins will be sufficient to cover fixed costs and make the required profit.

A particular problem with variable cost pricing is assembly of the various cost components. The common practice is not to include every direct cost of an item, but to use only food (or beverage) costs. Rather than calculate prices daily, taking account of shifts in ingredient costs, most restaurants use standard costs which assume that there is no short-term change. At intervals, these standard costs are recalculated and prices revised. A minority of operators incorporate the direct costs of labour and fuel—this is known as 'prime cost pricing'. Where the establishment makes heavy use of convenience or processed foods, labour and fuel costs tend to be relatively low and are, therefore, normally excluded from the calculation.

In the total cost approach the price-setter prepares a budget for the coming trading period, comprising both fixed and variable costs. Then, having forecast sales volume, he adds a margin for profit. This method is much easier to apply when products are homogeneous, as in the case of a motel without food and beverage facilities. For example, a 30-room motel with fixed costs of £70,000 and variable costs of £26,280 (calculated thus: £3 per room direct cost × 30 rooms × 365 days × 80% occupancy) would have to set a price to recover total costs of £96,280. Any price above £11.00 per room-night would produce a profit. A rate of £20 per night would produce a pre-tax net profit of just under £80,000, provided that the 80 per cent occupancy target was achieved. This return then can be considered against the capital invested in the motel. In multiproduct businesses, fixed costs have to be apportioned equitably between products. Menu pricing is particularly difficult under the total cost approach.

Now, the marginal cost approach. Marginal costs tend to decrease with volume until a stage is reached at which they start to rise. From that point the higher volume results in higher unit variable costs. If a percentage profit margin were added to marginal costs, then prices would vary according to the level of output—this would not lead to sufficiently stable prices. Consequently, for long-term pricing decisions variable costs or total costs are employed, but for short-term pricing problems marginal costs are used—e.g. in deciding whether it is economically worth while taking late bookings, accommodating a business meeting, or running a function. Each can be priced on its own marginal costs. This is an especially useful method if fixed costs have already been recovered by earlier sales. Morphis has suggested that hotels adopt load-factor pricing as used in the airline business.[2] This is essentially a marginal cost approach to pricing. Occupancy data from equivalent previous periods can be used to assess whether to offer discounted rates to today's prospective guests. Access to historical data held on a computer reservation system considerably simplifies the decision, and enables marginal costs to be used in the control of the mix of discounted and regular sales.

The profit margin which is added to costs is normally based on established industry practice, company tradition, or company profit objectives. There are a number of advantages to the cost-plus pricing method.

1. It is based on fact. Costings are concrete.
2. It has an air of precision.
3. Managerial judgement is not required as calculations are mechanical.
4. Provided that sales targets are met, profit is a certainty.

However, there are serious shortcomings.

1. It ignores the price elasticity of demand.
2. It may produce prices inconsistent with the positioning statement or desired image.
3. It fails to consider competitors' prices. The forecast sales volume may not be achievable at the cost-plus prices, given competitors' prices. Cost savings or margin reduction may be required.
4. Fixed costs can only be apportioned between products after estimating future sales volume. This leads to the anomaly of having to estimate sales volume *before*

establishing price, despite the fact that price is often an important determinant of demand.

5. There is a tendency to believe that a bigger margin gives bigger profits. A bigger margin will certainly create a higher selling price, and perhaps a fall in demand, with subsequent lower profits.

6. As input costs rise prices follow. These rises in price may mean loss of business. In periods of inflation business often goes to those who can keep prices stable (rather than low).

Factor pricing

Factor pricing is a simple variant of cost-plus pricing. Food costs are multiplied by a standard factor to produce a retail price. Factors vary by style of food service. In industrial contract catering the factor may be as little as 1 or 2; prices can be low when the client company underwrites all of the fixed costs and some of the variable costs of the service. As the derivative components of the meal experience, image and atmosphere, become more important the factor rises. A factor of 4 or more is not uncommon in highly fashionable high-status restaurants. Location and reputation also influence the factor.

A single factor is not normally applied to all menu items in an establishment. Management may consider the price sensitivity of guests, the prices of competitors, or the amount of labour/energy consumed. A coffee bar could apply a factor of 30 to tea or coffee but a factor of 2.5 to a ham sandwich. Factor pricing suffers from the same advantages and disadvantages as cost-plus pricing.

Breakeven pricing

The aim of breakeven pricing is to calculate the price which will enable the company to break even—i.e. neither make a loss nor a profit, but recover its total costs. The price-setter can then experiment on paper to see if it can be increased above the breakeven price with a view to producing profit.

In breakeven pricing costs are treated as either fixed or variable such that:

$$TC = FC + VC \qquad (12.2)$$

where TC = total costs
          FC = fixed costs
          VC = variable costs

We shall assume, for ease of demonstration, that variable costs are linear—i.e. that there is a standard variable cost per unit produced regardless of whether it is the first unit of output or the thousandth. We take no account of economies of scale or corporate learning, both of which tend to reduce unit costs as output increases.[3]

The second variable in the breakeven calculation is sales revenue. The formula for calculating sales revenue is:

$$TR = P \times Q \qquad (12.3)$$

where TR = total revenue
        P = price
        Q = quantity

Breakeven occurs when $TR = TC$. These two variables (TR and TC) can be plotted against each other to give a graphic representation of breakeven, as in Figure 12.1.

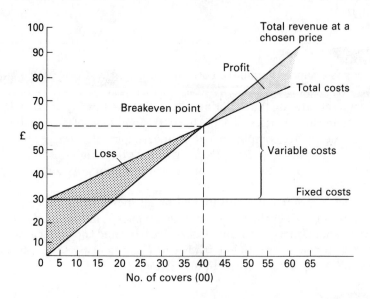

Figure 12.1   Breakeven chart.

   In the example $TC = TR$ at 4,000 covers. Breakeven, therefore, occurs where revenue of £60,000 (vertical axis) pays for the costs of serving 4,000-covers (horizontal axis). Total revenue is calculated on the basis of a selling price of £15 per cover (4,000 × £15.00 = £60,000). The fixed costs are £30,000 and the variable costs are £7.50 per cover. Any sales over 4,000 covers creates profits.
   A faster means of calculating breakeven point is to use the concept of unit contribution:

$$UC = P - VC \qquad\qquad (12.4)$$

where UC = unit contribution
        P = price
        VC = variable cost

and to apply it in the formula:

$$BEP = \frac{FC}{UC} \qquad\qquad (12.5)$$

Breakeven point in units (BEP) is the number of unit contributions it takes to recover fixed costs.

Using data from the example:

$$UC = £15.00 - £7.50$$
$$= £7.50$$

Therefore, BEP $\quad = \dfrac{£30,000}{£7.50} = 4,000 \text{ covers}$

There are a number of issues associated with using breakeven analysis which the marketing manager must consider when using it to set price, as follows:

1. How is the recommended ASP (in our example £15.00) reached? It should be based upon the understanding of the competitive dynamics of the market-place and should be consistent with the desired product position. The price-setter could attempt to see what effect raising or lowering the price would have on breakeven. At a higher price breakeven would occur earlier, and at a lower price later. For example, if the ASP were raised to £20.00, breakeven would be reached at 2,400 covers. If ASP were dropped to £12.50, breakeven would occur at 6,000 covers. Each of these differing output levels has corporate significance, in particular, with respect to capitalisation, staffing, atmosphere and food production.
2. Some marketing costs are difficult to determine in advance. For example, it may not be known how much expenditure is needed on advertising and promotion to sell 4,000 covers.
3. In periods of inflation skill in predicting movements of food and labour costs is necessary if breakeven pricing is to be of value.
4. Historical data are used when calculating the breakeven point. These may not be available for a new product. The best the new product marketer can do is to estimate selling price and contract for future deliveries of foods, beverages and other ingredients at negotiated prices.

Actual cost pricing

This method does not calculate price *per se*, but places a ceiling on the cost of food ingredients. The procedure is as follows:

1. Estimate sales revenue, given the style of operation and competitive position.
2. Set profit target as percentage of sales revenue.
3. Detail all costs except food costs.
4. Calculate food cost ceiling $(1 - (2 + 3))$.
5. Design menu to stay under food cost ceiling.

12.5 PROFITABILITY-ORIENTED PRICING TECHNIQUES

One criticism which has been levelled at cost-oriented pricing methods is that they take no account of the level of capital invested in the business. Profitability-oriented pricing techniques remedy this weakness.

Rate of return pricing (RORP)

Equally suitable for pricing existing or new products, RORP aims to find a price structure which will provide a satisfactory return on investment. The procedure is as follows:

1. Calculate capital invested in the venture.
2. Set target return on the investment, bearing in mind the risk level, opportunity costs and returns in similar competitive enterprises.
3. Estimate the number of covers/guests.
4. Estimate ASP/average guest expenditure.
5. Calculate sales revenue (3 × 4).
6. Estimate variable costs.
7. Calculate gross profit (5 − 6).
8. Estimate fixed costs.
9. Calculate net profit (7 − 8).
10. Does net profit meet the target rate of return?

If the rate of return is unsatisfactory, remedial courses of action include: reduction of target rate of return; variable cost savings; fixed cost savings; increased ASP; increasing number of covers or abandoning the venture.

Kotas illustrates how the technique applies to a venture with capital investment of £100,000, a target rate of return of 20 per cent, ASP of £4.00 and 50,000 covers.[4] Figure 12.2 demonstrates how the technique builds in consideration of the sales mix, gross and

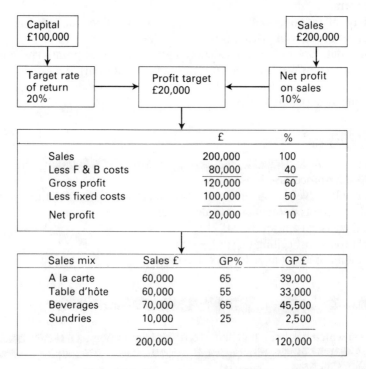

Figure 12.2 Target rate of return pricing.

net margins. It can be further refined to take into account differential gross profit margins for individual menu items.

The main strengths of this technique are its recognition that profit should be related to capital employed; its integration of costs, patronage, revenues, price and profit; and its mechanical simplicity. However, it ignores price elasticity of demand and the impact of local competition, and it regards pricing as independent of the rest of the marketing mix and irrelevant to overall marketing strategy.

A related technique, developed for the American Hotel and Motel Association, is known as the Hubbart formula.[5] The procedure is as follows.

1. Estimate total investment (fixed and working capital) required for the venture.
2. Set target rate of return on equity.
3. Estimate general and administration; advertising and sales promotion; heat, light and power; and repairs and maintenance expenses.
4. Calculate required gross operating income (2 + 3).
5. Estimate profits from all departments except rooms.
6. Calculate required rooms profit (5 − 4).
7. Estimate gross rooms department expense.
8. Calculate required rooms revenue (6 + 7).
9. Estimate number of room-nights per annum.
10. Calculate average room rate (8 ÷ 9).

The Hubbart formula is easily extended to build in the effect of double occupancies.

Base pricing

Base pricing hinges upon the development of a menu price list which is structured to achieve a target ASP. The procedure is as follows.

1. Estimate fixed costs.
2. Estimate variable costs.
3. Calculate total costs (1 + 2).
4. Set profit objective.
5. Calculate target income (3 + 4).
6. Estimate the number of covers.
7. Calculate target ASP (5 ÷ 6).
8. Structure menu prices to achieve target ASP.

The basic technique can be adapted to accommodate different target ASPs at breakfast, lunch and dinner.

This technique has an apparent logic and is both simple and mechanical to implement. Its main weaknesses are that it fails to relate profit to capital employed; it begs the question of how to structure prices to achieve the target ASP; and it, like target RORP, regards pricing as of no concern to marketing strategy.

IMPS

IMPS, which stands for the integrated menu pricing system, was proposed by Orkin as a means of bringing together pricing objectives, costs, margins, competition, and the elasticity of demand and profit into the pricing decision.[6] The procedure is as follows.

1. Calculate food costs.
2. Estimate direct production labour costs.
3. Estimate direct service labour costs.
4. Calculate direct costs (1 + 2 + 3).
5. Set objectives in terms of number of covers.
6. Estimate effect on demand of several alternative prices, bearing competitors in mind.
7. Calculate unit contribution at each price level (price − 4).
8. Select the item with highest unit contribution; record number of covers expected.
9. Repeat step 8 for second and third highest, etc. unit contribution until target number of covers is achieved.

According to Orkin, this method results in menu items being listed and priced for a higher overall contribution than would normally be achievable.

Marginal pricing

The marginal pricing method can be used when objectives are phrased in terms of either profits or sales. The method is very sophisticated because it requires the marketer not only to understand the cost structure of his product, but the relationship between price and demand.

There are practical difficulties in establishing a formula which expresses demand as a function of price. However, methods which help in its calculation are available; for instance:

- market surveys
- analogous product examination
- test markets
- market simulation
- laboratory testing
- management judgement

Calculation of the demand schedule requires that demand be treated simply as a function of price. Let us pursue a simplified example in which:

$$Q = 7,500 - 50P \tag{12.4}$$

where Q = quantity
         P = price

i.e. maximum sales volume, say, room-nights, is 7500. For every £1 hike in tariff we expect to lose 50 sales. This schedule is graphed in Figure 12.3.

The cost schedule is based upon the formula:

$$TC = FC + VC \tag{12.5}$$

In our example $TC = 100,000 + 5Q$
i.e. TC at any level of output includes £100,000 of FC plus £5 of VC per room sold. This relationship is shown graphically in Figure 12.4.

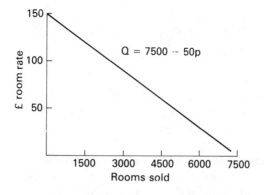

Figure 12.3 Estimated demand schedule.

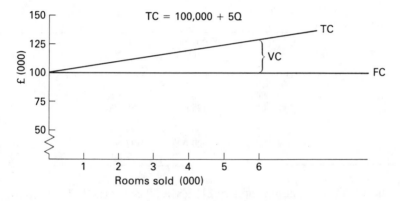

Figure 12.4 Cost curve.

In its own right the demand schedule provides an indication of the prices which will produce any desired volume of sales. By reference to the demand schedule, it is possible to detect what changes in price are required to maintain, increase, or decrease demand. For example, Figure 12.3 shows that a price of £75 produces sales of about 4,500 rooms and that £100 produces about 3,000 sales.

However, the two schedules—cost and demand—can be combined in the way shown below to provide details of the sales volume and price which will provide a required profit level. These calculations are based on the formula:

$$Z = TR - TC \tag{12.6}$$

where Z = profit
         TR = total revenue
         TC = total costs

Noting that $TR = P \times Q$:
        $Z = (P \times Q) - TC$

Substituting for *TC*:

$$Z = P \times Q - (100,000 + 5Q)$$
$$= PQ - 100,000 - 5Q$$

Substituting for *Q*:

$$Z = P(7,500 - 50P) - 100,000 - 5(7,500 - 50P)$$
$$= 7,500P - 50P^2 - 100,000 - 37,500 + 250P$$
$$= 7,750P - 50P^2 - 137,500$$

This last equation can be manipulated in various ways to give the profit levels which will be achieved at different prices. The simplest way for a non-mathematician to use the equation is to graph *Z* against *P* at different values of *P*. Profits can then be simply read off the resulting graph, which in this case would resemble an inverted 'U'.

Table 12.2 shows the levels of profit that are achieved at specified room rates.

Table 12.2 *Marginal pricing.*

Room rate (P) £	7750P −	Formula 50P² −	137 500	=	Profit £
10	77 500	5 000	137 500		−65 000
20	155 000	20 000	137 500		−2 500
50	387 500	125 000	137 500		125 000
75	581 250	281 250	137 500		162 500
77.50	600 625	300 312.50	137 500		162,812.50
80	620 000	320 000	137 500		162 500
100	775 000	500 000	137 500		137 500

The table shows that maximum profits of £162,812.50 are earned at an achieved room rate of £77.50; a hotel with a profit objective lower than this, say, at £162,500, has a choice of 2 prices which will give this result—either £80 or £75.

In order to discover how many rooms must be sold to create the desired profit level it is only necessary to substitute the value of *P* into the demand schedule. For instance, at maximum profit the price per room was £77.50. Substituting for *P*, this would give:

$$Q = 7,500 - 50P$$
$$= 7,500 - 3,875$$
$$= 3,625$$

Maximum profit of £162,812.50 is obtained from an occupancy of only 48 per cent (3,625 rooms) paying an average room rate of £77.50, giving a sales turnover of £280,937.50.

In principle, marginal pricing is quite simple. Yet there are problems, as listed below.
1. It is subject to all the frailties of the other methods which use cost data.
2. Demand schedules are costly to derive and can change at any point in time, in response to altered competitive conditions in the market-place. If a major rival drops his price, then this will also have an effect on others' sales. Marginal analysis can only be used with confidence in stable markets.
3. The method does not include any allowance for the influence of non-price variables on demand.

4. It ignores the interrelated cost and demand complexities which occur in multi-product companies.

Pound-per-thousand pricing

Kotas notes that until quite recently hoteliers have tended to use a rule-of-thumb method. This was to charge £1 for every £1,000 of the total cost of the hotel project. Thus where the total cost per bedroom was £20,000, average room rate was fixed at £20.

However, nowadays greater science is being applied to pricing rooms. Changes in construction methods, occupancy patterns, interest rates and competition have made this technique more or less redundant.

12.6 COMPETITOR-ORIENTED PRICING TECHNIQUE

Price followership

Many food service companies base their own prices on those of competitors. Indeed, in oligopolistic markets, it makes sense to do so. Price followership does not necessarily mean that price decision-making has been abandoned; it may simply be the only mechanism for the introduction of price changes by companies ranking no. 2 or 3 in a market. Profits are earned through strict cost control which enables margins to be maintained.

In the hotel business price followership is commonplace, particularly where price differentials have been established. One 3-star hotel sells rooms at £39.95, a second sells at £35.95. The 10 per cent differential is generally maintained, the lower-priced hotel following any price changes instituted by the price leader. Prices are generally reviewed twice per annum, in April and October.

The main weaknesses of price followership are that it takes no account of capital structure, profit objectives, or operating costs, all of which may be substantially different from the leader. It also inhibits innovation and risk-taking by management.

12.7 MARKETING-ORIENTED PRICING TECHNIQUES

We now look at 4 forms of marketing-oriented pricing techniques.

MOP

Marketing-oriented pricing (MOP) is particularly suitable for pricing decisions on new products marketed through several distribution channels, as are most new hotel developments. The technique involves consideration of costs, competition, the nature of demand, company objectives (including pricing objectives) and the form of distribution channel through which a product passes before reaching the consumer.[7] Figure 12.5 expresses MOP in flow-chart form.

Step 1 requires the initial identification of a target market. Company objectives may

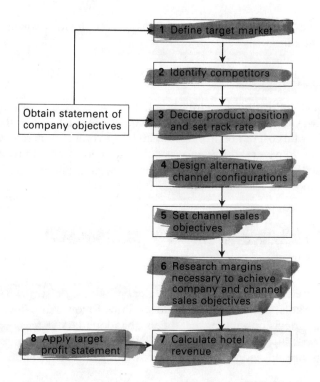

Figure 12.5   Market-oriented pricing.

well bear upon the choice by the imposition of sales volume or profitability criteria. Step 2 requires research: where do your prospective guests stay overnight? Step 3 requires the marketer to plot a product position appropriate for the competitive state of the target market, and to set a rack rate which will help to build a brand image complementary to the desired product position whilst satisfying company objectives.

In step 4 the stage of the MOP process is reached which requires the price-planner to list all possible channels through which the product could be made available to the consumer—e.g. direct sale to guests, through travel agents and through a voluntary association of similar establishments.

Step 5 recognizes that those channels which are realistic alternatives for the hotel will be limited by the hotelier's own marketing and distribution skills and resources. A hotel with no sales staff may well elect to sell a large proportion through travel agents. It is important to formalise this by estimating the sales volume that is to be shifted through each of the alternatives, so that 100 per cent occupancy is achieved.

In step 6 the task is to find out the margins necessary to achieve company and channel sales objectives. The hotelier must find out the conventional margins and discounts for similar products handled by each channel member; and considering his sales volume objective and desired product position, set the prices and discounts at which the product will move through the channel.

In step 7, calculation of the hotel revenue, the actual price calculations are relatively simple. Let us assume that the hotel is planning to sell through three channels: 50 per cent through direct sales to guests; 30 per cent through travel agents; and 20 per cent to tour operators. The discounts required off rack rate are 0, 10 and 30 per cent respectively. This information gives the price structure shown in Table 12.3. If the hotel has 100 rooms—i.e. 36,500 room-nights per annum—and sales targets are achieved, then hotel revenue would total £996,450 and average achieved room rate £27.30.

Table 12.3 *MOP calculations.*

Customer pays £	Travel agent receives £	Tour operator receives £	Hotel receives £
30————————————————————————————————————			30
30———————————— 3 ——————————————————————			27
Part of package	—————————————————— 9 —————————		21

Table 12.4 *Hotel revenue.*

Channel	Room nights %		Achieved room rate £	Revenue £
Direct	18 250	50	30	547 500
TA	10 950	30	27	295 650
TO	7 300	20	21	153 000
Total	36 500	100	27.30 (average)	996 450

Step 8 returns to the question of target profit. If the target profit for the hotel was set at £300,000 we can compute total costs of running the hotel for 1 year, given the sales mix, must not exceed £696,000 (£996,450–£300,000).

If total costs exceed this ceiling, profits will be below target and the hotelier must look for ways of increasing achieved room rate (perhaps by reformulating channel sales objectives or examining the discount structure), investigating new channels, reducing costs, or raising rack rate.

The hotelier can also calculate the effect of underachieving sales targets through each channel. Whilst the income from tour operators is assured, regardless of whether the tour operator manages to sell any inclusive tours, travel agents' sales and direct sales are not so certain.

The benefits of using MOP can be quite substantial. The company striving to be more marketing-oriented might find the first 4 benefits, listed below, attractive.

1. It combines demand, cost and competitive considerations in price setting.
2. It ensures that the rack rate is in line with the desired product position and brand image—this is something which cannot be guaranteed if the pricing procedure starts with costs and works forwards to retail price.
3. It requires some marketing research effort before embarking upon product development. This is standard procedure in better marketing-oriented companies.
4. It demands that the user appraises the suitability of alternative channels for his product and market, thus recognising that channel member support is necessary for success.

5. It can be combined with breakeven analysis to provide an idea of how long it will take the company to recover its fixed costs. The revenue curve in the breakeven analysis would, in the example above, be based on a price of £27.30.
6. It requires the user to set realistic rather than fanciful sales and profit targets, bearing in mind the needs of the company and the channel.
7. It integrates pricing objectives with the overall company profit and sales objectives.
8. It is flexible and a further benefit accrues, in that not only is it useful for new product pricing, but it can be used when pricing for a relaunch of an existing product or when an estimate is needed of the impact of a change in distribution channel design on profits or sales.

Prestige pricing

This involves taking advantage of the way in which price and quality are perceived by consumers to be interrelated. For some products, such as discothèques or the theatre, a high price reflects the subjective prestige value of the product. For these products the demand curve is shaped as in Figure 12.6. As price increases from P_1 to P_2, so there is an increase in demand from Q_1 to Q_2, contrary to the accepted laws of economics.

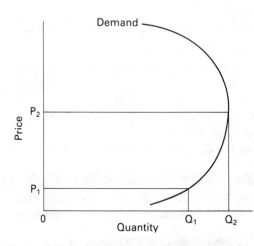

Figure 12.6   Demand curve of a prestige product.

Leader pricing

Some companies feel that of the mix of products they market, one in particular acts as an attraction and creates sales for the other, less attractive items. A similar strategy is called 'bait pricing' in which a low-priced article is promoted with a view to trading-up the customer. He is persuaded to make a more expensive purchase when he enters the outlet.

Psychological pricing

Psychological aspects of pricing seem to be more important where products are intangible or difficult to evaluate.[8] Forms of psychological pricing include the following:

1. Some consumers buy only between maximum and minimum prices which they find economically and psychologically comfortable. This tends to be reflected in the development over time of price lines. Price lining is the setting of price so it falls within 1 of these psychologically acceptable price brands.
2. Odd prices are a particular form of psychological pricing. An American survey of 242 restaurants revealed that 58 per cent of menu prices ended in 9, 35 per cent in 5 and 6 per cent in 0. The numbers 1, 2, 3, 4, 6 and 7 were never used as the terminal digit.[9]

The above practice, known as 'odd pricing', results in a bizarre form of demand curve, as shown in Figure 12.7. In low-ASP restaurants 9 is most frequently the terminal digit, creating an illusion of a discount—£1.79 seems much cheaper than £1.81. Indeed the latter may appear as money grabbing. In higher-ASP restaurants 5 dominates as the terminal digit. The diner is less price sensitive and the apparent discount is less appealing.

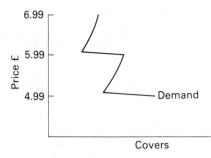

Figure 12.7 Effect of odd pricing.

There may be other 'magic numbers'. Some restaurateurs believe that diners respond to the first digit—69p is perceived as much less expensive than 71p. Others believe that the length of the price is vital: 95p (2 digits) appears much less expensive than £1.05 (3 digits). Similarly, £9.95 is perceived as much cheaper than £10.05. Other restaurateurs believe that customers round prices up or down. Prices between 86p and £1.39 are rounded to £1, and between £1.40 and £1.79 they are rounded to £1.50.

12.8 SPECIAL ISSUES IN PRICING

There are several pricing issues which are worthy of special mention:
1. Using price promotions.
2. Transfer pricing.
3. Product mix pricing.
4. Estimating consumer and competitive reaction to price changes.
5. Competitive bidding.

Using Price Promotions

The discussion on price promotions[10] is limited here to discussions about temporary reductions in price. Contrary to expectations, they do not always have a great impact on sales; indeed the major problem in creating successful price promotions is estimating the price reduction which is necessary to create the desired increase in sales.

Ten per cent may be too little to lift demand, whereas 25 per cent may stimulate overdemand, which in the case of a hotel with fixed supply would result in suboptimal profitability. Neither do temporary reductions often result in permanent shifts in brand preference. In short, price promotions can result in loss in profit unless they are used in a price-sensitive segment with an attractive saving offered to the customer.

The additional occupancy that needs to be generated by a price reduction in order for a hotel to maintain the same revenue varies according to the current level of occupancy. For example, if your current occupancy was 56 per cent and you instituted a 5 per cent rate cut, you would need to achieve a 60 per cent occupancy; a 15 per cent cut, 65 per cent occupancy; and a 20 per cent cut, 72 per cent occupancy. The effects of other cuts are detailed in Table 12.5. Clearly, price promotions may have disadvantageous effects on sales revenue. The bottom right-hand quadrant of the table shows how occupancy might actually have to exceed 100 per cent in order to maintain sales revenue! The direct costs of providing rooms for the additional guests have not been included in the calculations. Maintenance of current profitability levels, given the additional direct costs, would require an even higher occupancy than tabled.

Table 12.5   *Effect of cutting room rate.*

Current occupancy	Occupancy required to maintain sales revenue, following rate cuts of:				
	5%	10%	15%	20%	25%
50	53	56	59	63	67
52	55	58	62	65	69
54	57	60	64	68	72
56	59	62	66	70	75
58	61	64	68	73	77
60	63	67	71	75	80
62	65	69	73	78	83
64	67	71	75	80	85
66	69	73	78	83	88
68	72	76	80	85	91
70	74	78	82	88	93
72	76	80	85	90	96
74	78	82	87	93	99
76	80	84	89	95	101
80	84	89	94	100	107
88	93	98	104	110	117
90	95	100	106	113	120

Table 12.6 shows how many extra covers are required to make up for lost gross profits, given differing variable cost levels and price reductions. For example, where variable costs are 25 per cent of menu price (i.e. a price factor of 4 is applied) and a 20 per cent off-price promotion is launched, the restaurant would need to sell 36 per cent more covers in order to achieve the same level of contribution towards fixed costs and profits.

Table 12.6 *Effect of cutting menu prices.*

Variable cost as percentage of menu price	Percentage increase in covers required to maintain current gross profit level given cuts in menu prices of:				
	5%	10%	15%	20%	25%
25	7	15	25	36	50
30	8	17	27	40	56
35	8	18	30	44	62
40	9	20	33	50	71
45	10	22	38	57	83

Another problem associated with price promotions is their timing and frequency. Too frequent price promotions seem to lead to:
- price-sensitive purchasing behaviour, as consumers wait for price promotions
- a low level of consumer purchasing between promotions
- a tendency for competition to respond with similar price cuts, thereby reducing profits for all concerned

The timing of price promotions should be related to the promotion's tactical purpose. Price promotions are not often regarded as strategic weapons, but rather as tactical devices which can be used for specific purposes:
- to shift excess stock, thereby freeing dry goods store or refrigeration space
- to encourage trial
- to extend the season and fill rooms in shoulder periods
- to spoil a competitor's test market; price promotions on brands already on the market can inhibit trial of a competitor's newly launched product
- to counter a competitor's non-price promotion

A simple procedure for devising and executing a price promotion is shown in Figure 12.8. Most of the issues shown in the flowchart have been mentioned previously, but not that of obtaining channel support. This may be important to the success of hotel price promotions. The better price promotions improve profitability for both the hotelier and his agents. Travel agents' or hotel representatives' support is unlikely to be given unless proof can be offered of incremental sales.

Transfer pricing

A transfer price is the price at which products are traded between units in an organisation. Transfer pricing is particularly problematical in companies with decentralised profit responsibilities and where, unless there is an accepted transfer pricing system within the whole organisation, realistic comparisons of costs, profits and performances between subunits cannot be made. Transfer prices are a problem for vertically integrated organisations. Holiday Inns once had its own furniture-manufacturing division. How was it to price products transferred from the factory to hotels division? If a bar services both diners in a restaurant and drinkers at the bar, how can the relative profitability of bar and restaurant be assessed without a transfer pricing policy? Some hospitality organisations are vertically integrated, from farming through air transport to hotel accommodation, and experience highly elaborate transfer pricing problems.

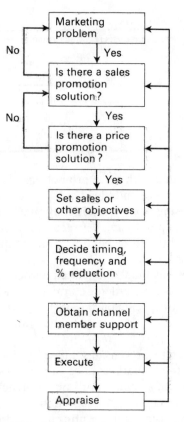

Figure 12.8   A procedure for price promotions.

The main problem is one of profit focus: should transfers be made at prices which benefit the entire organisation or should they benefit the subunits? In some companies this is of great importance because interunit trading can account for as much as 25 per cent of annual turnover.[11]

There are two basic methods used in setting interunit prices: those based on market prices, and those based on costs. Let us compare these two methods.

Interunit prices based on market prices
There are several overall advantages in basing interunit prices on market prices:
- it ensures that the units are operating in a realistic setting and are kept in close touch with current market prices
- it aids management in the evaluation of unit performance by keeping pricing methods in line with the concept of decentralised responsibility
- it increases the incentive to reduce costs as any increase in costs will mean a direct reduction in profits of the unit concerned
- it may help management to identify inefficiencies

On the other hand, there are some disadvantages to this system:
- it may lead to a loss of product–cost information as goods are transferred between units

- the inclusion and build-up of profit elements at each stage of production may mean that the final marketing unit is left with a very small profit margin, which can be a major problem if the market price for the finished product needs to be highly competitive

Some companies charge a modified market rate, particularly where interunit sales comprise a large part of sales turnover.

However, in favour of full market price are the following factors:

- it keeps prices in line with those charged to outside customers
- it treats buyers and sellers as though they were unrelated companies required to make profits in existing market conditions
- it neither interferes with normal marketing decisions nor distorts normal use of resources
- it acts as a check on operating efficiency

If a company favours a modified market price, adjustments can be made by negotiation or by applying a standard mark-down on market prices.

Interunit prices based upon costs

A major issue is whether to use average total costs, average variable costs, or marginal costs to determine price.

A second problem concerns whether or not costs only should be used as the transfer price or whether an element for profit should be included. The majority of companies do in fact modify their costs either by addition of a fixed mark-up or through negotiation with the purchaser.

An advantage of not modifying costs is that it is administratively simple, and the information required for arriving at the price is readily available. On the other hand, there is a major disadvantage: where no profit element is involved, the system can tend to diminish the apparent effectiveness of divisional heads, who are held responsible for the profitability of their units.

Product mix pricing

It is rare that a well-established company markets products whose cost or demand profiles are not interrelated. Difficulties arise in pricing a mix of products when some cost or demand interrelationship exists.

The 3 alternative problems are that:

1. Costs interrelate but demand does not, for instance, when a single room is used for both functions and conferences.
2. Demands interrelate but costs do not.
3. Both costs and demands are interrelated.

Demand relationships exist when products are regarded by consumers as substitutes for one another. This is called 'positive cross-elasticity'. Negative cross-elasticity occurs when goods are complementary. Zero cross-elasticity occurs when the goods are unrelated. The pricing difficulty occurs when positive or negative cross-elasticities exist. If the price of burger meat increases, demand for chicken will increase and the demand for burger buns will fall.

Cost relationships exist when the same resources are used to produce and market more than 1 product. Two important types of products where this problem arises are joint products and by-products. Pricing of by-products on a cost-plus basis is entirely inappropriate because it would lead to the product being given away.

Joint products face a similar problem—e.g. pricing bacon and ham is a difficult decision. A change in the cost of producing 1 of the joint products, or a main product from which some by-product is derived, often leads to an effect upon the cost of the associated products.

Forecasting reactions to price changes

Price changes, whether they occur as a result of a need to pass on cost increases, as a promotional tactic, or for any other reason, often influence consumer behaviour and provoke competitive reaction.

The shift in demand for a product caused by a price change is termed its 'elasticity of demand'. A product with high elastic demand responds decisively to a change in price. Products with lower elasticity tend to experience little change in demand when price changes. The terminology of demand elasticity is given in Table 12.7.[12]

Table 12.7   *The terminology of demand elasticity.*

Numerical measure of elasticity	Verbal description	Terminology
Zero	Quantity demanded does not change as price changes	Perfectly (or completely) inelastic
Greater than zero but less than one	Quantity demanded changes by a smaller percentage than does price	Inelastic
One	Quantity demanded changes by exactly the same percentage as does price	Unit elasticity
Greater than one but less than infinity	Quantity demanded changes by a larger percentage as does price	Elastic
Infinity	Purchasers are prepared to buy all they can obtain at some price and none at all at an even slightly higher price	Perfectly (or infinitely) elastic

Marketers who realise that price is not the only determinant of purchasing look for other factors to help them understand changes in behaviour which occur when prices change. A shift in price may be 'perceived' by the consumer in a way incompatible with the intent of the marketer. Over time the consumer may have learnt, through experience, to respond to a shift in price changes in a way inconsistent with economic theory.

Oxenfeldt has investigated psychological responses to price changes.[13] A price reduction may be perceived in many ways, as follows.
1. The item is about to be replaced by an improved version.
2. An attempt by a company in financial difficulty to stimulate demand.

3. The price may fall even further.
4. A reduction in quality.

A price increase may be perceived as follows:

1. A reflection of a sudden increase in demand—it is, therefore, wise to buy.
2. Profiteering.
3. An attempt to pass on increased costs.
4. A reflection of the quality of the product, which was previously undervalued.

Predicting the response of competitors to a price change is difficult. If a company's price change is likely to affect competitors' profit performance, sales targets, or achievement of other marketing objectives, then a competitive reaction can be forecast. The time, extent and nature of the reaction is less easy to predict. Knowledge of how competitors have behaved previously under similar circumstances is helpful. As pointed out in Chapter 11, companies are subject to several pricing influences. An examination of the 4 controllable, and 6 uncontrollable, influences upon competitors' pricing decisions will help to determine likely competitive response. For example, if price followership exists, there can be little doubt about the probable response.

Competitive bidding

Industrial and institutional catering contracts are often won or lost on the outcome of competitive tenders. The model outlined below can help companies with a history of bidding against known competitors to establish a price which will provide a desired level of long-term profits:

$$E(B) = Pr(\text{win})B - C \tag{12.7}$$

where $E(B)$ = the expected value of the bid
$Pr(\text{win})$ = the probability of winning the contract, given the bid price
B = the bid price
C = the cost of completing the contract

$B - C$, therefore, represents the gross margin that would be earned if the contract were won and completed.

The figures for B and C are obtainable from the company's own past records of bids, and the probability of winning can be calculated from the previous history of competitive bids. A 3-part table, a sample of which appears in Table 12.8, now can be produced. The figures in the body of the table illustrate the workings of the model. For example, the first horizontal line of figures (0.8, 0.01, and 1.00) tell us that on only 1 per cent (column 2) of past occasions has the competitor's bid been 0.8 (80 per cent) (column 1) of our own cost estimate. The probability of the competitor's bid being greater than, or equal to, that ratio (column 3) is the sum of all the probabilities for that ratio and higher ratios.

These figures enable the pricing executive to build a probability function of winning the contract (column 3 plotted against column 1). The function is shown in Figure 12.9. From the graph in the figure a marketer can read off the probability of winning the contract, given the profit percentage he has added to his costs. Given a 45 per cent profit margin (X_1), the probability of winning the contract is only 0.35 (Y_1). At a 25 per cent

Table 12.8   *Probability of winning competitive bids.*

1 Ratio of competitor's bid to own cost estimates	2 Relative frequency with which ratio has occured in past	3 Probability that competitor's bid is greater than, or equal to, the ratio in column 2
0.8	0.01	1.00
0.9	0.02	0.99
1.0	0.05	0.97
1.1	0.10	0.92
1.2	0.15	0.82
1.3	0.23	0.67
1.4	0.20	0.44
1.5	0.15	0.25
1.6	0.07	0.09
1.7	0.02	0.02

margin (X_2) the probability of winning rises to 0.75 (Y_2). This sort of calculation can take place at any point on the curve. By now substituting these figures back into the original formula we can establish the expected value of the bid. These results are shown in Table 12.9.

By way of explanation, the fourth row of figures in the table says that if a bid with a 10 per cent profit margin on costs is entered for a contract, then there is a 92 per cent chance of winning the contract. The expected outcome of the bid is, therefore, only a 9.2 per cent profit (92 per cent probability of achieving a 10 per cent margin). These calculations show that the maximum expected profit would occur if bidding consistently over time at 1.3 times cost. The expected profit margin would be 20.1 per cent of cost;

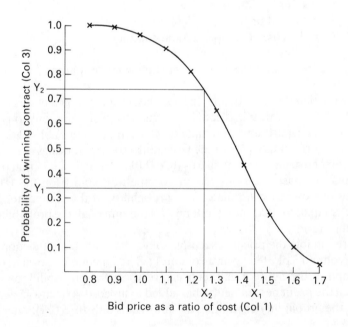

Table 12.9 *Expected payoff of various bid prices.*

$E(B) = P(\text{win})\,(B - C)$
$E(0.80) = 1.00(0.8C - 1.00C) = -0.200C$
$E(0.90) = 0.99(0.9C - 1.00C) = -0.099C$
$E(1.00) = 0.97(1.0C - 1.00C) = 0.000C$
$E(1.10) = 0.92(1.1C - 1.00C) = 0.092C$
$E(1.20) = 0.82(1.2C - 1.00C) = 0.164C$
$E(1.30) = 0.67(1.3C - 1.00C) = 0.201C$
$E(1.40) = 0.64(1.4C - 1.00C) = 0.176C$
$E(1.50) = 0.24(1.5C - 1.00C) = 0.120C$
$E(1.60) = 0.09(1.6C - 1.00C) = 0.054C$
$E(1.70) = 0.02(1.7C - 1.00C) = 0.014C$

and contracts would be won on 67 per cent of occasions, and lost on 33 per cent of occasions. Losses would be made on bids below cost, breakeven would occur when bidding at cost; thereafter is a pattern of rising and falling profit margins.

The main limitation of this model is that it requires a history of bidding against a known competitor but, on the positive side, it can be adapted to include more than 1 competitor (this requires the pricer to establish similar probability functions as if bidding separately against each competitor, then average out the probabilities); to bid simultaneously on more than a single contract; and to include non-price variables.

12.9 CHAPTER REVIEW

1. There are at least 14 methods of calculating price.
2. These methods can be classified as cost-oriented, profitability-oriented, competitor-oriented and marketing-oriented.
3. Cost-plus pricing is the most common form of price calculation.
4. Variable, total, or marginal costs are used in cost-plus pricing.
5. Variable or total costs are used for strategic pricing, marginal for tactical.
6. In factor pricing a multiplicative factor is applied either to food costs or to all direct costs.
7. The aim of breakeven pricing is to calculate the price which will enable a company to break even.
8. Actual cost pricing places a ceiling on the cost of food ingredients, so that a target profit is made.
9. Rate of return pricing aims to find a price structure which will produce a satisfactory return on investment.
10. The Hubbart formula is a particular application of rate of return pricing.
11. Base pricing aims to develop a menu price list which achieves a target ASP.
12. The integrated menu planning system (IMPS) develops a menu price list which is organised to achieve the highest overall contribution towards fixed costs and profit.
13. Marginal pricing integrates 2 mathematical expressions: demand as a function of price, and total costs as the aggregate of fixed and variable costs. The outcome is a price which will maximise profit.
14. The pound-per-thousand method is a rule-of-thumb which proposes that a room rate should be set on the basis of £1 for every £1,000 invested in the room.
15. Price followership is commonplace in oligopolies.
16. Marketing-oriented pricing (MOP) brings costs, competition, demand, marketing strategy, profit objectives, sales objectives and distribution considerations to bear on the pricing decision.
17. Prestige pricing occurs because the marketer expects to experience higher demand at higher prices.

18. Leader pricing is the practice of setting low prices for certain items to attract customers to one's premises.
19. Psychological pricing incorporates price lining and odd pricing.
20. Price lining is the practice of setting price between psychologically determined threshold and ceiling prices.
21. Odd pricing involves using prices which imply some advantage to the consumer—e.g. 99p rather than £1.01.
22. Price promotions do not always have a great impact on sales; consideration must be given to timing, frequency and depth of the cut. Their role is tactical.
23. Transfer pricing concerns the price at which products are traded between units in an organisation.
24. Market prices or costs are the 2 basic ways of establishing transfer prices.
25. Price changes are sometimes interpreted idiosyncratically by customers. A price fall does not always appear as better value for money.
26. Probability theory can be used to improve the success rate of competitive tenders.
27. Price decisions are more difficult when the costs or demands of individual products in a product mix are interrelated.

12.10 QUESTIONS

1. There is no difference between factor pricing and cost-plus pricing. Discuss.
2. In factor pricing is it preferable to use as the basis all direct costs (including labour) or food costs only?
3. What examples of by-products and joint products are there in the hospitality industry? How would you take account of such relationships in pricing decisions?
4. What tactical reasons are there for cutting rack rate?
5. Why do you think odd pricing has become the norm in both accommodation and menu pricing? Is odd pricing incompatible with VAT-inclusive prices?
6. Why is cost-plus pricing so widespread in restaurants?
7. How could you research the psychological impact on customers of price changes?
8. Under what circumstances would competitive-oriented pricing be desirable?

REFERENCES

[1] Horwath & Horwath (UK) Ltd, *UK Lodging Industry 1984*.
[2] Morphis, G. S. (1978) Load factor pricing and the lodging industry. *Cornell Hotel and Restaurant Administration Quarterly*, **19**(3), November, 34–7.
[3] See Kotas, R. (1977) *Management Accounting in Hotels and Restaurants*. Guildford: Surrey University Press, 56–68, for more detail.
[4] Kotas, R. (1975) *Market Orientation in the Hotel and Catering Industry*. Guildford: Surrey University Press, 27–9.
[5] See Kotas, R. (1977) op. cit., 112–13, for a worked example.
[6] Orkin, E. B. (1972) An integrated menu pricing system. *Cornell Hotel and Restaurant Administration Quarterly*, **19**(2), August, 8–13.
[7] Buttle, F. (1980) How to price by markets. *Management Today*, July, 52–3.
[8] Rogers, H. A. (1977) Psychological aspects of pricing. *HCIMA Journal*, January, 15–16.
[9] Kreul, L. M. (1982) Magic numbers: psychological aspects of menu pricing. *Cornell Hotel and Restaurant Administration Quarterly*, **23**(12), August, 70–5.
[10] Based partly on Livesey, F. (1976) *Pricing*. London: Macmillan.
[11] British Insitute of Management, Research Report, 1974.
[12] Lipsey, R. G. (1971) (3rd edn) *Positive Economics*. London: Weidenfeld & Nicolson, 102.
[13] Oxenfeldt, A. (1961) *Pricing for Marketing Executives*. London: Wadsworth.

SECTION 3
Distribution

—13—

Principles of Distribution and Channel Management

13.1 CHAPTER PREVIEW

This chapter and Chapter 14 will investigate the third of the Four Ps—i.e. Place, also known as distribution. The present chapter concentrates on the management of channels of distribution for hospitality products. It identifies the main function of these channels and the flows of information, persuasion and payment within them. We shall describe 12 types of channel intermediary. The trend towards vertically integrated marketing systems is explored, and a four-step process is recommended for the design of channels of distribution.

13.2 LEARNING OBJECTIVES

By the end of this chapter you should be able to:
1. Explain the scope of distribution.
2. Identify the main functions of (and flows in) channels of distribution.
3. Describe at least 10 types of channel intermediary for hospitality products.
4. Explain the differences between conventional and vertical marketing systems.
5. Follow a 4-step channel planning process.

13.3 SCOPE OF DISTRIBUTION

The distribution function in hospitality marketing has 2 dimensions: the distribution channel (or marketing channel), whose role is to make the product more accessible and convenient to the customer; and physical distribution, which is concerned with issues of location, inventory, warehousing and transportation.

This chapter discusses the distribution channel. (Chapter 14 investigates the physical side of distribution.) Whilst the location of any hotel or restaurant is obviously capable of a major impact on turnover and profitability, inventory, warehousing and transportation are not major issues in every hospitality organisation. However, some hotel companies have developed vertically integrated marketing systems (VMS) in which corporate-owned manufacturing plant supply the hotels with furniture and carpeting, thus making inventory, warehousing and transportation of concern to management. Similar arrangements exist in food service—i.e. farms and food-processing plant being owned by multiple operators. (More of this in Chapter 14.)

13.4 CHANNEL FUNCTIONS AND FLOWS

The distribution channel's function is to provide time and place utilities—i.e. to make the product available when and where required. Rathmell comments that:[1]

> in the recreation-tourism-hotel and motel-transportation complex of services, time and place utility appear to be the essence of the product itself . . . Any attempt to distinguish between the performance utility (i.e. the customer's receipt of the product), and time and place utility . . . is futile and meaningless.

The distribution channel is the configuration of organisations and individuals between the hospitality marketer and his potential customer which is used to make the product more accessible and convenient. Each organisation or individual is known as a 'marketing intermediary', or channel member.

In the UK there are millions of consumers and thousands of marketers of hospitality products. Each marketer could conceivably sell direct to each consumer but the cost in time and finance would be immense. Marketing intermediaries have, therefore, evolved to perform cost effectively the bridging function, bringing together buyer and producer.

Imagine an exchange system in which there are 3 marketers and 5 consumers. Each consumer wants to buy the product of each producer. Without intermediaries, 15 transactions would occur, as shown in Figure 13.1. With 1 intermediary, say, a travel agent, only 8 transactions occur, as shown in Figure 13.2.

For the channel to function properly there must be a flow of information and persuasion from marketer to customer—i.e. information about location, price, reservation system, or menu style, and persuasion in the form of, for example, personal selling or promotional literature. Equally there should be a reverse flow of payment and information. For instance, an hotel might contract a block of rooms to a tour operator. Payment would flow from holidaymaker to tour operator to hotelier. Further

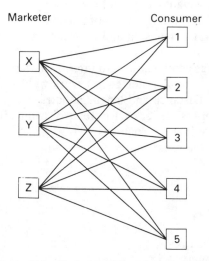

Figure 13.1   Marketing without intermediaries.

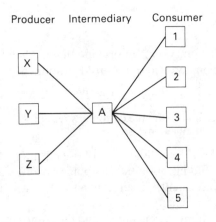

Figure 13.2   Marketing with one intermediary.

information about the specific requirements of the tourists would flow through the same channel.

13.5 CHANNEL MEMBERS

Most marketing writers generalise that because of the intangible and inseparable nature of services, direct sale is the only possible channel for distributing most of them.[2]

Direct sale is more common in food service than in accommodation, probably because potential channel intermediaries do not regard the distribution of seats at tables as a profit opportunity. A conventional distribution channel can be viewed as a loose coalition in which the objectives of all members must be more or less achieved for the channel to function. Channel members are almost invariably profit-oriented. Since there is little profit in distributing seats at tables, there is no established channel. Direct sale, however, does have advantages, as follows.

1. It can build a reputation for a high level of personal service.
2. It improves control over persuasion and information flows between company and customer.
3. It avoids payment of fees/commissions to intermediaries.

There are millions of potential hotel guests worldwide seeking rooms in tens of thousands of UK hotels. Distance and language barriers separate buyer from seller. This equation makes it impossible for each hotel to distribute its own products directly. Hence the development of indirect channels.

Intermediaries include the following:

- hotel representatives
- travel agents
- tour operators
- referral organisations
- tourist boards
- tourist information centres
- incentive travel planners

- airlines
- computerised reservation services
- convention bureaux
- car rental companies
- motoring organisations

The length of the distribution channel varies. The 2-member channel of hotel–customer is the direct sale; 3-, 4- and 5-member channels, as shown in Figure 13.3, are also common.

No. of members in channel	Channel of distribution
Three	Hotel ⟶ Travel Agent ⟶ Customer Hotel ⟶ Hotel Representative ⟶ Customer Hotel ⟶ Incentive Travel Planner ⟶ Customer
Four	Hotel ⟶ Tour Operator ⟶ Travel Agent ⟶ Customer Hotel ⟶ Airline ⟶ Travel Agent ⟶ Customer
Five	Hotel ⟶ Hotel Representative ⟶ Master Travel Agent ⟶ Local Travel Agent ⟶ Customer

Figure 13.3 Indirect channels of distribution for hotels.

Hotel representatives

Hotel representatives promote sales and accept reservations for non-competing properties. Many British hotels employ representatives in the USA and Middle East since these are regarded as productive markets. For example, Abercrombie and Kent (A & K) represent a group of British country house hotels, collectively called Pride of Britain in the USA. A & K receive a 15 per cent commission on each sale; if the sale is made by an A & K appointed travel agent, the agent receives 8 per cent whilst A & K retain the balance. A £1,000 fee is also payable to A & K annually by each group member.[3]

Travel agents

There are around 6,000 ABTA-registered travel agency offices in the UK. The Association of British Travel Agents registration implies the maintenance of ethical standards. These offices are embodied in about 2,700 travel agency businesses. The multiple groups—Thomas Cook, Lunn Poly, Pickford's, Hogg Robinson, Co-Op Travel and A. T. Mays—are growing by buying out the smaller groups and independents.[4]

A travel agent's business is to serve the consumer in all major aspects of travel. Among a travel agent's responsibilities are the following.[5]

1. Providing a wide range of unbiased travel advice—some clients will visit a travel agent with a specific plan in mind whilst others are looking for ideas.

2. Arranging transportation—air, sea, rail, bus, car rental, etc.
3. Arranging for hotel, motel and resort accommodation, meals, sightseeing, transfers of passengers and luggage between terminals and hotels, and special features such as music festivals or theatre tickets.
4. Preparing individual itineraries, personally escorting tours and group tours, and selling prepared package tours.
5. Arranging reservations for special-interest activities such as religious pilgrimages, conventions, incentive and business travel, student tours and sporting trips.
6. Handling and advising on the many details involved in modern-day travel—visa, health and passport requirements, travel baggage, insurance, traveller's cheques and language-study material.

The overall revenue mix of UK travel agents is 66 per cent from holidays and 34 per cent from business travel.[6] If the American experience is any guide, they will receive a greater proportion from business travel in future years. In 1982, 50 per cent of the American travel agent's revenue was from business travel; in 1977, it had been 25 per cent.[7]

The standard level of commission for booking accommodation is 8 per cent. Discounts apply to high-volume customers.[8]

Tour operators

Tour operators regard hotels as one of the raw materials necessary to create a marketable product, the others being transport, transfers, food, insurance and activities/attractions. Major UK tour operators, such as Thomson, Intasun and Horizon, concentrate on outward holiday traffic. They contract hoteliers to supply blocks of rooms at a much discounted rate. Tour operators differ from all other intermediaries in this list, in that they are wholesalers of accommodation. Unlike agents, wholesalers assume risk by advance ordering on behalf of tourists who have not yet booked holidays. Tour operators may negotiate a 'release date' clause into the contract under which, subject to penalty, unsold rooms may be returned to the hotelier.

Not all tour operators specialise in outward holiday traffic. Some specialise in domestic travel, often by coach. Others arrange tours for inbound travellers.

Referral organisations

A referral organisation is a group of hotels which agrees, out of mutual self-interest, to handle incoming reservation requests for one another. The organisation may be:
  • a corporate group
  • a voluntary association or consortium
  • a franchise group
Most referral systems are based upon computerised reservation systems, with a central data bank and remote terminals in each member establishment. Whilst the true cost of such installations is falling, members and customers experience a number of benefits: immediate confirmations, improved occupancies, convenience of booking procedure, rapid refilling of cancellations, instant analysis of occupancy data, computer manipulation of room rates for improved profitability and automated invoicing. Holiday Inns' system is called Holidex, Marriott's is Marsha. The major hotel groups,

Hilton, Sheraton, Marriott, Intercontinental, Holiday Inns and Hyatt, all operate corporate referral systems. One telephone call, frequently to a toll-free number, results in instant confirmation of a booking.

Many hotel groups, including Trusthouse Forte, Grand Metropolitan, Hilton, Ramada, Marriott and Sheraton, have entered into management contracts. Such a contract is a written, long-term agreement between a property-owner and an operator, which treats the operator as an agent. The agent pays all the operating expenses and retains a management fee, normally a percentage of gross income, remitting the remaining surplus to the owner. The owner provides the property, fixtures, working capital and assumes full legal responsibility.[9] Such operations are also tied in to corporate referral systems. There are a number of independent management contractors such as the American company Hospitality Management, whose ownership of hotel properties is insignificant. In these, referral systems are likely to be less sophisticated. Most of the independents receive 3 per cent of gross revenues, unlike the chains' 4 or 5 per cent.[10]

Some operators are offered the opportunity to participate in 'turnkey operations', where the entire business package of design, finance, construction and fixtures and fittings is provided by the developer. The operator merely turns the key and is in business.

As the power of the hotel chains grew in the 1960s smaller groups and independants began to form into co-operative groups or consortia. Defined as[11]

> an organization of hotels, usually, but not necessarily owned autonomously, which combine resources in order to establish joint purchasing/trading arrangements and operate marketing services

The hotel consortium affords several advantages to members: collective advertising and promotion, centralised reservations system, co-operative financing, group recruitment and training, better representation, economies in purchasing and brand image development.

Leading Hotels of the World, for example, is an association of 170 independently owned luxury hotels. It runs its own marketing company called Hotel Representative Inc. (HRI), which prints 1 million directories, operates a worldwide reservation system and spends about half a million pounds on advertising and promotion.[12] The first to emerge in Britain was Prestige Hotels (1966); other consortia are Best Western, Inter Hotels (3 star), Minotels (budget, 2 star), Guestaccom (small hotels) and Consort (3 star). Most consortia are organised on a non-profit basis, but are financed by annual dues proportionate to the number of rooms. Contributors to HRI also pay an annual marketing fee.

Members of each consortium share similar characteristics or marketing problems—e.g. they all may be located in the same resort area (Tenby) or they all may appeal to the same type of tourist. Consequently many of the consortia check applications for membership against strict criteria. Best Western reject over 90 per cent of applicants. Leading Hotels of the World's membership criteria are excellence of service, physical structure, cuisine and guest comforts. Even when accepted, periodic reviews are undertaken. Best Western, for example, assesses twice annually against a checklist each member property. If a minimum standard is not maintained, there is expulsion; therefore, loss of the benefits of the referral system are threatened. The 10 largest consortia worldwide are Best Western International (USA), Friendship Inns International (USA), Fédération Nationale (France), Supranational (Switzerland), Golden Tulip (Holland), Flag Hotels (Australia and New Zealand), SRS Hotels (Germany), HRI (USA), JAL Hotel System (Japan) and Inter Hotels (France).[13]

Franchise groups also operate referral systems. There have been many attempts to define the term franchise[14] but the following is adequate enough for our purposes: a franchise is a contractual arrangement between two parties whereby, for a consideration, one party (the franchisor) grants to the other (the franchisee) the right to use the franchisor's brand and commercial methods of operation. Many well-known hotel groups have franchised units—e.g. Hilton, Trust House Forte, Holiday Inns and Sheraton. Franchising is also widely applied in food service—e.g. Kentucky Fried Chicken, Wimpy, Burger King, Happy Eater, Oliver's and Pizza Express.

Franchising brings about a number of advantages and disadvantages for both the franchisor and franchisee.[15] Advantages to the franchisor are:
- rapid market penetration
- relatively little capital required for expansion
- pre-emption of competitors
- economies of scale
- strategic mobility (relatively easy to disengage from system)
- contribution of franchise fees to working capital
- no involvement in operating costs
- continuing source of revenue (often a percentage of sales)
- purchasing leverage
- highly motivated unit management
- avoidance of some legal responsibility for activities within units

Disadvantages to the franchisor are:
- difficult to enforce standards
- slower to introduce change than in wholly owned business
- franchisee complacency with performance
- franchisee's aim to secure short-term profit rather than longer-term stability or sales maximisation
- lower profit-to-sales ratios than in wholly owned properties
- locating suitable franchisees with adequate capital
- lack of clarity in legislation pertinent to franchising (there is no franchising legislation *per se*)

Advantages to the franchisee are:
- access to proven successful marketing strategy and brand image
- access to expertise and experience
- substantial advertising and promotion expenditure
- use of referral system
- reduced working capital required (no concept development costs)
- economic viability shortly after launch
- access to development funds because of connections with proven enterprise
- reliable product quality, stock control and delivery
- initial training
- sense of security

Disadvantages to the franchisee are:
- some franchises are inadequately tested and unproven
- public exposure of malpractices in other units
- payment of franchise fee prior to receipt of income
- continuing payment of royalties or other fees
- restrictions imposed by franchisor
- dependence upon viability of franchisor
- use of nominated suppliers
- franchisor's restriction on number of units operated per franchisee

Tourist boards

National Tourist Boards also distribute hotel accommodation. The British Tourist Authority (BTA) is the statutory body for the promotion of Britain in overseas markets. Tourists to Britain can book accommodation through any of the BTA's offices overseas. The English Tourist Board's (ETB) 'Let's Go' weekend-break programme markets hotel accommodation domestically. Each hotelier pays £300 to participate. The ETB estimates that 400,000 'Let's Go' breaks were sold in 1982–3, producing hotel revenue of £20 million.

Tourist information centres

There are over 700 tourist information centres (TICs) throughout Britain. One of the many services offered by TICs is an accommodation information and booking service. A small fee is levied when a booking is made.

Incentive travel planners

Incentive travel is a growth market. It straddles both business and leisure markets, in that the buyer is a business person, whereas the guest is a holidaymaker. Incentive travel planners design fully inclusive tours as motivational devices. Accommodation in an attractive hotel in a desirable resort is regarded by many as a major incentive.

Airlines

Airlines not only book accommodation for flight crews, but also act as intermediaries for passengers and travel agents who want the convenience of a single phone call to tie up all travel arrangements. Thus the channel could be hotel–airline–customer, or hotel–airline–travel agent–customer. Some airlines have their own hotel properties.

Computerised reservation services

In addition to the computerised reservation systems of corporate, voluntary, or franchise organisations, there are independent systems operated by other companies with close travel connections. The best known, perhaps, is the American Express Space Bank which can be accessed by travel agents.

Convention bureaux

The London Visitor and Convention Bureau is an example of a recently established agency whose function is to stimulate conventions, congresses, meetings, tours and seminars to assemble in the capital city. Most convention bureaux are funded by those who stand to gain most—e.g. hotels, restaurants, taxi operators and tourist attractions. Most bureaux provide the following services:
- central bureau to clear reservations for groups too big for 1 hotel
- registration staff to assist delegates upon arrival
- distribution of local information to convention delegates
- advice/assistance for hotel and convention management

Car rental companies

The major car rental companies—Hertz and Avis—offer their customers an accommodation booking service. Often they are able to offer specially negotiated rates. Hertz have a special joint marketing arrangement with the American division of Holiday Inns.

Motoring organisations

There are many organisations in the UK, the two biggest being the Automobile Association and the Royal Automobile Club. Some of these organisations offer an accommodation booking and itinerary planning service to their members.

13.6 ORGANISATIONAL PATTERNS IN HOSPITALITY MARKETING CHANNELS

The hospitality industry displays characteristics of both conventional and vertical marketing channel systems.
The conventional channel is defined as:[16]

> a piecemeal coalition of independently owned and managed institutions, each of which is prompted by the profit motive with little concern about what goes on before or after it is in the distributive sequence.

In comparison the vertical marketing system is defined as:[17]

> professionally managed and centrally programmed networks preengineered to achieve operating economies and maximum market impact.

We are witnessing the emergence of VMSs in the hospitality industry.
Co-ordination between members of the conventional channel is achieved through compromise and negotiation. The food service industry largely consists of independent farmers, food processors, distributors, wholesalers, cash-and-carry operators and restaurateurs who, despite their myopic focus, somehow manage to provide diners with satisfying meal experiences.
Three types of VMSs have been identified (see Figure 13.4): administered, contractual and corporate systems. The difference between the administered VMS and

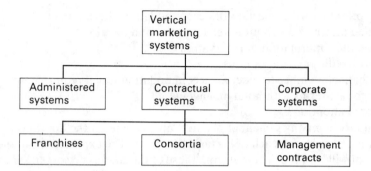

Figure 13.4   Vertical marketing systems.

the conventional channel is one of degree. Administered VMS channel members still pursue their own objectives but collaborate effectively to make decisions which are of mutual interest. For example, motels lacking food and beverage facilities will co-operate with local food service outlets to provide dining facilities for guests; coach-tour operators often arrange to stop at chosen food service outlets in return for a consideration.

Contractual systems take these relationships a stage further by legally defining formal roles in the channel. We have already discussed 3 forms of contractual relationship—i.e. franchises, hotel consortia and management contracts between property-owners and hotel management companies. Corporate systems exist when members at different stages in the distribution channel are owned by a single company.

The direction of integration may be forward or backward. Holiday Inns has integrated backwards, buying farmland to produce its own food. Singapore Airlines has integrated forwards, buying its own hotels. Marriott is in hotels, theme parks, airline catering and fast-food restaurants. The main aim of a corporate VMS is to reduce the suboptimisation which is common in conventional channels, therefore improving profitability.

13.7 CHANNEL PLANNING

Achievement of marketing objectives can be considerably hampered by the use of inappropriate marketing channels. However, a channel which has been specifically designed to deliver time and place utilities to a selected target market is a considerable marketing asset.

Channel design decisions should be related to the overall marketing plan and strategy and should, therefore, draw upon common information about the market-place. This is implied in Figure 13.5, which models the channel planning process. Channel planning starts by identifying target markets (part of the marketing plan) and defining the general level, and specific components, of service expected by these markets from channel members. Answers to questions such as the following help to frame channel objectives: Do customers want

- to meet with hotel management prior to purchase?

- to be offered a wide selection of accommodation alternatives?
- detailed information about hotel amenities and location?
- immediate confirmation of reservations?
- cash or credit payment options?
- one channel member to meet all accommodation/travel requirements?
- to negotiate terms with hotel management?
- personal attention?

The hospitality company's channel planner must decide on the appropriate level and components of service for each of his target markets. The expectations of the inclusive tour segment will be quite different from those of the conference organiser or transient one-nighter. Consequently different channels may be required for each segment.

Channel objectives should explicitly state the contribution that distribution is expected to make towards overall marketing objectives. Generally distribution objectives fall into 3 categories: sales objectives, profit objectives and service output objectives.

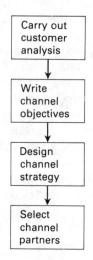

Figure 13.5   The channel planning process.

Sales objectives (volume or value)
- to fill 15 per cent of our rooms through our hotel consortium
- to shift from a 75–25 split between direct and indirect sell to 60–40
- to improve average achieved room rate by 2.5 per cent

Profit objectives
- to earn 25 per cent of our profit from sales to tour operators

Service output objectives
- to offer immediate confirmation of reservations
- to offer 2 months' credit to selected customers

Once these have been expressed, the general channel strategy for each segment can be formulated. The focus of the strategy is the level of market coverage—the number of outlets servicing a given geographic area or market segment. As indicated in Figure 13.6, the strategic alternatives are intensive, selective, or exclusive distribution.

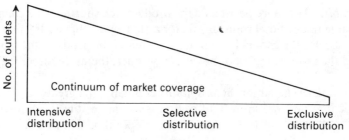

Figure 13.6 Market coverage.

A major Spanish group such as Sol Hotels, targeting British holidaymakers, may opt for intensive distribution through as many tour operators as possible. A highly esteemed gourmet restaurant may elect to use direct channels only (exclusive distribution). A city-centre hotel may use selective distribution to reach meetings planners but intensive distribution at all major travel termini to reach the transient one-nighter. Accepted practice is to use intensive distribution for convenience products and exclusive distribution for speciality products. When opting for intensive distribution, the hospitality marketer may face a number of adverse consequences: loss of control over the marketing of his product; falling prices as competition hots up; a slide in the quality of the channel members' service output; and deterioration of image. On the other hand, exclusive distribution arrangements involve careful negotiation of territories covered or markets served, products to be sold, sales quotas, co-operative advertising and promotion, duration of exclusivity and provisions for renewal or termination.

Having settled the coverage issue, attention must be given to selection of specific classes of channel partners. These are detailed in section 13.5. Their ability to achieve the objectives, provide suitable service outputs and reach the chosen target markets will largely determine whether they are to be included in the channel design. At this stage the channel planner will probably be considering a number of channel configurations for each target market. Club Med, for example, considered 2 main channel configurations for reaching their young, affluent target market:

Club Med————————————————————————————> Customer
Club Med——————————————>Travel agent ——————————> Customer

A number of factors can influence the suitability of each configuration. Rosenbloom identifies 6 categories:[18]

- market variables
- product variables
- company variables
- middlemen variables
- environmental variables
- behavioural variables

Market variables. The greater the distance between company and market, the less profitable is direct distribution; the smaller the market, the more direct the channel; the denser the market, the more direct the channel; and the smaller or more frequent the purchase, the more intensive the distribution.

Product variables. The more perishable the product, the shorter is the channel (what is more perishable than a hotel room unsold for a night?); the higher the unit value of the product, the shorter the channel; the more customised the product, the more direct the channel; and the more complex or novel the product, the more direct the channel.

Company variables. The larger the hospitality company, the greater is the flexibility in channel selection; and the more that capital is available, the less dependence upon intermediaries. Some firms lack managerial and operational expertise in distribution.

Middlemen variables. The key factors influencing channel structure are the availability, cost and service outputs of intermediaries.

Environmental variables. Economic, sociocultural, competitive, technological and legal factors.

Behavioural variables. Conflict, power, roles and communication within the alternative channels.

The channel designer is now at a stage where he must identify and select specific channel partners. The selection process involves evaluating each prospect against a set of criteria, often in checklist format. Questions such as these must be answered:
  - is the distributor profitable?
  - how well established is he?
  - does he sell complementary products?
  - what is his customer profile?
  - will he display our literature?
  - will he attend product training programmes?
  - does he sell competing products?
  - what is his reputation?
  - does he employ outside sales staff?
  - is he complacent or aggressive?
  - will he provide the required service outputs?
  - is his management sound?

13.8 CHAPTER REVIEW

1. Distribution has 2 dimensions: the distribution (or marketing) channel, and physical distribution.
2. The channel's function is to provide time and place utilities.
3. Information, persuasion and payment flow through the channel.
4. Channels can be classified as direct or indirect.

5. Channel members include hotel representatives, travel agents, tour operators, referral organisations, tourist boards, tourist information centres, incentive travel planners, airlines, computerised reservation services, convention bureaux, motoring organisations and car rental companies.
6. All channels have at least 2 members: the hospitality company and the customer; 3-, 4- and 5-member channels are commonplace.
7. The hospitality industry displays characteristics of both the conventional and vertically integrated marketing system (VMS); VMSs are professionally managed and centrally programmed networks.
8. Three types of VMS have been identified; administered, contractual and corporate.
9. There are 3 main types of contractual VMS in hospitality: franchises, consortia and management contracts between hotel proprietors and their managerial agents.
10. Achievement of marketing objectives is hampered by inappropriate marketing channels.
11. A 4-step channel planning process involves:
    ● customer analysis.
    ● writing channel objectives.
    ● design channel strategy.
    ● selecting channel partners.
12. The channel should be designed to provide the level and forms of service required by prospective customers of the hospitality company.
13. Channel objectives fall into 3 categories: sales, profits and service output objectives.
14. Channel strategy focuses on market coverage—the alternatives are intensive, selective, or exclusive distribution.
15. In choosing between alternative channel configurations the planner must consider market, product, company, middleman, environmental and behaviour variables.
16. The selection of individual channel members normally involves evaluating each prospect against a set of criteria.

13.9 QUESTIONS AND EXERCISES

1. Which channel intermediaries could contribute towards the effective marketing of:
   ● condominiums?
   ● private hospitals?
   ● college catering facilities?
   ● a gourmet restaurant?
   ● a theme park?
2. Draw up a checklist of criteria against which you would evaluate prospective individual, UK-based channel partners for a chain of Greek holiday hotels. Are some criteria more important than others?
3. What do you understand by the term 'time and place utility'?
4. Using the list of channel intermediaries in section 13.5, draw up a flowchart of 3-, 4- and 5-member channel configurations, starting with the examples in Figure 13.3.
5. What advantages and disadvantages could accrue to both property-owner and hotel operator from a management contract?
6. Why are VMSs of growing significance in hospitality markets?

REFERENCES

[1] Rathmell, J. M. (1974) *Marketing in the Service Sector*. Cambridge, MA: Winthrop, 105.
[2] Donnelly, J. H. (1976) Marketing intermediaries in channels of distribution for services. *Journal of Marketing*, **40**(1), January, 55–7.
[3] Kann, R. (1983) US connections which boost trade for the independent hotel. *Caterer and Hotelkeeper*, 10 November, 45–6.

[4] See: UK travel agents: who they are and their market. Pt II, the agents. *International Travel Quarterly*, 3, 40–56.

[5] Coffman, C. D. (1980) *Hospitality for Sale*. Educational Institute of American Hotel and Motel Association, 171.

[6] See: UK travel agents, op. cit.

[7] Bush, M. (1982) Capturing business travellers: the travel agency connection. *Cornell Hotel and Restaurant Administration Quarterly*, **23**(2), August, 58–61.

[8] See: UK travel agents, op. cit.

[9] Eyster, J. J. (1977) Factors influencing the adoption of management contracts in the lodging industry. *Cornell Hotel and Restaurant Administration Quarterly*, **17**(4), February, 17–26.

[10] Kiener, R. (1977) The management contract, in Brymer, R. A. (ed.) *Introduction to Hotel and Restaurant Management*. Des Moines, IA: Kendall-Hunt, 54 ff.

[11] See Littlejohn, D. (1982) The role of hotel consortia in Great Britain. *Service Industries Review*, **2**(1), Spring, 79–91.

[12] Kann, R. (1983) op. cit.

[13] *Service World International, 1981*, quoted in Littlejohn, D. (1982) op. cit.

[14] Housden, J. (1984) *Franchising and other Business Relationships in Hotel and Catering Services*. London: Heinemann.

[15] ibid., 206–39.

[16] Stern, L. W. and El-Ansary, A. I. (1982) (2nd edn) *Marketing Channels*. Englewood Cliffs, NJ: Prentice-Hall, 306.

[17] McCammon, B. C., Jr (1970) Perspectives for distribution programming, in Bucklin, L. P. (ed.) *Vertical Marketing Systems*. Glenview, IL: Scott, Foresman, 43.

[18] Rosenbloom, B. (1983) (2nd edn) *Marketing Channels: A Management View*. London: Dryden Press, 151–58.

—14—

Physical Distribution

14.1 CHAPTER PREVIEW

There is one dimension of physical distribution which is of overriding importance to hospitality marketers—location, the focus of this chapter. We shall examine how hospitality companies decide whether to locate in a particular area and which particular site to choose.

14.2 LEARNING OBJECTIVES

By the end of this chapter you should be able to:
1. Explain the difference between physical distribution in a fast-moving consumer goods context and a hospitality context.
2. Identify the key variables to be considered when selecting a trading area and a particular site for location.
3. Explain why demand is the most important factor in hospitality location.

14.3 SCOPE OF PHYSICAL DISTRIBUTION

Physical distribution (PD) is much better understood in the context of the marketing of tangible fast-moving consumer goods. It is also known as logistics and embraces activities such as inventory management, warehousing, facilities location, packing, transport, installation, customer service, materials handling and order processing. The costs of these activities reach 12 per cent or more of sales[1] and can, therefore, have a great impact upon the achievement of both corporate and marketing objectives. Most of these activities, however, are not of direct relevance to hospitality marketers.

Inventory in the hospitality business takes a variety of forms—i.e. the stock of rooms, prepared foods, beverages, raw ingredients and bed linen. In a vertically integrated organisation inventory might include aircraft in company hangars and carpets or furniture stocked at company factories. Such inventories are rarely the responsibility of marketing management. The most likely exception is the stock of rooms. A marketing decision may be made to reduce the stock of rooms available for sale in the low season, for example, by closing a wing or floor; equally the stock can be increased in certain types of hospitality businesses, for example, by installing additional caravan or canvas accommodation.

Warehousing of intangibles is impossible, as are packing, transportation and installation. In hotels order processing is the responsibility of reservations or front office management, whereas materials handling is managed within housekeeping, F&B or maintenance departments. Customer service is used to augment the basic hospitality product (see Chapter 8). The most important PD decision for marketers is that of location.

14.4 LOCATION OF SERVICES

Location is described by Rathmell as:[2]

the distribution of people and facilities prepared to perform services.

The location of services can be classified in 3 ways.
1. Location is irrelevant.
2. Services are concentrated.
3. Services are dispersed.

Location is irrelevant for gas, electricity, telephone and television. Supply and demand, custom, or inertia are the factors which determine whether services are concentrated or dispersed. Stud-farms, for example, are concentrated around Newmarket because of custom. Business hotels are concentrated in the main conurbations because of demand. Conversely, demand may also be the main reason for dispersion of services such as restaurants. Sometimes the service organisation is centralised but its operations are dispersed. For example, many national hotel companies are based in London but operate units from Inverness to Eastbourne. Figure 14.1 graphically summarises service location patterns.[3]

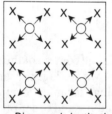

a Dispersed: institutionally and operationally

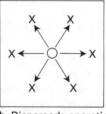

b Dispersed: operationally Concentrated: institutionally

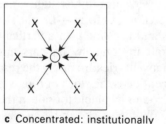

c Concentrated: institutionally and operationally

d Location irrelevant

Figure 14.1   Service location patterns.

14.5 LOCATING HOSPITALITY OUTLETS

As noted by Medlik and Airey, the traditional influences on the location of manufacturing industry—nearness to raw materials, parts and labour—have little bearing on the location of hotels and catering outlets. Demand is the most important (perhaps only) criterion. Hospitality services must be provided where demand exists.[4] Such is the proliferation of fast-food high-street locations in the USA that secondary sites such as hospitals, museums and military bases are being considered. (The basic approach to discovering whether demand potential exists is covered in Chapter 9, particularly in the section examining feasibility studies.)

Location decisions start by attempting to understand customers' search behaviour. For low-involvement convenience products, such as coffee shops, most consumers are not prepared to expend time and effort in search; for high-involvement shopping products, such as a gourmet restaurant or private club, search may be extensive. Location tends to be a more significant factor in the success of convenience products.

The location of retail outlets has been the subject of much experimental research. Consequently a number of models have evolved which either attempt to explain location decisions or predict which location, given a number of alternatives, will be most profitable. Similar models exist in hospitality, both for restaurants[5] and hotels[6], but as Akehurst observes, they are often simple developments of established retailing techniques.[7] However, since caterers retail meal experiences and hotels retail accommodation, the retailing parallel appears prima facie appropriate. There are 2 distinct, but interdependent, location decisions: (1) the selection of a trading area, and (2) the selection of a particular site within the trading area.

(1) Selecting a trading area

Pioneering work into the relative attractiveness of trading areas was performed by W. T. Reilly in the 1920s and 1930s. Reilly formulated the Law of Retail Gravitation, which states that 2 trading areas (*a* and *b*) attract trade from an intermediate point in proportion to the population of those trading areas, and in inverse proportion to the square of the intermediate point's distance from the trading areas.[8] The law is expressed mathematically thus:

$$\frac{Ta}{Tb} = \frac{Pa}{Pb}\left[\frac{db}{da}\right]^2$$

(14.1)

where a, b = the trading areas
P = population
d = distance
T = volume of trade

The amount of trade attracted to an area is, according to Reilly, a function of its accessibility (d) and its attraction (P).

Three recent developments have helped to modify and improve Reilly's law:
- Variables more specific than population and distance have been identified. These variables have come to be known as attraction and deterrence factors. Huff has

proposed retail floorspace and travelling time, in place of population and distance respectively.[9] Other factors specifically noted as indicators of an area's attractiveness have been durable goods sales retail, floorspace, the number of banks, variety of department stores, availability of parking-space, workforce size, entertainment facilities and retail sales volume

- More than 2 trading areas can be built, with ease, into modern computerised versions of the model
- The inverse-square relationship between distance and trade has been redefined more accurately.[10] The probability of using a hotel rises in proportion to the distance of the customer's residence from it, whereas the probability of using a restaurant decreases in proportion to distance

Notably, it has been proven that the travel-time exponent varies according to the class of trade. A gourmet restaurant will attract custom from a wider area than, say, a fish-and-chip shop. The attraction and deterrence factors for different types of hospitality establishment will vary. Examples appear in Table 14.1.

Table 14.1   *Attraction and deterrence factors.*

Snackbar

Attraction factors	Deterrence factors
Large numbers of office workers	Prosperity of office workers
Busy shopping centre	Absence of multiple retailers
Availability of public transport	Cost of public transport
Large population	Distance between residential areas
Parking space	Cost of parking
Number of banks	

Hotel

Attraction factors	Deterrence factors
Scenic attractions	Congestion
Prosperous businesses	Percentage unemployed
Affluent population	Distance from major centres of population
Rail terminus	Cost of rail travel
Entertainment facilities	Poor shopping amenities

The trading area decision, therefore, depends not only on the population of that particular area, but also on its attraction to the residents of other areas. Other demographic factors to consider are trends in population growth and structure. Population data are available from the electoral roll, government Censuses, newspaper circulation data and from school enrolments. Additional factors considered in area selection are:

- the extent of new homebuilding
- the income distribution within the trading area
- the number of children
- the volume of internal traffic and through traffic
- the sales potential measured as the sum of all competitors' revenues
- the nature and extent of competition
- the job security of the population
- the general health of other businesses in the area

- the presence of advertising media
- availability of staff-training facilities and suitable employees
- the closeness of supply sources
- the availability of banking services
- the reliability of public utilities such as gas, electricity and sewage

Having selected a trading area on the basis of this analysis, the choice of particular sites in the area now takes place.

(2) Selecting a site

Chain operations generally have formalised checklists of factors to be taken into account during site selection. Decisions are often taken by real estate or properties division staff, based on data collected from both secondary sources and market surveys. Even within a single company the criteria may vary for different styles of operation. Nordsee, the Germany-based fast-food chain applies quite different criteria to burger and fish operations.[11]

In rapidly expanding sectors it is not uncommon for 10 new sites a week to be considered by food service operators. Location decisions, therefore, tend to be made under time pressures which preclude extensive information acquisition. If sites are incorrectly assessed, investment may turn out to be unprofitable or a valuable site may be lost to a competitor.[12] Many operators, especially in those businesses whose customers are drawn to the trading area for other reasons such as shopping or entertainment, tend to use a heuristic approach or rules-of-thumb. This may take the form of a ratio between some measure of population size and floorspace or rentals at the sites under consideration.[13]

Where site selection is more carefully considered, 4 sets of variables are generally taken into account, as follows.[14]

1. Convenience/approachability.
2. Physical conditions.
3. Legal enactments.
4. Occupancy costs.

Convenience/approachability includes:
- visibility
- car-parking
- accessibility to pedestrian traffic
- proximity of rail, sea, or airport termini
- proximity to business, shopping and leisure attractions
- population size and structure
- ease of entry
- competition

Physical conditions include:
- external relief and terrain
- availability of utilities such as gas, sewerage, electricity and telephone
- load-bearing capacity of land
- architecture

- planned construction and roadbuilding
- standard of adjacent premises

Legal enactments include:
- zoning and land-use ordinances
- planning and building regulations
- fire precautions
- licensing regulations
- external signing

Occupancy costs include:
- acquisition costs
- rent and rates
- labour costs
- insurances
- heating and lighting
- leasing arrangements
- expected profitability and cash flows

Many companies have their own real estate or properties division responsible for seeking out and evaluating possible sites. However, property-developers, estate agents and solicitors also approach hotel and food service operators with site proposals. Rather than wait for sites to be vacated, the more aggressive companies will themselves court landowners and occupants of desirable premises or employ third parties to make discreet inquiries. The significance of location has been well summarised by Rathmell:

> Services which are not appropriately located may not be performed at all.

14.6 CHAPTER REVIEW

1. Most of the PD decisions made by fast-moving consumer goods marketers are irrelevant in hospitality marketing.
2. Location is the most important PD decision for hospitality companies.
3. The location of services can be classified in 3 ways: location is irrelevant; services are concentrated; or services are dispersed.
4. Hospitality companies locate where demand exists.
5. Much of what is known about site location is learned from retailing.
6. There are 2 distinct, but interdependent, location decisions: selection of a trading area, and selection of a particular site within the trading area.
7. The Law of Retail Gravitation explains that the trade done in an area is a function of the area's attraction and accessibility.
8. Attraction and deterrence factors vary according to the type of hospitality business.
9. Four sets of variables are generally considered when evaluating sites: convenience and approachability; physical conditions; legal enactments; and occupancy costs.

14.7 QUESTIONS AND EXERCISES

1. Why are location decisions of such importance to marketing management?
2. Is location of the following hospitality products concentrated, dispersed, or irrelevant? Why?
    - caravan park.

- private hospital.
- charitable rest-home.
- mobile fish-and-chip caravan.
- transport café.

3. It is possible for a single food service operation to offer a convenience product during the day and a shopping product in the evening, appealing to 2 different market segments. How would this influence the location decision?
4. Identify the major attraction factors which would make a trading area suitable for a sports-themed atmosphere restaurant with an evening ASP of £4.50 excluding liquor; an Indian take-away restaurant with an ASP of £2.20; and a budget motel with a room rate of £13.
5. Obtain a map of your local community. Mark the position of a well-known restaurant. Draw contours which represent driving times of 15 minutes and 30 minutes (these are called isochrons) from the site. How would you estimate the size of the population within these contours and the percentage falling into the restaurant's target market?
6. Draw up a checklist of variables which you would use to evaluate the prospective site for a new city-centre seafood restaurant. Which variables, if any, would you weight more heavily in your decision? Why?

REFERENCES

[1] Christopher, M. (1982) Remorseless logic in logistics ('Delivering the Goods' supplement). *Management Today*, November, 4.
[2] Rathmell, J. M. (1974) *Marketing in the Service Sector*. Cambridge, MA: Winthrop, 104.
[3] ibid., 106.
[4] Medlik, S. and Airey, D. W. (1978) (2nd edn) *Profile of the Hotel and Catering Industry*. London: Heinemann.
[5] Seltz, D. D. (1977) *Food Service Marketing and Promotion*. New York: Lebhar-Friedman Books.
[6] Peters, C. H. (1978) Pre-opening marketing analysis for hotels. *Cornell Hotel and Restaurant Administration Quarterly*, **19**(1), May, 15–22.
[7] Akehurst, G. P. (1981), Towards a theory of market potential with reference to hotel and restaurant firms. *Service Industries Review*, **1**(1), February, 18–30.
[8] Reilly, W. (1973) The law of retail gravitation, in Schwarz, G. (ed) *Development of Marketing Theory*. Southwest, 9–34.
[9] Huff, D. L. (1962) A note on the limitations of intraurban gravity models. *Land Economics*, **38**, 64–6.
[10] Davies, R. L. (1976) *Marketing Geography*, London: Methuen.
[11] Scholl-Poensgen, A. (1983) Management of fast-food chains, in Cassée, E. and Reuland, R. (eds) *The Management of Hospitality*. Oxford: Pergamon, 203–19.
[12] Guy, C. M. *Retail Location and Retail Planning in Britain*. Aldershot: Gower.
[13] Davies, R. L. (1973) Evaluation of retail store attributes and sales performance. *European Journal of Marketing*, **7**, 89–102.
[14] Davies, R. L. (1976) op. cit., 265–6.
[15] Rathmell, J. M. (1974) op. cit., 108.

SECTION 4
Promotion

—15———————————————

Principles of Promotion

15.1 CHAPTER PREVIEW

Promotion is the last of the Four Ps that we examine in Part III of this book. This chapter presents an overview of the role of promotion in marketing. It starts by defining the promotion mix as the set of tools used for demand manipulation, and then lists and defines each of the major types of tool. Promotion is used to solve communication problems, so the chapter presents a framework for their analysis which categorises them into 3 types: cognitive, affective and action.

Following this, we look briefly into communication theory and summarise a diverse and growing body of literature. We look at 4 major elements in the communication process—i.e. source, message, channel and receiver—and discuss how each of these and other causes can affect the fidelity with which messages are received. Finally, we examine the major practical problem of budgeting the promotion mix: first, in deciding how much to spend overall; and second, how much to spend on each tool.

15.2 LEARNING OBJECTIVES

By the end of this chapter you should be able to:
1. Define the 8 components of the promotion mix.
2. Explain the main function of promotion.
3. Distinguish between cognitive, affective and action problems.
4. Describe why high fidelity does not always occur in marketing communications.
5. Identify the main factors which influence the size of the promotion budget and the way in which it is deployed.

15.3 THE ROLE OF PROMOTION

The ultimate goal of all promotion is to obtain a level of demand which is favourable to the promoter—to increase, decrease, or maintain demand, and/or to influence the elasticity of demand by using channels of communication which allow access to a defined target audience. These goals are reflected in shifts in the demand curve for a product. Movements in the volume of demand are shown by the demand curves in Figure 15.1.

Graph (a) in the figure shows the position without promotion, in which sales volume

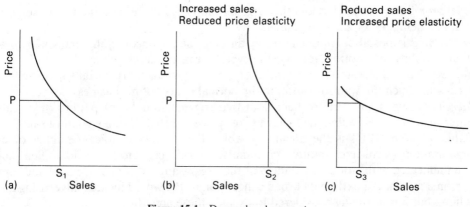

Figure 15.1   Demand and promotion.

S_1 is produced at price P. Given the same price, graph (b) shows what happens to the demand curve when the aim is to stimulate more demand and to reduce price elasticity; the demand curve has moved to the right and sales volume S_2 is produced. But not only are more sales produced; the curve is steeper, which means that demand has been made less price elastic, that is less responsive to price changes. Graph (c) shows what happens to the demand curve when the aim of promotion is to reduce sales and increase the consumer's price sensitivity.

15.4 THE PROMOTION MIX

The promotion mix is the set of communication tools which a marketing manager can use in his attempt to influence demand. It includes:
- advertising
- selling
- sales promotion
- direct mail
- sponsorship
- merchandising
- public relations
- publicity

Each of these is discussed elsewhere in the book, but at this stage it is necessary to define and distinguish between them.

Advertising is paid communication by an identified sponsor through a non-personal medium. It is also known as above-the-line promotion, all other forms of promotion being below-the-line.

Selling is of 2 major types. Personal selling is paid face-to-face persuasive communication by an identified sponsor. Telephone selling, sometimes inaccurately called telephone marketing, is paid persuasive communication by an identified telephone caller.

Sales promotion is any behaviour that triggers temporary incentive aimed at consumers, channel members, or sales personnel.

Direct mail is postal communication by an identified sponsor. Sometimes known as direct response promotion, it is one of several forms of direct selling.

Sponsorship is the material or financial support of some activity, usually sports or the arts, with which the sponsor is not, in the normal course of his business, associated.

Merchandising is any form of behaviour that triggers stimulus or pattern of stimuli, other than personal selling, and which takes place at retail or other point of sale.

Public relations (PR) is the means by which the various significant publics of an organisation (local community, customers, workforce, etc.) are identified and communicated with, to the advantage of the organisation through personal and non-personal media. An extremely broad conception of PR would include advertising and selling, but it is normally considered to exclude these activities.

Publicity is unpaid communication by an unidentified sponsor through non-personal media. It is crudely known as free advertising, and it is the predominant form of PR activity.

15.5 COMMUNICATIONS PROBLEMS

In Chapter 4 we identified the major audiences for communication. In the household their roles are initiator, influencer, decider, purchaser and user. In organisations they are user, influencer, buyer, decider and gatekeeper.

The communication problems a marketer could have with these audiences are extremely varied but can be categorised into 3 major types.

(a) *Cognitive problems*, such as
  • a low level of awareness about brandname, prices, location, benefits, etc.
  • a low level of comprehension—i.e. misunderstandings about prices, nutritional value of menu items, etc.

All cognitive problems are problems of *learning*.

(b) *Affective problems*, such as
  • a low level of interest in the brand
  • an unfavourable attitude towards a resort
  • disliking some of the features of the product—e.g. lack of variety in a menu

All affective problems are problems of *feeling*.

(c) *Action problems*, such as
  • not using a reservation system
  • not dining in an hotel restaurant

All action problems are problems of *doing*.

A hotel targeting both the corporate meetings market and the family weekend-break market could use the framework shown in Figure 15.2 to identify its communication problems. Such an analysis may show, for example, that in the weekend-break market although product awareness is high, decision-makers have misunderstandings about rates for family groups, and purchasers are not aware that credit cards are accepted. Analysis of the corporate meetings market might show than an hotel has a reputation

	Family weekend break					Corporate meetings				
	Initiator	Influencer	Decider	Purchaser	User	Gatekeeper	Influencer	Decider	Buyer	User
Cognitive problems										
Affective problems										
Action problems										

Figure 15.2 Material for analysis of communication problems.

for poor service of delegates' demands. This is an affective problem. User attitudes towards the hotel are unfavourable. Each cell of the matrix can be examined to find out what, if any, communication problems the marketer has with his audiences. Similar frameworks can be constructed by other hospitality organisations.

15.6 COMMUNICATION THEORY

Much of what we now know about communication has been borrowed from the social sciences, of which psychology in particular has contributed a great deal to our understanding of cognitive learning. However, there has been little debate and research into passive learning. The distinction between the 2 forms of learning is central to what follows.

Cognitive learning is active. Consumers face problems for which products are solutions. The consumer passes through a multistage problem-solving process, as has been shown in Chapter 4. Cognitive learning describes what happens with high-involvement products. Information is actively sought from a variety of sources, including marketer-dominant sources such as advertising, press releases and sales literature; it is then processed against a background of existing knowledge and predispositions and the consumer evolves a purchasing intention. So that intention becomes fact, the marketer uses merchandising material at point of sale.

Passive learning is different. The consumer is not an information-seeker, neither does he actively process the information to which he is exposed. He is not resistant to competing information and his attitude, if one exists at all, is weak and ill-defined. Passive learning is the norm for low-involvement products. The consumer attends to marketing communication only if it dominates the medium to which he is exposed for other, often recreational, reasons. Even if exposure does lead to attention, it is most unlikely that the message has any effect upon existing cognitive structure. Bettman calls this 'incidental learning'.[1] Such learning is unlikely to reflect in a consumer's ability to recall the content of a communication; more probably there will be a 'recognition' of the same communication when re-presented at a later date, with an 'Aha, I've seen that before!' response. The consumer will retain, if anything, a loosely defined feeling, sensation, or image.

Communication theory rests largely upon the implicit assumption that cognitive learning takes place. Therefore, communication has been described as 'establishing a commonness or oneness of thought between a sender and receiver',[2] and 'the sharing of meaning; it is the process by which an individual transmits stimuli to modify the behaviour or predispositions of other individuals'.[3] A simple model of such a communication process appears in Figure 15.3.

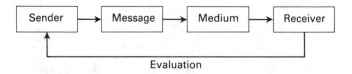

Figure 15.3   Communication process.

There are 4 main elements in the communication process; 2 are *always* human—the sender and the receiver—and 2 are not—the message and the medium, although the medium on occasion is human (e.g. a salesman). The sender decides what to communicate by putting into symbolic form his message. This is known as 'encoding', and it is carried to the receiving audience by a communication channel (the medium), the receiver then translating or decoding the symbols. True communication is said to have taken place when the decoder attributes the same meaning to the symbols as the encoder. The symbols used to convey meaning are both verbal and non-verbal—i.e. words, pictures and gestures. Since a person's life experience with these symbols determines how they are decoded, marketing communicators must have empathy with their audiences.

The sender normally wants his message to be understood as he intended. This is known as 'fidelity' and—as in the sound-reproduction business—it can be high or low. Occasionally low fidelity is intended. For instance, a company making public criticism of the products of a competitor may be called upon, under threat of legal action, to make a public retraction. The retraction may be deliberately encoded to be ambiguous, appearing overtly contrite, but on closer examination representing no such change in position. This is evidently the exception; the rule is that high fidelity is desired. 'Infidelity' results from fallible human (sender–receiver), message, or medium causes, as we enlarge upon below.

Human causes of infidelity

A number of such factors influence the fidelity of a communication: communication skills, attitudes, knowledge, group influence and needs.

(a) Communication skills. These are both intellectual (spelling, vocabulary, grammar, or reading skills) and physical (voice strength or clarity of writing). The more skilled the communicator, the better able he is to encode in easily understood symbols. Similarly,

the more educated the receiver, the more able he is to understand diverse communications.

(b) Attitudes. Attitudes are predispositions. If the audience actively processes communications, it is probable that the message will be decoded in the context of existing attitudes. Communications about low-involvement products are unlikely to interact with such predispositions. Every day thousands of commercially sponsored messages are encoded and issued. Consumers decode only a fraction. Selective processes operate which cause this to happen.

An example of selective exposure is that of the person who does not read, say, *Executive Travel* and who cannot, then, be exposed to its advertising matter. Selective attention is where attention is drawn towards some messages and not others either because the message dominates the perceptual field or because the audience is in a particularly receptive state (see Chapter 4). Selective perception is where the audience interprets messages and attributes meaning in the context of existing predispositions, so that message distortion occurs. In selective retention audiences remember what they want to remember, in the way they want to remember.

Attitudes affect fidelity in other ways. A favourable attitude towards the receiver means that the sender's message will probably be favourably decoded. Also a sender who has a positive attitude towards his message is likely to receive a positive response from his receiver towards the message.[4]

(c) Knowledge. Messages which match the receiver's level of understanding are more likely to be faithfully decoded. Messages which are too complex or sophisticated, or juvenile or patronising, are unlikely to be decoded faithfully.

(d) Group influence. Decoding is influenced by the receiver's role, family, peers, social class and culture. Messages should be encoded in symbols which are culturally and socially significant to the receiver.

(e) Needs. Messages which neither arouse needs nor appeal to already activated needs are unlikely to be faithfully decoded. Indeed they are unlikely to receive attention.

The message's causes of infidelity

Decoding of messages will probably display infidelity in the following conditions.
(a) When a 1-sided rather than 2-sided message is used to communicate with an audience holding the opposite view.[5]
(b) When a 2-sided message is used to communicate with an audience holding a view already supporting that of the sender. It is better to use a 1-sided message in these circumstances.[6]
(c) When the sender uses a 1-sided message knowing that his audience will later be exposed to counterinformation. If a 2-sided message is used, this counterinformation is seen in the context of the already learned 2-sided information and is, therefore, less powerful.[7]
(d) When the sender encodes a 1-sided message to send to a poorly-educated audience.

Single-sided messages are preferable.[8] A recent innovation in advertising has been the comparison advertisement in which 2 or more competing products are compared in a single advertisement. According to a *Media* report in 1978, 'empirical evidence to support or oppose comparisons is both scanty and questionable'.[9] However, comparison advertisements have been claimed to have the following advantages and disadvantages:

Advantages
- they point out meaningful differences to consumers
- they help the consumer to evaluate the product's performance
- they help the consumer to identify competitive products
- they reduce post-purchase dissonance
- they stimulate competitive product improvement
- they attract a higher number of readers by their novelty
- they are perceived as more honest than conventional advertisements

Disadvantages
- many claims are irreconcilable with competitive advertising
- presentation of too much information
- use of unvalidated or unrepresentative claims
- product testing raises the cost of advertising
- unfair use of competitor's name
- create divisiveness in the industry

(e) In presenting a 1-sided communication for a low-involvement product fidelity is enhanced by placing the most interesting and important points at the beginning of the message; otherwise audience attention is lost.

(f) For an interested audience, however, an order of presentation in which the main points conclude the message is more effective.

(g) Placing the main points in the middle of message transmission is least effective of all.

(h) Where the message is not structured so as to attract the attention of the audience at the beginning of the transmission, decoding will be based on reception of an incomplete message.

(i) If the message does not arouse a need in the audience prior to the presentation of information. Fidelity is enhanced where a need is first aroused.

(j) If the message does not draw a conclusion for the audience. Infidelity is far more likely when the audience is permitted to draw its own conclusions, especially for more poorly educated audiences, or when the message is complicated.

(k) If a strong appeal to fear is made. It appears that audiences are unable to faithfully decode strong fear appeals and psychologically distort or ignore the message. An intermediate fear appeal appears to work best because it is sufficiently strong to attract attention (unlike very weak fear appeals), yet avoids the rejection problems experienced by strong fear appeals.[10]

(l) If the humorous context of a message becomes more significant to the audience than the message itself. Humour is valuable for attracting attention and interest.[11]

Channel causes of infidelity

The nature of the channel or medium through which the communication is transmitted can affect fidelity of decoding. Factors include differences between personal and impersonal media; the status of the spokesperson, if personal; the 'halo'-effect; and the source credibility.

1. The media for transmission of a message can be classified broadly as personal or impersonal. Kotler distinguishes between 3 classes of personal channel: advocate channels (sales staff), expert channels (independent third parties with special expertise) and social channels (neighbours and friends).[12] Because of their strategic social location, independence and trustworthiness, word-of-mouth influences from social channels, despite their lack of expertise, can be extremely effective. All such personal channels, because of their interactive flexibility and instantaneous feedback, can enhance fidelity; they are particularly effective in bringing about attitude changes. Impersonal and, therefore, 1-way channels include newspapers, magazines, television, radio, cinema and posters.

2. It appears that the impersonal mass media are effective, largely because of the mediating influence of certain individuals who are known as opinion-leaders. These individuals are located in every stratum of society and act as gatekeepers, filtering information which they obtain from the mass media. They are regarded as sources of independent, product-specific expertise by members of their primary groups.

   This process has become known as the 2-step flow of communication. Information flows from mass media to opinion-leaders and then to the wider public.[13] Opinion-leaders are characterised as being more exposed to mass media, more cosmopolitan, more gregarious, of higher social status and more innovative than followers.[14] Information from an opinion-leader is more likely to be decoded faithfully than if obtained from another source (see also pp. 220–221).

3. The 'halo'-effect occurs when a communication is judged in terms of the general environment in which it belongs, rather than on its own merits. The same advertisement placed in quality and popular newspapers will be perceived quite differently. A private hospital's advertisement featuring a model dressed as a doctor will evoke positive feelings of care, comfort and security.

4. Certain media are more persuasive and, therefore, more capable of bringing about communication fidelity because they are more credible. Research has shown that credibility is a multi-faceted concept.[15] It combines elements of trustworthiness, expertise and status or prestige.

   Trustworthiness is a function of the medium's honesty and intent. If a spokesperson's motives are thought to be personal gain, he is perceived as less trustworthy. Expertise is a function of qualifications, experience and access to information. Specialised magazines which are circulated to a highly selective readership, for example, can be very influential in bringing about attitude change. Qualified, independent spokespersons are similarly credible. Personal or impersonal channels which occupy positions of higher prestige or status are more credible. A film-star promoting a health club or a leading business executive endorsing an hotel chain make the message more persuasive.

15.7 BUDGETING THE PROMOTION MIX

Let us now turn to the practical question of how much to spend on promotion, and how to divide such a budget between the various promotional tools. Some forms of promotion are free—e.g. word-of-mouth, publicity and some forms of merchandising—and it makes sense to use these tools constantly. However, most promotion has to be paid for.

Setting the promotion budget

Companies faced with budgeting their promotional mix have 2 problems: how much to spend on promotion overall, and how to divide this sum between alternative types of promotion.

Theory suggests that a company should shift funds into promotion, provided that the rate of return could not be improved if the funds were allocated to a different budget. This is the 'marginal productivity' rule. Similarly, within the promotion budget each pound should be spent where it will reap the greatest reward. In balancing, for instance, the proportions of the budget to be spent on selling and advertising the company should allocate enough to advertising (or selling) to ensure that the marginal return is greater than it would have been had the last pound of expenditure been used on the alternative.

In practice, due to difficulties of measurement of promotional effects, such theory is of little value; several rules-of-thumb can be identified. In general, the promotion budget should be higher where:
1. Consumers have difficulty in distinguishing between alternatives on the basis of their physical appearance; this is particularly true of service products.
2. Products are not well differentiated.
3. A new product is being launched and the target market has not had previous purchasing experience.
4. There are a large number of people having influence on the buying decision, as in some corporate purchases.
5. There is a strong need for consumer education; novel forms of food service face this problem.

Allocating the promotion budget

The manner in which budget is distributed between the various tools of promotion depends upon a number of factors. The most important are:
1. The communication problems faced by the company.
2. Involvement.
3. The level of investment.
4. The location of the market.
5. The type of market—household or organisational.
6. The stage of the product life cycle.

(1) Communication problems
This issue was addressed in section 15.5, above. Cognitive problems are more suitable

for non-personal communication. Where attitude change is the objective, personal communication is more effective; where action is required, sales promotion and merchandising can stimulate behaviour in the short term.

(2) Involvement

Promotion varies in its role and form, depending upon whether buying behaviour displays cognitive learning or dissonance reduction (high involvement) or variety seeking or inertia (low involvement). The main role of promotion in the cognitive learning model is to convey persuasive information, so that a buying intention is formed. Message content is important; it should stress differentiating benefits and take into account the audience's predispositions.

In the dissonance-reduction model promotion is largely used to provide post-purchase information which reassures the audience. Remember, perceived brand differences are absent.

The low-involvement consumer is not an active information-seeker because the product is less important. Consequently message content is less significant and brand choice is more prone to the influence of temporary incentives.

The applications of the main promotional tools, given differing levels of involvement, are discussed below.[16]

● *Advertising*

Advertising should build awareness and familiarity with low-involvement products, using symbolically meaningful and easily recognised content. Repetition is important. For high-involvement products carefully structured persuasive information should be conveyed. Long copy is more effective for this type of product.

● *Selling*

Selling has a major contribution to make in promoting high-involvement products. Salespersons can provide feedback to difficult inquiries and handle objections. Message content can be modified to suit audiences.

● *Sales promotion*

Sales promotion is more productive with low-involvement products. Continuous promotions can create repeat purchase, thus reducing variety-seeking. Consumers may be more attracted to the promotion than the product. More involved audiences are more resistant to sales promotion and less likely to switch brands.

● *Direct mail*

Direct mail has applications in both high- and low-involvement markets; it has an informational role in high-involvement markets. Already involved audiences are more likely to read print material, thus long copy can be used. In low-involvement markets direct mail can be used to deliver promotional incentives such as coupons or competition entry forms.

● *Sponsorship*

Sponsorship's main role is to build awareness. Generally the only information conveyed through sponsorship is the company (or brand) name which makes it more suitable for low-involvement products.

● *Merchandising*

Merchandising is more important for low-involvement products. Simple exposure to a product display or print material may stimulate purchase. As pre-purchase

evaluation does not occur with low-involvement products, purchase behaviour can be motivated at the point of sale.
- *Public relations (PR)*
Because of the diversity of activities classified as PR, it has applications in both high- and low-involvement sectors. An example of a high-involvement application is a familiarisation visit organised by an hotelier for tour operators. A low-involvement application would be a reminder by a lift attendant that the restaurant is on the top floor of the hotel.
- *Publicity*
A major problem with publicity is that it is non-purposive. Unlike advertising where messages can be devised to achieve specific promotional objectives, most publicity has to be newsworthy in its own right; PR is used for both high- and low-involvement products.
National newspapers may carry the story of an hotel's success in winning the contract to house a political party's annual conference. Conference purchase is high involvement. The story, and therefore the hotel's name, will be of interest to conference organisers. A local radio station broadcasting live from a garden fête will attract visitors indirectly to the catering concessions. Refreshments at such events are low-involvement purchases.
The strategic consequences of involvement for promotional strategy are as follows:
(a) The more involved the consumer, the more he is likely to repurchase the product despite the promotional efforts of competitors. Therefore, a goal of promotion should be to shift consumers from low to high involvement. Assael cites 5 tactics for achieving this objective:[17]
- link the product to some involving issue (e.g. fast food to nutritional values)
- link the product to some involving personal situation (e.g. promote a town-centre coffee shop in the morning before shoppers leave home)
- link the product to involving advertising. A value-expressive advertisement expresses consumers' central beliefs and values (e.g. diners at Mr Chow's are successful, non-traditional individualists)
- change the importance of product benefits; this is more difficult to achieve because it involves changing consumer need priorities—an educational process
- introduce an important characteristic into the product (e.g. convert the meat content of beefburgers from 80 to 100 per cent or introduce wholemeal buns)
(b) If dominant in a low-involvement market, stimulate inertia.
(c) If a minority product in a low-involvement market, stimulate variety-seeking. Once variety-seeking has occurred, promote inertia.

(3) Level of investment
Large-scale investments tend to be protected by heavy promotional expenditure. Loss of market share can turn 'cash cows' into 'dogs' (see Figure 7.3, p. 165). Successful products need to be protected, so that their positive cash flows can support tomorrow's breadwinners. Massive expenditures, on advertising in particular, are often used to prevent would-be rivals from attempting to gain market leadership. In effect, promotional budgets act as a barrier to both market entry and competitor initiative.

(4) Location of the market

Small, single-site companies can often rely on local reputation to build and support demand. Larger multisite companies serving geographically widespread markets cannot rely on word-of-mouth promotion to create brand awareness and trial. Advertising is often used to overcome the initial cognitive problems, and as new sites are developed, sales promotions used to stimulate trial.

(5) Type of market: household or organisational

There are major differences between household and organisational markets which affect the allocation of the promotional budget, as shown in Table 15.1. Personal contact, prior to purchase, for many organisational purchases is the norm. Prospective buyers want to sample, ask questions and negotiate before placing a purchase order. Personal representation is, therefore, more common in organisational markets.

Table 15.1 *Household vs organisational markets.*

	Household	Organisational
Customers	Families Individuals	Companies Government departments Military Convention organisers
Size of DMU	Few	Many
Customer's power in buying process	Weak	Strong
Buying expertise	Untrained, unspecialised	Trained and professional
Buying process	Ad hoc, subject to seller's terms	Negotiated, subject to contract
Cost of purchase	Normally low	Often high
Distribution	Bring customer to product	Bring product to customer
Location	Widespread market	Concentrated market
Product form	Standardised	Customised

However, advertising does have applications: it can be used to build awareness and interest, making it easier for the sales representative to make an appointment. Furthermore, much advertising is not read until after purchase when it is used to reduce post-purchase dissonance, and to legitimate the purchase by providing reassurances, for example, about quality and price. Advertising in organisational markets can also produce sales leads for coupon returns and inquiries. The division of promotional budgets between advertising and selling in multimarket companies tends to be as shown in Figure 15.4.

An additional refinement in budgeting for organisational markets can be made by considering the buying process, which, as noted in Chapter 4, comprises 8 phases. The significance of the various promotional tools in each phase will vary according to

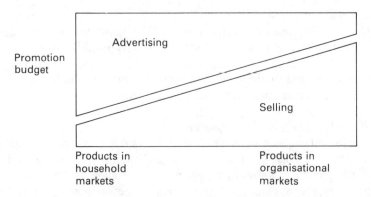

Figure 15.4   Promotional budgeting in household and organisational markets.

whether the purchase under consideration is a new task purchase, a straight rebuy (a previously bought product), or a modified rebuy. For example, a company making new task arrangements with a local caterer for the lunchtime entertainment of business guests may well have identified the need through exposure to advertising material. However, skilled personal selling by the caterer could help the prospect to identify the appropriate characteristics—i.e. menu, prices, etc.—of the problem-solving hospitality product; personal selling would also help to counter objections put forward about why his company should not be the selected supplier. Also at this stage a special offer or inducement to purchase may be valuable.

New task purchases tend to be slower in their passage through the 8 phases, whereas straight rebuys are the fastest. Each phase of the buying process can be studied in greater detail in order to gain clues about the appropriate types of promotional tool to use. For example, the search for suppliers may involve the buyer in:

- checking existing suppliers to the company
- checking existing suppliers to competitors
- checking previous suppliers
- identifying possible suppliers from Yellow Pages
- checking existing suppliers of similar products to the company

These methods of search suggest that catalogues, sample menus and pricelists should be produced to a size that is convenient for file records, and that advertising space should be bought in Yellow Pages.

The opposite pattern of promotion, reduced emphasis on personal selling and a greater emphasis on advertising, is apparent in consumer markets. This is because of the differences shown in Table 15.1. For instance, personal selling is generally inappropriate for widespread geographic markets because of the costs involved.

(6) Stage of the product life cycle
The type of promotional mix selected should vary between different stages of the product life cycle. This was discussed in detail in Chapter 8. To summarise that discussion, during the introductory stage personal selling and sales promotion are commonly used to introduce the product to intermediaries; consumer awareness is built up during the late introductory stage through advertising, whereas trial is encouraged

by sampling and other consumer deals. During growth informal word-of-mouth promotion prompted by advertising high in conversational value encourages the diffusion of the product. As market share comes under attack during the maturity stage various types of consumer deals are employed to reduce brand switching. During the decline stage it is not uncommon for advertising and promotional expenditures to be totally cut.

15.8 CHAPTER REVIEW

1. The ultimate goal of all promotion is to obtain a level of demand favourable to the promoter.
2. The promotion mix is the set of communication tools which a marketer can use in his attempt to shift demand.
3. The promotion mix comprises advertising, selling, sales promotion, direct mail, sponsorship, merchandising, public relations and publicity.
4. Communications problems are of 3 types: cognitive, affective, and action problems.
5. Communication audiences can be defined in terms of their role in the exchange process—e.g. as buyers, users, deciders, influencers, or initiators.
6. For true communication to take place the message received must duplicate the message sent and the desired outcome of the communication must be achieved.
7. There are 4 constituent elements in the communication process: the sender, message, medium and the receiver. (A fifth element, the response of the receiver, may be added.)
8. All 4 main elements in the communication process may contribute towards infidelity, that is, the communication not achieving what was intended.
9. The 2 main promotion mix decisions are, first, how much to spend, and second, how to apportion this budget between the various tools.
10. The principle of marginal return should be used to make both these promotion decisions.
11. Allocation of the budget between the various tools depends upon the communication problems faced by the company, the level of investment, involvement, the location of the market, the type of market (household or organisational) and the stage of the life cycle through which the product is passing.

15.9 QUESTIONS

1. You are a contract caterer entering a new geographical market segment. As usual, you are targeting the main employer, with the aim of supplying a lunchtime food service for employees. It is a large cottonmill with 2,200 employees. What communication problems would you anticipate encountering in trying to win the contract, and what promotion tools appear to offer the best solution?
2. Is it true that promotion can reduce price sensitivity?
3. What do you understand by the terms 'active learning' and 'passive learning'?
4. Poor communication skills can interfere with faithful encoding and decoding of messages. Are there any particular problems in international marketing, for example, in Burger King's implementation in the UK of its American promotional strategy?
5. How can selective processes affect the fidelity of communications?
6. You have read 2 reports about the relative market shares of the main competitors in the contract catering business:

	Report 1	Report 2
Gardner Merchant	8%	7%
Sutcliffe's	7.5%	7.5%

Report 1 came from a University of London survey, and report 2 came from Sutcliffe's advertising agency. How will source credibility influence your response to these conflicting reports?

7. A single product, such as an assembly-room, can be marketed to either household users (weddings and parties) or to organisational users (meetings and conferences). Should the promotion mix vary between markets?
8. To what extent does involvement affect the selection of promotional tools in hospitality markets?

REFERENCES

[1] Bettman, J. R. (1979) *An Information Processing Theory of Consumer Choice*. Reading, MA: Addison-Wesley.
[2] Schramm, W. (1955) *The Process and Effects of Mass Communications*, Urbana, IL: University of Illinois Press.
[3] Webster, F. E., Jr (1971) *Marketing Communication: Modern Promotional Strategy*. New York: Wiley.
[4] DeLozier, M. W. (1976) *The Marketing Communications Process*. Tokyo: McGraw-Hill, 25.
[5] Hovland, C. I., Lumsdaine, A. A., and Scheffield, F. D. (1949) *Experiments on Mass Communication*. Princeton, NJ: Princeton University Press.
[6] ibid.
[7] ibid.
[8] ibid.
[9] See: Pros and cons of comparison ads. *Media* (1978), May, 9.
[10] Ray, M. L. and Wilkie, W. L. (1970) Fear: the potential of an appeal neglected by marketing. *Journal of Marketing*, **34**, January.
[11] Sternthal, B. and Craig, C. S. (1973) Humor in advertising. *Journal of Marketing*, **37**, October.
[12] Kotler, P. (1984), (5th edn) *Marketing Management; Analysis, Planning and Control*. Englewood Cliffs, NJ: Prentice-Hall, 619.
[13] Lazarsfeld, P. F., Berelson, B. and Gaudet, H. (1948) *The People's Choice*. New York: Columbia University Press.
[14] Rogers, E. M. and Shoemaker, F. F. (1971) *Communication of Innovation*. New York: The Free Press.
[15] DeLozier, M. W. (1976) op. cit. 70–84.
[16] Based in part on Assael, H. (1984) (2nd edn) *Consumer Behaviour and Marketing Action*, Kent.
[17] ibid., 99–100.

—16————————————————

Advertising Theory

16.1 CHAPTER PREVIEW

Of the two chapters in this book on advertising, this, the first, describes what is known about how advertising works. The earliest attempts at explanation occurred in the 1920s. Today there is still disagreement about how advertising affects purchasing behaviour.

16.2 LEARNING OBJECTIVES

By the end of this chapter you should be able to:
1. Explain the aims of advertising.
2. Distinguish between informative, persuasive and confirmative styles of advertising.
3. List, in order, the 3 main stages of the conventional hierarchy of effects.
4. Find hospitality examples of products which are bought under conditions of high and low involvement.
5. Explain the various relationships between *learn, feel* and *do*.

16.3 INTRODUCTION

Advertising may be defined as:

> paid communication by an identified sponsor through a non-personal medium.

One of advertising's professional bodies has this to say:[1]

> Advertising is basically someone with something to sell telling potential customers about the product in such a way as to have them prefer his product to others. The job of advertising is to inform and persuade. It does this in space and time bought in media.

Whilst this is a reasonable description of much advertising, it should be said that not all advertising is concerned with selling (some is simply informative) or aimed at potential customers (some is aimed at past purchasers). Advertising excludes publicity because that is free; and selling because that is personal.

Many hospitality companies do not advertise and yet are successful businesses with satisfactory sales volumes and respectable profits. Other companies advertise widely and fail. Advertising expenditure does not guarantee a boost in sales—it must be used wisely and cost effectively as an integrated component of the promotional mix within the marketing mix. It is used widely in commerce and by government, and even by households, yet its dynamics are not well understood. Little is known about how or why it works, yet billions of pounds each year are spent on advertising.

16.4 THE AIMS OF ADVERTISING

No one knows for certain how advertising influences purchasing behaviour—or indeed why some advertising appears to, or not. There is empirical evidence to support the view that advertising can have an effect on sales turnover, but there is only one way to prove beyond doubt that advertising causes sales, and that is to conduct an experiment in which 2 matched groups of an audience are compared. Each of these groups is subjected to the same marketing mix, with one difference—advertising does not reach one of the groups. The difference between the volumes of sales made to these groups then can be attributed to the effect of advertising.

The vast majority of advertisers do not undertake this type of research. Any claim for the presence of an advertising–sales effect must, in these circumstances, be viewed as suspect.[2] In fact, as we noted earlier, advertising does not always have the aim of producing sales. It is true to say that most *consumer* or *trade* advertising has the long-term aim of influencing (not necessarily increasing) sales volumes, but this is not true of all types of advertising. The Institute of Practitioners in Advertising accordingly makes this claim about advertising's aims: 'the purpose of advertising is to influence a person's knowledge, attitude and behaviour in such a way as to meet the objectives of the advertiser.' Perhaps the only claim which can be made about the general aim of all advertising is that it is intended to *influence the behaviour* of its target either in the short term or the long term.

Most classified advertising (e.g. readers' ads placed in local newspapers) is intended to produce a short-term effect on behaviour. On the other hand, corporate image advertising is not usually intended to influence behaviour in the short term, but to create awareness, correct misimpressions, project positive truths, or enhance morale. The belief is generally held that if the advertiser creates a favourable image, then in the long term this will have a favourable effect on customer behaviour. Most informational advertising, such as the government's campaign advising the hospitality industry on how to save energy, is also designed to produce long-term behavioural change.

16.5 ADVERTISING STYLES

It is possible to identify 3 styles of advertisement which are all intended to influence behaviour either in the long or short term:
- informative advertising
- persuasive advertising
- confirmative advertising

Informative advertising
This is mass-media communication with the aim of influencing the audience's cognitions

(i.e. what the audience knows) about a product. Its purpose is educational, and its success can be measured by the ability of the audience to recall pieces of information and explain the content of the advertisement.

Much informative advertising emanates from bodies which have a duty to provide information. Legislation compels some organisations to advertise. There are plenty of examples of such compulsion in the public notices columns of local newspapers.

Persuasive advertising

This is mass-media communication with the aim of inducing purchasing behaviour. Most hospitality product advertising is of this type.

Confirmative advertising

This is mass-media communication with the aim of reducing post-purchase dissonance. After purchasing a product which is physically, socially, psychologically, or economically risky, many consumers feel anxiety about the purchase and its outcomes. Post-purchase dissonance occurs when the anxiety experienced by the consumer is more than was expected. By referring to advertising material after the purchase has been made the consumer can reduce the experienced level of anxiety.

Most advertisements contain elements of all 3 forms: informative, persuasive and confirmative.

16.6 HOW DOES ADVERTISING WORK?

Whether advertisers admit it or not, they place advertisements on the basis of beliefs they have about how advertising influences behaviour. Many advertisers would not be able to express how they think advertising works, but the fact that they are prepared to spend time, effort and money advertising is sufficient evidence to support the view that they think it does! The mental model they have may be simple or sophisticated. It may be as simple as:

$$\text{Sales} = f(\text{advertising})$$

(therefore sales are a function of advertising)
or they may believe that advertising influences behaviour only if it permeates through a system of psychological barriers and defences, which protect the buyer's psyche from information which is incongruent with current beliefs and behaviour.

16.7 HISTORICAL REVIEW

In 1925 Daniel Starch, the founder of an advertising research company, proposed the view that an effective advertisement must move a consumer nearer to purchasing, and that to do so, 5 conditions had to be met. He wrote: 'An advertisement, to be successful (a) must be seen (b) must be read (c) must be believed (d) must be remembered (e) must be acted upon.'[3]

This was still the view in 1961, when Cox made the following statements; he said that

In order for an audience to be influenced in the desired manner by a communication several conditions must be met:[4]
1. The audience must somehow be exposed to the communication.
2. Members of the audience must interpret or perceive correctly what action or attitude is desired of them by the communicator.
3. The audience must remember or retain the gist of the message that the communicator is trying to get across.
4. Members of the audience must decide whether or not they will be influenced by the communication.

These models have not met the test of time. A review of 13 studies on the relationship between recall of advertising information and behaviour, summarised by Haskins as long ago as 1964, made this claim about Starch's step (d) and Cox's point about memory:[5]

All thirteen studies had this in common: they showed no relationship between what a person learned, knew or recalled on the one hand, and what he did nor how he felt on the other. The teaching and learning of factual information was not related to behaviour.

The act of remembering was, therefore, shown not to be a sufficient condition for behaviour to occur.

In 1961 Colley had this to say about how advertising works:[6]

All commercial transactions that aim at the ultimate objective of a sale must carry a prospect through four levels of understanding. From unawareness to:

Awareness: The prospect must first be aware of the existence of a brand or company.
Comprehension: He must have a comprehension of what the product is and what it will do for him.
Conviction: He must arrive at a mental disposition or conviction to buy the product.
Action: Finally, he must stir himself to action.

Colley's summary of advertising's role was that its 'job is to increase *propensity* to buy—to move the prospect, inch by inch, closer to a purchase', and that advertising and other communications should strive to move prospects through the 4 stages. Of awareness, he writes: 'it is inconceivable that people buy products . . . whose names are unknown to them.' Of conviction, he writes that it is typified by the consumer who says: 'I intend to buy this product in the future.' Action does not necessarily mean purchase; according to Colley, it may mean 'he has visited a dealer's showroom . . . asked for literature or for a salesman to call . . . reached for a brand'. Further, 'Consummation of the sale may have been beyond the power of advertising'.

This work of Colley's was the first of a number of similar attempts to map the psychological steps a consumer passes through from exposure to an advertisement to purchase. Others were produced by Lavidge and Steiner,[7] Wolfe, Brown and Thompson,[8] Sandage and Fryburger[9] and Rogers.[10] These models, known collectively as hierarchies of effects, are remarkably similar and can be reduced to 3 basic stages (see Table 16.1). The first stage is cognitive development; the second stage involves the development of affections towards or against the advertised item; and the final stage requires action. This is the learn–feel–do process introduced in Chapter 4.

All these models suggest that it is necessary for a consumer to acquire and process information about the product *before* evaluation which, in turn, precedes action. There

Table 16.1 *Hierarchies of effect models.*

Basic stages	Lavidge and Steiner (1962)[8]	Wolfe, Brown and Thompson (1962)[9]	Sandage and Fryburger (1962)[10]	Rogers (1962)[11]
Cognitive	Awareness ↓ Knowledge ↓	Awareness ↓	Attention ↓	Awareness ↓
Affective	Liking ↓ Preference ↓	Acceptance ↓ Preference ↓	Interest ↓ Desire ↓	Interest ↓ Evaluation ↓
Action	Conviction ↓ Purchase	Intention to buy ↓ Provocation of sale	Action	Trial ↓ Adoption

is still considerable practitioner support for these approaches. An article by a senior staff member at a major international advertising agency supported this view:[11]

> Sustaining awareness of a brand among its target market is usually considered to be the first requirement of an advertising campaign. Awareness does not equal motivation to buy, but without it nothing can be achieved

Another attempt to explain how advertising works was made by Joyce in 1967, who reflected upon 'the absence of empirical support' for the hierarchy type of model.[12] He produced the diagram shown in Figure 16.1, and an explanation which explores the apparent interrelationship between attitudes, purchasing behaviour and advertising.

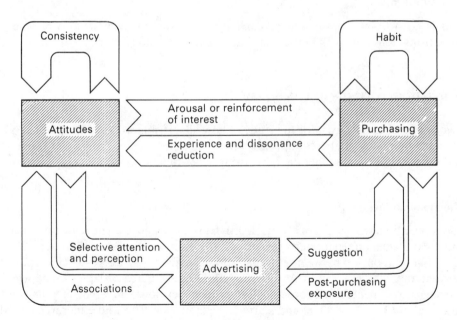

Figure 16.1 Joyce's advertising–sales model.

Joyce makes these explanatory remarks in the conclusion of his work:

> We might take as our starting point a simple model of advertising consisting of just two arrows joining three boxes—an arrow from advertising to attitudes, showing that advertising changes or reinforces attitudes by investing the product with favourable associations, and an arrow from attitudes to purchasing showing that favourable attitudes lead to interest in the product being aroused when there is an opportunity to buy it or to a reinforcement of a purchasing habit.
>
> However, it seems that it would also be correct to put in arrows going the other way. Purchasing may influence attitudes, partly as a straightforward reflection of product experience but partly by the drive to reduce dissonance, which leads to favourable attitudes in justification to oneself of the decision. Equally, the impact of advertising on the consumer is very much affected by preconceived attitudes: both attention and perception are selective, and this selectivity is affected by them.
>
> It also appears legitimate to put in arrows linking advertising and purchasing directly. [There is a] possibility that advertising may work partly by suggestion, a process in which attitudes need not necessarily function as an intermediary. Also, there is evidence that the fact of having bought a particular product may in some circumstances heighten attention to advertisements for that product, again as a part of the phenomenon of the drive to reduce dissonance.
>
> Finally, it seems appropriate too to introduce two loops in the system. [There is] a certain amount of evidence that there is a drive towards consistency amongst attitudes even when advertising stimuli and purchasing intentions are absent, and we therefore put a loop in around attitudes. Also we have recognised that much purchasing is habitual and apparently unaffected by advertising or by attitude changes, at any rate below some sort of threshold level. This is represented by a loop around purchasing.
>
> The precise direction of the arrows and the labelling of arrows and boxes is perhaps less important than the general impression conveyed by the diagram, which is surely correct—that the advertising–attitudes–purchasing system is a complex system of interacting variables. The model itself is tentative, but this general conclusion seems unlikely to be overthrown.

This is not too far from being the current view. Modern theorists also believe that advertising does not work in the one simple learn–feel–do sequence.

16.8 THE CONTEMPORARY VIEW

Two approaches now exist for the study of how advertising works, one of which builds upon the hierarchy of effects approach whilst the other totally ignores that framework and relies solely on mapping the advertising–sales function.

The modified hierarchy

The conventional hierarchy of effects, learn–feel–do, began to come under attack in the mid-1960s, when one marketer's review of the literature established that there need be no causal relationship between attitudes and behaviour.[13] The feel–do element of the conventional hierarchy was being questioned. Other research had questioned whether learning was a necessary precedent for attitude development or behaviour, raising doubts about both learn–feel and learn–do sequences.[14] The whole hierarchy needed review.

The 4 hierarchies proposed by Assael are typical of contemporary attempts to reformulate the original hypothesis.[15]

1. Complex buying behaviour: learn–feel–do.
2. Dissonance–reducing buying behaviour: do–learn–feel.
3. Variety-seeking behaviour: learn–do–feel.
4. Inertia: learn–do.

These were detailed in Chapter 4, where variety-seeking and inertia were identified as 2 forms of low-involvement purchasing behaviour, whereas complex buying and dissonance reduction were seen as 2 forms of high-involvement purchasing behaviour.

There are 2 quite different audience profiles of the high- and low-involvement consumer.

Information seeking

The high-involvement consumer seeks information actively; the low-involvement consumer is an information-catcher, who acquires information passively.

Information processing

Highly involved consumers process information cognitively, striving to avoid cognitive dissonance. New information is processed so it fits into the existing cognitive structure and is, therefore, consistent with existing beliefs. Low-involvement consumers pick up random advertising stimuli and may retain them despite their being incongruent with existing beliefs. Krugman first hypothesised the concept of passive learning in experiments on the effects of television advertising. He discovered that viewer's brainwave patterns showed a lack of involvement in what was being transmitted.[16] Viewers were relaxed and did not pay attention. Learning occurred because of repetition but had little effect upon brand attitudes.

Audience involvement

The high-involvement audience is psychologically active; selective exposure, attention, perception and retention are operative. The low-involvement audience is passive, susceptible to advertising and retentive of frequently repeated messages.

Pre-purchase evaluation

The involved audience uses advertising to help form buying intentions. The uninvolved audience, conversely, either responds to advertising because it has created a high level of awareness due to repetition or ignores it.

Group influences

Involved audiences are more likely to seek advice from opinion-leaders and be susceptible to reference-group influence than uninvolved audiences.[17] The 2-step flow of communication is pertinent only for high-involvement products. Hence advertising audiences need to be defined differently for each type of product.

Personality and lifestyle influences

These factors appear to have influence over high-involvement purchases. Where products are unimportant and the self-concept is not at risk, they are of little significance.[18]

Because of these variations in audience advertising of low-involvement products should differ.[19]

1. Emphasis on a few key points should be made rather than full information.
2. Frequent repetition of short messages encourages passive learning.
3. Television, a low-involvement medium, is more suitable than print.

4. Advertising may be the basic means of differentiating the product, there being few (or insignificant) brand differences.
5. Advertising should contain easily understood and highly visible symbols; long copy is inappropriate and visual images are more suitable.
6. The basic advertising objective should be brand recognition.

In a similar vein Ehrenberg has proposed an awareness–trial–reinforcement (ATR) model of advertising. He claims that 3 steps can account for the known facts of brand choice behaviour: (1) gaining awareness of a brand; (2) making a first or trial purchase; and (3) being reinforced into developing and keeping a repeat-buying habit.[20] He has produced data which indicate that trial purchase need not be preceded by a favourable attitude towards the brand: 'Evidence shows that most attitudinal variables are largely of an "evaluative" kind, plus some highly "descriptive" differences for certain brands.'

Evaluative attitudes, such as 'I like it', differ between users and non-users of a brand, but not between brands. Such an evaluative attitude depends largely upon whether the consumer is already a brand-user. 'Descriptive' responses to brands, such as one brand being described as more comfortable or more nutritious than another, are present in both users and non-users of a brand and, therefore, do not relate to whether one is actually a user.

Ehrenberg claims that attitudes primarily develop after trial, not before. Trial can be brought about through sales promotion, merchandising, and so on, and occasionally this will precipitate a repeat-purchase sequence. Such a sequence is, according to Ehrenberg:

> primarily a matter of reinforcement after use. Any feeling of satisfaction—that the brand is liked at least no less than previously bought ones—has to be nurtured. Evaluative attitudes have to be brought into line with the product class norms. But no exceptional 'liking' need arise because . . . the consumer does not inherently care whether he buys Bingo or Bango.

The vital factor in repeat purchasing is experience of the brand. Advertising's role varies at each stage of the ATR process. First, it can create, reawaken, or strengthen awareness. It may also stimulate trial. However, the main role for advertising is to make the trial a success by reinforcing the satisfaction a brand delivers. It is a defensive role in which the aim is to prevent brand switching once trial is achieved. Consequently a cut in advertising expenditure may well result in reduced reinforcement and lost sales. An increase in budget may well reach some marginal target consumers, raising their awareness and stimulating trial, but according to Ehrenberg, this 'would not by itself have much effect on sales'.

The advertising–sales function

Some marketers do not feel it is worth while using the concepts of comprehension, awareness, interest, or preference to understand how advertising works. They believe that if the aim of advertising is to increase sales, then the advertising–sales response should be measured empirically without reference to these intervening variables.

An American state-of-the-art study has examined the literature on sales response to advertising and drawn these general conclusions:[21]
- an upward response of sales takes place soon after increased advertising

- a relatively slower sales decay occurs on withdrawal of advertising, which is attributed to customer satisfaction
- sales saturation occurs at high advertising levels
- a possible threshold-like effect occurs at low levels
- a change of effectiveness over time takes place because of media and copy changes
- a loss of sales is experienced due to competitive advertising
- an advertising increase sometimes only brings a temporary sales increase

The author of the study was unable to reach any general conclusion about the shape of the sales response curve because of conflicting information obtained from the experiments he reviewed. These used different products in many different markets, at different stages of their life cycle under different competitive conditions, and applied conflicting definitions of advertising and sales: 'it is presumptuous to expect a regularity that can be reduced to models with only a few parameters.'

16.9 CHAPTER REVIEW

1. Advertising's general aim is to influence the behaviour of its audience in the short or long term.
2. There are 3 styles of advertisement: informative, persuasive and confirmative. Most advertisements contain elements of all of them.
3. The conventional hierarchy of effects, the learn–feel–do sequence, has been substantially revised. Additional hierarchies are: learn–do–feel, learn–do and do–learn–feel.
4. Contemporary investigations into how advertising works either favour explanations in terms of effects at each stage of the modified hierarchy or attempt to quantify the advertising–sales response function.
5. The behaviour of low-involvement audiences towards advertising differs from that of high-involvement audiences.
6. Ehrenberg has proposed an awareness–trial–reinforcement (ATR) model of advertising.
7. The choice of advertising media and message content varies between high- and low-involvement products.
8. There is no single universal advertising–sales response function.

16.10 QUESTIONS

1. What relationship exists between a consumer's attitude towards hotels competing for his expenditure and his choice of accommodation?
2. Does Ehrenberg's ATR model apply to hospitality products?
3. You are marketing manager for a large hotel's F&B operations. You have a coffee shop with off-street access and an à la carte restaurant offering a very high standard of service and cuisine. You believe the former is a low-involvement product with a local market, whereas the restaurant is a high-involvement product drawing traffic from up to 50 miles away. Given freedom to advertise as you wish, how would your style of advertising, media selection and message content vary in view of these essential differences between products and markets?
4. The 3 basic stages in the hierarchy of effects can be ordered in various ways other than those suggested in the text:
   - feel–do–learn.
   - feel–learn–do.
   - do–feel–learn.
   What validity have these new sequences?

5. Joyce's explanation of how advertising works incorporates 3 main elements: attitudes, purchasing and advertising. He postulates a 2-way relationship between each paired combination of these elements. Explain these relationships.
6. AIDA is a well-known mnemonic, standing for attention–interest–desire–action. What hospitality products would you buy in this way?
7. Clip some press advertisements for hospitality products. Are they informative, persuasive, or confirmative? Why?

REFERENCES

[1] Association of Accredited Advertising Agencies of New Zealand Inc. *Advertising: its purpose and performance*.
[2] See Channon, C. (1985) *Advertising Works 3*. Eastbourne: Holt, Rinehart & Winston, for a series of cases illustrating how research can be used to demonstrate advertising's effects.
[3] Starch, D. (1925) *Principles of Advertising*. London: Shaw.
[4] Cox, D. F. (1961) Clues for advertising strategists: pt II. *Harvard Business Review*, **39**, November–December, 160–82.
[5] Haskins, J. B. (1964) Factual recall as a measure of advertising effectiveness. *Journal of Advertising Research*, March, 2–8.
[6] Colley, R. H. (ed.) (1961) *Defining Advertising Goals for Measured Advertising Results*. New York: Association of National Advertisers of New York.
[7] Lavidge R. C., and Steiner, C. A. (1961) A model for predictive measurements of advertising effectiveness. *Journal of Marketing*, **25**(4), 59–62.
[8] Wolfe, H. D., Brown, J. N., and Thompson, G. C. (1962) *Measuring Advertising Results*. National Industry Conference Board.
[9] Sandage, G. H. and Fryburger, V. (1963) *Advertising Theory and Practice*. Homewood, IL.: Irwin, 240.
[10] Rogers, E. M. (1962) *Diffusion of Innovations*. New York: The Free Press, 79–86.
[11] See: Single medium or multi-media? *National Business Review* (New Zealand), 15 February 1978, 16–17.
[12] Joyce, T. (1967) *What Do We Know about How Advertising Works?* London: J. Walter Thompson.
[13] Palda, K. S. (1966) The hypothesis of the hierarchy of effects: a partial re-evaluation. *Journal of Marketing Research*, **3**, February, 13–24.
[14] Haskins, J. B. (1964) op. cit.
[15] Assael, H. (1984) (2nd edn) *Consumer Behaviour and Marketing Action*. Kent.
[16] Krugman, H. E. (1965) The impact of TV advertising: learning without involvement. *Public Opinion Quarterly*, **29**, Fall, 349–56.
[17] Cocanougher, A. B. and Bruce, G. (1971) Socially distant reference groups and consumer aspirations. *Journal of Marketing Research*, **8**, August, 378–81.
[18] Kassarjian, H. H. and Kassarjian, W. M. (1979) Attitudes under low involvement conditions, in Maloney, J. C. and Silverman, B. (eds) *Attitude Research Plays for High Stakes*. AMA.
[19] Based on Assael, H. (1984) op. cit., 100–1.
[20] Ehrenberg, A. S. C. (1974) Repetitive advertising and the consumer. *Journal of Advertising Research*, **14**(2), April.
[21] Little, J. D. C. (1979) *Aggregate Advertising Models: The State of the Art*, The Marketing Centre, Massachusetts Institute of Technology, Cambridge, MA, April.

—17—

Advertising Management

17.1 CHAPTER PREVIEW

This chapter starts with a description of the structure of the advertising industry and the role of an advertising agency. However, the bulk of the chapter reviews the 10 decisions faced by advertising management. These are objective setting, budget determination, developing basic copy strategy, execution, pre-testing, adjustment, media planning, media buying, post-testing and implementation.

17.2 LEARNING OBJECTIVES

By the end of this chapter you should be able to:
1. Describe the structure of the British advertising industry.
2. Draw a flowchart detailing the 10 key decisions made by advertising management.
3. Describe the most significant characteristics of the advertising media.
4. Defend as best the objective-and-task method of budgeting.
5. Write advertising objectives.
6. Recommend methods for pre- and post-testing advertising effectiveness.
7. Define and explain the relationships between reach, frequency, OTS, TVR, weighting and CPT.

17.3   THE ADVERTISING INDUSTRY

The Advertising Association, a body representing the interests of all those connected with advertising, annually surveys advertising expenditure.[1] The data in Table 17.1 show that over £4 billion (4,000 million pounds), or about 1.26 per cent of gross national product, was expended on advertising in 1984. Recent expenditure through the various media is shown in Table 17.2, which distinguishes between display and classified advertising. Classified advertising occurs exclusively in the press and consists of space bought by the single-column centimetre, normally by households, and categorised into sections. Display advertising is all other space and time. If the data in Tables 17.1 and 17.2 were inflation adjusted, they would still show an industry growing in real terms.

The industry consists on the one hand of media-owners who have advertising space to sell, and on the other advertisers who wish to communicate with their target audiences. Very often advertisers will buy space direct from the media-owners (classified

Table 17.1　*Total advertising expenditure.*

	£m	Total expenditure as percentage of: Consumer expenditure	Gross National Product
1952	123	1.15	0.87
1962	348	1.84	1.35
1972	708	1.76	1.25
1975	967	1.50	1.00
1982	3126	1.88	1.12
1983	3579	1.96	1.18
1984	4055	2.08	1.26

Source: Advertising Association *Advertising Statistics Year Book* (1985)

Table 17.2　*Advertising expenditure by media.*

	£m 1982	1983	1984	Percentage of total advertising expenditure 1982	1983	1984
Display						
Press	1 297	1 436	1 622	41.5	40.1	40.0
TV	928	1 109	1 245	29.7	31.0	30.7
Poster, transport, cinema, radio	212	234	252	6.8	6.5	6.2
Total display	2 437	2 779	3 119	78.0	77.6	76.9
Classified	689	800	936	22.0	22.4	23.1
Grand total	3 126	3 579	4 055	100.0	100.0	100.0

Source: As Table 17.1.

advertising is an example) but most large-budget advertisers use intermediaries such as advertising agencies, commercial artists, or independent media buyers.

Typically an advertising agency has an account management department (each client being an account). One account executive normally handles 3 or more accounts and reports to an accounts director. The account executive's job is to represent the client's interest in the agency. He often helps in developing the client's marketing plan, advising on the role of advertising and other elements of the promotional mix. Account executives will use an account group, that is a group of agency staff, to help in creating advertisements. They may be a designated set of people with group responsibility for the account, or the account executive may have freedom of choice about which staff to use.

The resources of the agency are normally grouped into departments such as these:
- Accounts—client liaison
- Media—planning, buying and research
- Creative—copywriting and artwork
- Marketing—consulting and research
- Production—advertising materials
- Administration—personnel, accounting and secretarial staff

The industry is represented by a variety of professional and craft bodies. The major organisations are listed in Table 17.3.

Marketers venturing into advertising for the first time need to decide how to organise

Table 17.3 *Organisations in advertising.*

Abbreviation	Name	Address	Functions
AA	Advertising Association	Abford House 15 Wilton Road London SW1V 1NJ	Represents the common interests of all members of the advertising industry in all sectors of society
ABC	Audit Bureau of Circulations	13 Wimpole Street London WC1M 7AB	Provides an independently certified audit of circulation and readership data
ASA	Advertising Standards Authority	Brook House 2–16 Torrington Place London WC1E 7HN	Controls print and cinema advertising through British Code of Advertising Practice
BARB	Broadcasters' Audience Research Board	Knighton House 56 Mortimer Street London W1N 8AN	Measures viewership of television stations and programmes
CAM	Communication, Advertising and Marketing Education Foundation Limited	Abford House, 15 Wilton Road London SW1 1NJ	Provides professional training and qualifications for those entering the marketing communications industry
IBA	Independent Broadcasting Authority	70 Brompton Road London SW3 1EY	Controls advertising standards in TV and radio through Code of Advertising Standards and Practice
IM	Institute of Marketing	Moor Hall Cookham, Maidenhead Berkshire SL6 9QH	Establishes and maintains standards of professional competence in marketing
IPA	Institute of Practitioners in Advertising	44 Belgrave Square London SW1X 8QS	Represents collective interests of advertising agencies and maintains/improves standards of service offered to clients
ISBA	Incorporated Society of British Advertisers Ltd	44 Hertford Street London W1	Represents collective interests of advertisers, promotes freedom within the law to advertise and high standards of advertising practice
JICNARS	Joint Industry Committee for National Readership Surveys	44 Belgrave Square London SW1X 8QS	Evaluates issue readership for all major publications analysed by age, sex, social grade, survey region and ITV region; profiles publication readership; known as NRS (National Readership Survey); equivalent bodies exist for posters (JICPAS) and radio (JICRAR)

for advertising. The alternatives are to establish an in-house advertising department, to use a full-service advertising agency, or to recruit specialist creative and media buying resources as required.

The advertiser's selection of an agency depends largely upon the accumulated experience and skills of the alternatives.[2] Advertising agencies' main source of revenue is the commission they receive from the media in which advertisements are placed; however, this sometimes causes conflict with clients. The commission system tempts agencies to buy media indiscriminately, operating against the best interests of the client. Furthermore, advertising is a more productive source of revenue than sales promotion or publicity, although these may offer better promotional, if non-commissionable, solutions to clients' problems. In recognition of this some agencies prefer to earn their income in fees from clients.

In a survey of European advertising agency remuneration systems the Incorporated Society of British Advertisers (ISBA) found that the overwhelming majority of consumer advertising vehicles across all media categories pay 15 per cent agency commission.[3] The Office of Fair Trading has recently investigated the traditional system of agency remuneration whereby only 'accredited' advertising agencies received commissions from media-owners. This system of approving some agencies but not others was deemed a restrictive trade practice. As a consequence media-owners have withdrawn the offending condition for recognition of agencies.

17.4 MANAGING THE ADVERTISING FUNCTION

Given that most marketers believe advertising to be worth while, even if they cannot be sure about how it works, management of the advertising function poses several practical, interrelated problems. Figure 17.1 shows the major advertising decisions and their relationship to one another. These decisions are examined in sections 17.5–17.14.

17.5 MANAGING THE ADVERTISING FUNCTION: ADVERTISING OBJECTIVES

Advertising is just one element of the marketing mix and its objectives should, therefore, be derived from the overall marketing objectives. They should be precisely formulated, specifying details of both the target audience and the desired effect. Target audiences for hospitality advertising include families, business executives, secretaries, travel agents, conference organisers, and so on. These objectives are, or should be, based either upon one of the hierarchical models of communication effects, as described in Chapter 16, or upon a sales target if the marketer holds the view that the sole concern of advertising is to create sales. In practical terms the problem is whether objectives should be stated in terms of learning, feeling, doing, or a mixture of these elements. Objectives are vital because they determine the type of message to be transmitted, the media to be used and the evaluation procedure to be followed when gauging the effectiveness of the advertising. Examples of advertising objectives appear in Table 17.4.

If the marketer feels that his consumers are following a complex decision-making process, he will probably phrase his advertising objectives in cognitive terms, perhaps leaving the inducement of behaviour to other elements of his promotion mix such as sales promotion and merchandising.

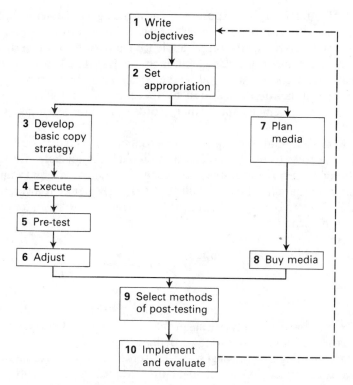

Figure 17.1   Advertising decisions.

Because of the cost and difficulty of undertaking research into the sales effectiveness of advertising, many marketers feel compelled to set their objectives in relatively simple communication terms. Thus, advertisers commonly use:

- exposure
- awareness
- comprehension

Table 17.4   *Advertising objectives.*

'Learning' objectives
1 To increase awareness of the group as a luxury hotel company that caters to the business community (Four Seasons Hotels, Canada; winners of the 1982 HSMA Advertising Awards)
2 By December 40% of major conference organisers will know that we offer tele-conferencing facilities
3 By December 60% of travel agents will know the main selling features of our hotel

'Feeling' objectives
1 To increase consumer preference of our brand to 15% by December
2 To make our restaurant the preferred venue for children's parties
3 To shift the attitude of schoolchildren towards wholefood to a quantifiably more favourable position by December

'Doing' objectives
1 To obtain 10,000 applications to join our hotel's executive club within 12 months
2 To lift average number of covers on Tuesday evenings from 15 to 25
3 To obtain 500 sales leads from coupon returns within 2 months of placement of the advertisement

as measures of effectiveness. Exposure to advertising is the least demanding of advertising objectives. The exposure effectiveness of an advertisement is measured by its reach (the total number of the target audience exposed to the advertisement) and, frequency (average number of times a member of the target audience is exposed to the advertisement). Awareness, measured by the consumer's ability to recall advertising content, and comprehension, measured by the consumer's ability to translate the content of an advertisement into other words, are also used as indicators of effectiveness.

Some marketers view advertising as an investment, the value of which depreciates over time. Unless advertising expenditure is intended for immediate effects, long-term objectives should be set. For example, a concentrated campaign might want to achieve a 60 per cent awareness level in 2 months but only a 10 per cent awareness level 12 months hence. Objectives may differ according to strategic situation, for example, by:

- nature of the product
- stage of product life cycle (PLC)
- position of product against competitors

Product

Service products, because of their intangibility, perishability, heterogeneity and inseparability, face particular advertising problems. George and Berry recommend that service advertisers adopt the following guidelines.[4]

- Use clear, unambiguous messages. Advertisers find it difficult to capture the range and quality of services in words and pictures. Many advertisements tend to be too wordy and make little use of visual illustrations to demonstrate quality
- Emphasise benefits, not technical details of the service
- Only promise what can be delivered. A Holiday Inn campaign under the headline 'No surprise' had to be withdrawn because this could not be guaranteed.[5] Variability in service performance causes heterogeneity of service products
- Advertise to employees. The service provider is inseparable from the service product
- Obtain and maintain customer co-operation in the service production process. Restaurant customers entertaining guests must work as hard as the chef to make the meal experience a success
- Build on word-of-mouth promotion. Interpersonal communication is relatively more important for intangibles. Word-of-mouth promotion can be stimulated by targeting opinion-leaders
- Provide tangible clues which give the intangible product a concrete dimension
- Develop continuity in advertising. This helps to overcome the disadvantages of intangibility and heterogeneity
- Remove post-purchase anxiety. Since the consumer owns no tangible product after purchasing the service, advertising must reassure the customer of the soundness of his choice

PLC

During the introductory stage of the PLC advertising objectives may be phrased to encourage trial, to obtain a certain level of distribution, penetration of influential segments, brand awareness and brand comprehension. During growth attention is given to repurchase levels, penetration of new segments, developing market share and widening distribution. At the maturity stage attention is often given to maintaining market share, reinforcing brand image and establishing reasons for a price differential. At decline the focus is often on lengthening the life cycle through promotion to new segments.

Positioning

For an up-market aimed product advertising may be asked to establish an image to support a high price ('feeling' objective). For a 'me-too' product positioned alongside competitors the objective may be to stress consumer benefits at the same price ('learning' objective); and for a down-market product the advertising may aim to build a value-for-money, no-nonsense image ('feeling' objective).

17.6 MANAGING THE ADVERTISING FUNCTION: THE ADVERTISING APPROPRIATION

Determining the budget is the next stage in the management of advertising. This order suggests that the budget is determined by the advertising objectives. Often this is not the case, as when a specific budget or maximum level of advertising expenditure is set first, and the marketer is then obliged to determine how best to spend it!

Where a single promotion budget is fixed, advertising often finds itself competing against sales and sales promotion management for an adequate share. Generally speaking, advertising deserves a larger share where:

- repeat business is insignificant. Since hotels and restaurants largely survive on a high level of repeat business, advertising is seen as less appropriate than direct mail or sales promotion
- specific media allow.cost effective access to the target audience
- the market is too large or too dispersed for salesmen economically to contact consumers
- the market is segmented on image. Grohmann comments that the larger the hotel or hotel group and the higher its tariff, the bigger should be the advertising budget, largely because of the need to develop image[6]
- the market is expanding too quickly for personal selling to be effective

The method of allocating funds to advertising after setting objectives has become known as the *objective-and-task method*.

Other methods are as follows.

1. Percentage of sales method. Some companies will spend only a certain percentage of last year's sales turnover or this year's forecast on advertising (known as the advertising sales or A/S ratio). As a method it is somewhat flawed since it does not allow for exploitation of new profit opportunities or response to competitive threats for which advertising is appropriate. Additionally, it is based on obscure reasoning—presumably advertising is meant to cause sales, yet by this method sales cause advertising! Had this method been employed, there would have been no advertising of the first weekend breaks. However, £1,000 was spent (in 1964) and 300 bookings were received.[7]

2. Profits excess method. Under this method what remains from profits, after other claims have been made, is allocated to advertising. Its major weakness is that it means that advertising is not regarded as an integral part of the company's marketing strategy—it is superfluous and subject to withdrawal of funding.

3. Matching competitors. This appears to be used quite widely as a means of ensuring that market share is not lost because of competitive advertising expenditure. It encourages stability but does not allow the company to be a leader, or to be the first to develop a new market.

4. Risk-reduction approach. In this method probability is used to calculate the budget. Suppose that the product in question stands a 50 per cent chance of losing market share valued at £100,000 a year in contribution if not backed by advertising. If this situation were encountered over many years, the company would expect to lose, on average, £50,000 per year; some years it would lose £100,000 and in other years nothing. The expected loss of contribution can be calculated by multiplying the total amount at risk by the chance of losing it. If the company believes that maintaining advertising will eliminate the risk of losing market share, then it should be prepared to spend up to £50,000 in this simplified example.[8]

How do these models compare with actual practice? Quite well, in some respects, but poorly in others. One study of 40 advertising and marketing managers showed that they asked for the same amount as the previous year, with an adjustment to allow for changes in the current year's advertising task, expectations of competitors' advertising and an allowance for inflation.[9] A mail survey of 92 British companies found that 'most managers do not use advanced models for advertising budgeting'.[10] The findings are tabulated in Table 17.5.

Table 17.5 *British advertisers' budgeting practices.*

Method	N	%
Percentage of expected turnover	32	35
Percentage of previous year's turnover	14	15
Percentage of previous year's profit	13	14
Percentage of expected profit	11	12
Analysis of marketing opportunities	6	7
What the company can afford	5	5
Guesswork	4	5
Competitive parity	3	3
Use of decision model	2	2
Other	2	2
	92	100

Whatever the means of budget calculation, it needs to be sufficient to pay the following:

- Costs of buying media space and time
- Fees to external agencies such as advertising agents, photographers and copywriters
- Production costs
- Administrative and managerial costs

Sometimes small advertisers co-operate by pooling budgets in a campaign designed to achieve objectives of mutual interest. Such co-operation underpins franchise advertising. Each of Spud-u-Like's franchises contributes 3 per cent of sales to advertising.

Details of advertising expenditure by the hospitality industry are available in the quarterly reports of Media Expenditure Analysis Ltd (MEAL). The MEAL figures are based upon the published cost of media space and time known to have been bought by the advertiser and thus exclude any specially negotiated discounts or premiums. In addition, the reports name the agency handling the account.

Expenditure of hotels is classified by MEAL under 'Holidays, travel and transport'. Table 17.6 brings together entries for 4 consecutive quarters, showing a hotel annual expenditure of over £6 million. The data show Trusthouse Forte (THF) to be the biggest advertiser, accounting for nearly one-quarter of the industry's expenditure. Other than

Table 17.6   *Hotel advertising expenditure.*

		Quarter ended (£)			Year ending
	June 1984	September 1984	December 1984	March 1985	March 1985
Best Western Getaway	15 900	19 700	29 200	62 000	126 800
Best Western Hotels	11 300	—	—	—	11 300
Calotels	—	—	—	21 300	21 300
Ciga Hotels	—	—	—	121 100	121 100
Crest International Hotels	212 400	123 800	109 700	180 800	626 700
Forum	—	—	7 400	—	7 400
Gleneagles Hotels	—	—	—	69 500	69 500
Grand Metro Stardust	1 700	—	—	—	1 700
Hilton Hotels	20 300	49 500	—	—	69 800
Hilton International (Business)	—	—	26 400	4 300	30 700
Hilton International Hotels	—	12 400	11 000	—	23 400
Intercontinental	25 800	8 500	3 500	48 200	87 000
Ladbroke Hotels	9 000	18 100	5 900	—	33 000
Marriott Hotels	—	—	—	64 300	64 300
Meridien Hotels	—	—	48 000	45 300	93 300
Metropole Conference	—	—	—	28 300	28 300
Rank Hotels	—	—	53 200	1 500	54 700
Sol Holiday Hotels	—	—	192 600	406 400	599 000
Sheraton Business	38 200	25 400	49 300	30 000	142 900
Sheraton Hotels	50 400	48 700	58 200	64 200	221 500
Thistle Business	—	—	92 300	—	92 300
Thistle Hotels	—	—	—	32 700	32 700
Thistle Highlife	—	—	—	172 200	172 200
THF Bargain Breaks	50 300	31 800	88 000	456 700	626 800
THF Hotels	220 600	238 800	204 400	72 700	736 400
THF Hightime	34 400	42 100	19 500	1 800	97 800
Grouped brands	218 800	163 400	218 500	305 700	906 400
Other brands (up to 80 hotels)	248 600	227 500	280 400	367 900	1 174 400
Total	1 157 800	1 059 800	1 497 500	2 556 900	6 272 000

THF, only Best Western, Crest, Hilton, Sol (Spain), Sheraton and Thistle had 6-figure budgets. The figures also show: (1) how budgets are apportioned between hotel products—Thistle Hotels, for example, spent nearly 60 per cent of its budget on promoting its Highlife weekend-break product; and (2) how expenditure is scheduled throughout the year—the Sol Hotel group, faced with low bookings for its Spanish resort hotels, spent a massive £600,000 over winter and spring to boost trade. Also recorded by MEAL are food service advertising expenditure. Other MEAL tables show how the expenditure breaks down between media.

The trade press occasionally features advertising league tables. One such table showed THF (the leading hotel advertiser) in sixth place, in terms of advertising expenditure, behind Kentucky Fried Chicken (1st, £5.25 million), McDonald's (2nd, £4 million), Wimpy (3rd, £2 million), Pizza Hut (4th, £600,000) and Watney Combe Reid (5th, £550,000).[11]

Hospitality advertising appropriations are very small compared to major fast-moving consumer goods manufacturers who may budget over 30 per cent of turnover. The AA's 1985 *Statistics Yearbook* shows toothpastes, shampoo and deodorants to have A/S ratios of 38, 28 and 27 per cent respectively. Budgets, as a percentage of turnover, are typically as shown in Table 17.7.[12]

Table 17.7   *Typical hospitality advertising budget.*

Company/product	Advertising as percentage of turnover
Pizza Express	0.5
Superfish	0.5
Casey Jones	1.1
Happy Eater	2
Oliver's	2
Kentucky Fried Chicken	3 (UK); 4.5 (USA)
Spud-u-Like	3
McDonald's	3.5
Burger King	4
Pizza Hut	4.5 (USA)
Roast Inns	11

There are many problems which the hospitality marketer faces in calculating a budget, even if using the more acceptable objective-and-task method. Some of them are outlined below.

1. Lack of experience. He may not know how much to spend to achieve an acceptable awareness or purchase level because he has no experience in that market, or with that product.
2. There may be alternative media and message combinations for achieving the desired objective, each of which may be more, or less, costly than the others.
3. Relatively more money may need to be spent converting the late majority and laggards to product use. These prospects may be unwilling to change their purchasing behaviour because of strongly held attitudes which are not easy to change with advertising.
4. Estimating the rate of decay amongst brand-loyal consumers. If the aim of advertising is to reduce the number of consumers lost to competitors, the advertiser

will need to quantify the likely number of losses during the budget period before setting his budget.

5. Interaction of advertising with other marketing mix variables. An attempt to link other aspects of the marketing mix to trial rates has been developed by David Learner. His model, named DEMON, views trial as a function of 3 factors: advertising, sales promotion and distribution.[13] It is illustrated in Figure 17.2.

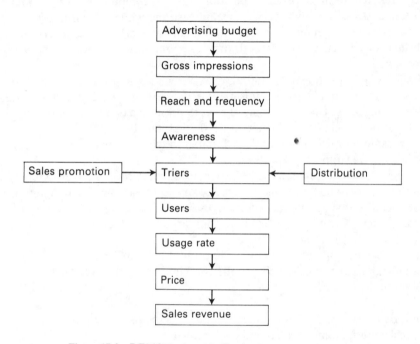

Figure 17.2   DEMON advertising budgeting model.

Examination of the model shows that the number of gross impressions (total impacts) is a direct function of the size of the advertising budget. Gross impressions are translated into reach and frequency equivalents and this, in turn, is used to estimate the level of awareness. The relationship of awareness to trial rates is then considered in conjunction with the impact of sales promotion and distribution. A relationship is established between trial, repurchase levels and price to calculate the effect on sales revenue. (See pp. 349–350 for a detailed explanation of the terms 'gross impressions', 'reach' and 'frequency'.)

6. Inability to predict competitor's responses to advertising.

17.7 MANAGING THE ADVERTISING FUNCTION: BASIC COPY STRATEGY

The next stage in management of the advertising function is to decide on the basic message to be communicated. The type of message will vary according to the objectives, and there is no single acceptable way of generating messages, translating the messages into creative proposals, or testing them. The basic message which is chosen to achieve the objectives is known as the basic copy strategy, copy platform, or campaign theme.

Basic copy strategy (particularly for new products) should aim to differentiate the product from others, so that it:

- acquires the desired product position against competitors. McDonald's, for instance, stresses quality, service, cleanliness and value to consumers
- appeals to the target market; 5 key benefit appeals were isolated in a survey of 270 restaurant advertisements—food quality, menu variety, price, atmosphere and convenience[14]
- provides a basis for behavioural change, where appropriate—i.e. motivates behaviour, normally by promising the delivery of some benefit. A leading advertising agency believes that: 'it pays to promise a benefit which is unique and competitive. And the product must deliver the benefits you promise. Most advertising promises nóthing. It is doomed to failure in the market place'[15]
- obtains trade support

Sometimes several campaign themes are considered before one is selected by client or agent for execution. Ray claims there are 'no formulas [sic] for judging proposed message ideas', but suggests that alternatives can be judged against 9 criteria:[16]

1. Is it consistent with the other elements of marketing and promotional strategy?
2. Is it relevant to the target audience?
3. Can the idea be applied throughout the promotional mix?
4. Does it stand out from the noise of the communications environment?
5. Is it simple?
6. Is it specific?
7. Can it be translated for communication through the mass media?
8. Is it resistant to counterattack and counterclaim?
9. Is it durable?

17.8 MANAGING THE ADVERTISING FUNCTION: EXECUTION

This stage of the advertising management process involves translating copy strategy into a creative form suitable for the particular mass medium chosen for the campaign. This is usually undertaken by the creative staff of advertising agencies.

Many agencies have creative philosophies about the way that campaign themes should be executed. In effect, this is the core of what agencies offer their clients—a particular way of presenting commercial messages in the mass media distilled from hundreds of successful campaigns over many years.

Agency 1 Ted Bates
Rosser Reeves, a former president of the American advertising agency Ted Bates, developed a number of 'immutable principles of advertising'.[17] His most lasting conceptual contribution has been the unique selling proposition (USP). He believed in identifying a single, unique product characteristic and promoting this USP single-

mindedly. The USP concept can be criticised for being highly product-oriented; indeed it did not seem to matter to Reeves that the USP was not a consumer benefit.

Reeves was hard-nosed about measuring advertising effectiveness in terms of sales. He developed a technique known as 'usage pull'—this being the proportional difference in purchasing between those who can recall the USP and those who cannot.

Reeves's philosophy of advertising, particularly the USP concept, seems more appropriate to low-involvement products.

Agency 2 Ogilvy & Mather

David Ogilvy, founder of O & M, believes in factually informative executions of copy strategy:[18]

> If all advertisers would give up flatulent puffery and turn to the kind of factual informative advertising, which I have provided for Rolls-Royce, KLM Royal Dutch Airlines and Shell they would not only increase their sales, but they would also place themselves on the side of the angels. The more informative your advertising, the more persuasive it will be.

Unlike Reeves, who had made his reputation with TV advertising, Ogilvy is essentially a 'print' man, where long copy is not only possible, but often necessary.

Agency 3 Leo Burnett

Leo Burnett's executions always sought to emphasise the 'inherent drama' in the product. He believed that the advertisement would have to compete in media which carried much more exciting material, and that to be noticed it would need to be dramatised with bold, interesting copy and illustrations.

Readers who wish to know how the findings of communications researchers relate to these agency philosophies should refer back to Chapter 15, particularly to the review of factors which promote or inhibit fidelity of communication in section 15.5.

Copy

Copywriters produce the words, known as copy, used in advertisements. Copy and illustrations, plus sound-effects for broadcast ads, together comprise the complete advertisement. The copywriter has to be knowledgeable about the product and the market. He must know what the product is made from; what benefits it can convey; and how it can be identified. Of consumers, he must know who are the prime prospects; who influences the purchase; who buys; who consumes; what motives dominate their purchase of the product; and what will attract them to an advertisement.

Copywriters have 4 main elements to consider:

1. The headline, which is to attract the attention and arouse the interest of the audience: 'On the average, five times as many people read the headline of an advertisement as read the body copy', and 'headlines that promise a benefit sell more than headlines that don't'.[19]
2. The headline extension, which directs the reader to product-related information.
3. The body copy, which develops the headline extension and details the benefits.
4. The close, which exhorts action and distils the purpose of the advertisement.

These basic elements are present in both print and broadcast copywriting, yet not all advertisements carry all of these elements. Indeed some carry none because visual symbols are regarded as more communicative than text. Headlines are written in a variety of styles, for example:

- news headlines, which relate the advertisement to current editorial matter
- questions, which provoke involvement by demanding an answer
- narratives, which lead the audience right into the body copy
- instructions, which demand action

The body copy amplifies the headline and headline extension, detailing consumer benefits and, where necessary, reducing perceived risk with proofs in the form of demonstrations or testimonials, and assurances in the form of trial offers, warranties and money-back guarantees. The copywriter's contribution is more significant when the product is a learn–feel–do or do–learn–feel type of purchase and the copy has to promote learning or reduce post-purchase anxieties.

Illustrations

Illustrations and copy jointly execute the basic copy strategy and, therefore, should be in harmony. During development illustrations generally progress by stages from broad visualisations through to finished art.

There appear to be few generalised laws which describe a well-executed advertisement.[20] An advertisement should:

- satisfy all demands of the basic copy strategy
- command attention
- be balanced—all elements (headline, illustrations, coupon, body copy, etc.) should direct attention to the advertisement's focal point
- be well proportioned—the available space should be attractively apportioned between the various elements for a pleasing visual effect
- be unified—all elements should contribute to the advertisement's objective
- be legible, understandable and, in most cases, credible
- be consistent with the image of the product

Technical aspects, such as the advertisement size, method of reproduction and typeface can have a considerable impact on ad effectiveness.

Copy controls

Not all copy is acceptable. The Advertising Standards Authority's Code of Advertising Practice controls print and cinema advertising; the Independent Broadcasting Authority performs in like capacity in respect of television and radio advertising.

The British Code of Advertising Practice is a self-regulating system designed to uphold standards of advertising. In essence, the code demands that advertisements should be legal, decent, honest and truthful. The code also contains standards relating to specific product groups such as cigarettes, alcohol and vitamins.

Complaints about print and cinema advertising are referred to the Advertising Standards Authority. For example, a claim by the Carlton Hotel, Weymouth, that full board was available was found, upon complaint, to be misleading because it was only provided in the early and late season. Advertisers may obtain copy clearance in advance by submission to the Copy Panel of the Code of Advertising Practice Committee.

17.9 MANAGING THE ADVERTISING FUNCTION: PRE-TESTING

The next stage of the advertising management process is to test the advertisement. We already have objectives, and we may have several alternative executions. We need to find out whether the advertisement is likely to achieve its objectives, and if not, why not.

Practically all pre-testing is concerned with measuring the communication effects of the advertisement. Does it attract attention and what parts of the advertisement can be recalled? What meaning does the advertisement convey? Is the advertisement understood, is it credible? Does the advertisement encourage the audience to read through? Does it imply action? Are there any words which are ambiguous? A simple 3-stage pre-test process involves selecting a sample of the intended audience for the advertisement, exposing it to one or more executions, then questioning in the foregoing way.

Because much of the production cost of an advertisement is incurred in the finishing stage, most pretesting uses paste-ups (rough versions of print advertisements), narrative tapes (scripts on audio tape), storyboards (hand-drawn versions of television advertisements), or 'animatics' (videotaped storyboards with a rough soundtrack) to test the executions.

Pre-tests vary in a number of ways, as follows.
1. Personal interviews or group discussions may be used.
2. Use of a structured questionnaire or informal techniques.
3. Use of a randomly selected sample or a small judgemental sample.
4. Taking the advertisements into the audience's homes or bringing the audience together into a trailer or hall.
5. Examination of the effectiveness of the advertisement as a whole or examination of parts only (e.g. the slogan or presenter).
6. Testing either the basic copy strategy or the way that the strategy has been executed.
7. Within-medium testing (i.e. placing the test advertisement in a medium), or out-of-medium tests.

Infrequently actual sales effects of alternative advertisments may be tested experimentally but this is very costly because of the necessity to produce commercials of broadcast or print quality.

The pre-tester can draw on a number of technological aids. The eye-camera tracks the movement of a subject's eyes when exposed to stimuli such as print advertisements. A videotape recording is made of the stimulus as seen by the respondent and a moving dot, corresponding to eye position, is superimposed. This information is computer-analysed following exposure of a number of subjects. The tester is able to judge where the eye rests longest, how much time is spent looking at each of several alternative advertisements, which element of the ad is dominant and the order in which subjects look at elements on a page.

A tachistoscope is an instrument which allows subjects to view an advertising stimulus for a timed period from ¹⁄₁₀₀th of a second upwards. It is basically an illuminated box with a peep-hole. Linked to recall tests it can be used to test the relative strength of alternative layouts.

Also used are a number of physiological measures of response to advertising, including pupil dilation and variations in the conductivity of the skin. The pupil of the eye has been shown to dilate when levels of arousal are high—measurement of pupil dilation is based on the premiss that high arousal correlates with greater advertising effectiveness. The psycho-galvanometer measures the resistance of the skin to a mild electrical current passed through the subject's body. As arousal occurs variations in resistance are recorded. Technological aids are not widely used.

Adjustments

Any communication problems the advertisement contains should by now be identified. At this stage necessary alterations are made to the advertisement and the final version is created, ready for release to the advertising media.

17.10 MANAGING THE ADVERTISING FUNCTION: MEDIA PLANNING

Two media decisions must be made. Firstly, which major advertising media categories, if any, should be excluded from consideration. The major categories are:

Broadcast media	television
	radio
Print media	newspapers
	consumer publications
	business publications
Other media	transport
	posters
	cinema

Second, within each of the remaining categories, which specific vehicles should be chosen? These questions can only be answered in the light of knowledge about the British advertising media, to which we now turn.

British advertising media

There are 2 guides to the advertising media of Great Britain: BRAD (*British Rate and Data*) and the *Advertisers' Annual*. Updated monthly, BRAD details rates and technical data for advertisements in business publications, cinemas, consumer publications, electronic media, feature-advertising media, foreign-language daily newspapers, national daily newspapers, newscasters, posters, radio, regional daily newspapers, ship's newspapers, Sunday newspapers, television, transport media and weekly newspapers. In addition, it quotes rates for door-to-door deliveries. The *Advertisers' Annual* is less current and less detailed.

Print media

BRAD lists over 400 pages of print publications from *The Times* to *Jewish Vegetarian*. We shall examine newspapers, consumer and business publications.

Newspapers

The UK has one of the highest newspaper circulations in the world, with 388 daily newspapers per 1,000 people.[21] New Zealand has 365, Japan 526, Australia 394 and the USA 287. BRAD lists 10 fully national daily newspapers, 9 national Sunday newspapers, 12 regional Sunday newspapers, 120 regional daily newspapers, 2 foreign-language daily newspapers, 1 ship's newspaper and 1,100 regional weeklies and local free-distribution publications. Newspapers can be distinguished from magazines because they contain news, advertisements and other literary matter, whereas magazines are predominantly filled with articles by identified authors and advertising material. Newspapers may be tabloid (36 cm or less column depth) or broadsheet (56 cm column depth) in format, with paid circulation or free distribution and with national, regional, or local readerships, be independent or part of a group and, with respect to news, be internationally or locally oriented.

Most newspapers separate their advertising into 2 types: classified and display. In the former advertisements are placed in categories and are printed in a classified section of the paper. Display advertisements appear throughout the editorial pages, and a large variety of size of space is available. This latter type is of greater interest to most hospitality companies. Customer analysis can help select appropriate regional newspapers. Food and beverage sales can be promoted through local newspapers. The volume of advertising appearing in newspapers is shown in Table 17.8.

Table 17.8 *Newspaper advertising.*

| | National newspapers | | Regional newspapers | |
	£m	Percentage of total advertising expenditure	£m	Percentage of total advertising expenditure
1982	515	16.5	737	23.6
1983	584	16.3	817	22.8
1984	678	16.7	921	22.7

Source: Advertising Association *Advertising Statistics Yearbook* (1985).

In 1984, 39.4 per cent of all advertising expenditure was used to buy space in newspapers. This is £1,599 million, the majority of which was placed with regional newspapers. Details of further interest to marketers are:

- column widths (measured in ems, 10 ems being 42 mm) vary between newspapers
- some national papers offer regional readerships and accept display advertising for national or regional insertion
- special locations, such as specified pages, lugs (the advertisements alongside the paper's name—the masthead—on the front page), back page, top of columns and front page, are more costly than the flat rate, which is based on a per column centimetre charge
- special colour rates apply
- most daily papers have regular features into which advertisements can be placed; occasional special-interest supplements may be issued to attract specific advertisers
- each newspaper has standard sizes of display advertisement which they are prepared to accept

- volume discounts are available for multiple insertions
- advertisements are accepted at short notice
- all papers specify the form in which advertising materials must be presented, such as zincs, bromides, or art pulls, the form being dictated by the printing process
- photographic reproduction is poor

Consumer publications

BRAD lists over 1,200 consumer publications (including directories), classified into 54 categories, from advertising-only publications through do-it-yourself to women's interest and youth publications. Many of these publications are not members of the Audit Bureau of Circulations and cannot, therefore, provide audited circulation figures (see Table 17.3). They are increasingly used to attract special-interest groups to hotels.

A class of publication of particular value to hotel and food service advertisers is the consumer guide or directory. Most of these combine editorial matter about destinations, hotels or restaurants with advertising matter. Some publishers place restrictions on the type of advertising carried; for example, some restaurant guides do not carry restaurant advertisements: space will be sold to hotels and breweries. A sample of titles appears below.

AA: *Around Britain's Seaside.*
AA: *Guesthouses, Farmhouses and Inns in Britain.*
AA: *Guide to Stately Homes, Museums, Castles and Gardens in Britain.*
AA: *Hotels and Restaurants in Britain.*
AA: *999 Places to Eat Out.*
BHRCA: *Hotels and Restaurants in Britain.*
Egon Ronay: *Good Pub Guide.*
Egon Ronay: *Lucas Guide.*
Egon Ronay: *Raleigh Pub Guide.*
English Tourist Board: *Hotels in England.*
English Tourist Board: *Let's Go.*
English Tourist Board: *Self-Catering Holiday Homes.*

Business publications

In over 200 pages BRAD classifies 2,500 business publications and directories into 213 categories, varying from accountancy through the environment to the wines and spirit trade. An advertiser wishing to reach a catering readership has a choice of 27 print vehicles. The total advertising revenue earned by consumer and business publications inclusive of trade and technical journals appears in Table 17.9.

Table 17.9   *Advertising revenue for magazines and periodicals.*

	£m	Percentage of total advertising expenditure
1982	456	14.6
1983	500	14.0
1984	561	13.8

Source: As Table 17.8

Consumer and business publications have a number of features of interest to marketers:

- unlike newspapers, which generally aim to appeal to all groups of people in a specific geographical area, magazines aim to appeal to specific groups of people throughout the country, or internationally; business travel magazines such as *Executive Travel* or *Business Traveller* attract a lot of hotel advertising; new hospitality products are often launched through the pages of the travel press; the *Travel Trade Gazette*, for instance, uses a lot of publicity material released by hotels and tour operators
- magazines have a longer active life than newspapers; therefore, an advertisement tends to work for a longer period
- they often accept full-colour advertisements
- they often use better quality paper than newsprint, giving improved reproduction
- advertisements are accepted on a per page basis, or part thereof
- preferred positions may be available at extra cost—e.g. outside back cover and inside back cover
- special facilities are often available—e.g. gatefolds (triple pages), booklet insertions, business reply-card insertions, double-page spreads with no white paper division between the pages (i.e. no 'gutter'), full pages with no white paper border (i.e. 'bleed' pages, the advertisement being bled to the edge) and choice of glossy paper or newsprint

Radio

Britain boasts 50 commercial radio stations and the number is growing. In addition, Radio Luxembourg is broadcast to British audiences. Rates vary according to the day, the time of day and length of commercial. Stations offer packages of spots—e.g. Piccadilly Radio in Manchester runs housewife, daytime and total-audience packages for advertisers wishing to reach these markets. Another popular package is the Drive Time (rush-hour) package. Discounts are made available to bulk purchasers. Advertisers spending £100,000 over a 365-day period with Radio Luxembourg, for example, qualify for a 20 per cent discount.

Radio is widely used to promote local trade for restaurants. The Grosvenor House Hotel, for instance, promoted its Pavilion Restaurant on Capital Radio. Advertisers wishing to use local radio to reach a national audience can buy network time through co-ordinating sales agents. The 2 main sales agencies are Independent Radio Sales Ltd and Broadcast Marketing Services Ltd. National television and press campaigns are often supported by radio. Stations commonly load spots adjacent to news broadcasts as preferred time spots; rates for sports events and specialised programmes are often negotiated.

Each station attempts to attract certain listener groups by adopting a format, or style, with a specific appeal. Most stations are able to provide full details of their audience appeal, hour-by-hour variations in listenership and assistance with production of commercials. Although commercial radio can be received in only 70 per cent of homes in the UK, the penetration of radio is at saturation level, many homes owning several sets. In addition, the in-car audience has recently assumed greater importance. Other advantages of radio are its low relative cost and its flexibility. Its disadvantages are its lack of visual appeal and its lifespan. Revenues from radio advertising are shown in Table 17.10.

Table 17.10   *Radio advertising revenues.*

	£m	Percentage of total advertising expenditure
1982	70	2.2
1983	81	2.3
1984	86	2.1

Source: As Table 17.8.

Television

Television is a highly powerful, dramatic medium which can deliver a common message simultaneously to very large audiences. Its main drawback is cost, and the true, inflation-adjusted, cost of buying television time is rising. Over 90 per cent of homes in the UK are equipped with television sets, two-thirds of them colour sets. Advertising aimed at the television viewer produced the expenditures, inclusive of production costs, shown in Table 17.11.

Table 17.11   *Television advertising revenues.*

	£m	Percentage of total advertising expenditure
1982	928	29.7
1983	1109	31.0
1984	1245	30.7

Source: As Table 17.8.

BRAD details data for 14 television stations (known as contractors) in the UK and Eire. These are Thames, London Weekend, Anglia, Central Independent, Granada, Link, TVS, Harlech, TSW, Border, Grampian, Scottish, Ulster and Irish. Each contractor has its own advertising sales department which handles accounts for both the Channel 4 and main regional television frequency. Thames Television, for instance, sells weekday time on Thames and Channel 4; and London Weekend sells weekend time on both channels. Rates vary according to time of day and length of commercial. The lowest basic rate for Thames at the time of writing is £365 for a 10-second commercial broadcast between 10 minutes past midnight and closedown. The highest basic rate is £20,720 for a 60-second commercial between 6.00 p.m. and 11.05 p.m.

However, these are only basic rates. A Thames advertiser wanting a *guaranteed* transmission spot has to pay a 75 per cent surcharge on basic rates, subject to the spot's availability. Fixed spots can be bought at lower surcharges, but these may be resold by the television company at a higher rate to any other advertisers. These spots are open to pre-emption. They are fixed in the sense that an advertisement will be transmitted in the agreed time segment, provided that no other advertiser offers a higher rate for the time spot. White comments, 'I have heard several attempts to justify this method of doing business, but none which succeeds in avoiding the suspicion that this is a highly opportunistic version of having your cake and eating it'.[22] Broad (or segment) spots are also open to pre-emption. The advertiser buys a spot in a given time segment but the contractor decides—sometimes in negotiation with the advertiser or his agency—in which particular break the commercial is to appear.

In addition to broad and fixed spots, contractors offer a wide variety of packages and discounts. Guaranteed audience packages promise to deliver a certain number of opportunities to see a commercial. Should the package fail to deliver, costs are adjusted accordingly. Spot packages are offered by television companies to advertisers who buy a certain number of spots, and discounts apply. Contractors may also offer run-of-day, run-of-week, run-of-month, run-of-campaign, or run-of-year schemes whereby, at a discounted rate, the contractor reserves the right to broadcast the commercial at any break during the chosen time segment. Filler spots, which are 10-second commercials, are offered by contractors to advertisers who are prepared to permit their commercials to be broadcast at any time to fill a gap in an otherwise complete break.

Special rates and facilities are usually available for advertisers making their first use of television, to those trading mainly in a chosen television area and those wishing to use the station's production facilities. Quantity discounts are also available for advertisers spending upwards of £1.5 million in the year. Some contractors offer discounts for advance (early) booking, new product launches, or test markets.

National television has been used by Kentucky Fried Chicken, THF and Grand Metropolitan. Regional campaigns have been run by hoteliers as large as Hilton International and as small as the 96-room Carlton Hotel in Great Yarmouth.[23]

The penetration of homes claimed by television contractors includes those located in overlap areas. Some homes are located in areas which can receive 2 or 3 signals from commercial stations. In practice, each or all of these contractors claim to deliver the overlap audience, despite the fact that in many cases television sets are not tuned in to all available channels. This introduces difficulties into campaign planning. Most advertising agencies, in comparing alternative budget allocations, will split the duplicated audiences 50:50 between adjacent contractors and triplicated audiences 33:33:33.

Cinemas

About 1.5 million people visit the cinema in an average week. The Cinema Advertising Association calculates that there are over 1,600 screens throughout the UK and an additional 187 in Eire. It is possible to buy access to an audience with a minimum 15-second commercial. Increments of 5 seconds up to 1 minute may be bought. It is also possible to tie in with television advertising by buying only in certain ITV areas. Break-outs by metropolitan county are also available. Local advertisers may only wish to buy a single screen, and this too is available.

All commercials in the UK are on film; some other countries have slide options. Stock films which are available from cinema advertising contractors' libraries can be bought and re-edited to include a personalised ending.

The cinema audience is heavily weighted at the younger end of the age-spectrum: 51 per cent are aged 15–24 (compared to 17 per cent of the national population). The upper social strata (ABC1) account for 53 per cent of attendances (compared to 39 per cent of the national population). Restaurants are frequent cinema advertisers. Cinema advertising expenditure fell to £16 million in 1984 (see Table 17.12).

Table 17.12   *Cinema advertising revenues.*

	£m	Percentage of total advertising expenditure
1982	18	0.6
1983	16	0.4
1984	16	0.4

Source: As Table 17.8.

Transport advertising

British Rail, bus companies, vans, taxis, the London Underground, ships and airports all offer advertisers space. British Rail offers station sites for posters and exhibitions/displays; on-train distribution; advertising on ships; at hoverports; the National Exhibition Centre in Birmingham; and buses. A special option is the 'colour bus' in which the entire bus is painted according to an advertiser's instructions. British Rail is also active in roadside hoardings and bridge spans.

Bus advertisers offer both internal and external sites. Underground advertising on station posters, escalator panels and tube car panels is managed by London Transport. Surcharges are payable for selected stations and lines.

Nationally, local authorities have made available their vansides as advertising media. Taxis have advertising sites available inside and outside the vehicles. Every passenger sea-line serving the UK makes space available to advertisers. In 1984 some £47 million was expended on transport advertising, compared to £36 million in 1982.

Posters

Hoardings are available in the UK at 180,000 sites either grouped along road and rail routes or solus. Solus sites, where a single hoarding is available, are fewer; the best are named 'Supersites' and are more expensive. Many of the best sites are committed under contract for some time ahead. The advertiser has a number of purchase options both in terms of poster size and locations.

The size of a poster is measured in sheets, a single sheet being 30 in × 20 in. This single sheet is called, contrarily, double crown. Normal sizes for posters are:

4 sheet   60 in × 40 in
12 sheet   60 in × 120 in
16 sheet   120 in × 80 in
32 sheet   120 in × 160 in
48 sheet   120 in × 240 in
64 sheet   120 in × 320 in

An advertiser can buy from a selection of ready-assembled packages, known as preselected campaigns (PSCs) or key plans. These are designed to reach certain audiences such as housewives or adults. If these are not suitable for a given advertiser's objectives, he can buy individual sites or groups of sites. This is known as line-by-line or site-by-site buying.

Rates vary according to site location, poster size and whether or not a package is bought; and with some contractors, the time of the year. Most contractors lease sites from land or building owners, erect poster panels and post bills once the space is sold. Contractors comply with standard trading conditions laid down by the British Poster Advertising Association.

Various attention-winning ploys can be used on hoardings: 3-dimensional effects, back-lighting, cut-outs, frontal illumination and reflective discs. The value of hoardings is directly related to their visibility. This, in turn, depends upon:

- length of approach; the longer the approach, the more exposed the audience is to the hoarding
- speed of traffic; some hoardings are aimed at pedestrian traffic, and others at car, bus, or train passengers—the slower the better
- the angle of the hoarding to the traffic; some hoardings are parallel to the traffic, some at right angles and others with parallel signs employ angled boards, so that the display is visible to traffic approaching from both directions
- presence of other posters; the more isolated a panel is, the more readily is it seen

Posters are popular with food service operators having premises on main roads. Copy, unless addressing a static audience as in a tube station, should be brief and bold. In 1984 £103 million was spent on poster advertising at hoardings, compared with £88 million in 1982.

Feature-advertising media

The term feature advertising is used to describe the minority media. Minority they may be in terms of revenue received, but there is an enormous variety: calendars, year planners and term planners; desk pads, pens and pencils; launderette sites; football programmes; rate demands; bus tickets; swimming-bath tickets; bookmarks; litter-bins; car-park tickets; envelope franking; bookmatches and matchboxes; programmable electronic signs; cricket grounds, football stadia and racecourse sites; supermarket trolleys; and parking meters!

Media development

A number of new developments are extending the conventional media mix; cable television, videotex or teletext and video cassette advertising are the leading developments.

Cable television
Penetration of UK homes by cable television is approximately 10 per cent but could rise substantially, given government support. In the USA cable television is received in 38 per cent of all homes, giving improved reception of conventional broadcast stations and access to several cable-only channels. Some cable television systems, notably QUBE, are interactive. The viewer can respond immediately to advertising using a key-pad. There has been experimentation with advertising-only cable television.[24]

Videotex/teletext
Teletext presents textual matter in alphanumeric and graphic form on the television

screen. Videotex extends this technology by combining teletext with the telephone network to provide 2-way communication between viewer and teletext data bank. The commercial television contractors offer advertising space in their teletext system. Oracle, the ITV system, has carried advertising for Thomas Cook.

Video cassette recorders (VCR)

Penetration of VCRs into British homes is expected to reach 70 per cent by 1990.[25] Television programmes recorded for later viewing normally retain advertisements; however, recent technological developments permit their omission during recording. Conventional television advertising rate structures are allied to viewership data. The advent of VCRs has presented a new set of measurement problems to audience researchers. Pre-recorded video cassettes are also carrying advertisements.

Media planning

Now let us return to the two problems we posed before describing the various media. First, whether to exclude any media from consideration, and second, which vehicles within each medium to select. These 2 decisions are generally made simultaneously:[26]

> The basis of sound media selection is dependent upon: (1) the people or market to be reached and (2) the nature of the message to be conveyed. Thus, facts about sales prospects are accumulated which may be generalised into a consumer profile. These target group data, along with the basic copy strategy and copy requirements, modified by any need for seasonal or geographical emphasis, and taking into account the size of the advertising appropriation, are analysed. This analysis is followed by a matching of the audience characteristics of various media with the market profile and by evaluating the adaptability of the physical format of the media to the copy requirements. Finally, through the exercise of judgement concerning the dimensions of coverage, reach, frequency, and ad size, the media plan emerges.

This description of media planning is based on American experience but it is also true of most European advertising agents' practice.

Media planning starts by evaluating the available media against the objectives, basic copy strategy and recommended execution of the campaign. The objects are to sort out which media are feasible, to pick the main medium, to help the media buyer (the person who actually buys particular spaces or times in the recommended media) prepare for purchase and to select supporting media if required.[27]

The criteria considered include the following:

Creative suitability

Advertising style (informative, persuasive, or confirmative), including the need for colour, coded coupons, demonstration, explanation, movement, sound, or long copy

Marketing considerations

Size and location of the market, market share, market dynamics (growth or decline), product (low or high involvement), level of distribution, channels of distribution, seasonal patterns, timing of buying decision, geographic differences, competitive advertising, the budget, and other promotional activities

Qualitative media differences

Atmosphere, quality, lifespan, style, consumer attitudes to the medium, context in which audience is exposed to the medium (home, work, or travel), or tone: 'The difference between print and television is the difference between Understanding and Experience. Print is linear; A is followed by B which is followed by C and so on. One sentence proceeds to another in orderly fashion. Print is rational; it engages the mind. We understand print; TV on the other hand, [is] a mosaic medium. It is both non-linear and non-rational. And the viewer participates in a non-rational way. We experience television';[28] in similar vein it has been remarked that newspapers inform, whereas television entertains[29]

Quantitative media differences

Several quantitative measures of a medium's suitability are employed; they are discussed in detail in the following section.

Media mathematics

The media planner's job is to achieve the campaign objectives by using media as cost effectively as possible. Consequently measures of media efficiency are widely employed. The fundamental concepts are *reach* and *frequency*.

Reach, also known as 'coverage', is the total audience delivered by a medium; in print reach equals readership, not circulation, since there is normally more than 1 reader per copy.

Frequency is the total number of times a member of the audience is exposed to the medium. Frequency is strategically more important than reach when purchase decisions are made at short notice, as is often the case with hotels. The term 'opportunities-to-see' (OTS) is used to describe the average number of exposures received by the audience.

Readership and television-audience data are available through JICNARS and BARB respectively (see Table 17.3). Multiplied together, reach and frequency indicate the total number of exposures (also known as gross impressions and total impacts) delivered by a medium.

If planners were only to use reach and frequency to make their recommendations, all advertisements would be placed in the same media. However, planners value some media more highly because

- they give access to a larger number of the target market; consideration of total audience figures alone could lead to wasteful media buying
- they give access to a larger number of heavy users of the product
- their qualitative characteristics give added impact to the advertisement
- campaign objectives make them intrinsically more suitable
- discounts make them more cost effective

Those media valued more highly are accordingly weighted when the cost of reaching the audiences is computed.

In principle, planners use the following formulae to compare media efficiencies before buying space. Formula 17.1 calculates the cost of each thousand exposures delivered by a medium:

$$CPT = \frac{\text{cost} \times 1,000}{R \times F} \qquad (17.1)$$

where CPT = cost-per-thousand exposures (also abbreviated to CPM)
         cost = cost of buying specific advertisement time or space
         R = reach
         F = frequency

Formula 17.2 calculates the weighted cost of the audience delivered by each medium:

$$WCPT = \frac{\text{cost} \times 1,000}{R \times F \times W} \qquad (17.2)$$

where $WCPT$ = weighted cost-per-thousand exposures
         W = weighting

By using formula 17.1 alone, two different media might deliver quite different audiences for exactly the same CPT. Only by applying the weight can a valid medium be selected. This principle is illustrated in the following expressions:

		Medium 1	*Medium 2*
(1)	*Unweighted CPT*	$\frac{£15.00 \times 1,000}{125,000 \times 2.0}$	$\frac{£25.00 \times 1,000}{200,000 \times 2.08}$
		$= £0.06$	$= £0.06$
(2)	*Weighted CPT*	$\frac{£15.00 \times 1,000}{125,000 \times 2.0} \times 0.75$	$\frac{£25.00 \times 1,000}{200,000 \times 2.08} \times 0.95$
		$= £0.08$	$= £0.063$

Therefore, because medium 2 is weighted more favourably than medium 1, it is more cost effective.

Computers in media selection

Computers are becoming more widely used in media planning; this is not surprising since the huge variety of media vehicles, rate structures, circulation data and weighting considerations have become extremely difficult to grasp.

The advertising agencies Leo Burnett and D'Arcy-MacManus respectively use BAR and BOAST media selection models. They generally allow the manipulation of media effectiveness and efficiency for the optimum allocation of advertising budgets.

17.11 MANAGING THE ADVERTISING FUNCTION: MEDIA BUYING

The purchasing of time and space in particular vehicles is called scheduling. Final decisions are made on the following.
1. Which media to omit from the schedule.
2. Which particular vehicles are to be used within each medium.
3. How many purchases of time/space to make.
4. When to place the advertisements.

There are 6 different types of schedules which can be used.
1. Steady pulse. Insertions occur at regular intervals throughout the advertising period. Suitable for transient accommodation.
2. Seasonal pulse. Insertions are made to vary according to seasonal purchasing periods. Suitable for resort hotels.
3. Periodic pulse. Advertisements appear in regular blocks at different times throughout the schedule.
4. Erratic pulse. As above, but the blocks occur at irregular intervals.
5. Start-up pulse. Heavy advertising at the beginning of the schedule, tapering off later.
6. Promotional pulse. Advertising is timed to coincide with sales promotions run by the marketer.

Which of these types of schedules is chosen is normally a matter for media planning staff to ponder in advertising agencies. They are likely to consider issues such as these:
- the objectives of the campaign. If the objective is to fill a coastal hotel during the shoulder season, then the seasonal pulse is self-evidently correct
- competitors' advertising schedules. If these are known, a small company may wish to avoid the period of time when the larger advertiser is spending; this produces an erratic pulse
- carry-over effects. On the assumption that the effect of a pulse is felt over the long-term, an agency may choose to open a campaign with heavy advertising (start-up pulse) to create a high level of awareness and then top up the awareness levels with erratic pulses at ever-longer intervals. It does appear that over-repetition of an advertisement can have adverse effects; one literature review concluded that: 'Repetition does not influence the retention of information content of a communication in any simple manner. While the usual effect is to increase retention in some circumstances, too frequent repetition without any reward leads to loss of attention, boredom and disregard of the communication'[30]
- habitual purchasing. If the advertising is intended to break habitual purchasing behaviour, it may be linked to a sales promotion campaign in a promotional pulse
- purchase frequency. When purchasers buy frequently, continuous advertising is necessary, especially if there is little brand loyalty
- number of trial purchasers. The greater the number of first-time purchasers in the market, the more regular should be the schedule, especially if no seasonal peaks exist
- the 'sleeper'-effect. This effect describes the eventual loss from memory of factual information, whereas evaluative or emotional information can be retained longer; the sleeper-effect suggests that if factual learning is required, regular pulsing is essential
- the 'threshold'-effect. Research has shown that there is a threshold below which advertising does not produce sales effects; the start-up pulse must cross the threshold
- diminishing returns. This is the opposite to the threshold-effect; as advertising volume is increased a point is sometimes reached at which the sales return per unit of advertising expenditure makes further advertising uneconomical—i.e. diminishing returns have set in
- media discounts offered for bulk purchases or purchase of packages of spots

- active life of the medium; newspapers generally have a persuasive life of 1 day whilst magazines are retained longer and television delivers an audience to the advertiser only fleetingly

17.12 MANAGING THE ADVERTISING FUNCTION: POST-TESTING METHODS, IMPLEMENTATION AND EVALUATION

This part of campaign planning requires the advertiser to choose how to measure the success of his campaign. (This topic was introduced during the earlier paragraphs on advertising objectives in section 17.5.) It is only against objectives that effectiveness can be measured. The 2 forms of effectiveness research which predominate will be discussed here:
1. Communications-effect research.
2. Sales-effect research.

Communications-effect research

Communications-effect research is used when objectives are of the 'learning' or 'feeling' variety. Tests of learning include:
- unaided brand recall; following Crest Hotels' 1984–5 campaign, unaided brand recall by the target audience rose to 45 per cent from a pre-campaign 4 per cent
- aided brand recall
- message comprehension
- recognition tests

Daniel Starch has developed a recognition test which is widely used. The Starch technique (available through Gallup in the UK) asks the following questions of readers.

'Did you see or read any part of this advertisement?' The responses are percentaged for the number of readers in the sample who have
1. 'Noted'—seen any part of the advertisement.
2. 'Seen associated'—seen or read anywhere in the advertisement the name of the product or service being advertised.
3. 'Read most'—read half or more of the written material in the advertisement.

'Noted', 'seen associated' and 'read most' scores have their own individual significance: first, as to the actual size of each score; second, as to the actual sizes of the scores in relation to one another; and third, as to their importance in relation to differing advertising objectives. These scores are of differing importance to advertisers depending on their objectives. When an advertiser's purpose is simple brand recognition, he will want to direct the reader's attention to the illustration and the headline. This is not thorough reading, but it has significance for the advertiser. 'Noted' and 'seen associated' are the most important readership measurements for this type of objective.

Tests for the 'feeling' objective include:
- intentions-to-buy surveys

- attitude studies
- surveys of brand preferences

Sales-effect research

The value of checking the sales effectiveness, rather than communications effectiveness, of an advertisement is reflected in this quotation:[31]

> When people praise a programme, they say things like: entertaining, informative, well-made, credible, sincere. A commercial however, may display shoddy workmanship, lack of intelligence, amorality, embarrassingly bad taste—and still be a 'good commercial'. The only criterion is: does it increase sales? Good is profitable.

Sales effectiveness can be measured either in a small-scale test market or in a full implementation of the campaign.

As with other forms of post-testing, it is necessary to use an appropriate experimental design to isolate the effects of the advertising. In addition to the sales effects of the advertisement, it may also be possible to obtain other behavioural indicators such as coupon response levels and written/telephone inquiries received from would-be customers and distributors.

Implementation and evaluation

The finished advertising material is sent to the media with instructions for insertion, and the marketer checks that the desired effects are achieved.

17.13 CHAPTER REVIEW

1. The British advertising industry is structured on similar lines to the American industry with advertisers and media-owners being brought together by advertising agents and other intermediaries.
2. Advertisers spent over £4 billion in 1984.
3. Managers of advertising make 10 interrelated decisions. These concern objectives, appropriation, basic copy strategy, execution, pre-testing, adjustment, media planning, media buying, post-testing, and implementation and evaluation.
4. Advertising objectives need to be phrased either in sales or communication terms and specifically define the target audience.
5. Objectives vary according to the type of product, the stage of the product life cycle and the product's position against competitors.
6. The appropriation is best decided upon after advertising objectives have been set.
7. Various methods of setting advertising budgets have been used: objective-and-task, percentage-of-sales, profits excess, matching competition and risk reduction.
8. Problems faced by budget-setters include inexperience, variations in costs of different media, interaction of advertising and other marketing mix variables, and the prediction of trade and competitive responses.
9. The primary task in developing basic copy strategy is to determine what the advertising is intended to communicate.
10. The execution of an advertisement translates the basic copy strategy into a form suitable for use in the chosen media.
11. Agencies often have their own philosophies to guide execution.

12. A well-executed advertisement is usually balanced, proportioned and harmonised in both copy and illustration.
13. Copywriters need to be knowledgeable about the product, the market and the type of purchase that the product represents for most of its customers—complex buying, dissonance reduction, variety seeking, or inertia.
14. The ASA and IBA impose standards on the content of copy. In essence, ads should be decent, legal, honest and truthful.
15. Advertisements can be pre-tested for communications and sales effects, the former by recall and comprehension tests and the latter in an experimental design. Testers can draw on technological assistance. After this, final adjustments should be made before the advertisement is placed.
16. Britain has the full set of advertising media, the most prominent being newspapers, consumer and business publications, radio, television, cinema, transport and hoardings. Cable television, teletext/videotext and video cassettes offer new advertising opportunities.
17. The 2 main media guides are BRAD (*British Rate and Data*) and the *Advertisers' Annual*.
18. Media selections are made following consideration of 4 main factors: creative suitability, marketing issues and the qualitative and quantitative differences between media.
19. Two media selection decisions are made: (1) which media types should be totally excluded from the schedule?; and (2) within the remaining media which vehicles are preferable?
20. Mathematically the better vehicles are those which deliver most cost effectively (in terms of CPT) the desired audience.
21. Media planners use reach and frequency to evaluate alternative media plans.
22. Weighting considerations are taken into account in media evaluation.
23. Computers are becoming more widespread in assisting media planners to make effective decisions.
24. An advertisement can be scheduled to appear in one or more of 6 ways: steady pulse, seasonal pulse, periodic pulse, erratic pulse, start-up pulse and promotional pulse.
25. Before the advertisement finally appears, the advertiser must decide how best to check that its objectives are achieved. Researchers investigate either communications or sales effects.

17.14 QUESTIONS AND EXERCISES

1. Clip an hotel or restaurant ad. What appears to be its basic copy strategy? How would you assess its execution?
2. Obtain a copy of BRAD. Calculate the CPT of a standard-sized ad in all motorcycling magazines. Say you owned a 4-star hotel in the Isle of Man and wanted to attract international celebrity riders to stay with you during the TT race meeting, what media weights would you attach to each advertising vehicle and why?
3. Write advertising objectives for:
   - a new themed restaurant.
   - a recently refurbished and upgraded 3-star hotel.
4. What classes of media would you exclude from consideration in the following cases, and why?
   - a national food service chain opening a new outlet in Leeds, Yorkshire.
   - a change of ownership for a Tandoori restaurant in Balham, South London.
   - the launch of a timeshare complex at Aviemore in the Scottish Highlands.
   - the introduction of a new corporate rate structure for a national hotel chain.
5. How are pre-testing and post-testing methods related?
6. How would you describe a 'good' advertisement?
7. Obtain a copy of the ASA's *Code of Advertising Practice*, and review it for issues particularly relevant to the hospitality industry.
8. How do the concepts of intangibility, inseparability, heterogeneity and perishability affect basic copy strategy, execution and media selection?

REFERENCES

[1] Advertising Association (1985), *Advertising Statistics Yearbook*.

[2] See Fisher, W. P. (1982) Choosing an advertising agency, in Fisher, W. P. *Creative Marketing for the Foodservice Industry: A Practitioner's Handbook*. New York: Wiley, 229–52, for a review of some important issues in advertising agency selection.

[3] Incorporated Society of British Advertisers (1980) *Survey of Agency Remuneration*.

[4] George, W. R. and Berry, L. L. (1981) Guidelines for the advertising of services, *Business Horizons*, **24**(4) July–August, 52–6.

[5] Nykiel, R. A. *Marketing in the Hospitality Industry*. London: CBI, 89.

[6] Grohmann, H. V. (1975) Ten keys to more successful advertising. *Cornell Hotel and Restaurant Administration Quarterly*, **22**(2).

[7] Ryan, C. (1980) The success of weekend promotions. *Hospitality*, January, 60.

[8] Corkindale, D. (1979) Putting budgets on the line. *Media*, March, 33–4.

[9] ibid.

[10] Gilligan, C. (1977) How British advertisers set budgets. *Journal of Advertising Research*, **17**(1), February, 47–9.

[11] See: First of the big spenders. *Hospitality*, September 1984, 2–3.

[12] See *Popular Food Service*, December 1983; and Seltz, D. (1977) *Food Service Marketing and Promotion*. Lebhar-Friedman Books.

[13] Learner, D. B. (1968) Profit maximization through new products, in Bass, F. M. *et. al. Application of the Sciences to Marketing Management*, New York: Wiley, 153.

[14] Lewis, R. C. (1980) Benefit segmentation for restaurant advertising that works. *Cornell Hotel and Restaurant Administration Quarterly*, **21**(3), November, 6–12.

[15] Ogilvy, D. and Mather (1978) Creative advertising that sells', *National Business Review* (New Zealand), 15 February, 12.

[16] Ray, M. L. (1982) *Advertising and Communication Management*. Englewood Cliffs, NJ: Prentice-Hall, 212–16.

[17] Reeves, R. (1961) *Reality in Advertising*. New York: Knopf.

[18] Ogilvy, D. (1963) *Confessions of an Advertising Man*. New York: Atheneum.

[19] Ogilvy, D. and Mather, (1978) op. cit.

[20] See Fuller, J. (1975) Sales promotion in hotels. I, external selling, in Kotas, R. (ed.) *Market Orientation in the Hotel and Catering Industry*. Guildford: Surrey University Press, 138–9, for advice on the execution of hotel advertising.

[21] *New Zealand Official Yearbook*, 1980.

[22] White, R. (1980) *Advertising: What it Is and How to Do it*. London: McGraw-Hill, 120–1.

[23] See: Ever tried local TV. *Marketing Monitor, Caterer and Hotelkeeper*, 25 May 1978.

[24] Yuspeh, S. and Hallberg, G. (1983) The radical potential of cable advertising. *Journal of Advertising Research*, **23**(4), August–September.

[25] ibid.

[26] Wright, J. S., Warner, D. S., and Winter, D. L. (1971) (3rd edn) *Advertising*, London: McGraw-Hill, 611.

[27] Broadbent, S. (1979) (3rd edn) *Spending Advertising Money*. London: Business Books.

[28] Bruce, D. (1978) TV: Let your pictures do the talking. *National Business Review* (New Zealand), 15 February, 18.

[29] Egbert, H. A. (1981) Newspapers: the bread and butter medium for hotel and restaurant advertising. *Cornell Hotel and Restaurant Administration Quarterly*, **21**(4) February, 34 ff.

[30] Hovland, C. I., Janis, I. L., and Kelley, H. H. (1953) *Communication and Persuasion*. New Haven, Conn: Yale University Press, 249.

[31] See: Ad nauseam, ad nauseam, NZ. *Listener*, 21 April 1979.

—18—

Selling and Sales Management

18.1 CHAPTER PREVIEW

This chapter starts with a definition of selling before considering who is involved in selling (all customer-contact staff) and what can be sold (both the organisation and its products). The roles of salesman and sales manager are described. The sales manager's job involves deciding upon salesforce size and structure; recruiting, training, controlling, supervising, motivating and evaluating sales staff; and designing the salespersons' job and remuneration system.

18.2 LEARNING OBJECTIVES

By the end of this chapter you should be able to:
1. Define selling.
2. Write an outline job description for a salesman.
3. Identify hotel and food service staff who have the opportunity to sell.
4. Describe the main functions of the sales manager.

18.3 INTRODUCTION

Selling can be defined as:

   Paid communication by an identified sponsor through a personal medium.

An equally sound explanation of selling is that it is an interpersonal confrontation where at least 1 party has the aim of influencing an exchange. A broad interpretation of 'interpersonal' would include telephone selling, a technique which is widely applied in hotel marketing.

   Selling differs from advertising by virtue of being personal and from word-of-mouth promotion by being paid. In the USA it is estimated that for every $2 spent on advertising, $5 is spent on selling.[1] A similar ratio in the UK would produce a national sales bill of £10 billion.

18.4 WHO SELLS?

Where products are intangible or service dominant, the customer's perception of service personnel assumes greater significance both in delivering satisfaction and in influencing brand choice and corporate image. Where the service provider and the service product are inseparable, as in the case of banking or dentistry, this is more pronounced. In hotels and food service the product is less service-dominant, there being the tangible dimensions of food, drink and accommodation to influence customer perceptions. None the less, service personnel still have an important role to play.

In the service sector generally, unlike manufacturing, customers come into contact with 2 classes of personnel: those whose primary job is to sell the service, and those whose primary job is to perform the service. Purchasers of conference facilities, for example, will meet with hotel sales management to negotiate terms and requirements but on the day of the conference will deal with reception, housekeeping and food service personnel. In some cases the service seller is also the service performer. Both groups are in a position to enhance customer satisfaction and help achieve marketing objectives.

Who sells? The answer is anyone who has customer contact. Even in organisations with no sales department, the selling function must be performed. When buying and consuming service products customers may have contact with a dozen or more personnel, only some of whom have formal responsibility for selling. Table 18.1 shows the degree to which selling is formally incorporated into job descriptions.

Table 18.1   *Who sells?*

Major responsibility for selling:	Sales and marketing director Sales manager Sales representative Hotel representative Travel agent
Moderate responsibility for selling:	Food and beverage manager Banqueting manager Front office manager Reception staff Table service staff
Minor responsibility for selling:	Chef Lift attendant Kitchen staff Chambermaid Maintenance engineer

Even staff with moderate responsibility for selling can be highly productive. For example, by suggestive selling—e.g. 'A bottle of Beaujolais would go very well with your beef, sir'—a skilled waitress could raise the total bill for a meal experience quite dramatically, as Figure 18.1 shows. Nearly £20 of potential revenue was lost because of missed selling opportunities. Table service staff can be trained to suggest additional items to accompany each major dish. For example, if the customer orders steak, the waitress suggests mushrooms; if a burger, a side salad is suggested; and if fruit pie, ice cream.

Sales staff can be classified in 2 other ways. Internal or external, employee or agent, as in Figure 18.2. The vast majority of hospitality sales staff are either internal employees or external agents. The former sell only their employer's products, are subject to contract of employment and are generally easier to direct and motivate.

	£
Actual bill for table of 4:	32.60
Missed sales opportunities	
Extra pre-meal drink × 4	3.20
1 additional low-calorie starter	0.90
Trade-up to higher-priced main course × 4	4.00
Wine sale	6.50
2 additional low-calorie desserts	3.20
Trade-up to Irish coffee × 4	1.80
Potential bill for table of 4:	52.20

Figure 18.1　Suggestive selling.

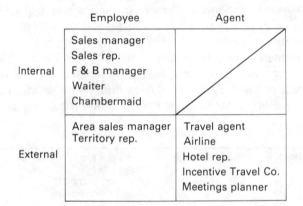

Figure 18.2　Classification of sales staff.

External agents, however, often sell competing products and are more independent of the hospitality company's influence.

Regarding what is sold, contact staff sell both the service organisation and its products. Directly, sales staff may be charged with responsibility for selling a given number of rooms or covers per month. Indirectly, through interaction with customers, all employees can sell their organisation. Consequently marketing management in high customer-contact service companies are very concerned with the interpersonal skills and customer orientation of all staff—whether having major or minor responsibility for selling.

18.5 THE SALES TASK

Many food service organisations take a passive view of selling, preferring to wait until a prospect calls them. Consequently function rooms remain underused. Managements who have profit responsibility should be actively seeking function, banqueting and meeting business.

The role and title of the salesperson varies between hospitality companies. In conventional family restaurants the salesperson is a waiter, whose basic role is to deliver food from kitchen to table; in fast-food service the seller is a counter assistant, whose role is primarily order-taking; and in banquet or function marketing the salesperson may be a departmental manager, whose main role is to advise on customer catering problems.

Whatever the title, sales staff perform 1 or more of the following tasks:

1. *Prospecting.* Prospectors find new sources of business.
2. *Information distribution.* Sales staff may provide oral information about forthcoming advertising campaigns, new products and sales promotions, or give literature to customers/prospects.
3. *Information acquisition.* Where marketing staff are office-bound or remote from the market-place, the salesperson can act as an intermediary, feeding back information about customer tastes or competitors' sales promotions and prices.
4. *Client service.* The salesperson may service the customer in a variety of ways which are not directly sales productive—e.g. advising on finance or helping to assemble a brochure.
5. *Selling.* The salesperson must be able to convert prospects into customers and maintain a long-term relationship, so that marketing objectives are achieved.
6. *Administration.* Planning sales calls, making out call reports and submitting of weekly/monthly summaries to management are essential tasks.

The types of task actually performed by salepersons are likely to vary according to the role of selling in the overall promotional strategy. In a 'pull' strategy advertising is used to influence consumer demand and the salesman may not have to prospect—i.e. he becomes more of an order-taker. Under a 'push' strategy the salesman may find himself cold-canvassing new prospects and concentrating on the selling, rather than the client service, task. The tasks of the salesman also vary according to the type of demand his company is trying to create. If raising demand, the salesman will attempt to prospect, open new accounts, create interest in the product, present benefits, demonstrate the product and improve sales through existing customers. Not all of these tasks would have equal priority. One job of the sales manager in these circumstances would be to establish whether new business selling or servicing of existing customers had priority. If trying to reduce demand, the salesperson would be involved in withdrawing sales literature and point-of-sale material; there would be no prospecting, no selling!

18.6 THE ROLE OF THE SALES MANAGER

Essentially the sales manager has only 1 job: that is to ensure his staff effectively and efficiently fulfil the role assigned to them in the promotional mix. But this job involves the manager in 7 tasks, as follows.

1. Determining salesforce size.
2. Determining salesforce structure.
3. Selecting sales personnel.
4. Designing the salesperson's job:
    - setting quotas
    - designing territories
    - identifying key accounts
    - providing sales aids

5. Training salespersons.
6. Devising remuneration systems.
7. Controlling, supervising, motivating and evaluating salespersons.
We shall examine each of these in greater detail in sections 18.7–18.13.

18.7 THE ROLE OF THE SALES MANAGER: SALESFORCE SIZE

For the small hotelier and most food service organisations, large or small, salesforce size is not a major issue. However, for large single-unit hotels (the London Dorchester has 3 sales managers, one having overall responsibility, the others being charged with international and commercial sales), national hotel groups, international hotel chains, hotel representative companies and hotel consortia salesforce size is a critical issue which affects both the cost and revenue side of the profit equation.

Fuller observes that the size of a hospitality sales organisation is determined by a number of influences:[2]

- magnitude of the hotel or catering operation
- financial limitations
- nature of sales—e.g. available space and facilities for group business and functions
- future plans for development and the timing of their implementation
- possibilities for reciprocity in bookings and recommendations (as in chains or hotel consortia)
- availability of outside sales service or representation

Although a number of techniques have been advanced, most companies appear to use variations of the workload method to establish salesforce size.[3] This method attempts to answer the question: how much selling can a representative accomplish over a specific period of time.

Work study has shown that the salesperson often spends time in unproductive ways. For instance, a territory sales representative will spend time on these activities:

- waiting to meet prospects
- selling to prospects
- eating
- travelling in car
- walking to and from car
- merchandising
- report-writing
- telephoning
- preparing for the sale
- prospecting
- relaxing

Time study will reveal how long is spent on each of these activities; motion study should show how the sales representative could improve his efficiency. Between them, time and motion studies enable the sales manager to determine how many calls a sales representative can make in the course of his working year.

The basic formula underlying the workload approach is as follows:

$$\frac{\text{Number of actual and potential customers} \times \text{call frequency}}{\text{Average daily call rate} \times \text{number of working-days per annum.}}$$

Its application is:

1. Classify existing customers according to their value to the company—e.g. by volume of business written or contribution to profit.
2. Establish the level of call frequency required in each class for sales objectives to be achieved, having obtained objectives from the marketing plan.
3. Calculate total number of calls on existing customers per annum (2 × 3).
4. Estimate number of new customers required to replace lost business or achieve growth.
5. Estimate number of prospects and calls required to generate new business.
6. Calculate total number of new business calls per annum.
7. Calculate grand total of sales calls (3 + 6).
8. Divide activity 7 by average daily call rate to calculate total number of sales personnel required.

An example showing how it might be applied in a hotel's corporate sales department appears in Figure 18.3.

Step 1 *Calculate total number of sales calls*

Customer category	No. of customers	Call frequency pa	Total calls
A over £50,000	20	12	240
B £25,000– £49,999	30	8	240
C under £25,000	60	4	240
D new business	60	8	480
		Total number of calls	1 200

Step 2 *Calculate number of working-days*

Days in year		365
less weekends	104	
holidays	15	
training	5	
sickness	5	
conferences/meetings	11	
	140	(140)
Working-days available		225

Step 3 *Estimate average daily call rate*
Average daily call rate = 3 (from time-and-motion studies)

Step 4 *Calculate number of sales staff*

$$\frac{1{,}200}{225 \times 3} = 1.78$$

Therefore, 2 sales staff are needed

Figure 18.3 Calculating sales personnel requirements.

The major weaknesses of the workload approach are its assumptions that the number of sales calls made is the major sales-producing factor (not the quality of the call); also that there are differences between customer classes, but no differences within classes; and that each salesperson can produce the same number of calls.

18.8 THE ROLE OF THE SALES MANAGER: DETERMINING SALESFORCE STRUCTURE

Having decided on the number of sales persons to employ, the manager now needs to decide how to deploy them. The main alternatives are to assign them by:
1. Geographical area.
2. Product or product group.
3. Customer type.

Geographical areas, called 'sales territories', are the usual basis for assigning sales personnel. The salesperson will be responsible for the sales of the full range of his company's products. This structure is suitable when the product mix is homogeneous and where there are no major demand differences between the customer groups. There are several advantages to this, as to both of the other ways of deploying salespersons. Advantages of territorial division of salespersons are:

- travelling time is reduced
- the salesperson becomes part of the local 'business scene' and might meet his clients socially, making the prospecting role easier
- it is easier for management to spot a weak salesperson because direct comparisons can be made—e.g. on the basis of sales per customer within the territory

The disadvantages are:

- when the company extends its product mix, the salesperson may find himself calling on prospects with whose needs he is not familiar
- many buyers like to deal with sales staff who know their particular problems; with a wide product range, the salesperson's product knowledge may be inadequate

Where a representative is assigned to the national sales of a special product or product group, these advantages are lost. However, the relative increase in product knowledge he experiences means that:

- he is more able to handle objections and answer questions and, therefore, much more likely to be able to close the sale
- he perceives himself as more of an expert; his self-esteem rises as his confidence in his product knowledge grows
- he is more able to convert product features into consumer benefits; it is a maxim of selling that consumers buy benefits, not features
- the sales manager often finds it easier to identify training needs where sales of specific products are weak
- sales representatives become more able to sell to expert members of the decision-making unit

Disadvantages of sales staff being organised on a product basis are:

- more costly travel as the representative attempts to open new accounts and service his existing clients

- several salespersons working for the same company may call on the same prospect; this is particularly likely where the hospitality company is diversified into a wide range of products; the buyer may well interpret this as a sign of inefficiency

The third form of salesforce organisation is by customer group. In this case each representative sells all the company's products but only calls on specific customer groups. Customer groups may be segmented by the following factors.

1. Industrial classification—electrical appliance manufacturers or food processors.
2. Account size—large or small accounts.
3. Age of account—existing accounts or new business.
4. Company—in some circumstances one salesman or indeed a team may represent a supplier to a particularly large customer.

The special advantages of this method are:

- the representative quickly becomes conversant with his customer's decision-making process, and finds out who are the members of the decision-making unit
- the representative may become regarded as an industry consultant who is able to identify and resolve problems
- as new industries emerge the salesforce can be expanded without disruption to other sales staff

Disadvantages are:

- travel costs can be exceptionally high if the customer group served is not concentrated geographically
- the advantage of product knowledge is lost where the product mix is extensive

In fact many companies have variations on each of these 3 themes. Combinations are commonplace; for example, a representative may sell the complete range of hospitality products—rooms, banquets and conferences—to a limited number of customers within a specific territory.

18.9 THE ROLE OF THE SALES MANAGER: SELECTING SALESPERSONS

Hospitality sales representatives are less well paid than their counterparts in other sectors. In 1983 one estimate claimed that a typical f.m.c.g. sales representative cost his employer £18,000 per annum in salary, bonus, commissions, expenses and perks, whereas a capital goods salesperson cost £30,000 per annum.[4] Most representatives in the hospitality industry cost substantially less than the lower of these 2 figures.

None the less, sales representatives are valuable assets and the best are likely to move between employers at levels of remuneration equalling those of the capital goods salesperson. A successful sales representative can make a major contribution towards the achievement of corporate and marketing objectives, whereas a bad representative can irreparably damage customer relations. Consequently great care should be exerted when selecting sales staff.

There are 2 alternatives open to the sales manager. He can advertise and recruit the salesman himself, or he can employ an outside agency to do the same. An outside agency will normally charge a fee based on a percentage (normally between 9 and 13 per cent) of the salesman's expected first-year income. This procedure is often swifter and cheaper than the manager's advertising and interviewing applicants himself. Which of these alternatives is chosen depends upon the relative costs of each, and upon the confidence that the manager has in his own ability to select good salesmen.

In practice, recruitment is a systematic process comprising 7 steps as follows.

1. Writing the job description. This should incorporate details of job title, sales, or other objectives; duties and responsibilities; remuneration structure, reporting requirements; and method of evaluation.
2. Writing the personal profile. An attempt should be made to describe the ideal candidate for the job.
3. Recruiting candidates.
4. Shortlisting the better applicants from their application forms.
5. Interviewing and testing the shortlist.
6. Checking references.
7. Offering the position to the best applicant.

But how can a sales manager predict who will make a good sales representative?

There have been 3 major approaches to this problem:

- the traitological approach
- the sales formula approach
- the dyadic approach

The traitological approach associates sales success with individual differences in personality (sociable, aggressive, or extrovert), education, intelligence and appearance. One effort to identify key traits in intangibles sales staff mentions imagination, drive and self-management.[5] Coffman believes successful hotel sales staff have the following traits: courtesy, deportment, conservative appearance, product knowledge, willingness to work and personality.[6]

Reid suggests that successful food service salespeople possess the following traits:[7]

- Spirit of hospitality; courtesy, tact and concern for people
- Appearance; conservative dress is preferred
- Product knowledge; banquet menus, room sizes, dates and times available, etc.
- Determination
- Above-average commonsense and personality

Apart from the ambiguity of many of these terms, the major assumption and weakness of this approach is that it only considers 1 party in the sales interaction—the salesperson. The prospect is seen as a puppet responding to strings pulled by the representative.

The sales formula approach associates sales success with the behaviour of the salesperson during his presentation; AIDA (attention–interest–desire–action) is typical of the formulae proposed as the key to success. Salespersons who know how to progress their prospects sequentially through the 4 stages are viewed as likely to be more productive. Again the major weakness of this approach is that it assumes a simple stimulus–response relationship between seller and buyer.[8]

The dyadic approach is fundamentally different. It highlights the interaction between seller and prospect. The foundations of this approach were laid by Mayer and Greenberg.[9] They have proved (to their own satisfaction, and to that of several clients for whom they have worked) that a successful salesperson needs only 2 attributes. He needs:

- a high level of empathy with the customer

• a strong ego-drive

According to the authors, a seller with high empathy[10]

> senses the reactions of the customer and is able to adjust to these reactions. He is not simply bound by a prepared sales track, but he functions in terms of the real interaction between himself and the customer. Sensing what the customer is feeling, he is able to change pace, double back on his track, and make whatever creative modifications might be necessary to home in on the target and close the sale.

The second basic quality, ego-drive, makes the salesman 'want and need to make the sale in a personal or ego way, not merely for the money to be gained. His feeling must be that he has to make the sale; the customer is there to help him fulfil his personal need'.

Figure 18.4 shows how these 2 attributes combine to produce different types of salesmen. The 'bulldozer' and the 'nice guy' can both sell, but the bulldozer will build no long-term relationship with his prospects and the nice guy will only sell because people befriend him. The worst salesperson scores low on both empathy and ego-drive, whereas the top salesperson scores high on both dimensions. The authors claim to have produced a battery of tests which, if administered during the selection process, cannot be faked and can predict which applicant will be a successful salesman. Mayer and Greenberg also believe that it is extremely difficult to develop these 2 traits in trainees, and that it is better to recruit staff in whom both qualities are present.

	EMPATHY	
	Low	High
Low	The worst salesman	Nice guy
EGO DRIVE		
High	Bulldozer	Top salesman

Figure 18.4   Classification of Sales Staff.

A recent development of the dyadic approach regards the good salesperson as being an expert negotiator, one who is able to interactively resolve a prospect's demands and proposals with concessions and counterproposals, so that both parties perceive mutual benefits in the transaction.

18.10 THE ROLE OF THE SALES MANAGER: DESIGNING THE SALESPERSON'S JOB

The fourth task of the sales manager is to design the salesperson's job. We have already in this chapter listed the 6 main elements of that job—prospecting, information distribution, information acquisition, client service, selling and administration. Sales managers generally are involved in setting sales quotas, designing sales territories, identifying key accounts and providing sales aids.

1. Setting sales quotas

A quota is a salesperson's required contribution towards total sales volume—his personal sales target. Most representatives are set sales quotas. The field sales staff, regional managers and general sales manager may meet annually to set these targets, which are normally the minimum acceptable sales volumes (but may be maxima). If a representative is not rewarded for exceeding his quota of sales with either bonus or commission, then his sales productivity is likely to cease when he meets the quota. A solution to this problem is to operate a sliding scale of commissions or bonuses, so that higher productivity over and above the minimum is met with higher rewards.

2. Designing territories

Territory designers need to produce sales areas which, by virtue of their size and shape, are
- serviceable—all categories of accounts must have their needs met; a territory which is too large to service properly will result in calls not being made on prospects who could be profitable customers for the company
- provide equal-earnings opportunities to sales representatives—if sales quotas are more easily exceeded in a particular territory, there is sure to be dissatisfaction in others if this results in unreasonable differences in earnings
- require approximately the same labour input from the salesman.

3. Identifying key accounts

Key accounts, those which are especially important, can be defined in a number of ways:
- major present accounts; these are major customers to whom sales are substantial, in comparison to the cost of servicing the account
- major potential accounts; these are accounts which at present may be unproductive, but which offer good prospects for the future
- opinion-leading accounts; these are accounts which may be either small or large in their own right, but which have considerable influence on the purchasing of other accounts

The importance of key accounts is that they offer the opportunity for high sales at relatively little cost. New salespersons can not hope to identify key accounts in their own territories without help. The sales manager and the territory's former representative are ideally placed to help the new recruit avoid offending important customers or losing goodwill.

4. Providing sales aids

The sales manager should be able to provide leadership and guidance on selling matters. It is his job to equip his team with the tools for them to satisfactorily service their territories.

Sales aids include:
(a) lists of prospects, or guidance about how to obtain prospects. THF identify the following sources of prospects: directories such as *Kompass* and *Dunn & Bradstreet*; regional development boards; trading estate directories; local and

national newspapers and trade magazines; chambers of commerce; and the local town hall.[10]

(b) details about product features and their associated consumer benefits. The salesman should be able, during a presentation, to ascertain what benefits are important to the prospect, and point out or demonstrate them by reference to features.

(c) information which will help the salesman to identify the prospect's problems and needs and the relevant benefits which will meet these needs. This should enable the salesman to become a good problem-solver.

(d) aids to help the salesman present the product benefits, such as
   - case histories of satisfied customers
   - introductions which gain the prospect's attention and raise his interest

(e) demonstration aids such as floor plans and sample menus.

(f) aids for handling objections and closing the sale. A good sales manager should be able to tell new recruits what objections to expect and how to handle them. Equally, techniques for closing the sale should be provided by the sales manager.

(g) aids which help in administration. Record cards detailing the prospect/customer's address and phone number, contact name, members of DMU, previous sales, preferred call day and time and special needs must be designed by the manager.

18.11 THE ROLE OF THE SALES MANAGER: TRAINING SALESMEN

It is the responsibility of sales management to ensure that sales-volume targets are met by the salesforce, and this often requires training. Due to the high costs both of laying off poor sales personnel and recruiting new salesmen, it is frequently wiser to invest in training. Such training can take one of 2 forms—either the salesman is subjected to training which improves his performance in the sales confrontation, or his sales-support skills are improved. Included in these 2 forms of sales training are the following.

Sales confrontation training
This includes:
- how to approach a prospect
- how to present the product's benefits
- how to demonstrate the product
- how to anticipate and handle objections
- how to negotiate
- how to use bargaining tactics
- how to close the sale[11]

Sales support training
This includes:
- how to find prospective customers and sources of prospects, and how to weight them significantly for the company
- how to prepare for the sale by inquiring about the prospect and his needs prior to the confrontation

- development of product knowledge in order to increase confidence and enable the seller to negotiate with even the most knowledgeable customer
- improvement of communication skills—both from the point of giving information (talking, phrasing and speech-making) and receiving information (listening, attending and responding)
- improving administrative skills—such as record-keeping and report-writing
- improving knowledge about human behaviour—i.e. about how attitudes are formed and how they can be changed; and about motivation, personality and the many other aspects of human behaviour which can influence selling results
- improving knowledge about the company and its systems, so that orders may be efficiently obtained and processed
- improving knowledge about competitors' strengths and weaknesses

18.12 THE ROLE OF THE SALES MANAGER: DEVISING REMUNERATION SYSTEMS

There are several forms of remuneration systems for salesmen. They include:
- salary only
- commission only
- salary plus commission or other incentive

Commission is defined as:[12]

> payment which varies according to the level of achievement of sales, either by the individual or by a group of salesmen.

Commission is only one of 3 types of financial incentive which may be part of a salesperson's remuneration. The others are general bonus and incentive bonus. A general bonus is:[13]

> usually related to the profitability of the company and is often paid, not only to salesmen, but to all eligible employees in the company.

Marriott Hotels operates such a scheme.

An incentive bonus is:[14]

> directly linked to the efforts of the salesman or group of salesmen.

It may be paid for performance against quota, sales value, gross margin, profit on sales, or opening new accounts. A survey of 85 staff in 10 British hotels showed 16 to be on a productivity bonus or incentive scheme, 9 in a profit-sharing scheme and 3 on an annual bonus scheme.[15]

Incentives can be offered to the bellboy who sells most dry cleaning/laundry, the waiter who sells most wine and the telephone operator who sells most room service, in addition to those with major responsibility for selling. Incentives need not take the form of money: public recognition of performance, travel vouchers, free weekend accommodation, invitations to the hotel floor-show, or gifts can be equally effective. Intercontinental Hotels rewarded staff in 9,000 USA travel agents with a coupon allowing 2 nights' free accommodation at any American unit.[16]

A salary-only remuneration system has a number of benefits. First, management can change the nature of the selling task, by requesting more non-selling duties be performed, without affecting salesmen's income. Second, it is a far cheaper system to operate, not incurring the clerical or computing costs of commission-based systems. However, sales skills and performance go unrewarded, a greater supervisory burden is placed on management and competing companies who operate commission systems may attract the best sales staff. Some hotel representatives operate on a retainer-plus-commission basis, the retainer being equivalent to a salary.

A commission-only system often produces the 'bulldozer' type of salesperson, who is reluctant to perform his non-selling duties. Sales staff under this system may feel insecure because they lack the reassurance of a regular income. Additionally, good salesmanship often involves building a long-term relationship with clients; this is not encouraged by a commission-only system. It is difficult to estimate commission costs of selling at the beginning of the budget period. It is not widely used in the hospitality industry because (1) a high proportion of sales is repeat business (according to Horwath & Horwath, between 30 and 50 per cent of hotel guests are repeaters);[17] and (2) it is frequently impossible to identify individuals responsible for making a sale. The system does have a number of points in its favour—the incentive to sell is at a maximum, so it is particularly useful for a firm wishing to take advantage of a fast-growing market and productive sales personnel tend to feel they are well rewarded, whereas the less effective are more likely to quit.

Commission rates vary between companies in a number of dimensions:

- different rates for different products, in recognition that some products require more sales effort, time, or skill
- different rates for different customer types, especially when the sales potential of a new group of prospects is being explored
- different rates for new business selling, especially when the company wants to expand its number of customers
- different rates for different territories
- different rates for different account sizes

Methods for payment of commission also vary between companies—e.g. quarterly payments, monthly payments, payment on invoice, twice yearly, annually, on receipt of payment, or on receipt of order. Together with salary, commission, bonus and expenses, some hospitality companies offer fringe benefits—e.g. life insurance, pensions, medical insurance and paid holidays.

A survey of British hotel workers in 1982 identified 39 different forms of fringe benefit. The most common was meals on duty; the least common benefit was a car. Other employees were offered discount holiday schemes, travel expenses, or a Christmas bonus.[18]

The best form of remuneration scheme, it has been reported, incorporates the following features.[19]

1. A basic salary, which provides a significant proportion of total earnings and which is high enough to attract the right staff and provide an adequate sense of security and loyalty to the company.
2. Incentive elements, which should be related solely to the selling skills and achievements of the salesperson. The incentive element should only be influenced by factors or conditions over which the salesperson has control.

3. The incentive should be high enough to reward extra effort and achievement.
4. The time-lapse between receipt of the incentive and actual achievement should be as short as possible.
5. The system should be as simple as possible and easily understood by the staff.

The final choice of remuneration system must result in sales effort being directed towards areas which are profitable for the company, in the stimulation of a consistently high level of sales performance, and in the attraction and retention of a high-quality sales team.[20]

18.13 THE ROLE OF THE SALES MANAGER: CONTROLLING, SUPERVISING, EVALUATING AND MOTIVATING

Control and supervision of salesmen are necessary in order to ensure the following.
1. Individual quotas are met.
2. Total sales targets are achieved.
3. The salesperson's problems are identified and solved.
4. The total sales effort and direction is consistent with company policy and objectives.
5. The sales aids and training provided by the manager are being properly and effectively used.
6. The salesman is making productive and efficient use of his time.

When evaluating an individual salesperson or a salesforce, a number of factors need to be considered. The list below, suggested by Robinson and Stidsen,[21] consists of 3 criteria—the salesperson's physical activity, his adaptive behaviour and his instrumental performance.

(a) *Physical activity or efficiency*:
- number of calls made?
- how much time spent with prospects?
- how much company money did the salesman cost?
- how many orders did he produce, and at what value?
- how many miles did he travel?
- how many new accounts were opened?

(b) *Adaptive behaviour*:
- can he change his selling style according to the needs of different customer types?

(c) *Instrumental performance*:
- does he need much supervision?
- has he worked out ways of handling objections?
- how many closing techniques does he know?

In evaluating the performance of a salesforce as opposed to an individual, with the aim perhaps of making intercompany comparisons, the manager might consider the following points: whether sales targets have been met; the number of new accounts opened or competitors' accounts taken; whether market share has been improved; whether special target markets have been penetrated as desired; the costs of running the salesforce; the relative costs of salaries, commissions and bonuses; whether there has been a high turnover of staff; whether there is satisfaction with sales management's performance and supervisory style; whether a growth in the number of sales staff has been matched by a parallel increase in sales; and whether or not the career aspirations of salespersons are being met.

As can be seen, there are a host of ways of evaluating both salesmen and salesforce. The critical point is that evaluation of a salesperson should be in line with what was expected of him originally. It is damaging to admonish him for irregular reporting if he was not informed that this was part of his sales duties. Equally, there is little value in evaluating either individual or salesforce unless such evaluation, if it shows unfavourable results, indicates appropriate remedial action.

Some sales representatives will be highly productive regardless of the conditions under which they work; others will need motivating to achieve a satisfactory level of performance. Motivation is an important supervisory job for sales management.

According to Smallbone,[22] a general explanation for a salespersons's performance is:

$$P = M(A + K) \tag{18.1}$$

where P = performance
  M = motivation
  A = ability
  K = knowledge

and M, in turn, can be explained by:

$$M = I - Di \tag{18.2}$$

where I = incentives
  Di = disincentives

To motivate sales staff management must, therefore, maximise the incentives and minimise the disincentives.

Motivation is a major area of investigation for organisational psychologists. Herzberg's work is of major significance.[23] He distinguishes between factors which provide satisfaction to employees, and thus motivate high performance, and those which do not. Major motivators identified are:

- sense of achievement
- recognition
- the work itself
- responsibility
- opportunities for personal growth and advancement

Major demotivators identified are:

- company policy and administration
- supervisory standards
- inadequate salary
- poor working-group relationships
- poor working conditions
- job security

Motivation is drawn from the job itself, whereas demotivation stems from the job context or environment.

To apply these principles Herzberg recommended the following: remove some controls over employees whilst retaining accountability; assign the employee a complete unit of work; create additional authority for the employee (job freedom); improve employee access to management; introduce more challenging tasks; and assign employees specific tasks which enable them to become experts.[24]

In one survey of sales representatives the factors shown in Table 18.2 were identified as contributing to job satisfaction.[25] The table lends support to Herzberg's contention that job content is the major source of satisfaction.

Kotler suggests that management can influence salesforce morale and performance through its organisational climate, sales quotas and positive incentives.[26] Organisational climates which hold sales representatives in high esteem, give opportunity for advancement and provide supportive supervision are more effective. Sales quotas are normally either high or modest for the entire salesforce, although some companies, recognising the individual motivational differences between representatives, will set high targets for some and modest targets for others.

Table 18.2 *Contributions to salesperson's satisfaction.*

	Percentage of respondents mentioning
The challenge of selling	41
The sense of freedom	41
Pride in the product	41
Interest in the product	36
Variety of the job	36
Amount of responsibility	32
Type of customer	27
Promotion prospects	9
Company reputation	5
Pay	0

18.14 CHAPTER REVIEW

1. Selling is paid communication by an identified sponsor through a personal medium.
2. The aim of all selling is to influence an exchange.
3. In service-dominant markets the sales person, rather than the product, may become the focus of the customer's attention.
4. Any person with customer contact can sell.
5. Sales staff can be classified by degree of formal responsibility for selling, location (internal/external) and status (employee/agent).
6. A salesman's job has 6 principal parts: prospecting, information distribution, information acquisition, client service, selling and administration.
7. The sales manager commonly faces the following decisions: how many salesmen to employ; how to structure them; and how to select, train, pay and control/supervise/evaluate/motivate them. He also has to design the salesman's job.
8. The main technique for determining the size of the salesforce is based upon the workload of a typical salesperson.
9. The 3 most common ways of deploying salesmen are to allocate them by geographical area, product, or customer. Mixes of these 3 approaches are possible.
10. There have been 3 approaches to the selection of sales staff. The traitological approach, the sales formula approach and the dyadic approach.
11. Research has shown that a good salesperson has 2 main characteristics—that he is high on empathy and high on ego-drive.
12. The manager is generally held responsible for devising the salesperson's job—setting sales quotas, designing territories, identifying key accounts and providing sales aids.
13. Sales training takes 2 forms: training in skills to be used in the sales confrontation, and sales support skills.

14. Sales remuneration systems take 3 forms: salary only, commission only, or salary plus commission or other incentive. Each has its own advantages and disadvantages.
15. One system for evaluating individual salesmen takes account of their physical activity, their ability to adapt selling approaches and their instrumental performance.
16. Management must motivate sales staff by maximising incentives and minimising disincentives.
17. Motivation is drawn from the job itself, whereas demotivation stems from the job context or environment.

18.15 QUESTIONS AND EXERCISES

1. Why does the intangibility of service products make the service provider a more important instrument of customer satisfaction?
2. Draw up a list of criteria which you would use to evaluate the performance of a hotel salesperson.
3. Are empathy and ego-drive enough to make a good hospitality salesperson? Give reasons for your answer.
4. Write a job description for a group business salesperson stationed in a 6-unit hotel group's head office.
5. Is there a role for a function salesperson in a fast-food restaurant company such as Wendy's? Give reasons for your answer.
6. What do you understand by the following expression?
$$P = M(A + K)$$
Break down each component in the formula.
7. Do you favour salary only, commission only, or other incentive as the preferred method of remuneration for:
   - Hotel representatives?
   - Wine waiters?
   - The sales director of a family restaurant chain?
   - The owner-manager of an independent 2-star hotel?
   If incentives are involved, what form should they take?
8. Should sales quotas be generally set high and challenging or low and achievable? Why?

REFERENCES

[1] Kotler, P. (1984) (5th edn) *Marketing Management: Analysis, Planning and Control.* Englewood Cliffs, NJ: Prentice-Hall, 674.
[2] Fuller, J. (1975) Sales promotion in hotels. I, External selling, in Kotas, R. (ed.) *Market Orientation in the Hotel and Catering Industry.* Guildford: Surrey University Press, 127.
[3] Kingwell, P. (1974) Sales force size and allocation: progress in the application of quantitative methods, in Shapiro, S. J. and Chebat, J. C. (eds) *Marketing Management: Readings in Operational Effectiveness.* London: Harper & Row, 163–69.
[4] Lidstone, J. (1983) Putting force back into sales. *Marketing*, 22 September, 29.
[5] Young, J. R. and Mondy, R. W. (1982) (2nd edn) *Personal Selling: Function, Theory and Practice.* London: Dryden Press, 61.
[6] Coffman, C. D. (1970) *Marketing for a Full House.* Ithaca, NY: Cornell University Press, 183–84.
[7] Reid, R. D. (1983) *Food Service and Restaurant Marketing.* London: CBI, 266.
[8] This is still at the heart of THF's sales training, for instance: 'To achieve success involves an understanding of the four main segments of persuasive communication (AIDA).'
[9] Mayer, D. and Greenberg, H. M. (1964) What makes a good salesman. *Harvard Business Review*, July–August, 119–25.

[10] THF's sales training manual for Plaza Hotels.
[11] See Greene, M. (1982) *Marketing Hotels into the 90s*. London: Heinemann, for discussion of some interesting closing techniques as well as comment on telephone and face-to-face selling generally.
[12] See: Methods of remunerating salesmen: a survey of 197 companies. Information Summary No. 146, British Institute of Management, London, March 1970.
[13] ibid.
[14] ibid.
[15] Johnson, K. (1982) Fringe benefits. *Hospitality*, June, 2–6.
[16] See: Marketing and media. *Caterer and Hotelkeeper*, 13 September 1984, 148.
[17] Horwath & Horwath Ltd (1984) *UK Lodging Industry 1984*.
[18] Johnson, K. (1982) op. cit.
[19] See: Methods of remunerating salesmen, op. cit.
[20] Smallbone, D. (1971) *How to Motivate and Remunerate your Salesmen*. London: Staples, presents a wide-ranging discussion on the relative merits of different remuneration schemes.
[21] Robinson, P. J. and Stidsen, B. (1967) *Personal Selling in Modern Perspective*. Boston, MA: Allyn & Bacon, 227.
[22] Smallbone, D. (1971) op. cit.
[23] Herzberg, F., Mauser, B., and Snyderman, B. (1959) *The Motivation to Work*. New York: Wiley.
[24] Herzberg, F. (1968) One more time: how to motivate your employees? *Harvard Business Review*, January–February.
[25] Smallbone, D. (1971) op. cit., 57.
[26] Kotler, P. (1984) op. cit., 694–95.

Sales Promotion, Direct Mail and Sponsorship Management

19.1 CHAPTER PREVIEW

This chapter discusses 3 promotional tools: sales promotion, direct mail and sponsorship. First, sales promotion is defined and the main management decisions investigated—i.e. budgeting and the design, implementation and evaluation of individual sales promotions. Choosing from the dozens of sales promotion techniques necessitates a clear understanding of their application and strengths and weaknesses. Second, direct mail is defined, together with its advantages and disadvantages, and the 2 key factors in its success—the mailing-list and the print piece—are investigated. Finally, sponsorship is defined and its uses and limitations noted. Management decisions about sponsorship objectives are introduced, together with the choice of activities to sponsor, the budget, contractual terms and evaluation.

19.2 LEARNING OBJECTIVES

By the end of the chapter you should be able to:
1. Define sales promotion, direct mail and sponsorship.
2. Produce a shortlist of sales promotion techniques for solving tactical promotional problems.
3. Describe the main decisions which sales promotion managers make.
4. Identify the principal advantages and disadvantages of direct mail and sponsorship.
5. Define the qualities of a good mailing-list.
6. Describe how to choose between sponsorship options.
7. Identify the main sources of cost in both direct mail and sponsorship.

19.3 INTRODUCTION

The 3 subjects of this chapter—sales promotion, direct mail and sponsorship—are not easy bedfellows. They differ, in that they have their own applications, strengths and weaknesses. Yet they are similar in 2 ways: none of them involves the purchase of time or space in media owned by others, which makes them dissimilar from advertising; nor do any of them involve face-to-face interaction between promoter and customer, which makes them dissimilar from personal selling. Sales promotion is examined in section 19.4; direct mail in section 19.8; and sponsorship in section 19.9.

Sales promotion may be defined as:

any behaviour-triggering temporary incentive aimed at consumers, channel members, or sales personnel.

A few words of explanation are required. Sales promotion (SP) is generally used to achieve 'doing' objectives. However, the behaviours triggered by SP extend beyond purchasing alone. Consumer behaviours include sending for information, asking for a representative to call and picking up a brochure. Channel member behaviours include recommending the promoted hotel, using point-of-sale material and attending a seminar. Salesforce behaviours include selling a promoted line, prospecting for new business and calling on a targeted group of customers.

Sales promotions are very rarely used to achieve 'learning' or 'feeling' objectives. However, learning may be incidental to purchasing—e.g. a sales promotion for a themed weekend break will obviously only succeed if customers process promotional information. Also attitude development may be a consequence of product experience. The term 'temporary', used in the definition, can be stated arbitrarily as a period not longer than 9 months. Beyond this period promotions run the danger of becoming an expected part of the product and losing their incentive value.

19.4 MANAGING SALES PROMOTION

Sales promotion—whether run at unit, area, or group level—needs managing. The responsible individual is usually a sales manager, marketing manager, or advertising manager. In exceptional circumstances a sales promotion specialist may have control.

Whoever manages, the following decisions have to be made
1. How much of the overall promotion budget to allocate to sales promotion.
2. Of this allocation, how much to devote to promotions for consumers, channel members (trade promotions) and sales personnel.
3. Planning individual sales promotions—i.e.
     • identifying target audiences
     • specifying objectives
     • generating sales promotion ideas
     • screening ideas by costing them and estimating probabilities of success
     • executing the chosen promotional idea
     • timing its implementation
     • implementation
     • evaluation of effectiveness

Each of these decisions will be examined in sections 19.5–19.7.

19.5 MANAGING SALES PROMOTION: BUDGETING FOR SALES PROMOTION

Sales promotion is big business. Estimates suggest that expenditure on SP exceeds that on advertising. But how are individual budgetary decisions made?

Sales promotions have a special contribution to make towards marketing objectives under certain conditions, as follows.

1. Where there are low-involvement products.
2. Where products are not well differentiated.
3. Where channel members list or display only a fraction of the products available. Thomas Cook, the multiple travel agency, for instance, only gives shelf-space to 120 travel products, whereas independents may display well over 300.
4. Where total market demand is static.
5. Where impulse buying is prevalent.
6. Where an hotel or restaurant is operating below capacity.
7. Where there is intense oligopolistic competition.
8. Where there is a high proportion of marginal customers.

Under these conditions SP warrants a bigger slice of the promotional budget.

In principle, the 'marginal productivity' rule should be used to determine the sales promotion budget. In practice, however, because of difficulties in applying the principle, a number of rules-of-thumb are substituted. Most companies set their promotion budgets in the light of predetermined marketing objectives. Consideration is then given to expenditure on long-term (advertising) and short-term promotion (sales promotion).[1] Some companies feel their products can only bear a limited number of sales promotions in a year; others keep to a predetermined percentage of sales.

Three major weaknesses of SP budgeting practice have been identified.[2]

- failure to consider SP's cost effectiveness
- widespread use of simple rules-of-thumb such as a predetermined percentage of sales or a fixed ratio between advertising and SP
- advertising and SP budgets being prepared independently

It is recommended that management apply an objective-and-task approach such as the following.

1. Establish sales objectives.
2. Identify communication/promotional problems facing the product.
3. Assign gross budget for solution of problems.
4. Identify all potential solutions, including selling, advertising, merchandising, PR and sales promotions.
5. Estimate costs of alternative promotion mixes.
6. Estimate incremental sales arising from each promotional mix.
7. Adopt most cost-effective mix.
8. Assign proportion of budget to sales promotion as determined by stage 7.

19.6 MANAGING SALES PROMOTION: APPORTIONING THE BUDGET

This decision calls for SP priorities to be established. How much should be spent on consumer, channel member and sales-staff promotions respectively?

One difficulty is that the ideal SP is often a tripartite assault on consumer spending. First, the salesforce must be motivated to sell to channel members (known as selling-in); second, channel members must be motivated to display point-of-sale material, stock and persuasively sell the product. Third, consumer purchasing must be triggered directly.

Whilst the tripartite view of SP is accurate for products using channel intermediaries, a high proportion of hospitality products, especially in food service, are sold direct to customers, thus making trade sales promotions redundant. However, if indirect channels are employed, SP priority normally goes to channel and salesforce promotions in order to *establish* distribution. Once established, the emphasis transfers to consumer promotions (known as selling-out). Some marketers leave a proportion of their SP budgets to meet contingencies. For example, if hotel room bookings are lower than forecast, SP can be used at short notice to lift occupancy.

19.7 MANAGING SALES PROMOTION: PLANNING INDIVIDUAL SALES PROMOTIONS

Identifying the target audience

As noted in the definition of SP, there are 3 main audiences: the consumer, the channel member and the salesforce. Audiences can be defined even more tightly: 'independent American business travellers' gives much clearer guidance for the selection of SP ideas than 'hotel guests'.

Specifying objectives

Objectives in SP derive from promotion objectives which derive, in turn, from marketing objectives. They take many forms:
1. Obtaining trial of new or existing products.
2. Generating repeat purchasing.
3. Increasing frequency or volume of consumer purchase in the short run.
4. Reducing inventory levels.
5. Getting prospects to visit a location.[3]
6. Obtaining wider distribution.
7. Encouraging display.
8. Correcting a seasonal imbalance.
9. Undermining competitive promotions.
10. Stimulating brand switching.
11. Motivating prospecting by salesforce.
The objectives must also state the duration of the SP.

Sales promotion is predominantly used to achieve tactical objectives because management by and large believes that long-term changes in consumer behaviour cannot be brought about through SP: 'There is a growing body of evidence that companies who switch their marketing expenditure exclusively [to sales promotion] make temporary gains in volume at the expense of permanently undermining their brand image and the loyalty of their most regular buyers.'[4]

Generating sales promotion ideas

There are a huge variety of sales promotion techniques. Table 19.1 identifies the most common.[5] Each has its own applications, advantages and disadvantages.

For example, consumer trials, free premiums, money-off discount vouchers and free samples are particularly potent. To obtain repeat purchasing free premiums on surrender of continuous coupons, or competitions and self-liquidating premiums requiring proof of purchase, are preferable.[6] What is appropriate depends upon the promotion's objective, target audience, the available budget and competitive sales promotion (see Table 19.2).[7]

Table 19.1 *Sales promotion techniques.*

1 *Consumer sales promotions*
Competitions
Free premiums (gifts) with purchase
Free mail-in premiums
Free premiums on surrender of continuous coupons
Self-liquidating premiums ('gifts' at reduced prices; consumer pays reduced price and usually surrenders proof of purchase)
Money off
Discount vouchers (coupons)
Free samples
Package deals (e.g. rail/accommodation packages at advantageous single price)
Bonus deals (e.g. double room for price of single)
Charity promotions (e.g. Olympic tie-in)
Personality promotions

2 *Trade promotions*
Competitions
Free samples
Gifts
Coupons
Bonus offers
Push money (special payments for giving extra sales effort to a product)

3 *Salesforce promotions*
Commission rates
Special bonus
Sales contests
Points schemes

Consumers generally prefer promotions which offer:
● something free
● instant gratification
● convenience
● no long-term commitment

The most popular forms of food service SP are free samples, free premiums and money off.[8]

Both legislative and voluntary controls apply to sales promotion. Legislative controls include the Consumer Credit Act 1974, the Fair Trading Act 1973, The Lotteries and Amusements Act 1976, the Trading Stamps Act 1964 and the Unsolicited Goods and Services Act 1971. Voluntary controls are administered by the sales promotion subcommittee of the Code of Advertising Practice Committee, which issues the *British Code of Sales Promotion Practice*. Its basic principles are that:

all sales promotions should be legal and should conform to the principles of fair competition . . . they should deal fairly and honourably with the consumer. In particular, as far as the consumer is concerned the terms of any offer should be clear and honest and its administration should be swift and efficient.

Table 19.2   *Advantages and disadvantages of 5 sales promotion techniques.*

Advantages	Disadvantages
Competitions	
Attract publicity	May require advertising support
Generate excitement	Finding suitable prizes
Costs predetermined	Administration of entry forms
Free premiums	
Flexibility	Costs depend on uptake
Encourages repeat purchase	May require advertising support
Popularity	Existing customers also benefit
Money off	
Immediate benefit to customer	Only deep cuts are effective
Cost predetermined	Non-selective: all customers benefit
No consumer effort required	Easy to copy
Free Samples	
Immediate benefit to consumer	Very expensive
Encourages trial	Wasted on existing customers
No consumer effort required	Administration
Self-liquidating premiums	
Flexibility	Supplies of premium
Breaks even financially	Administration
Encourages repeat purchase	Consumer effort/cash required

The code operates general rules of conduct relating to integrity, protection of privacy, safety, children and young persons, presentation, the quality and suitability of goods, the worth and value of claims, the terms of the offer and administration. Specific rules of conduct are applied to free offers, prize promotions, charity promotions and trade promotions.

Screening

There are normally a number of sales promotion solutions to a given problem. The job of screening is to help select the optimal solution. Costs and probability of success are the 2 key criteria.

For some promotions costs are known in advance. The costs of a competition include the following: prizes, packing/postage for prize distribution, administration, judge's fees, advertising of promotion and results, printing of entry forms, dispensers and point-of-sale material and incentives to participating channel members and sales staff. The cost of a promotion such as a free mail-in premium are unknown—it depends entirely upon the number of customers mailing in their proofs of purchase to obtain the free gift. Uptake can vary between 1 and 50 per cent of consumers, depending upon the nature of the target audience and the attractiveness of the premium.

The probability of success can be estimated in 3 ways.
1. Comparisons with similar promotions in similar markets. Successful sales promotions tend to be copied or modified by competitors. An example is the hotel Executive Club; THF was not the first company to introduce such a scheme. However, they recently launched the Premier Club; 80,000 Premier Club 'passports' were mailed out to business travellers. Every time a club member stayed at a THF

hotel the passport was stamped. Free premiums were awarded to those who collected 15 stamps (2 nights free in a THF hotel), 30 stamps (weekend break for a couple) and 60 stamps (5-night touring holiday for a couple). The collector of the largest number of stamps won a sports-car. Many hotel groups including Swallow and Crest run similar schemes, despite plagiarism and lack of creativity being major causes of SP failure.[10]
2. Consumer rankings. Members of the target audience can be asked to rank the attractiveness of the alternatives.
3. Market test. A small-scale, regional implementation of the alternatives.

Execution

Suppliers of promotional materials now need to be briefed. The larger hospitality companies employ specialised sales promotion agencies or consultancies to generate and execute ideas. The client's role is to brief, then direct and control, the agency. Most agencies are well connected and obtain competitive quotations for supply of promotional materials such as premiums, prizes and print.

Timing the promotion's implementation

This issue is often decided by the objectives; for example, to raise occupancy to 75 per cent in the early season shoulder month would require a promotion to be launched, at the latest, 2 months before the first promotional guests book in. Given the tactical nature of SP, promotions are often introduced at short notice for immediate implementation.

Measuring effectiveness

An SP which achieves its objectives is effective. If the objective of opening 20 new accounts is achieved, the promotion is a success. Success can be measured experimentally and by undertaking consumer surveys.[11] A prize-winning SP by London caterers Hotstuff had as its objective the generation of leads for Hotstuff staff to follow up. Four butlers and four maids, in full uniform, called on identified prospects and handed out truffles in return for business details. Over a 10-week period 816 leads were generated, 230 brochures were mailed out on request and Hotstuff sales staff converted 71 prospects into customers.[12]

19.8 DIRECT MAIL

Direct mail (DM) is defined as postal communication by an identified sponsor. It is also nicknamed, inaptly, advertising by post. It is particularly useful for achieving 'learning' and 'doing' objectives, although it may take a series of planned mail shots to do so. A single mailing may be inadequate.

Post Office estimates show that DM is growing. Over 1.25 billion items were direct-mailed in 1984 at an estimated total cost, inclusive of postage, of £324 million. It is not known what proportion had hospitality origins (see Table 19.3).

Table 19.3   *Direct mail expenditure.*

	1982	1983	1984
Volume (millions of items)	1 102	1 084	1 262
Mail-order origins (millions of items)	333	264	276
Other origins (millions of items)	769	820	986
Postal expenditure (million pounds)	120	112	121
Total expenditure (million pounds)	341	299	324

Source: Advertising Association *Advertising Statistics Yearbook* (1985)

Direct mail offers considerable advantages to the promoter:[13]
- selectivity. Messages can be tailored to suit target readerships from one person upwards
- personalisation. Word processors, computers and advanced printing techniques can produce mail shots which address individuals personally
- limited competition. Although DM is becoming more popular, postal deliveries do not produce the promotional noise found in broadcast or press advertising
- fewer mechanical restrictions. Size, length and colour are unrestricted
- convenient scheduling. Deliveries and production have total flexibility
- ease of response. Many mail shots include return postcards, envelopes, or coupons
- ease of measuring effectiveness. Response rates can be used to evaluate effectiveness. Response rates vary. Whereas a mail shot to prospective independent restaurant guests would be deemed a success if producing a 2.5 per cent response rate, a professionally interested audience, such as conference organisers, should respond in greater numbers to a mail shot in their area of competence

However, there are a number of disadvantages:
- mailing-lists. A well-designed print piece mailed to the wrong person or address is utterly wasted. Contemporary, accurate mailing-lists are essential for DM success
- 'junk mail' image
- mail-shot content needs creative, eye-catching design and may need to employ specialist expertise
- cost. Postage, printing, paper, copywriting and list compilation or purchase can be costly. Lists are normally sold on a per 1,000 names basis
- postal regulations regarding size, weight and content

Direct mail has many potential applications and, in consequence, is widely applied by hospitality marketers. It can be used to build room or F&B sales, to generate inquiries, to make special announcements (e.g. restaurant refurbishment), to supply information (e.g. mailing brochures to potential channel members), or to acquire information (e.g. guest surveys). The 2 key factors in successful DM are the list and the print piece. A poor print piece mailed to a top-quality list may be productive, whereas a poor list simply wastes resources.

The list

Lists for DM can be compiled internally or acquired from external agents, known as list brokers. Hospitality companies, particularly hotels, are in a very strong position to produce repeat business by direct mail. Guests' registration details are a valuable asset. Food service operations are less well endowed.

List sources include the following: guest register, inquiry file, club memberships, school and college directories, travel agents, directories, trade magazines, exhibitions, credit card companies, Yellow Pages, Chambers of Commerce, the electoral roll, professional association membership, hotel representatives, car-hire firms, magazine subscriptions, tour operators and marketing research organisations (e.g CACI, which sells the ACORN list). The buyer acquires rights to use, rather than retain, lists available through brokers. Prices vary according to the list's exclusivity; costs of compilation; demand; standards of completeness, accuracy and contemporaneity, and response rate. Up-to-date, exclusive lists with a proven high response rate are more expensive to buy. Many list brokers have connections with direct-mail specialists, having expertise in print piece design and production, and envelope addressing, stuffing and distribution. Lists date very quickly. Up to 20 per cent redundancy occurs annually due to removal from the area, retirement, or death. Consequently lists need regular purging, correcting and updating. It is generally possible to assess the quality of a list by mailing a randomly selected sample prior to full-scale use.

The print piece

Because DM is used for many purposes, the contents of mail shots vary considerably, including letters, postcards, birthday/Christmas cards, questionnaires, brochures, vouchers, free gifts and magazines. Sometimes a number of non-competitive organisations share a single mail shot.

Most mail shots consist of 4 print pieces: the envelope, letter, brochure and return card or return envelope. Response rates improve when a number of simple rules-of-thumb are followed.[14]

1. Envelopes with provocative copy/illustrations stand a better chance of being opened.
2. Personalise the letter.
3. Use conversational and credible copy. Retain the letter reader's interest.
4. Remember the cover of a brochure is just like the headline of a print advertisement. Four-fifths of readers never progress beyond it. Keep copy brief and succinct. Use illustrations.
5. Build promises into brochure copy. Focus on claims and proofs.
6. Pre-code return items. Keep them functional and simple to complete. Use Freepost or reply-paid envelopes.

The AIDA (attention–interest–desire–action) formula is widely recommended for mail-shot copywriters.

Managing direct mail

As with other components of the promotion mix, direct mail needs to be planned. This involves identifying DM opportunities; establishing priorities, target audiences and objectives; budgeting; deciding upon timing; assigning responsibility for execution; and selecting methods of evaluation.

The Dorchester Hotel's 1984–5 marketing plan called for 8 mail shots at a total cost of £15,500. Amongst the audiences were Dorchester guests, chief executive officers in the top 300 Australian companies and all 12,000 names on Regent International Hotels' mailing-list.

19.9 SPONSORSHIP

Sponsorship may be defined[15] as:

> the material or financial support of some activity, usually sports or the arts, with which the sponsor is not, in the normal course of his business, associated.

It is of growing significance in hospitality marketing. Table 19.4 list some recent sponsorships. Sponsorship takes a variety of forms: international/national/local, series/event/team/individual, and sports/arts/environment/community interest.[16]

Table 19.4   *Hospitality sponsorship activities.*

Company	Sports	Involvement
Tennants Breweries	6-a-side indoor soccer	£47,000
THF	Ladies' golf	£40,000
Beefeater Steak Houses	Equestrian	£25,000
Happy Eater	3-day-eventing	Financial support; own horse: Jolly Eventer

Sponsorship provides a number of benefits:[17]
- media coverage. The company/brand name obtains media exposure in editorial matter. If measured by cost-per-thousand, sponsorship sometimes makes more efficient use of promotional resources than advertising
- customer relations. Invitations to attend the sponsored event can be issued to key customers/prospects
- community relations can be enhanced by local sponsorships—e.g. take-away food service operators sponsoring rubbish-bins
- employee morale may be lifted.
- provision of promotional opportunities—e.g. linkages to advertising or selling points for representatives

The major management decisions for sponsorship are:
- setting objectives
- deciding what to sponsor
- budgeting for sponsorship
- negotiating the sponsorship contract
- evaluation

Setting objectives

Sponsorship objectives derive from overall promotional objectives which, in turn, derive from marketing objectives, and should lend themselves to evaluation. Sponsorship is more suitable for achieving 'learning' and 'feeling' objectives than 'doing' objectives. Examples are:

1. Raise brand awareness.
2. Improve the corporate image.
3. Increase goodwill amongst channel members.

Deciding what to sponsor

Sponsorship deals either arise from approaches by activity organisers or from formal search for suitable activities by a potential sponsor. Many sponsorship opportunities are presented to marketing management and they need to be carefully considered against a set of criteria such as these:

1. Does it already attract television, press, or radio coverage?
2. What sort of exposure would be obtained?
3. Does the activity's image match the sponsor's?
4. Would coverage reach the target audience?
5. Would it contribute to promotion objectives—and cost effectively?
6. Can the sponsor's name be incorporated into the title?
7. Is the activity's management efficient and professional?
8. Would the sponsorship be exclusive?
9. Could sponsorship be integrated with other promotional activities?
10. What financial commitment is required? Over what period?

Budgeting for sponsorship

Sponsorship costs include the following: prizes; provision and erection of display materials; wages/salaries of employees at the event; hospitality to guests; administration charges; travel; advertising of the sponsorship; and costs associated with evaluation.

Negotiating sponsorship contract

Large-scale sponsorships are usually undertaken under binding contractual terms. Local or community sponsorships are less formal. Contracts should specify mutual expectations, financial obligations and the terms of the arrangement.

Evaluation

Evaluation is undertaken to find out if sponsorship has achieved its objectives. Experimental designs are preferable. However, informal evaluations are often undertaken. Crude measurements—e.g. the number of column centimetres reporting the event; the number of seconds the sponsor's hoardings are visible on television; the number of visitors attending the event; and the number of mentions of the sponsor's name in press reports—are often used in lieu of more formal evaluations.

19.10 CHAPTER REVIEW

1. Sales promotion is any behaviour-triggering temporary incentive aimed at consumers, channel members, or sales personnel.

2. Sales promotion is generally used to achieve 'doing' objectives.
3. Many companies use simple rules-of-thumb to set their SP budgets.
4. There are over 2 dozen SP techniques, each having its own applications, advantages and disadvantages.
5. Originality and creativity are major factors in SP success.
6. Consumers prefer promotions which offer something free, instant gratification, convenience and no long-term commitment.
7. Sales promotion ideas should be screened for costs and probability of success.
8. The effectiveness of SP can be assessed experimentally or through consumer surveys.
9. Direct mail is defined as postal communication by an identified sponsor.
10. The major advantages of DM are its selectivity, personalised appeal and the ease with which its effectiveness can be measured. Its disadvantages are the difficulty of obtaining good-quality mailing-lists and its 'junk mail' image.
11. The quality of the mailing-list and the standard of the print piece determine the effectiveness of direct mail.
12. Sponsorship is defined as the material or financial support of some activity, usually sports or the arts, with which the sponsor is not, in the normal course of his business, associated.
13. Sponsorship is used for 'learning' or 'feeling' objectives.
14. The main criterion in selecting sponsorship opportunities is the media coverage attracted to the activity.
15. Large-scale sponsorships are usually subject to contract.

19.11 QUESTIONS AND EXERCISES

1. What role could sponsorship perform for:
   - a high-street take-away outlet?
   - a private hospital?
   - a chain of 3-star hotels?
2. Do activities such as Crest's Frequent Guest programme, which last longer than 9 months, still retain their status as sales promotions, or do they lose their impact?
3. What factors, other than originality and creativity, are likely to contribute towards SP success?
4. Scan the trade press and collect examples of SP objectives. Are they expressed in terms of learning, feeling, or doing? Does their phrasing suggest ways in which they could be evaluated?
5. Go through Table 19.1 and come up with applications in the hospitality industry.
6. Why is direct mail so popular in the hotel industry? Could other promotional tools perform the same function as cost effectively?
7. Produce a set of criteria to judge the quality of a mailing-list.
8. What is the difference between sponsorship and patronage?
9. As owner-manager of an independent coastal hotel you have been asked to sponsor:
   - one cricket match for the local team.
   - a team of marching girls aged 6–16.
   - a swimming marathon in aid of Help the Aged.
   - the World Tiddlywinks championship.
   How would you select which, if any, of these sponsorships to undertake?

REFERENCES

[1] Christopher, M. G. (1972) *Marketing Below-the-Line*. London: Allen & Unwin.
[2] Strang, R. A., Prentice, R. M., and Clayton, A. G. (1975) *The Relationship between Advertising and Promotion in Brand Strategy*. Cambridge: Marketing Science Institute.

[3] Thistle Hotel's recent promotion pursued this objective; see Upton, G. (1984) Thistle in promotion first. *Marketing*, 22 November, 5.

[4] See: *A Guide to Consumer Promotions*. London: Ogilvy, Benson & Mather, n.d.

[5] ibid.

[6] See Williams, J. (1984) Picking the winners. *Marketing*, 26 April, for a review of the applications of each technique.

[7] *A Guide to Consumer Promotions*, op. cit., defines each sales promotion tool, cites its advantages, disadvantages and essentials for success, and costs and the decisions to be made by the sales promotion manager.

[8] Axler, B. H. (1979) *Food Service: A Managerial Approach*. Lexington, MA: D. C. Heath.

[9] See Advertising Standards Authority (1980) (3rd edn) *British Code of Sales Promotion Practice*. London: ASA, March.

[10] Spillard, P. (1975) (2nd edn) *Sales Promotion*. London: Business Books, 198–201.

[11] ibid., 217–46.

[12] See: Guinness's pint size champion (Sales Promotion supplement). *Marketing*, **16**(13), 29 March, i–iv.

[13] Reilly, R. T. (1982) Rediscovering direct mail: a primer for hospitality firms. *Cornell Hotel and Restaurant Administration Quarterly*, **23**(1), May, 45–51.

[14] Compiled partly from recommendations in Mass, J. (1980) Better brochures for the money. *Cornell Hotel and Restaurant Administration Quarterly*, **20**(4), February, 21–34; Blomstrom, R. L. (1983) Strategic marketing planning in the hospitality industry. Education Institute of AHMA, 267–73; and Coffman, C. D. (1970) *Marketing for a Full House*. Ithaca, NY: Cornell University Press.

[15] Unlike patronage, which may be similarly defined, sponsorship is undertaken in return for commercial benefit.

[16] Compiled from: Happy Eater's £30m 5 year expansion. *Caterer and Hotelkeeper*, 1 May 1984, 10; see also *Marketing*, 18 April 1985, 12, 21 March 1985, 12 and 21 February 1985, 12.

[17] Incorporated Society of British Advertisers (1984) *Guide to Sponsorship*. London: ISBA.

—20—

Merchandising

20.1 CHAPTER PREVIEW

This chapter investigates the management and techniques of non-personal promotion at the point of sale. It starts by defining the term 'merchandising', then moves on to examine the purposes for which merchandising can be used and how and why it works. The main part of the chapter describes the application of merchandising techniques in the hospitality context, and it ends with a discussion of merchandising planning.

20.2 LEARNING OBJECTIVES

By the end of the chapter you should be able to:
1. Define merchandising.
2. Describe 20 different types of merchandising stimuli.
3. Explain why and how merchandising works.
4. Distinguish between 3 categories of product merchandisable in hospitality establishments.
5. Identify merchandising opportunities.
6. Follow a step-by-step approach to merchandising planning.
7. Write merchandising objectives.

20.3 MERCHANDISING DEFINED

Merchandising is:[1]

> any form of behaviour-triggering stimulus or pattern of stimuli, other than personal selling, which takes place at retail or other point of sale.

Self-service retailing is the field in which merchandising skills are at their most sophisticated, whereas their application in the hospitality industry is not yet fully developed. The stimuli may take various forms, as shown in Table 20.1. Furthermore, they may be intended to evoke behaviour singly or through their combined and cumulative impact.

The term 'merchandising' is one which is attributed a variety of meanings in the marketing literature. It is used to describe many activities. Hughes defines it in the context of retailing as:[2]

> the selection and promotion of goods to meet the needs of the market.

Table 20.1 *Hospitality merchandising stimuli.*

Fascia-boards	Electronic broadcasters
Display cards	Place mats
Posters	Tent cards
Directional signs	Brochures
Displays of food and drink	Lighting
Tabletop	Illuminated panels
Menu	Restaurant layout
Bulletin boards	Open/shut signs
Drink mats	Price tickets
Information packs	Door cards

Elvy describes it as:[3]

> all those sales promotion activities which aim to generate the customer's interest in the product or service other than conventional press and television advertising or the use of public relations.

In wholesaling and retailing it is used to describe the selection and buying process as well as promotion at point of sale. A similar interpretation in hospitality would include the selection and purchase of the fixtures, fittings, foods and beverages which, when combined, provide customer satisfaction.

However, in a marketing management sense, our first definition is a truer reflection of its meaning. Merchandising is non-personal promotion at the point of sale; it has the aim of motivating behaviour in the short term; in hospitality this could include ordering room service, phoning for a taxi, drinking in the bar, or booking a dinner table.

Hospitality merchandising is also known as 'cross-selling', 'in-house selling', 'cross-advertising', 'in-house advertising', 'criss-cross selling' and 'internal promotion'. Strictly speaking, these terms are inaccurate. Merchandising is neither selling—it uses non-personal means of communication—nor is it advertising—it does not involve the purchase of time and space in media vehicles owned by others. The term 'internal promotion' is so broad that it encompasses both personal selling and merchandising.

20.4 MERCHANDISING OBJECTIVES

Every customer is a business opportunity. In retailing, once a shopper has entered a store, his movement around the store and his shopping behaviour is determined in large part by the way in which the retailer has planned the physical environment. The retailer attempts to convert patronage into sales by stimulating purchasing behaviour. So it is in hospitality. A hotel's guest is a business opportunity. If a guest books in for 2 nights at £30 per night and pays a £60 bill on departure, the hotel has failed to capitalise on the opportunity. Similarly, in catering if a café customer buys a drink but no food, then the opportunity for making that incremental sale has been missed.

Advertising, public relations, direct mail and personal selling can be productive in delivering customers to hospitality outlets, but once delivered, merchandising takes on an important role in creating sales. Sales volume, as we have seen, is the product of multiplying the number of customers by their average expenditure. Merchandising's primary task is to improve the average expenditure per customer.

The hotel guest could be subjected to merchandising stimuli, persuading him to dine in the hotel's restaurant, drink in the hotel's bar, hire a videotape for in-room entertainment, relax in the jacuzzi, play squash in the hotel's club and purchase souvenirs from the hotel's shop. Furthermore, once in the restaurant, the guest is stimulated to purchase the food which produces the best profits; in the bar he is encouraged to drink high-margin beverages and in the shop he is subjected to the merchandising techniques which are so expertly applied by many self-service retailers.[4]

Merchandising objectives can be specific or general. Specific objectives can be set for:
1. Departments. A food and beverage department may be expected to increase average spend from, say, £9 to £10 per cover.
2. Products. The bar may be expected to sell 10 per cent more cocktails, or the restaurant 20 more desserts per day.

General objectives can also be set. One hotel analyst believes that for the Ritz Hotel (London) to achieve a 15 per cent return on investment, given a 70 per cent occupancy level, it needs to take £130 per room let per day. Given a room rate of £60, merchandising would have to stimulate £70 of incremental sales. It is a simple task to gather sales data; however, to attribute the cause of sales movements to merchandising is rather more complicated as it requires an experimental design which controls the impact of all other variables.

What of merchandising's role in welfare catering? We have seen that merchandising stimuli are used to evoke immediate behaviour. The welfare caterer could use merchandising to:
1. Encourage staff to patronise the works canteen more frequently.
2. Stimulate consumption of foods with high nutritional value.
3. Promote a reduction in alcohol consumption by factory workers at lunchtime.

Merchandising does have a behaviour-stimulation role in welfare catering but its applications appear less well understood than in the commercial sector.

20.5 HOW MERCHANDISING WORKS

There is no established body of knowledge about the mechanics of merchandising, but commonsense suggests that successful merchandising employs 3 tactics to generate sales. Readily recalled through the mnemonic ASDA, they are A = accessibility, SD = sensory domination, A = appeal. Products which are accessible sell better than those which are not. *Accessibility* can be enhanced in a large number of ways: room service, self-selection wine displays, racks of newspapers, multiple access to restaurants, car-parking facilities and vending machines all serve to enhance accessibility.

The 4 main *senses* through which merchandising stimuli are received are sight, hearing, smell and touch. If a product can gain the attention of a prospective consumer by dominating 1 or more of these senses, it is more likely to be bought. Displays, mobiles, signs and posters are all intended to draw the consumer's eye. In-hotel discothèques attract custom by relaying music into public assembly areas; ice-cream vans tinkle 'Greensleeves'; and a department store entices lunchtime shoppers to dine out by broadcasting recorded announcements over its public address system. Sound sells! Smell and touch are particularly important in catering—the smell of roasting coffee, the sweet bouquet of fresh herbs and spices, the delicious aroma of the chargrill, or the texture of an avocado pear and the firmness of tomato can all contribute to sales.

Appeal in merchandising occurs when the consumer feels aroused by the stimuli and motivated to buy. Such motivation can function at a physiological level. For example, demonstration of food preparation methods may arouse the hunger drive. Learned motives, such as the need for achievement or affection, also can be aroused through appropriate communication at the point of sale. In psychological terms the merchandiser must cue behaviour—i.e. employ an external stimulus (the cue) to arouse a need; this, in turn, creates tension which is reduced through purchase and consumption.

One recent attempt to explain how merchandising works draws heavily on the science of environmental psychology.[5] The science of environmental psychology (EP) is concerned with the effects on man of physical and social environments. Typically it has dealt with the effects of urban congestion, industrial/residential zoning, suburb development and pollution on behaviour. The science is not only concerned with long-term effects, but immediate responses to environmental stimuli; it also attempts to investigate the effects of both simple (a single display) and complex (a complete merchandising plan) stimuli.

Environmental psychology is still in a formative stage of development. At the outset researchers investigated the effects of physical stimuli on comfort, fatigue, or anxiety. More recently they have examined the effects of environments on emotions such as pleasure or arousal, and the consequences of such emotional responses for behaviour. As in most developing sciences there is considerable disagreement about definitional issues. Indeed, in EP, there is little agreement about the boundaries of the science, the way in which environments can be described, measured and categorised, or the appropriate classification systems for human responses and the best way in which behavioural responses can be measured. The basic framework around which the functioning of merchandising is discussed is shown in Figure 20.1.

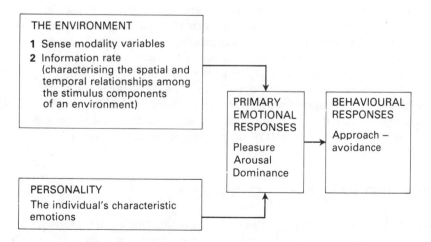

Figure 20.1 Conceptual framework of environmental psychology.

Based on Mehrabian and Russell,[6] the framework suggests that primary emotional responses of an individual can be seen as an outcome of the quality and quantity of environmental stimuli set against the individual's personality. Behaviour derives from this emotional response. A hospitality merchandising scenario may illuminate the framework.

In his room a business traveller is resting. He notices the information pack on the bedside table, the welcome note on his pillow, the sticker on the mirror, the tent card on the television set and the pictures on the wall. They all draw his attention to the exciting variety of activities he could enjoy as a guest. An announcement interrupts the in-house radio broadcast; the hotel's golf professional is offering coaching. The guest practises his swing a couple of times, then leaves his room to seek out the pro. The information pack, note, sticker, tent card, pictures and announcement are all environmental stimuli. His desire to achieve success, in golf as in business, is a dimension of personality. He is aroused by the announcement, anticipating pleasure. His behaviours are to seek out the golf pro and buy coaching lessons.

The theory of merchandising suggests that stimuli received via the senses produce intermodal responses, that is responses which cut across sense modalities. Thus a red and orange display (visual stimulus) may be described as warm (tactile response). There is considerable evidence that an individual's emotional response to environmental stimuli is independent of the sensory mode through which the stimuli are received. Mehrabian and Russell suggest that:[7]

> variations in pleasure, arousal, and dominance constitute the core of human emotional responses to all situations . . . Additional terms describing a diversity of emotional reactions to situations may be defined in terms of these three basic dimensions. Thus . . . the feeling of boredom or fatigue may be described as one that is low on pleasure, arousal and dominance . . . excitement may be characterized as an emotional state of high pleasure, arousal and dominance.

These emotional responses of pleasure, arousal and dominance are viewed as intervening variables between stimuli and behavioural response.

One concept which serves to draw together all behavioural responses into a single dimension is approach–avoidance. This includes all behaviours which suggest either preference for, or dislike of, the stimuli. In principle, therefore, the theory suggests that behaviour (assessed in terms of approach–avoidance) is determined by emotional responses to environmental (i.e. merchandising) stimuli. These responses (pleasure, arousal and dominance) are tempered by the personality of the individual.

The majority of hospitality managers are employed to make profits for their employers. Management of the environment and manipulation of merchandising variables, therefore, should be part of their decision responsibilities.

20.6 WHY MERCHANDISING WORKS

We have seen how merchandising works—by stimulating emotional responses which, in turn, cause purchase behaviour. But why does merchandising work? Are we able to identify any enabling conditions which foster effective merchandising? Again there is no established theory, but a number of factors do appear to explain why merchandising is effective.

(a) Low-involvement purchasing
A large number of purchases are unimportant to the purchaser. As we have seen in earlier chapters, the consumer has weak or non-existent attitudes towards the low-involvement product and tends not to actively seek out and process information prior to purchasing. Consequently merchandising stimuli may be sufficient to evoke purchase.

(b) Disposable income
As his level of disposable income rises a consumer is able to indulge his whims and fancies, gratifying aroused desires instantly without concern for budget.

(c) Need fulfilment
Research has indicated that spending money or making shopping trips is a way of killing time. In addition, it can be a way of role playing, obtaining social contact, increasing the level of arousal through sensory stimulation, demonstrating status and authority, communicating with others with similar interests, or enhancing a special occasion.[8] Merchandising can function through motivating these needs and providing the means for their gratification.

(d) Consumer values
As we noted in Chapter 4, consumer values are changing. Society is becoming more inner-directed. Consumers are more experimental, participative, artistic and impulsive. This reflects in a number of behaviours and attitudes. We participate in more sports, make constructive use of leisure-time and experiment with exotic foods and drink. Merchandising can inform consumers how these values can be expressed through consumption.

(e) Unplanned purchasing
With the shift towards self-service retailing has come recognition of the importance of unplanned purchasing. Engel and Blackwell, the consumer behaviour experts, reckon that nearly 40 per cent of department-store purchases and two-thirds of supermarket purchases are unplanned.[9] A large proportion of these are caused by exposure to merchandising stimuli. Some food service businesses, particularly those offering self-service, are in a position to provoke unplanned purchases.

20.7 MERCHANDISING STIMULI

Table 20.1 lists 20 different merchandising stimuli. The majority of merchandising media (a term synonymous with merchandising stimuli) can be classified as visual, audio or audio-visual. A minority also work through the senses of touch and smell.

Visual media include displays, electronic broadcasters, signs, posters, menus, blackboards, bulletin boards, wine lists and tent cards. Audio media include public address systems and promotional inserts in radio broadcasts. Audio-visual media include film, tape/slide and video presentations.

The hospitality products which can be merchandised fall into 3 categories, as follows:
1. Main products: accommodation, food and beverage.
2. Associated products (products which are directly associated with being away from home): tobacco, transport, books, newspapers, magazines, maps, stationery, theatre and cinema tickets, pens, lighters, toys, games, sports facilities, stamps, dry-cleaning, laundry, beach accessories, car accessories, baby-sitters, hairdressing, medical and dental services, secretarial services and personal requisites such as razors, razor blades, contraceptives, shower caps, toothpaste and toothbrushes, darning kits, snacks, take-away foods, video cassettes, films and souvenirs.
3. Other products: tourists are a market for jewellery, rugs, paintings, clothing, ceramics, silverware, fruit, flowers, confectionery and sports and health clubs.

Merchandising can take place in 4 locations, as follows:
1. Public areas such as the front desk or reception area, the lobby, lifts, corridors, toilets, cloakrooms, stairwells and lounge which are all internal. External merchandising takes place through window displays, posters and directional signs in streets and car parks, notices in courtesy cars and fascia boards.
2. Guest rooms.
3. Dining areas such as coffee lounges, snackbars and restaurants.
4. Bars—public, lounge and cocktail.

Let us now examine how a hospitality outlet might construct a merchandising environment. What makes public areas so attractive for merchandising is that there are often large numbers of people waiting—to check in, to check out and talking with friends.

Between a hotel's front door and reception desk customers can be routed past free-standing or wall-mounted displays, posters, vending machines and bulletin boards; elsewhere they may be routed through a mall of in-hotel shops, either concessions or hotel owned, selling 'associated' and 'other' products—a news-stand, video cassette library, boutique, or sporting goods shop for those hotels boasting sporting facilities. The most profitable lines can be displayed attractively at eye level where customer traffic is most frequent. To encourage such traffic a lobby could double as a coffee lounge. If it became busy enough, concessions could be sold to car-hire firms, florists, or banks. At the front desk an illuminated display board and brochure rack could show how the guest might make use of the premises; the receptionist could also present every guest with an information pack, luggage labels and a hotel map, and point out the free-standing signs which have been installed to indicate the locations of lounge bars and restaurant.

Lift lobbies and the lift itself can both be fruitful locations for merchandising stimuli. People waiting at a lift would be most likely to read a bulletin board announcing, say, a special in-house entertainment; and the lift could house a wall-mounted panel of information about the bars, and alongside the illuminated floor indicator could be a brief note about restaurant specials.

Some establishments position name boards so as to be seen by all potential customers, be they pedestrians or road or rail users. The windows of a hotel or restaurant often play much the same role as those of the supermarket or liquor store.

They are dressed to make 'passers buy'! The window shape need not be a constraint on creativity—glass can be painted or masked to add to the attraction. If the everyday activity behind the window, say, in a Chinese restaurant, is interesting and attracts prospects into the premises, then no further dressing may be required. Restaurants may profit from externally displayed menus, particularly if they aim to attract pedestrians.

Once in his room, the guest can be exposed to a wide variety of merchandising stimuli. It is now standard for hotels to provide directories in each room. Of more use to holidaymakers than businessmen, this will list all restaurants, bars, room service, valet, laundry, dry-cleaning and other facilities available on site. Where the hotel has negotiated terms with other off-site services such as florists, art galleries, or theatres, these are often promoted. Many hotels earn revenue from referrals.

Pictures of the hotel's facilities or other group hotels could decorate the walls, a tent card listing breakfast options could sit on the television set and stickers might be placed on the telephone handset and mirror. The bathroom is a suitable place for a notice about availability of shower caps, razors, soap and other personal requisites.

Many hotels install a small fridge containing complimentary milk and a known stock of miniatures, mixers and beers. A stocktake occurs daily and the guest's account is updated accordingly and stock replenished. Doorknob hangers can be used to promote room service and the complimentary laundry-bag the linen service. There is much scope for merchandising in eating areas, both of food and drink, and of 'associated' products.

There are a variety of print and display options, in particular, which can create incremental sales. On-table merchandising is normally print; off-table merchandising is normally display. On-table print merchandising vehicles are the menu, wine list, placemats, coasters, napkins, ashtrays, tent card, menu extenders, inserts and clip-ons. Even the table top itself could perhaps carry a message. The menu is the primary vehicle for merchandising the most profitable meals and drinks. Many diners look no further than the first half-dozen items on the menu, so this is obviously the place for profit-earners. They can be made to stand out by astute use of white space, larger typeface, mouth-watering descriptions and colourful illustrations. Poorer earners should be less ambitiously treated.

Many menus are sequenced to follow a meal pattern, starting with aperitifs and ending with digestifs. Sometimes, depending upon type of customer, it is advisable to list ingredients, calorific value, or fibre content. Some menus mention how long it takes to prepare each dish. In the case of long preparation times the serving staff can take the opportunity to suggest a drink. Today's healthier and more weight-conscious consumer is eating fewer desserts. Menus can highlight low-calorie treats.

Chef's specials or other high profit-earners can be highlighted by menu inserts, tent cards, wall posters or table-edge clip-ons. Further off-table print merchandising vehicles are the blackboard, door-mounted menus and wall posters.

If the dining area is expected to promote secondary sales like take-away meals, home deliveries, packed lunches, or room service, the menu is a convenient vehicle. Liquor sales can be promoted through table-top merchandising; some establishments display wine on the table in addition to using a wine list. Wine suggestions can be listed alongside food items on the menu. A selection of different wine glasses can be incorporated into the place setting. Off-table display can play an important role in sales stimulation. Wine can be merchandised by using wine racks as room dividers, hanging decanting baskets from the ceiling, exhibiting wine in a free-standing display, or operating a wine cart.

Food can be merchandised through hors-d'œuvre displays, dining-room cooking stations, guèridon, salad bars, smorgasbord and dessert trolley. Where consumers serve themselves, the most profitable items should be nearest the entry point; trolley service should exhibit the most profitable items on the top tier, nearest to the diner. This can overcome the inhibitions of the weight-conscious diner and generate considerable impulse sales. The same is true of the liqueur cart. A glass-fronted chiller cabinet can be useful in merchandising juices, beers, salads and cheeses.

At the cashier's desk displays of mints, matches, lighters and tobacco will stimulate sales whilst a promotional message can be printed on the bill. Wall space is not frequently exploited, although it can be used to merchandise paintings, batik, or craftwork.

Brewers, vintners and distillers are generally sophisticated marketers. However, their primary objective is to enhance sales of their own brands whilst a bar manager's objective is to merchandise the more profitable lines regardless of origin. Selective use of merchandising materials, such as ashtrays, stickers and beermats provided by brewery representatives, can contribute towards this objective, as can the controlled allocation of shelf and display space. Bar snacks, tobacco and 'pub grub' can be merchandised by means of blackboards, posters and menus, as can other non-bar products. Related-item displays of whisky with soda and dry ginger or gin with tonic or bitter lemon can promote impulse sales.

20.8 PLANNED MERCHANDISING

Much of this chapter has been concerned with the techniques and theory of merchandising. Management of the merchandising component of the promotional mix implies the need for a coherent plan with measurable objectives and reasoned selection of merchandising techniques. Such a planning scheme, consisting of 10 stages, is proposed below.

1. Fact-gathering:
   - sales analysis (departments and products)
   - profit analysis (departments and products)
   - customer movement
2. Identification of merchandising problems.
3. Objectives.
4. Merchandising techniques to be used.
5. Timing of implementation.
6. Departments, staff and material suppliers involved.
7. Training requirements.
8. Likely competitor reaction.
9. Budget.
10. Means of evaluation.

Fact-gathering, the opening stage, furnishes the planner with all the details he needs to execute the plan. The sales analysis of departments and products will indicate which areas of business make the most contribution to turnover. The profit analysis tells the planner where profit contributions are earned. Two measures are important: gross margin and net margin. Gross margin, the difference between bought cost and sold price, is not an adequate indication of an item's actual contribution to profit. The planner should deduct the direct costs of ordering, receiving, stocking, displaying and transporting an item in order to calculate its net margin.

Items found to be frequent sellers can be located so as to draw customers past high-margin or impulse items. In a self-service restaurant, high-demand items such as cold meats can be displayed alongside high-margin lines such as mixed salads. Impulse items such as biscuits and confectionery sell best when customers are stationary or moving slowly; self-service restaurants often place impulse items near the cash register. The merchandising planner, therefore, needs to know how traffic moves through the establishment—i.e. where people enter and exit, assemble, move slowly, or walk briskly. Customer traffic is manipulable by astute placement of room fixtures and display material.

The planner's second task is to identify merchandising problems. He may find, for example, that whole departments are operating so far below capacity that they are actually making losses, that high-demand items are grouped so closely together that customers are not exposed to the high-margin and impulse lines, or that point-of-sale print material is soiled. In a retail experiment to measure the effect of deterioration of props and point-of-sale material on display productivity it was found that sales in the second week of a promotion fell by 30 per cent below the first week's level in a well-maintained display; however, where the display was allowed to deteriorate, sales fell by a significantly higher amount.[10]

Having identified the problems, the planner needs to assign priorities and set objectives. If he has a 100-seat hotel restaurant averaging only 25 covers per night when hotel occupancy is sufficient to fill it twice over, he is likely to regard this as a major problem. Highest priorities are attached to major problems. Objectives in merchandising have already been treated in section 20.4.

The merchandising techniques listed in Table 20.1, and discussed in section 20.7, can now be studied with a view to selecting the most appropriate stimuli. Timing the implementation of the plan depends very much upon the objectives: does the planner want to generate more sales to existing custom or generate more customers? If the former, then the plan for a hotel restaurant should be implemented so that existing customers are exposed to stimuli whilst dining; if the latter, public area, bar and guest-room merchandising is required, so that prospective diners are exposed to stimuli whilst considering where they should dine.

Departments, staff and material suppliers involved in the plan must be briefed, co-ordinated and motivated. Staff training requirements must be identified and accomplished. For example, bar staff might need instruction in bar layout, and housekeeping staff in how to furnish guest rooms with merchandising materials.

If competitive reaction is anticipated, the planner would be well advised to make contingency plans. If in-house dining facilities are merchandised, local restaurants may lose custom and take recovery action. On the revenue side the budget for the plan includes the gains expected in sales; on the cost side the major expenditures are on print, labour and training. Finally, the means of evaluation needs to be written into the plan. This is generally implied by the objectives and usually requires sales and profit data to be collected both before and after implementation of the plan.

20.9 CHAPTER REVIEW

1. Merchandising is any behaviour-triggering stimulus, or pattern of stimuli, other than personal selling, which takes place at retail or other point of sale.
2. Merchandising stimuli tend to fall into 3 main categories: visual, audio and audio-visual.
3. The main role of merchandising in the commercial sector is to improve average expenditure per customer.
4. Merchandising objectives may be applied to entire establishments, departments, or individual products.
5. The mnemonic ASDA attempts to explain how merchandising works—A = accessibility, SD = sensory domination, A = appeal.
6. One theory explaining how merchandising works draws on environmental psychology. The theory suggests that a person's behaviour derives from emotional responses to environmental stimuli, set against the individual's personality. Emotional responses may be classified as arousal, pleasure and dominance.
7. A number of factors appear to explain why merchandising works: the volume of low-involvement purchasing, the level of disposable income, merchandising's ability to highlight avenues offering immediate need gratification, shifts in consumer values and the prevalence of unplanned purchasing.
8. There are 3 categories of product that can be merchandised in hospitality establishments: the main products of accommodation, food and beverage; products directly associated with being away from home; and other products, particularly those appealing to tourists.
9. Merchandising takes place in 4 locations: public areas, bars, dining areas and guest rooms.
10. Management of merchandising implies the need for a coherent plan with measurable objectives and reasoned selection of merchandising techniques.

20.10 QUESTIONS

1. Take a catering outlet known to you. List the array of merchandising stimuli it employs and suggest others which you consider might be productive.
2. What distinguishes between sales promotion and merchandising?
3. To what extent can the responses pleasure, arousal and dominance explain the emotional effect of merchandising stimuli?
4. The text suggests that 5 factors appear to explain why merchandising works: the extent of low-involvement purchasing; the level of disposable income; the ability of merchandising stimuli to suggest avenues of need gratification; the shift in consumer values; and the extent of unplanned purchasing. To what extent do these factors derive from deep-seated trends in society? Are there any other significant reasons why merchandising works?
5. What behaviours can be triggered by merchandising stimuli?

REFERENCES

[1] Buttle, F. (1984) How merchandising works. *International Journal of Advertising*, 3.
[2] Hughes, G. D. (1978) *Marketing Management: A Planning Approach*. London: Addison Wesley, 412.
[3] Elvy, B. H. (1982) *Marketing Made Simple*. London: Heinemann, 174.

[4] Buttle, F. (1984) Merchandising. *European Journal of Marketing*, June–July. Elaborates on the merchandising techniques employed in retailing.

[5] Buttle, F. (1984) How merchandising works, op. cit.

[6] Mehrabian, A. and Russell, J. A. (1974) *An Approach to Environmental Psychology.* Cambridge, MA: MIT Press.

[7] ibid., 17.

[8] Buttle, F. (1984) Shopping motives. *Service Industries Journal.* Vol. 4, March, 71–81.

[9] Engel, J. F. and Blackwell, R. D. (1982) (4th edn) *Consumer Behaviour.* London: Dryden Press.

[10] See: The magic of merchandising. *Progressive Grocer*, November 1980, 98–101.

—21—

Public Relations

21.1 CHAPTER PREVIEW

Public relations (PR) can make a significant contribution to the solution of communications problems. This chapter details PR's distinctive advantages and its function, and explains a number of techniques, showing how PR can be managed effectively.

21.2 LEARNING OBJECTIVES

By the end of the chapter you should be able to:
1. Distinguish between PR and publicity.
2. Detail 5 classes of PR technique.
3. Use an 8-stage flowchart to establish a PR programme.

21.3 INTRODUCTION

Public relations may be defined as:

> the means by which the various significant publics of an organisation are identified and communicated with, to the advantage of the organisation, through personal and non-personal media.

The publics of greatest interest to marketers are the consumer and channel member. However, PR experts have a much broader conception of the term 'publics'.

One survey of PR's role in the service sector has identified a number of additional publics; in order of perceived importance they are: customers/consumers, the general public, Whitehall/Westminster, media/journalists, management/employees, the City/shareholders and opinion-formers.[1] Public relations, then, identifies publics inside and outside the organisation and has a corporate, rather than a mere marketing, communications role.

However, it is with its marketing applications that we are concerned. Haywood identifies several marketing roles for PR:[2]

> improving awareness, projecting credibility, combating competition, evaluating new markets, creating direct sales leads, reinforcing the effectiveness of sales promotion and advertising, motivating the sales force, introducing new products, building brand loyalty, dealing with consumer issues and in many other ways.

It is undertaken both in-company and by consulting organisations on behalf of clients. In 1984 the Public Relations Consultants' Association reported total combined fee billings of £25 million.[3] This is probably only the tip of a very large iceberg because (1) many PR consultants are not registered; (2) most PR is in-house; and (3) some PR activities may not be formally recognised or costed as such.

Public relations is used in 2 ways by marketers. It has:

- a problem-solving role
- a problem-avoidance role

The former is probably more common. The marketer, faced with a communications problem, launches a PR solution. When a well-known, highly esteemed London restaurant received unwelcome publicity, having been charged with keeping a dirty, unhygienic kitchen, it rapidly put together a PR response which involved: issuing press releases to national daily newspapers, inviting opinion-formers into the kitchens and purchasing advertising space.

There is also for PR a pre-emptive, problem-avoidance role. When New Zealand ski-field operators Alex Harvey Industries were developing a new slope, 3 publics were identified as potential opponents—conservationists, the press and the New Zealand government's Parks Board, whose function is to balance the demands for public use against conservation. The PR solutions included the issue of film and press material portraying the company as environment-conscious and offering a fellowship to a member of the Parks Board operational staff to study ski-field management overseas.

21.4 PR TECHNIQUES

There are an enormous number of PR techniques, some well established, others novel.[4] The more common methods are discussed below.

(a) Print media relations
The provision of materials for editorial use in the print media, including:

- news (or press) releases. Also known as 'tip-sheets', these are news stories written in the style of the medium or vehicle to which they are submitted
- press kits. Complete packages of background material, which may be distributed with or without news releases—a restaurant might compile a press kit comprising name, address and telephone number; menu; wine list; exterior photograph and interior photographs; biography of proprietor and chef; testimonials; business card; location map; and details of capacity, parking and opening hours
- letters to editors
- meetings with editors
- writing articles
- provision of information for feature writers
- columns—e.g. recipe columns
- establishing a press office
- calling occasional press conferences
- photographs

(b) Radio and television relations

The broadcast media also provide opportunities for public exposure, including:

- programme opportunities. The range covers news, features and special-interest programmes; many shows such as *The Food Programme* or consumer and holiday programmes use commercially initiated material
- radio interviews—studio or telephone
- television interviews
- panel discussions

(c) Publications

These include:

- leaflets
- brochures
- house journals
- corporate publications
- sponsored books—e.g. cookbooks
- other print such as calendars, diaries, posters, wallcharts, stickers and educational leaflets—e.g. nutritional details of fast food

(d) Special events

These include:

- seminars
- exhibitions
- openings/launches
- celebrations—e.g. Christmas party
- competitions
- tastings
- conferences
- open day
- familiarisation tours—e.g. Warner's holiday camps invited travel agency staff to sample the product in order to combat their poor image
- filmshows
- stunts
- speeches

(e) Community involvement

This includes:

- professional bodies
- sports/social clubs
- charitable organisations
- school visits
- grants or fellowship awards

Publicity

The most common form of PR in hospitality marketing is publicity, the provision of newsworthy stories normally taking the form of a news release and/or press kit to the print and broadcast media. Publicity has been nicknamed 'free advertising'.

Many opportunities present themselves for such publicity such as opening new premises, accommodating VIP guests, or launching new products. A number of novelty weekend-break products have attracted national publicity; in Norwich, Hotel Nelson's 'Fed-up-with-Xmas', 'Bureaucracy' and 'Walk-a-Plank' weekends; in Hove, Imperial Hotel's 'History of the Dirty Weekend'; and in Teignmouth, Strathearn's 'Rain-lovers' Weekend' have all been themed around oddball ideas which have attracted media interest.[5]

The opening of a new hotel shows how a single event can provide many opportunities for publicity, as follows.[6]
1. Announcement of construction plans and site selection.
2. Ground-breaking ceremony.
3. Cornerstone ceremony.
4. Topping-off ceremony.
5. 'Soft' opening to which members of the press and key opinion-formers are invited.
6. Ribbon-cutting.
7. Press opening.
8. Grand opening 1 or 2 months after opening for business.
9. Restaurant opening.

Publicity has a number of advantages which make it valuable to marketers:
- credibility. Good publicity is perceived as editorial matter, not advertising
- objectivity. Publicity is apparently independent from sponsor's influence, and catches the reader off-guard when his psychological defences—selective exposure and attention—are down. Publicity therefore is used to change attitudes
- low cost. Space is not bought. However, it may be necessary to employ freelance copywriters or journalists to write the story in usable form
- contemporaneity. Publicity can be obtained at any time in a product's life, from the entrepreneurial struggles of the product developer to the quest for funds to finance growth in overseas markets. Topicality makes publicity interesting to news media

However, there is no guarantee that the publicity generated by a company will be used in the mass media. Newsworthiness is the prime consideration of most editors. Much publicity is so poorly written, and would be clearly perceived by readers as partial, that it is not even considered for publication. Much of what is used is edited. Thinly veiled ads are not welcomed.

News releases should be brief (2 pages maximum), concise, factual, bear the date, and be written specifically for an identified audience. Editors prefer copy on 'news release' letterhead with wide margins and spacing. If photographs are enclosed, captioned black-and-white prints are more likely to be used.

21.5 MANAGING PR

For PR to deliver its considerable potential planning is advisable. Figure 21.1 charts the major decisions. The planning cycle commences with identification of relevant publics. Marketers' main publics are customers, prospective customers and channel members. Second, current or anticipated communication problems with these publics are noted.

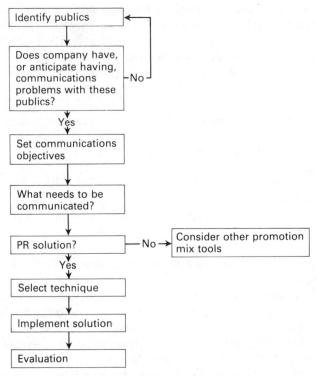

Figure 21.1   PR management.

An analytical framework has already been proposed in Chapter 15 (see especially Figure 15.2, p. 303) listing 3 varieties—cognitive, affective and action problems. Since PR is particularly useful for solving the first 2 classes, communication objectives are typically phrased as follows.

Cognitive objectives
To make the general public aware that the term 'junk food' is a totally inappropriate description of our products because of their high nutritional value and our concern for quality control.

To inform business travellers that we are opening a 190-bedroom hotel in Vancouver within 9 months.

Affective objectives
To convince prospective customers that our commitment to the motto 'We care to serve' is the best reason for preferring our company to our main competitor. To change young persons' attitudes towards vegetarian food.

These objectives, then, imply that certain types of information need to reach the specified publics. Whether or not there is a PR solution depends upon the suitability of other promotional tools for this purpose. The main determinants of PR's suitability are the size of the promotional budget and the need for objectivity and credibility. For any communications problems there are normally several PR solutions. The list in section 21.4 of this chapter should stimulate idea generation.

Once implemented, the PR solution should be evaluated for effectiveness. However, it has been estimated that only 40 per cent at most, of PR campaigns are so evaluated.[7] Many of those which are evaluated use crude measures of effectiveness such as counting the number of times the company/brand name appears in editorial matter or the number of column centimetres or television/radio time obtained. Press-cutting agencies perform this job. The equivalent cost of buying this space or time can be calculated by reference to the advertising rates for the media in which the exposure occurred.

A preferable form of evaluation is the experimental measurement of PR's effects. However, the experimental design must allow for all other possible causes of awareness, attitude, or other dependent variable change to be isolated.

21.6 CHAPTER REVIEW

1. Public relations has been defined as the means by which the various significant publics of an organisation are identified and communicated with, to the advantage of the organisation, through personal and non-personal media.
2. Public relations has two main roles:
    * a problem-solving role.
    * a pre-emptive, problem-avoidance role.
3. The main marketing publics for public relations are customers and channel members.
4. There are many PR techniques which can be classified under
    * print media relations.
    * radio and television relations.
    * publications.
    * special events.
    * community involvement.
5. Publicity is the most common form of hospitality PR.
6. Publicity's main advantages are its credibility, objectivity, contemporaneity and low cost.
7. Management in PR identifies publics, analyses communication problems, sets communication objectives, selects and implements appropriate techniques and evaluates their effectiveness.

21.7 QUESTIONS AND EXERCISES

1. What are the differences between PR and publicity?
2. Clip articles from the travel trade press which you think were initiated by PR. Calculate what it would have cost to buy this space. Use BRAD.
3. What would you put in a press kit for an hotel?
4. What PR objectives would you set and techniques would you use (if any) in these situations?
    * you run a private nursing-home and 1 of your staff is accused of maltreating elderly patients.
    * you intend to demolish dockland high-rise flats and build a new 4-star hotel.
    * you are opening a new atmosphere restaurant, styled in the Elizabethan manner, in a country town.
    * you run a meals on wheels service and want to attract volunteers.
5. Your company has decided to offer a travelling scholarship to a young person to study hotel operations in Europe. How could you capitalise on the PR value of the proposal?

REFERENCES

1 McLaughlin, N. (1984) PR's place in the sun. *Marketing*, 23 February, 22–4.
2 Haywood, R. (1984) *All about PR*. London: McGraw-Hill.
3 McLaughlin, N. (1985) PR fee billings hit new high. *Marketing*, 7 February, 12.
4 Interesting PR applications and techniques are cited in Rotman, M. B. and Rotman, R. E. (1982) Public relations for a restaurant enterprise, in Fisher, W. P. (ed.) *Creative Marketing for the Foodservice Industry*. London: Wiley, 275–93; Nykiel, R. A. (1983) *Marketing in the Hospitality Industry*. London: CBI, 99–111; and Coffman, C. D. (1970) *Marketing for a Full House*. Ithaca, NY: Cornell University Press, 230–52.
5 See Whitehall, B. (1983) Promotional gimmicks can boost occupancy. *Caterer and Hotelkeeper*, 15 December, 33–9, and Marketing and Media, *Caterer and Hotelkeeper*, 13 September 1984, 145.
6 Zive, J. D. (1981) Public relations for the hotel opening. *Cornell Hotel and Restaurant Administration Quarterly*, **22**(1), May, 19–28; see also Cossé, J. C. (1980) Ink and air time: a PR primer. *Cornell Hotel and Restaurant Administration Quarterly*, **21**(1), May, 37–40; and Bird, C. (1978) Your light beneath a bushel. *HCIMA Journal*, October, 39–44.
7 Haywood, R. (1984) op. cit., 248.

Index